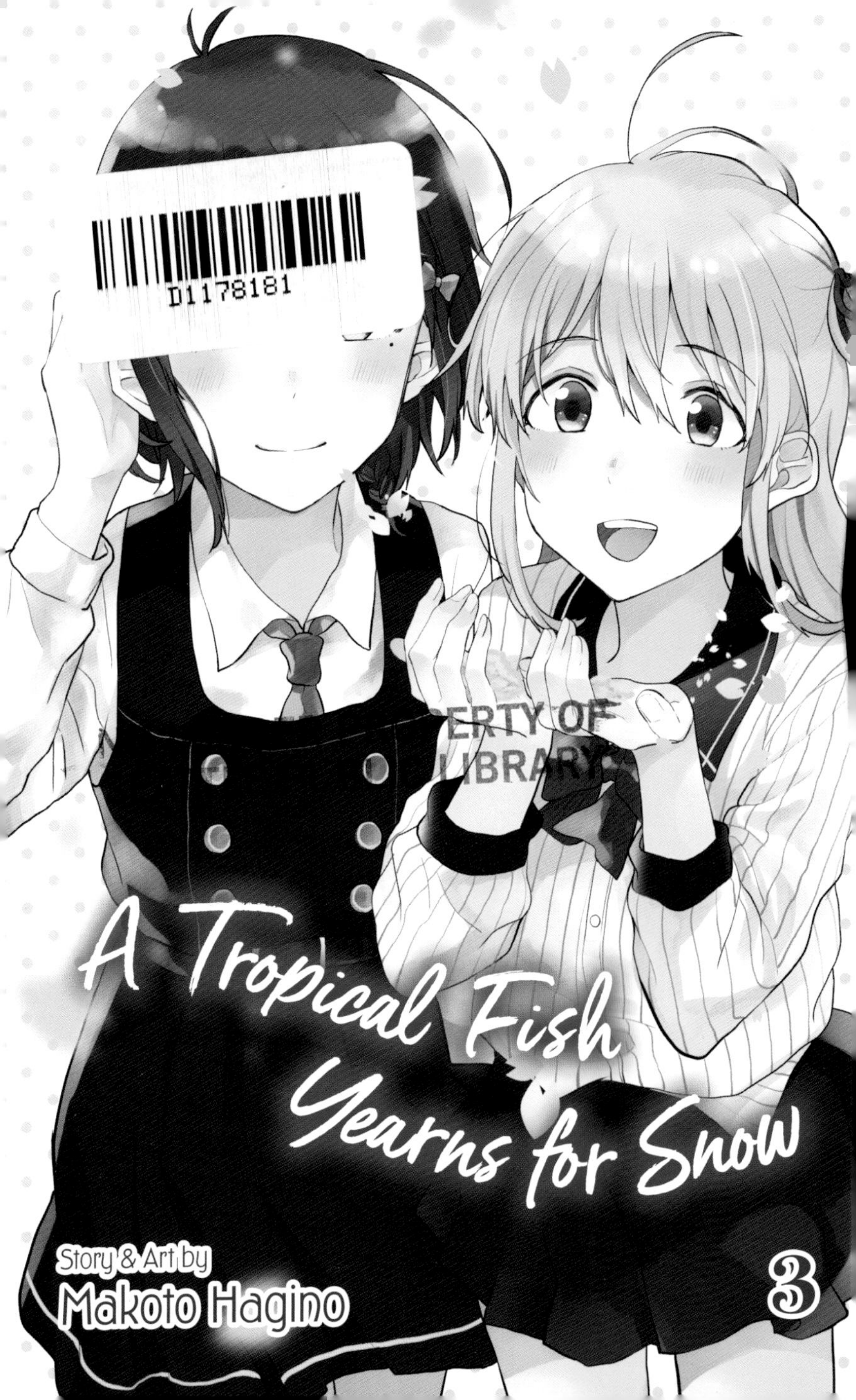
A Tropical Fish Yearns for Snow
Story & Art by
Makoto Hagino
3

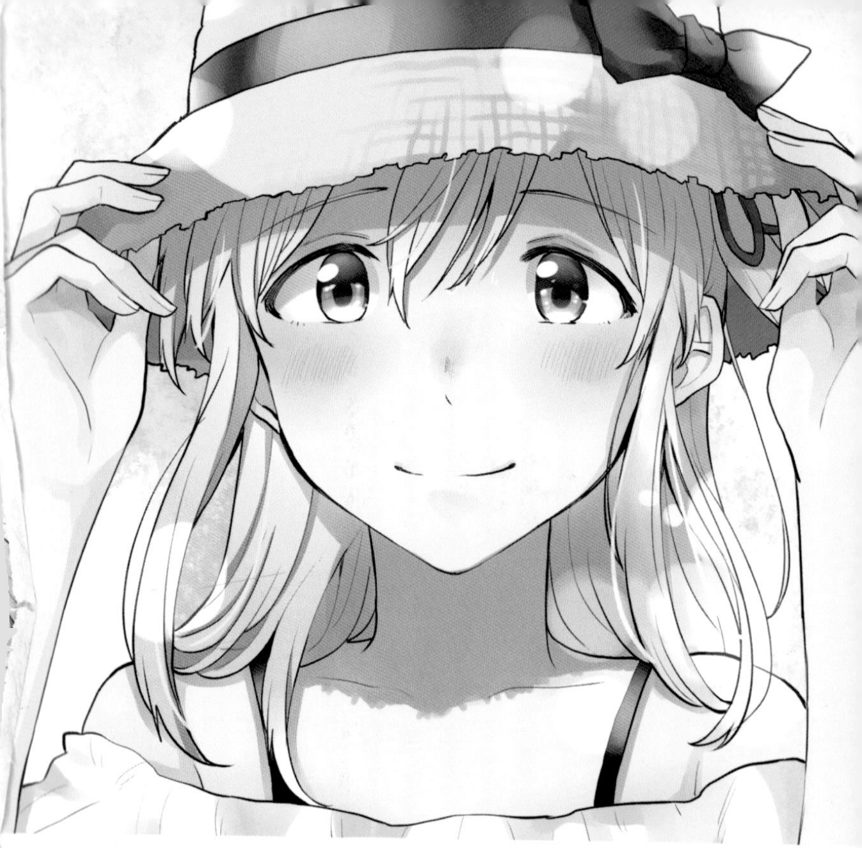

The Story So Far

Konatsu transfers to Nanahama High School from the city and meets Koyuki, the only member of the Aquarium Club. The two girls naturally take a liking to each other because they're both lonely, so Konatsu ends up joining the club. One day, they go to the town summer festival together, and Konatsu asks something that has been on her mind: "Why did you speak to me on the day we first met?" Presented with such a direct question, how will Koyuki respond?

Characters

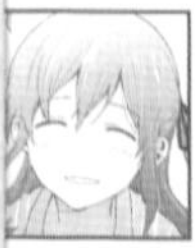

Konatsu Amano

A first-year transfer student. She has trouble adapting to her new surroundings until she decides to join her new friend Koyuki in the Aquarium Club.

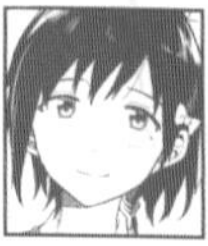

Koyuki Honami

Head of the Aquarium Club. Everyone puts her on a pedestal, and she tries to satisfy their expectations even though she finds them suffocating and feels lonely.

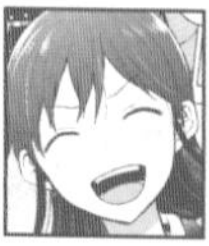

Kaede Hirose

Konatsu's classmate. Due to her perky personality, she has many friends and doesn't hesitate to extend a hearty welcome to Konatsu.

A Tropical Fish Yearns for Snow

A Tropical Fish
Yearns for Snow

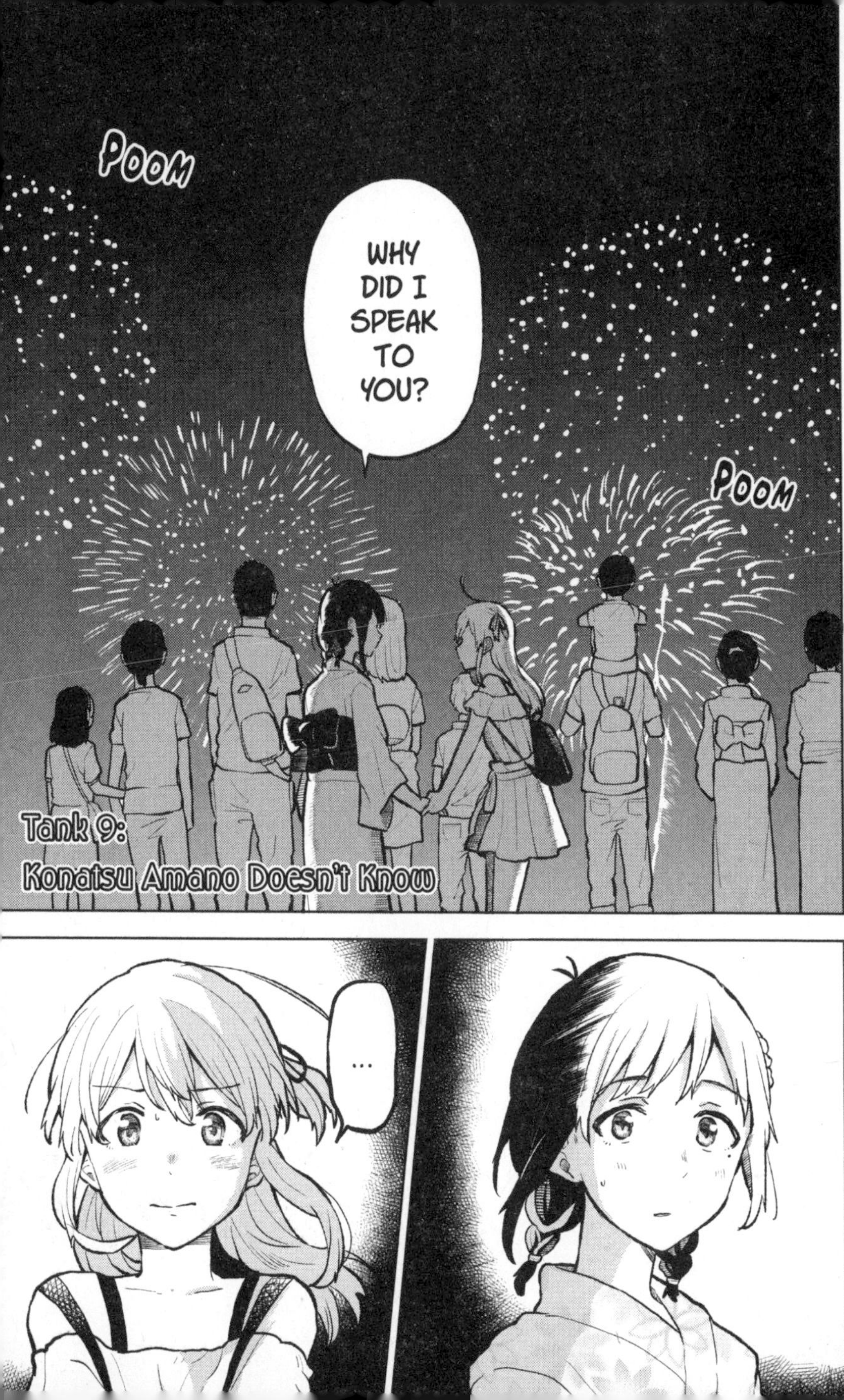
POOM
WHY DID I SPEAK TO YOU?
POOM
Tank 9:
Konatsu Amano Doesn't Know
...

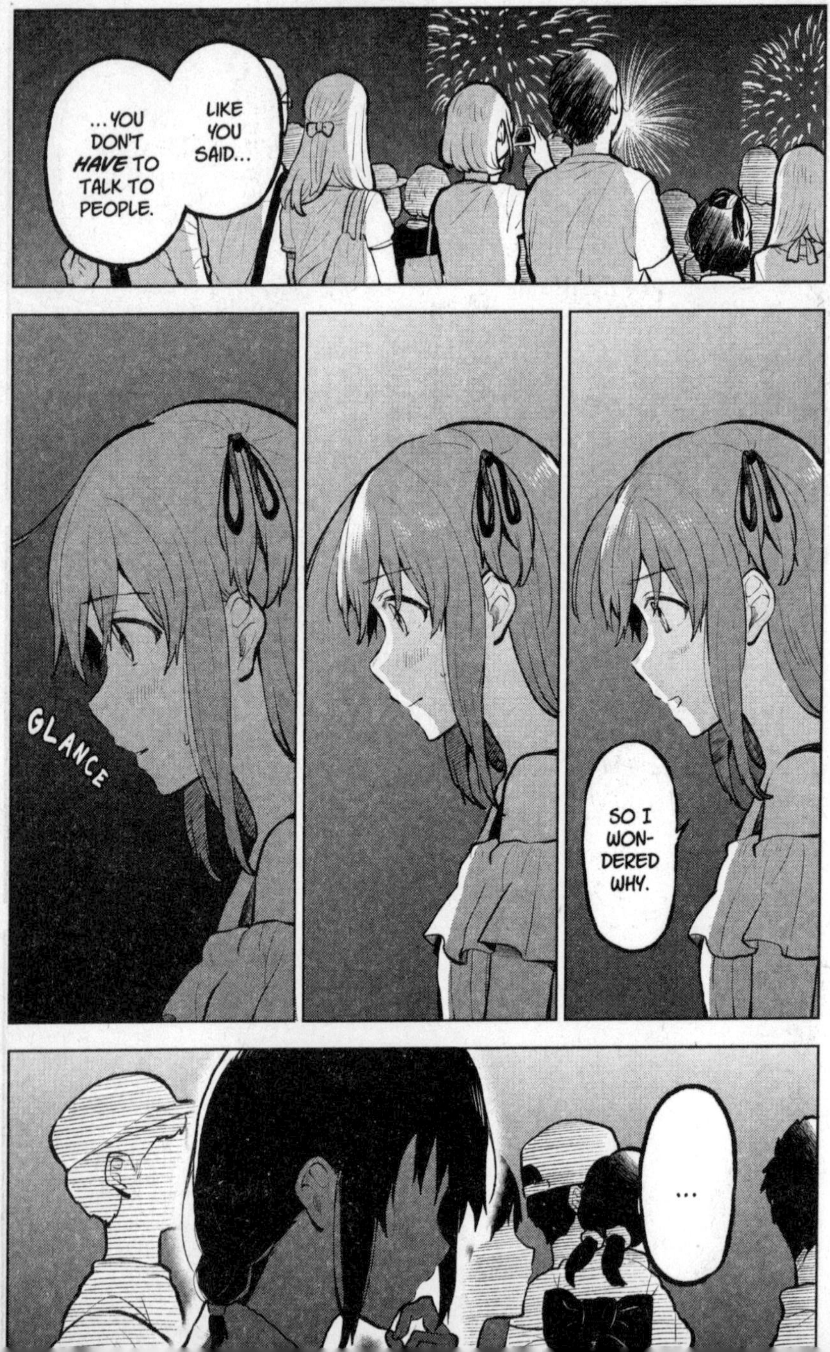
LIKE YOU SAID...
...YOU DON'T *HAVE* TO TALK TO PEOPLE.
SO I WONDERED WHY.
GLANCE
...

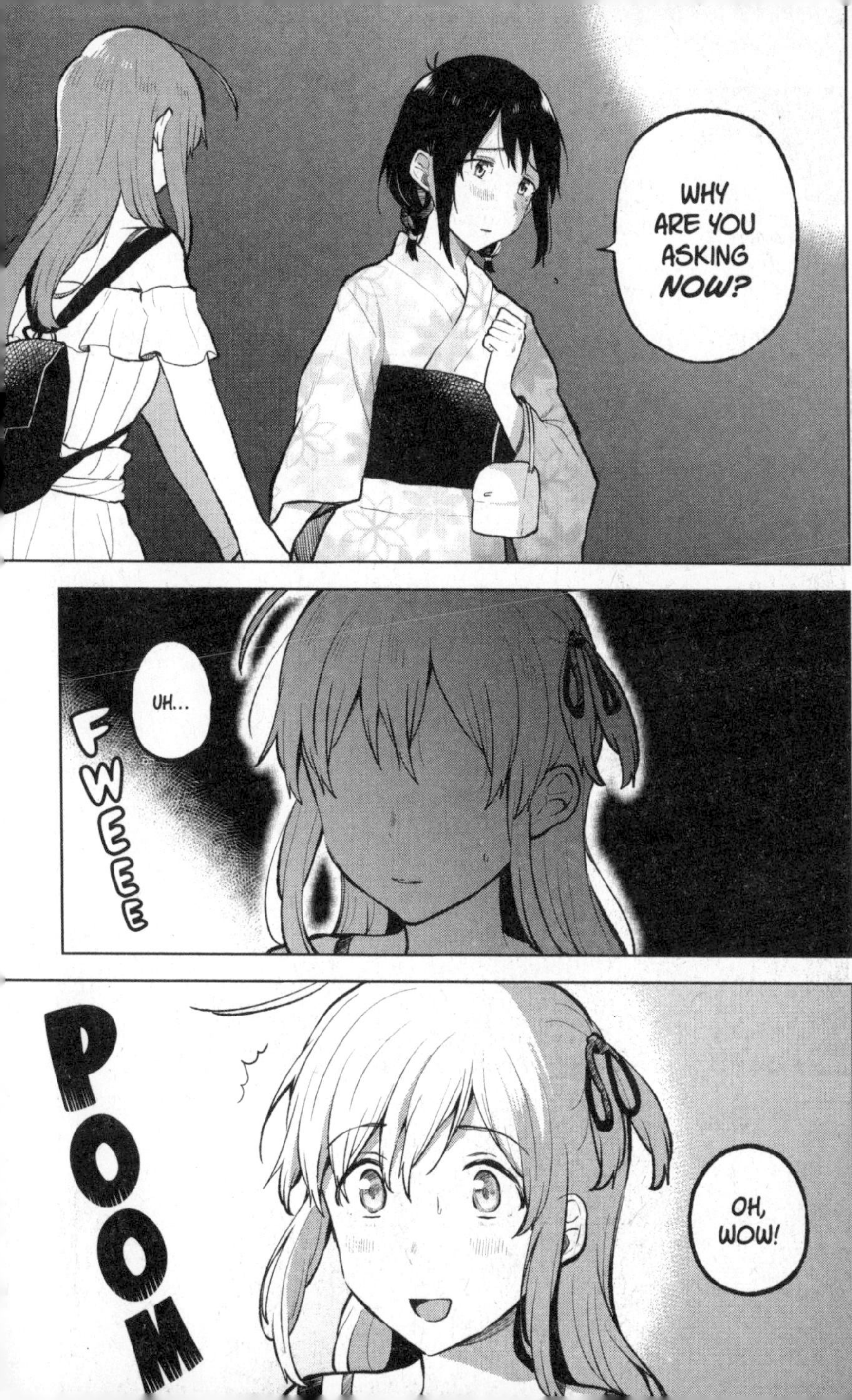
WHY ARE YOU ASKING NOW?
UH...
FWEEE
OH, WOW!
POOM

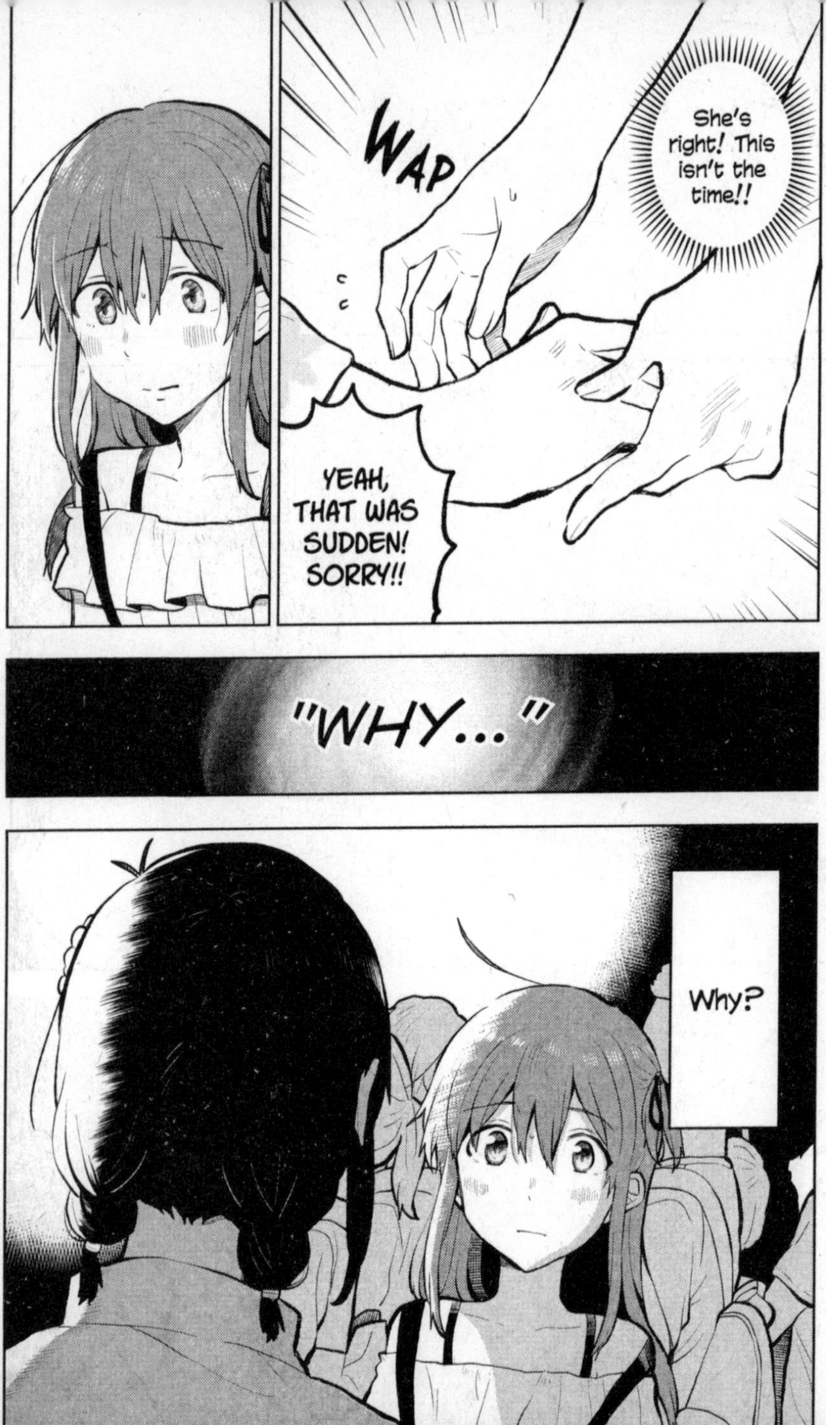
She's right! This isn't the time!!
WAP
YEAH, THAT WAS SUDDEN! SORRY!!
"WHY..."
Why?

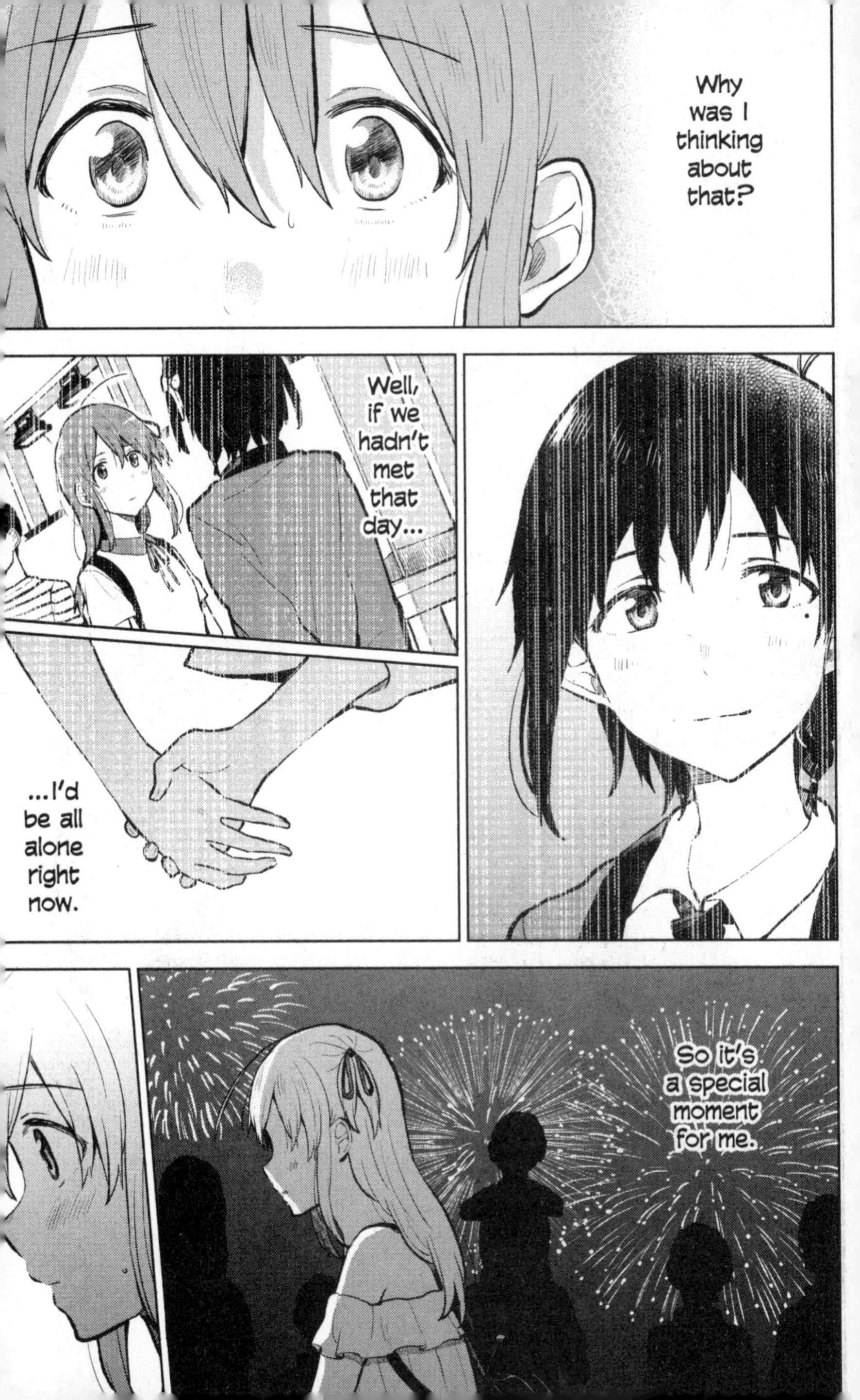
Why was I thinking about that?
Well, if we hadn't met that day...
...I'd be all alone right now.
So it's a special moment for me.

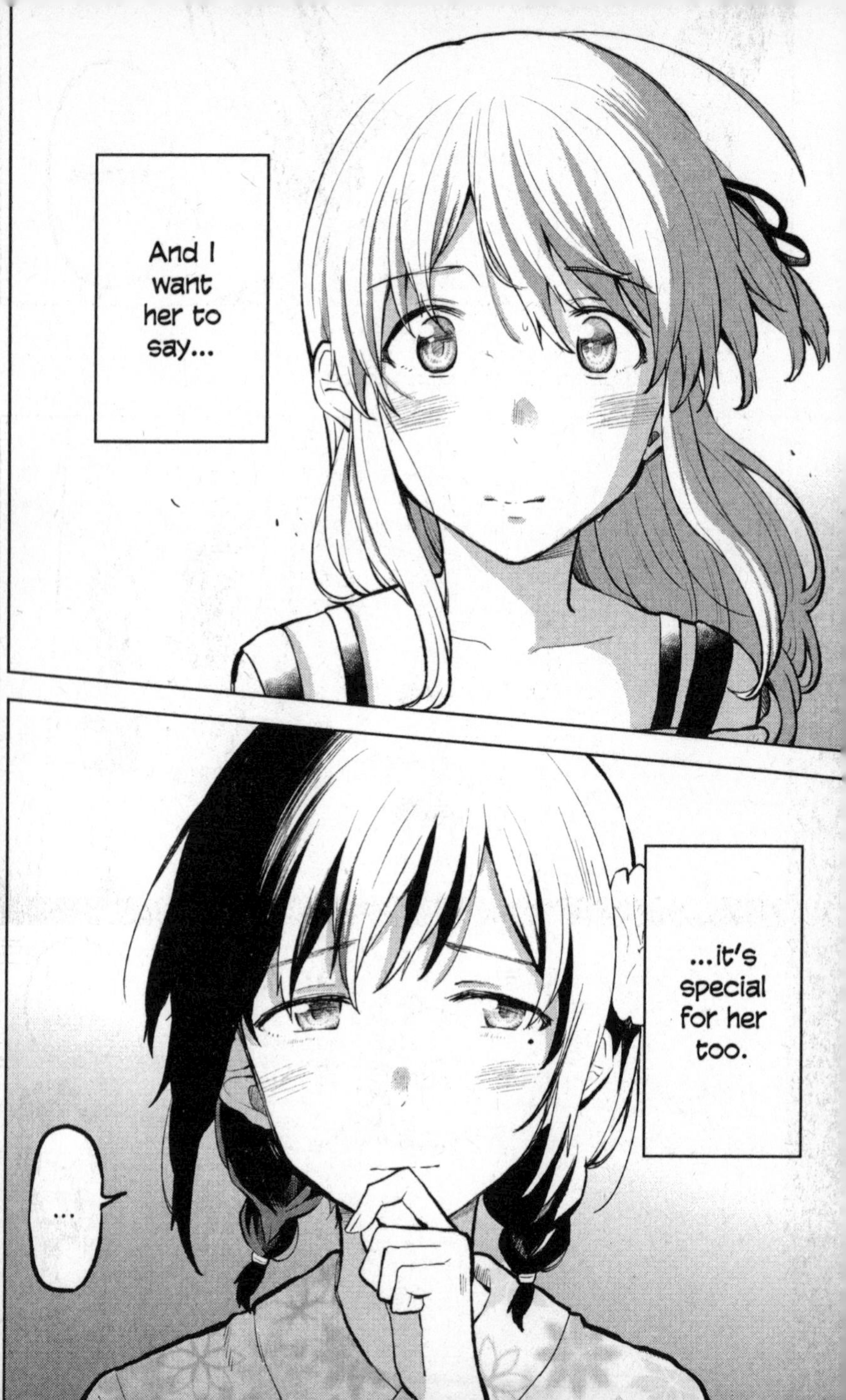
And I want her to say...
...it's special for her too.
...

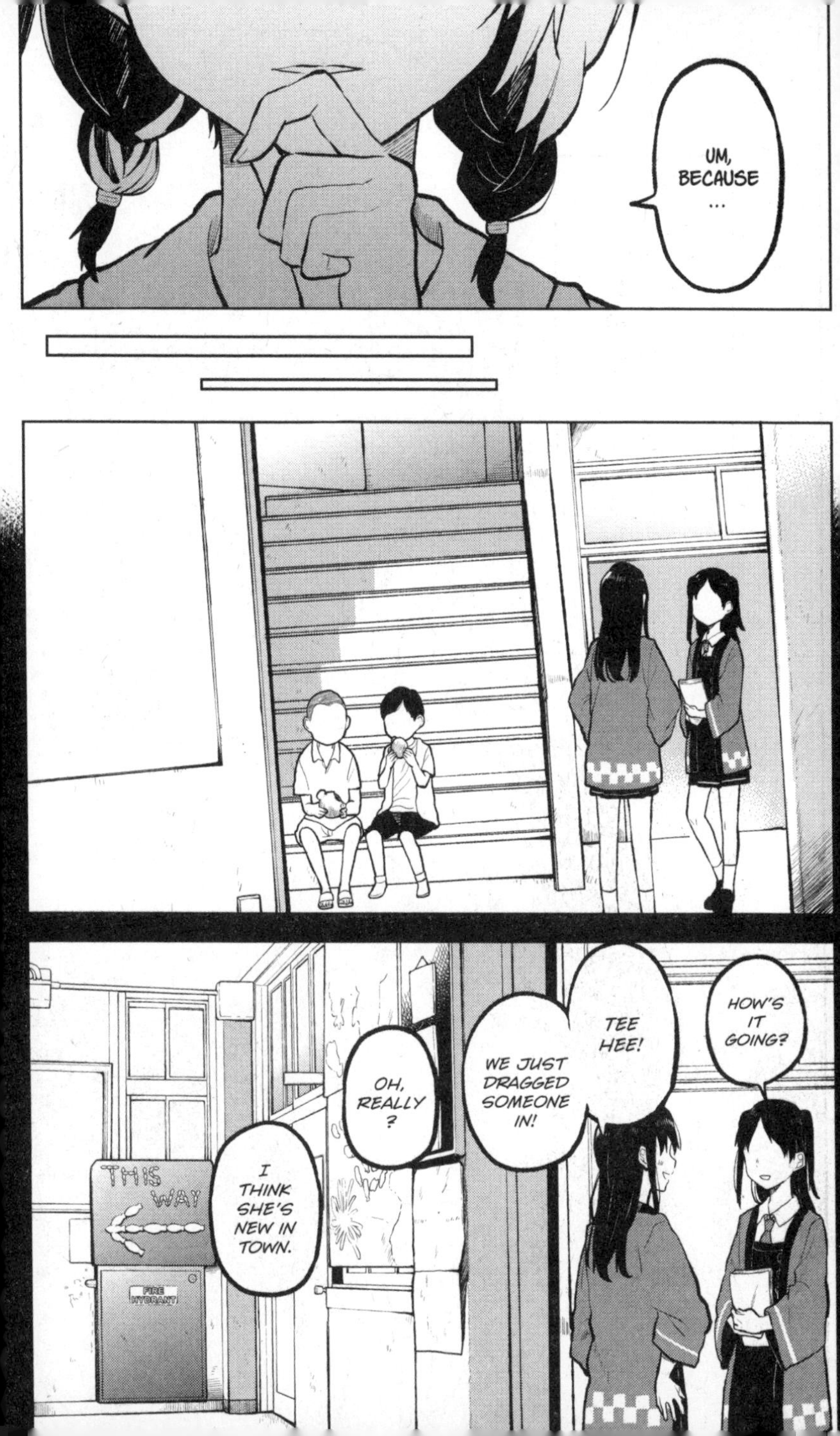
UM, BECAUSE ...
HOW'S IT GOING?
TEE HEE!
WE JUST DRAGGED SOMEONE IN!
OH, REALLY?
I THINK SHE'S NEW IN TOWN.
THIS WAY
FIRE HYDRANT

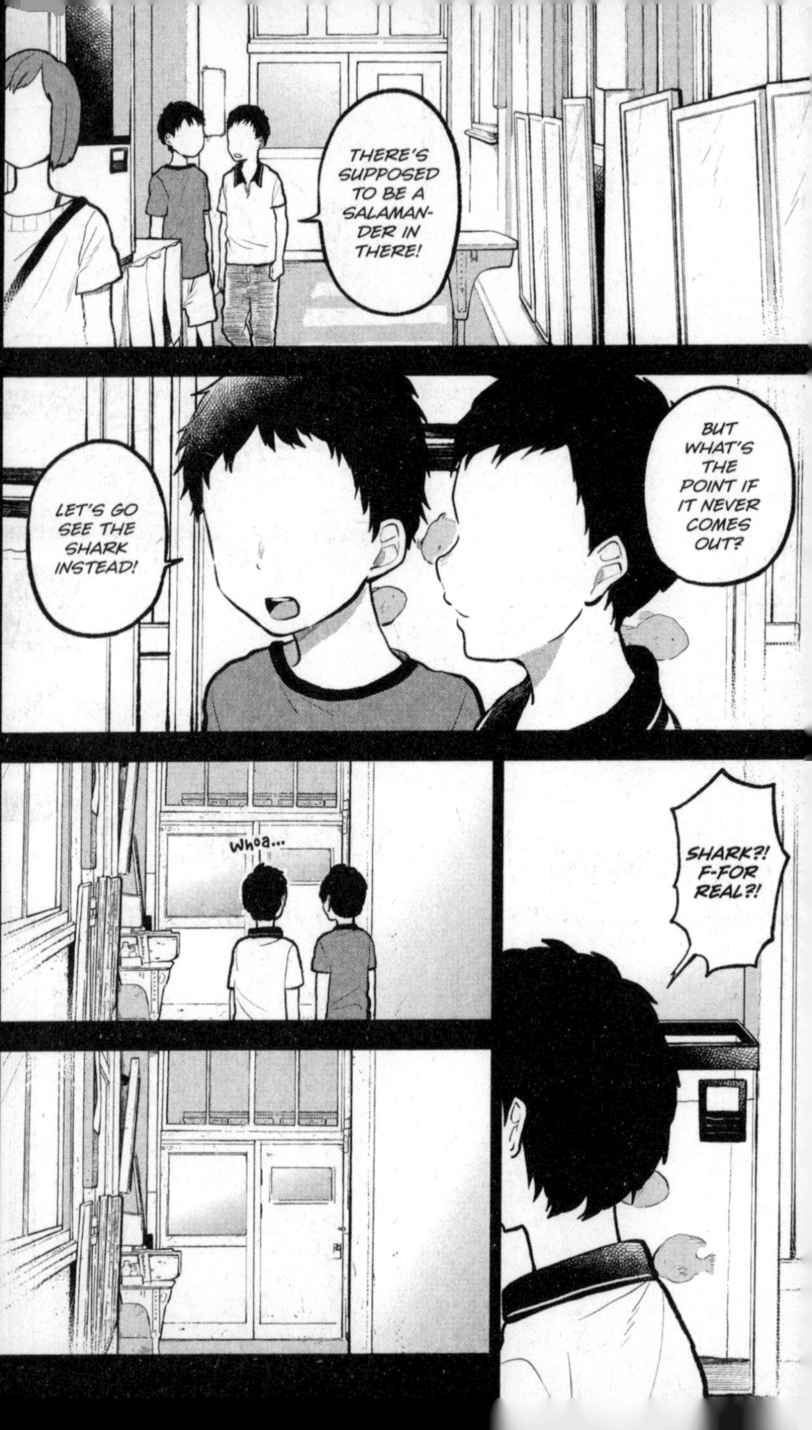
THERE'S SUPPOSED TO BE A SALAMANDER IN THERE!
BUT WHAT'S THE POINT IF IT NEVER COMES OUT?
LET'S GO SEE THE SHARK INSTEAD!
SHARK?! F-FOR REAL?!
Whoa...

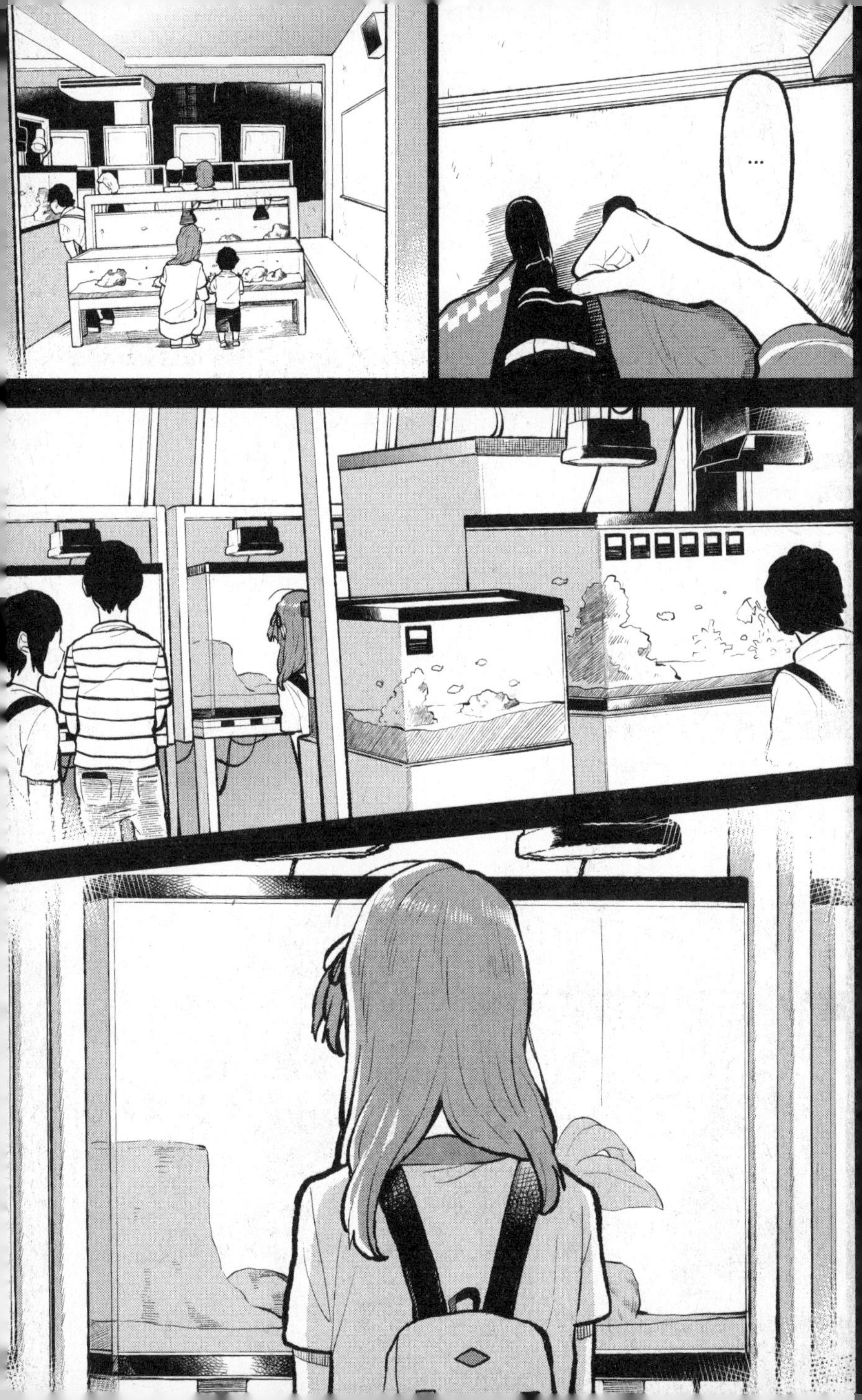
...

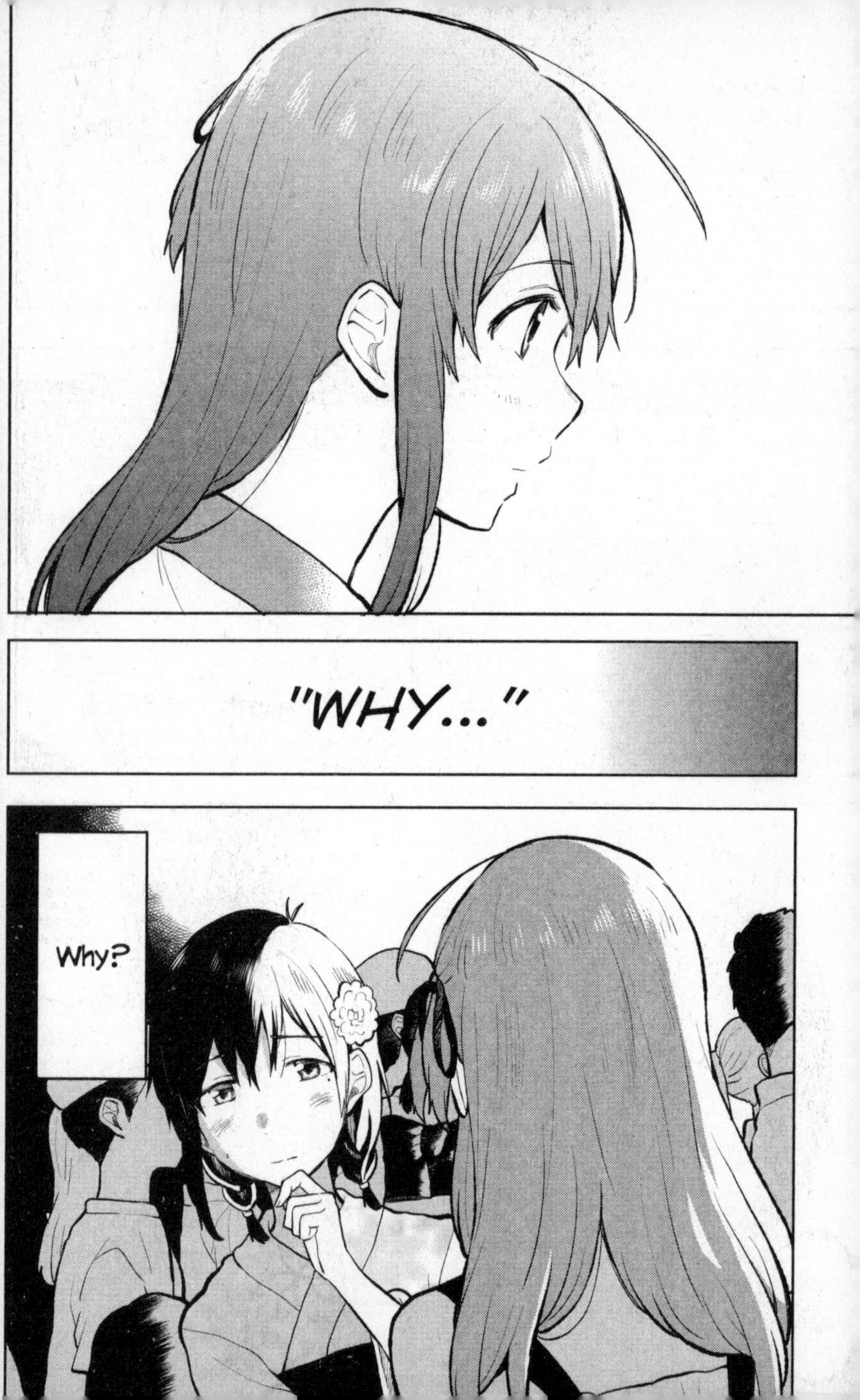
"WHY..."
Why?

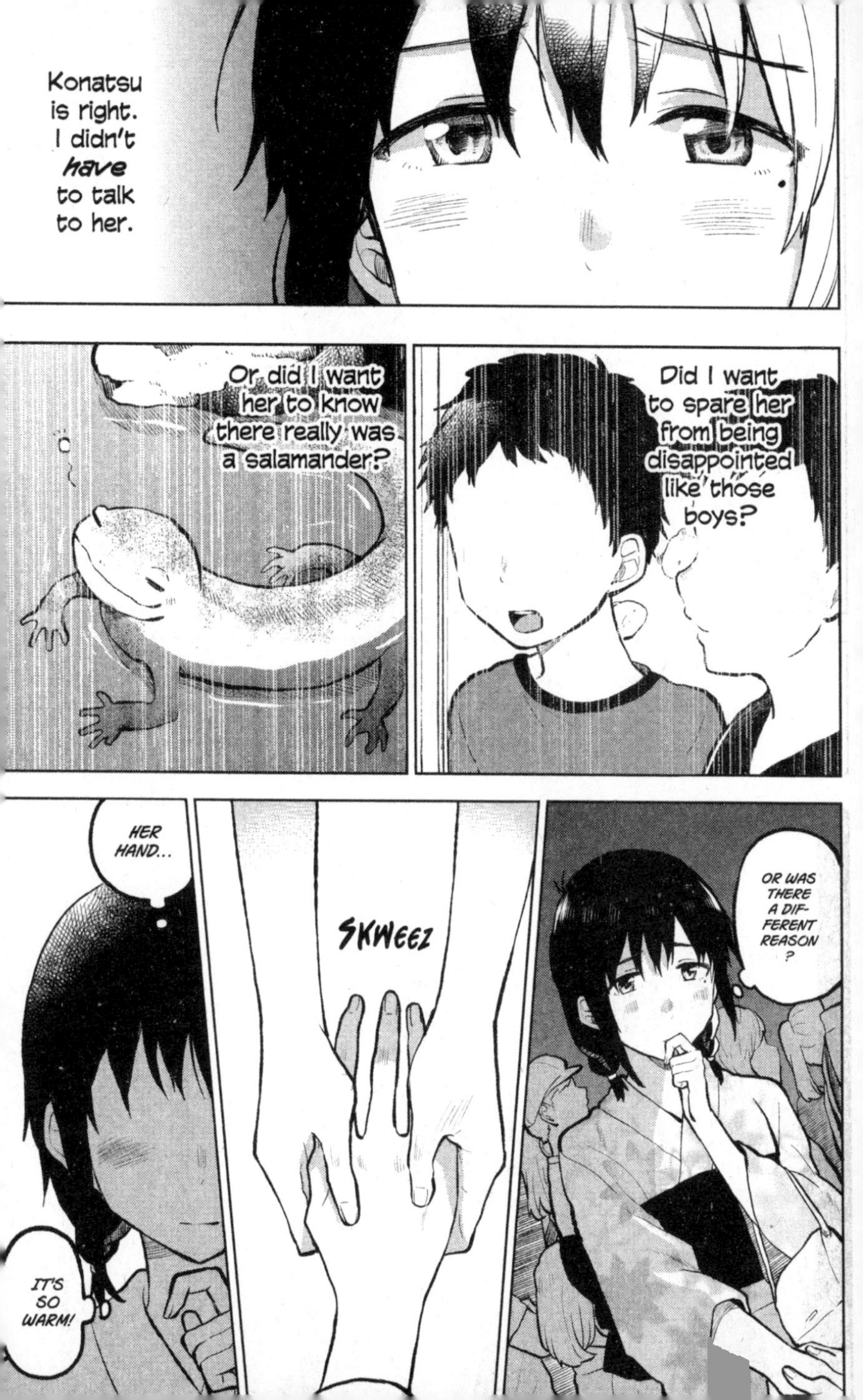
Konatsu is right. I didn't *have* to talk to her.
Did I want to spare her from being disappointed like those boys?
Or did I want her to know there really was a salamander?
OR WAS THERE A DIFFERENT REASON?
SKWEEZ
HER HAND...
IT'S SO WARM!

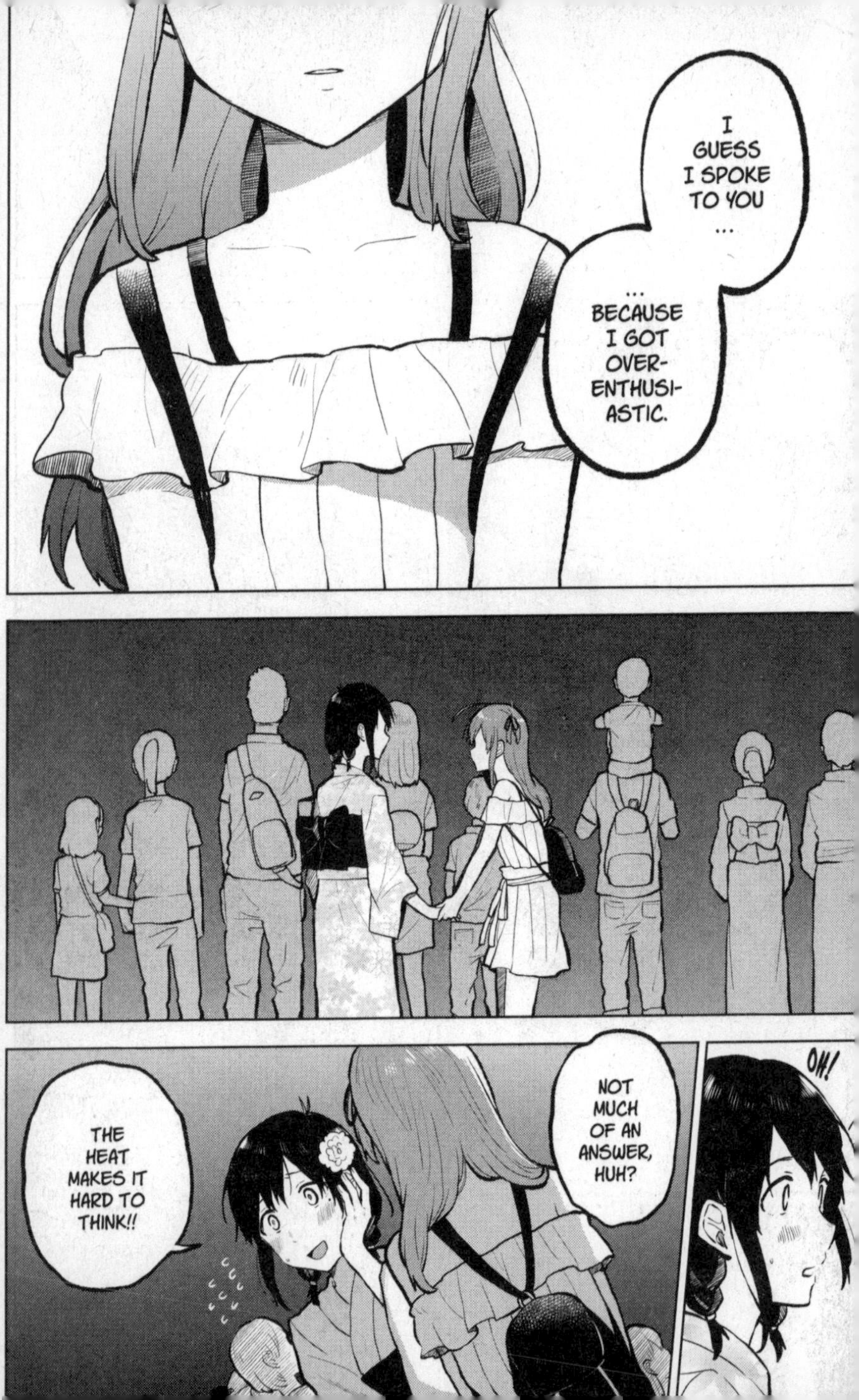
I GUESS I SPOKE TO YOU ...
... BECAUSE I GOT OVER-ENTHUSIASTIC.
OH!
NOT MUCH OF AN ANSWER, HUH?
THE HEAT MAKES IT HARD TO THINK!!

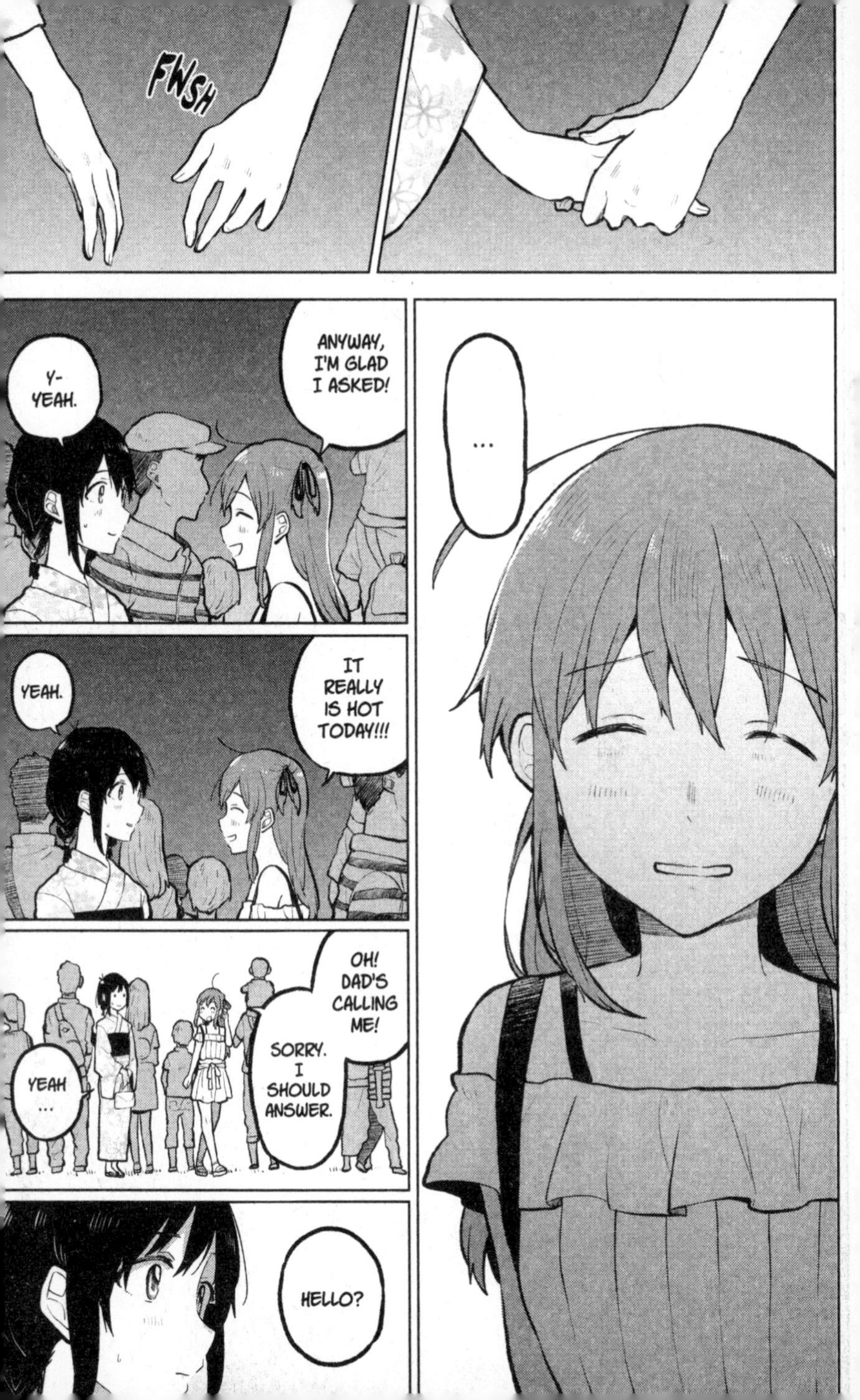
FWSH
...
ANYWAY, I'M GLAD I ASKED!
Y- YEAH.
IT REALLY IS HOT TODAY!!!
YEAH.
OH! DAD'S CALLING ME!
SORRY. I SHOULD ANSWER.
YEAH ...
HELLO?

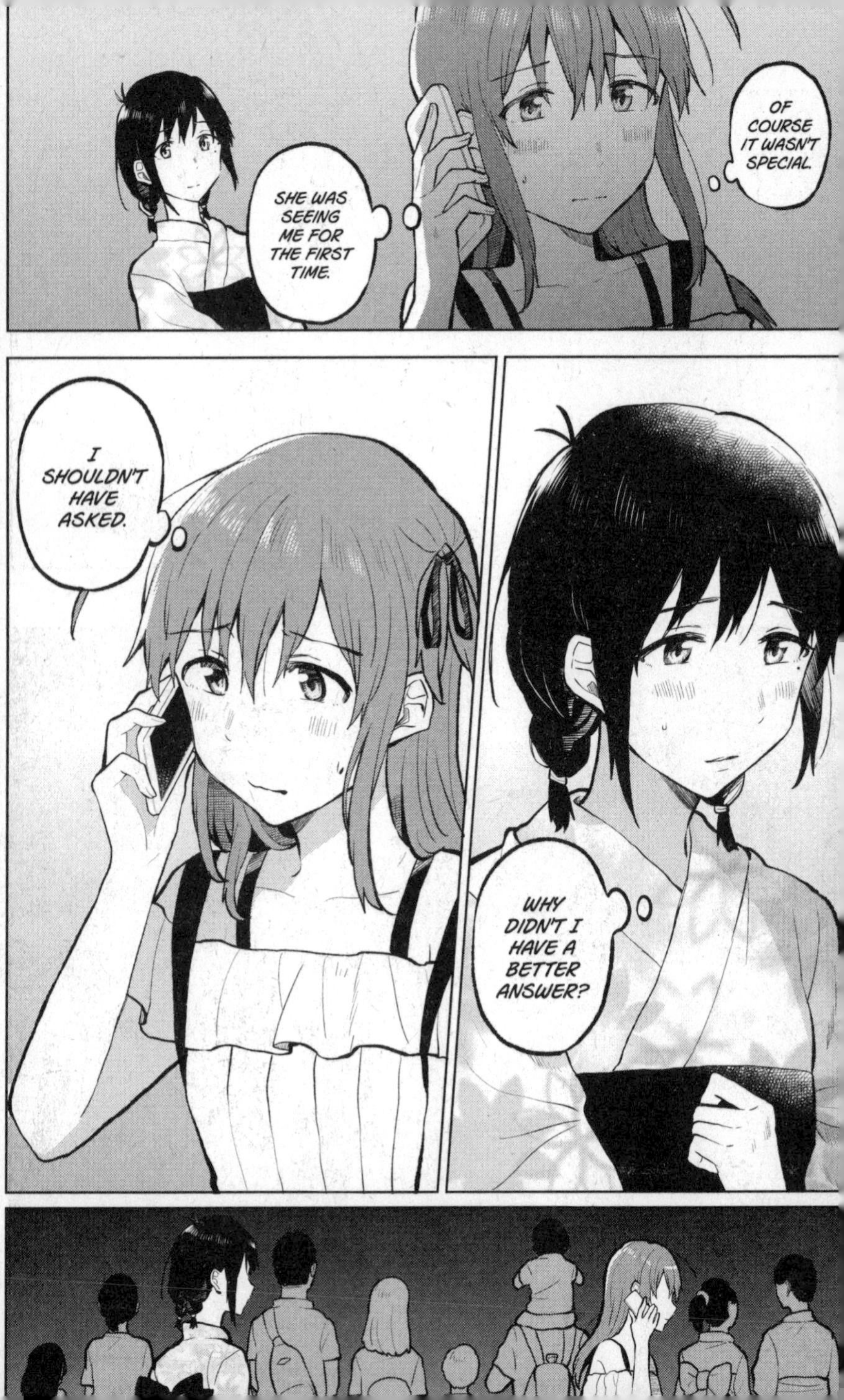
OF COURSE IT WASN'T SPECIAL.
SHE WAS SEEING ME FOR THE FIRST TIME.
WHY DIDN'T I HAVE A BETTER ANSWER?
I SHOULDN'T HAVE ASKED.

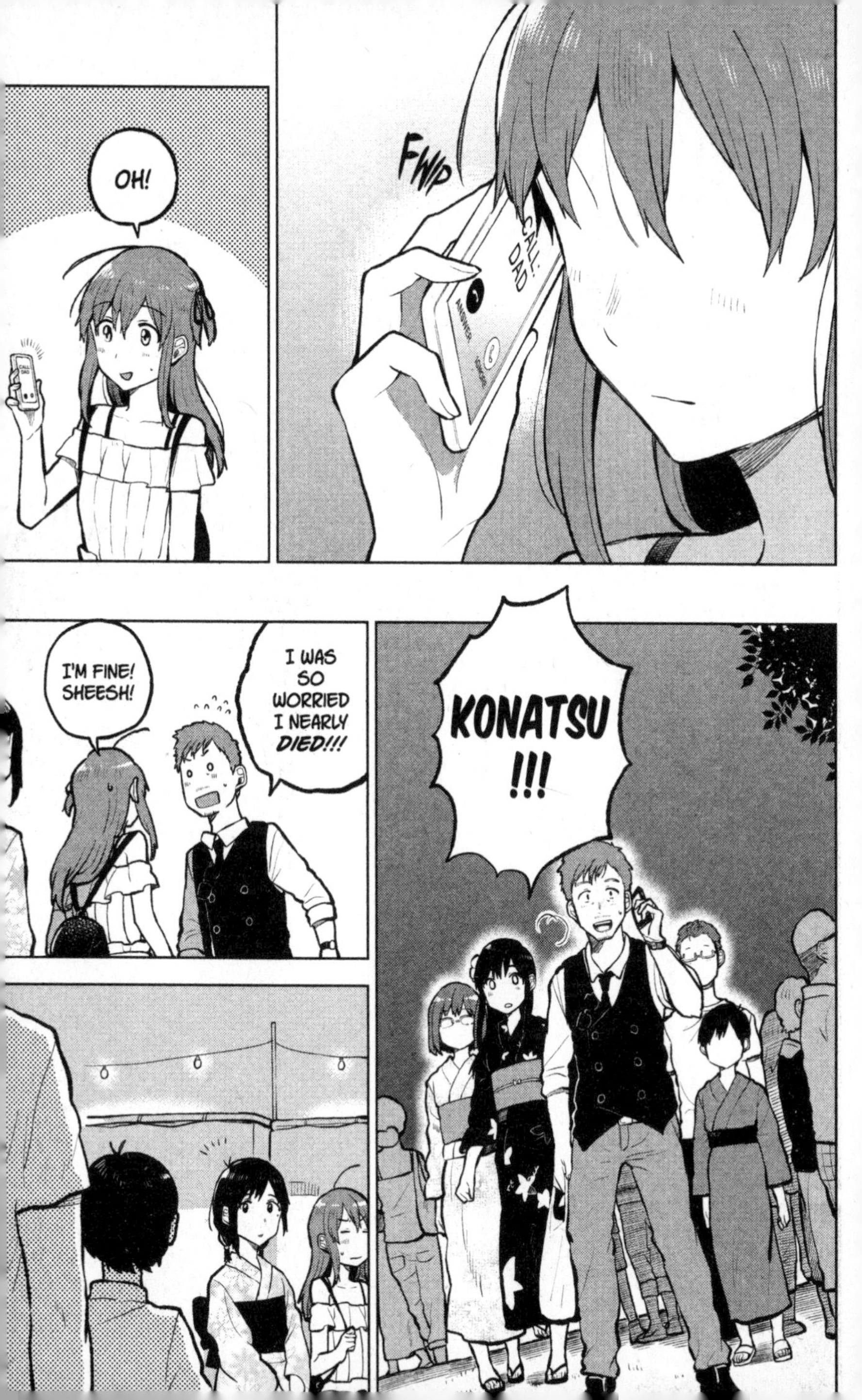
FWIP
CALL: DAD
OH!
KONATSU!!!
I WAS SO WORRIED I NEARLY DIED!!!
I'M FINE! SHEESH!

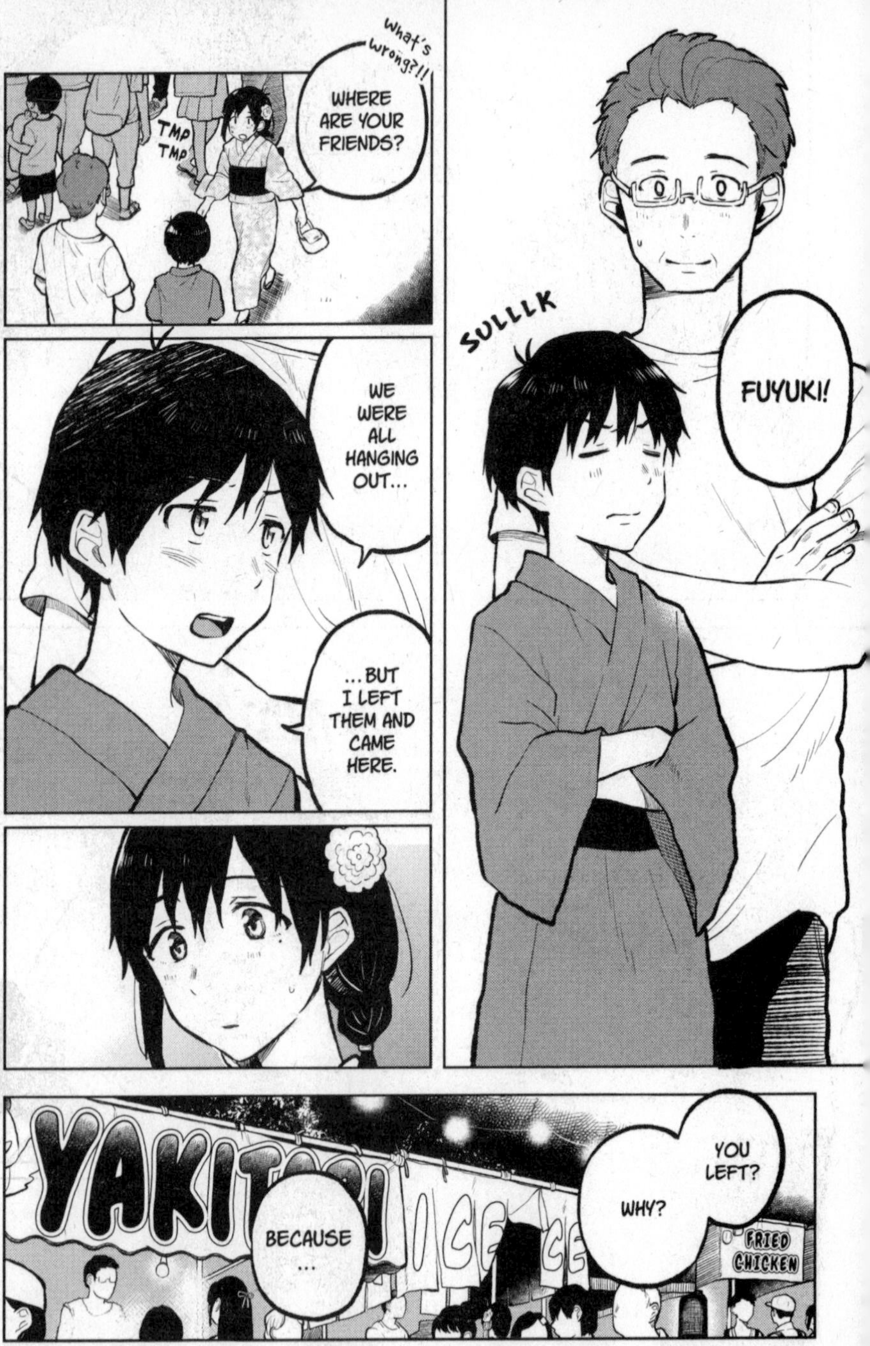
SULLLK
FUYUKI!
What's wrong?!!
WHERE ARE YOUR FRIENDS?
TMP TMP
WE WERE ALL HANGING OUT...
...BUT I LEFT THEM AND CAME HERE.
YOU LEFT?
WHY?
FRIED CHICKEN
ICE
BECAUSE ...
YAKITO

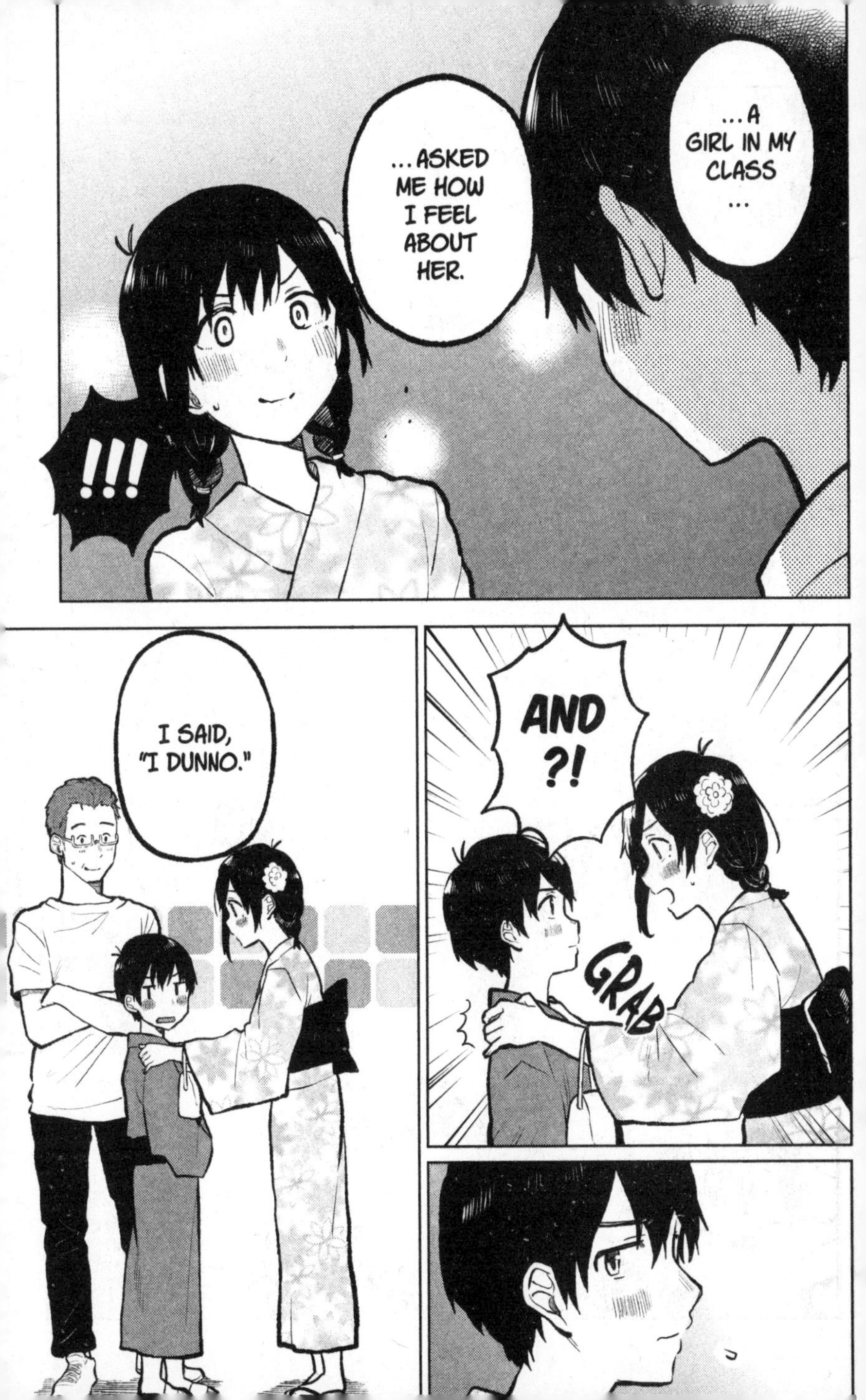
...A GIRL IN MY CLASS ...
...ASKED ME HOW I FEEL ABOUT HER.
!!!
AND ?!
GRAB
I SAID, "I DUNNO."

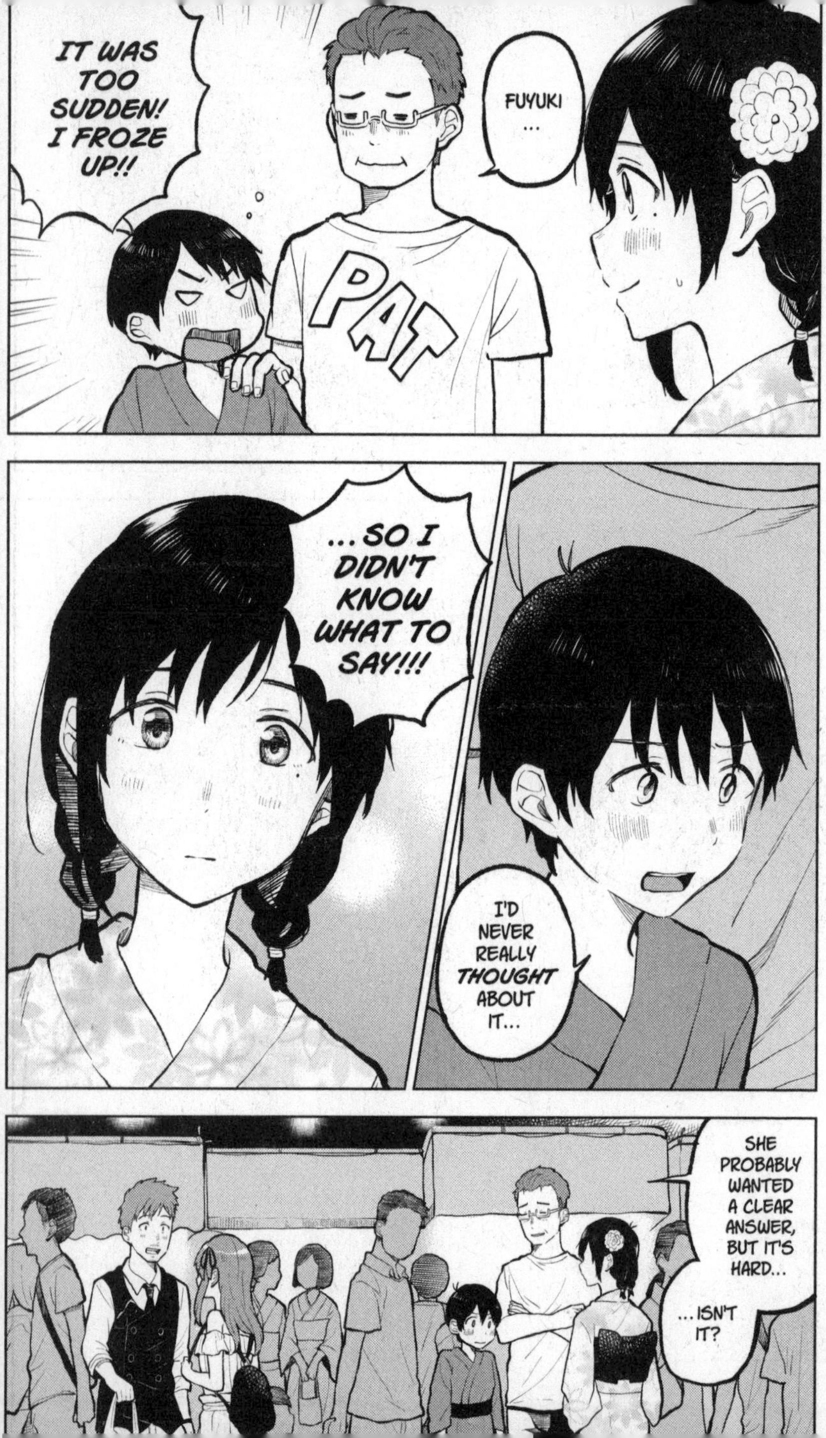
FUYUKI ...
IT WAS TOO SUDDEN! I FROZE UP!!
PAT
I'D NEVER REALLY THOUGHT ABOUT IT...
...SO I DIDN'T KNOW WHAT TO SAY!!!
SHE PROBABLY WANTED A CLEAR ANSWER, BUT IT'S HARD...
...ISN'T IT?

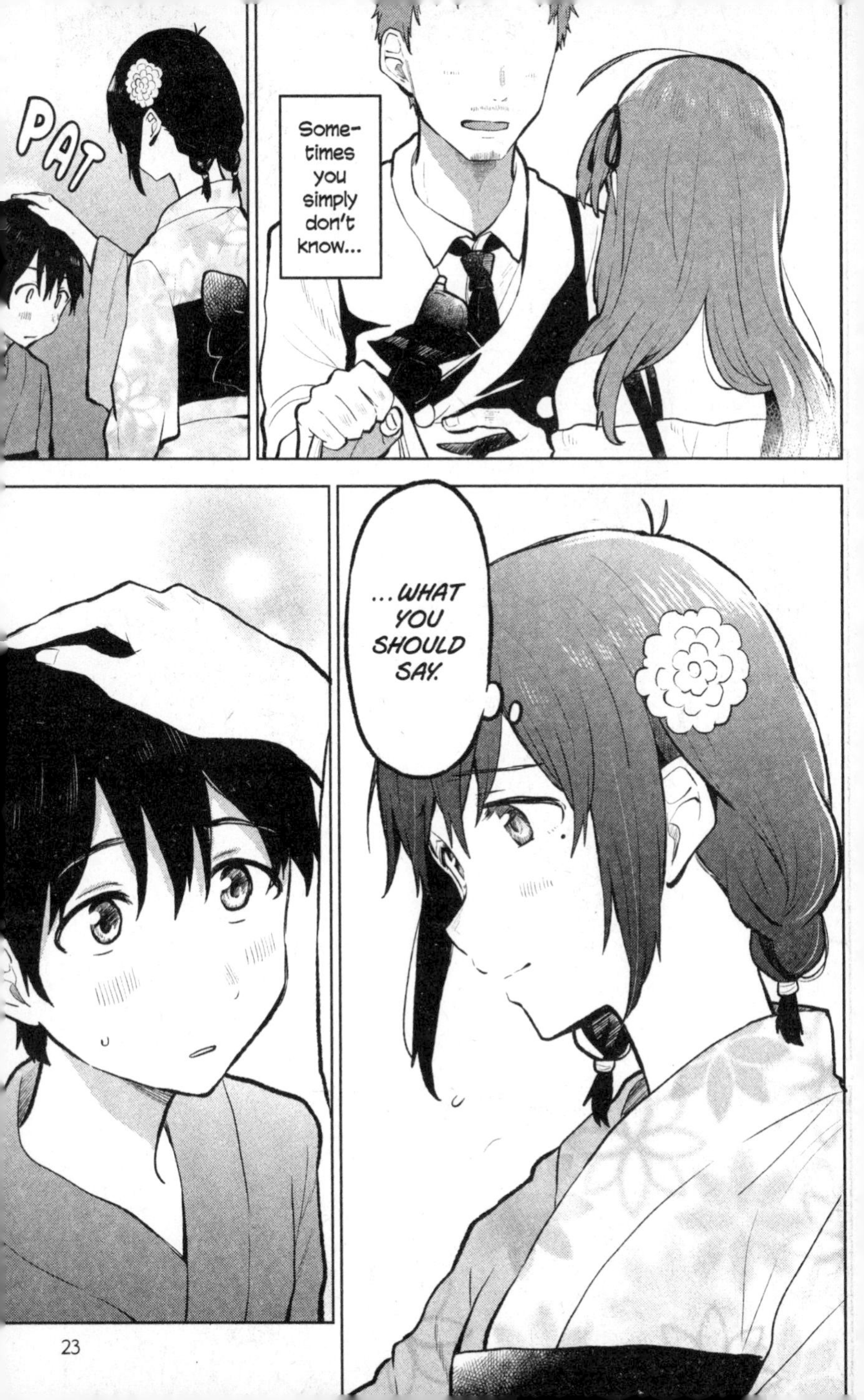
Some- times you simply don't know...
PAT
...WHAT YOU SHOULD SAY.

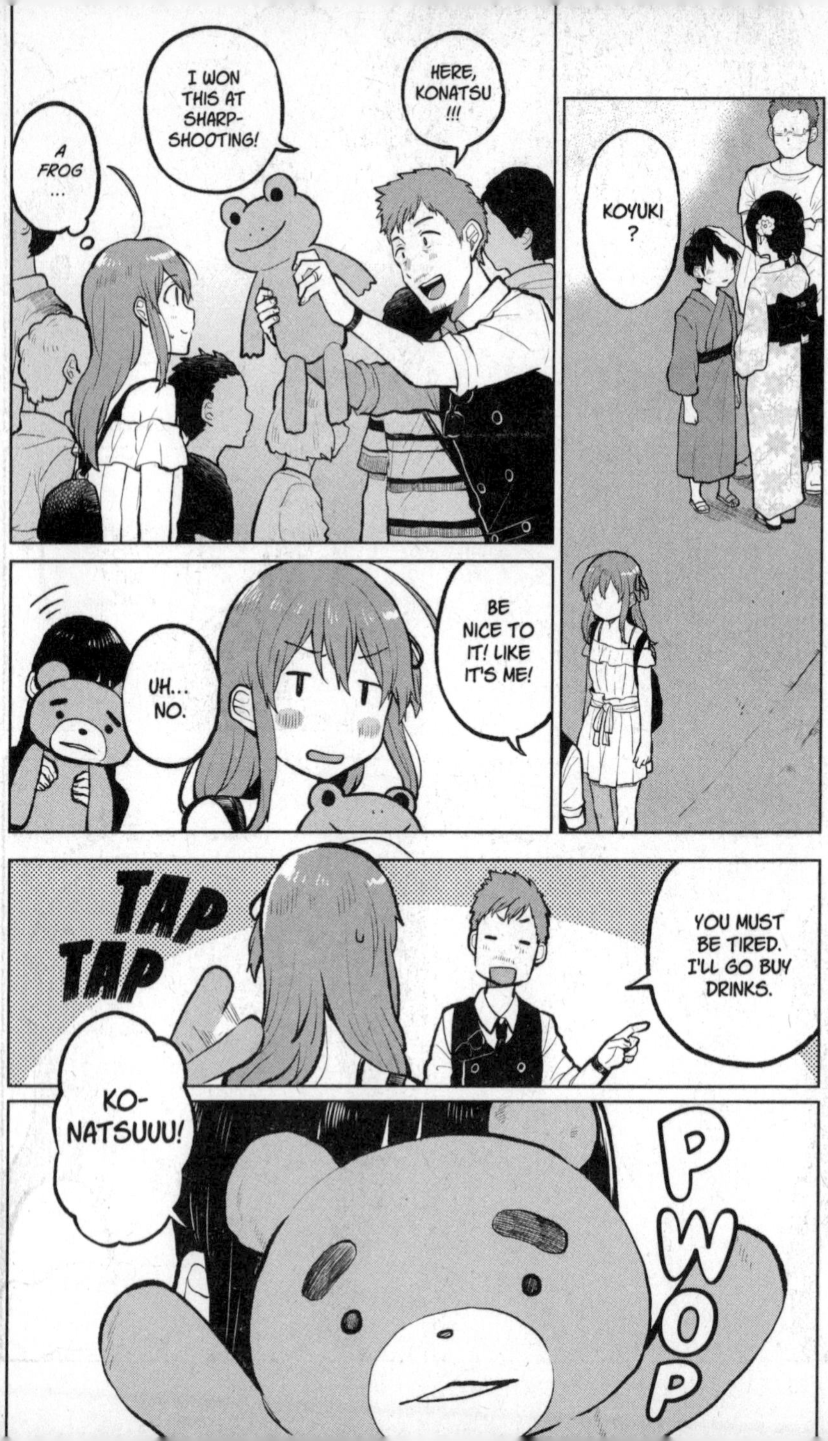
KOYUKI?
HERE, KONATSU!!!
I WON THIS AT SHARP-SHOOTING!
A FROG...
BE NICE TO IT! LIKE IT'S ME!
UH... NO.
YOU MUST BE TIRED. I'LL GO BUY DRINKS.
TAP TAP
PWOP
KO-NATSUUU!

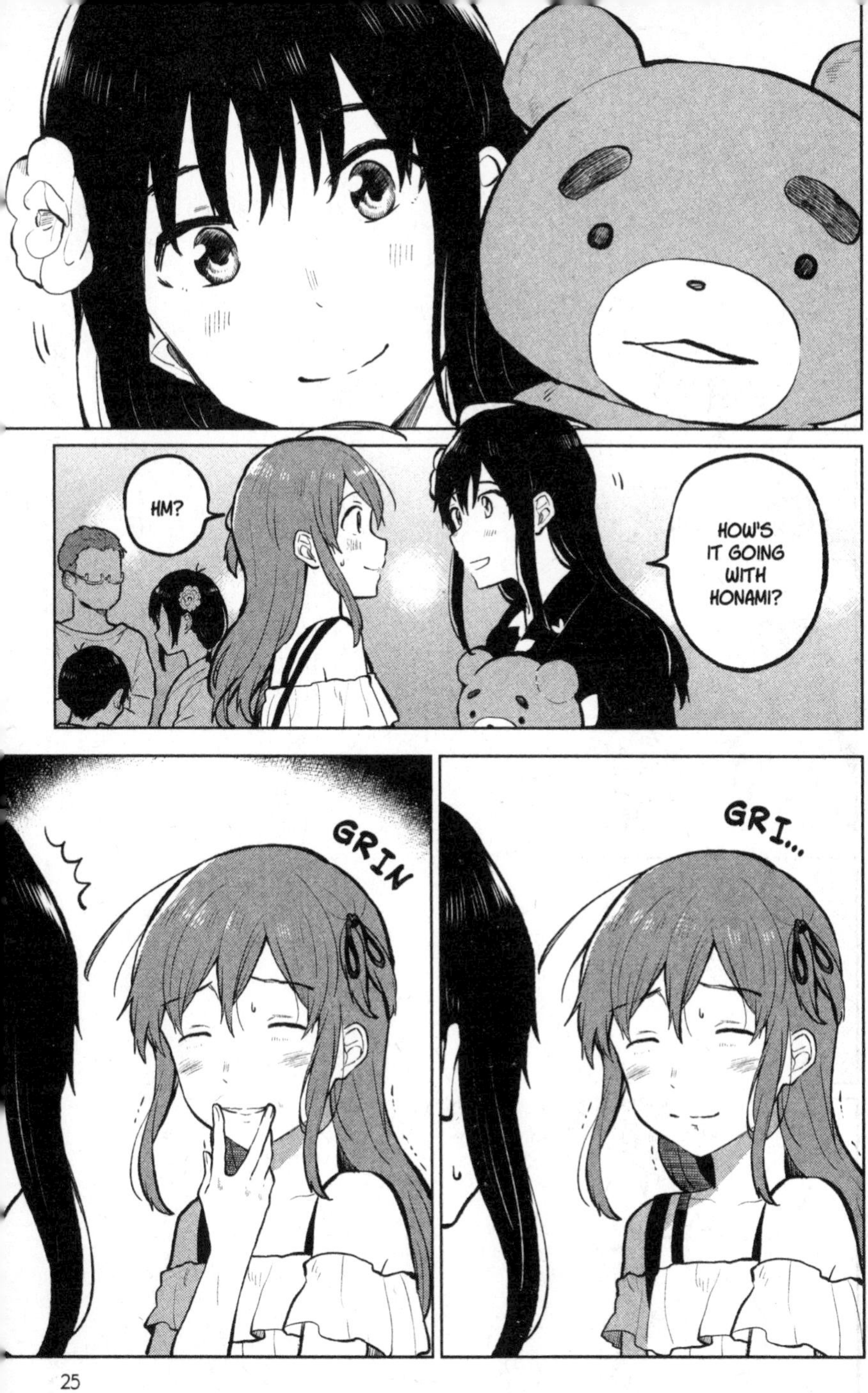
HOW'S IT GOING WITH HONAMI?
HM?
GRI...
GRIN

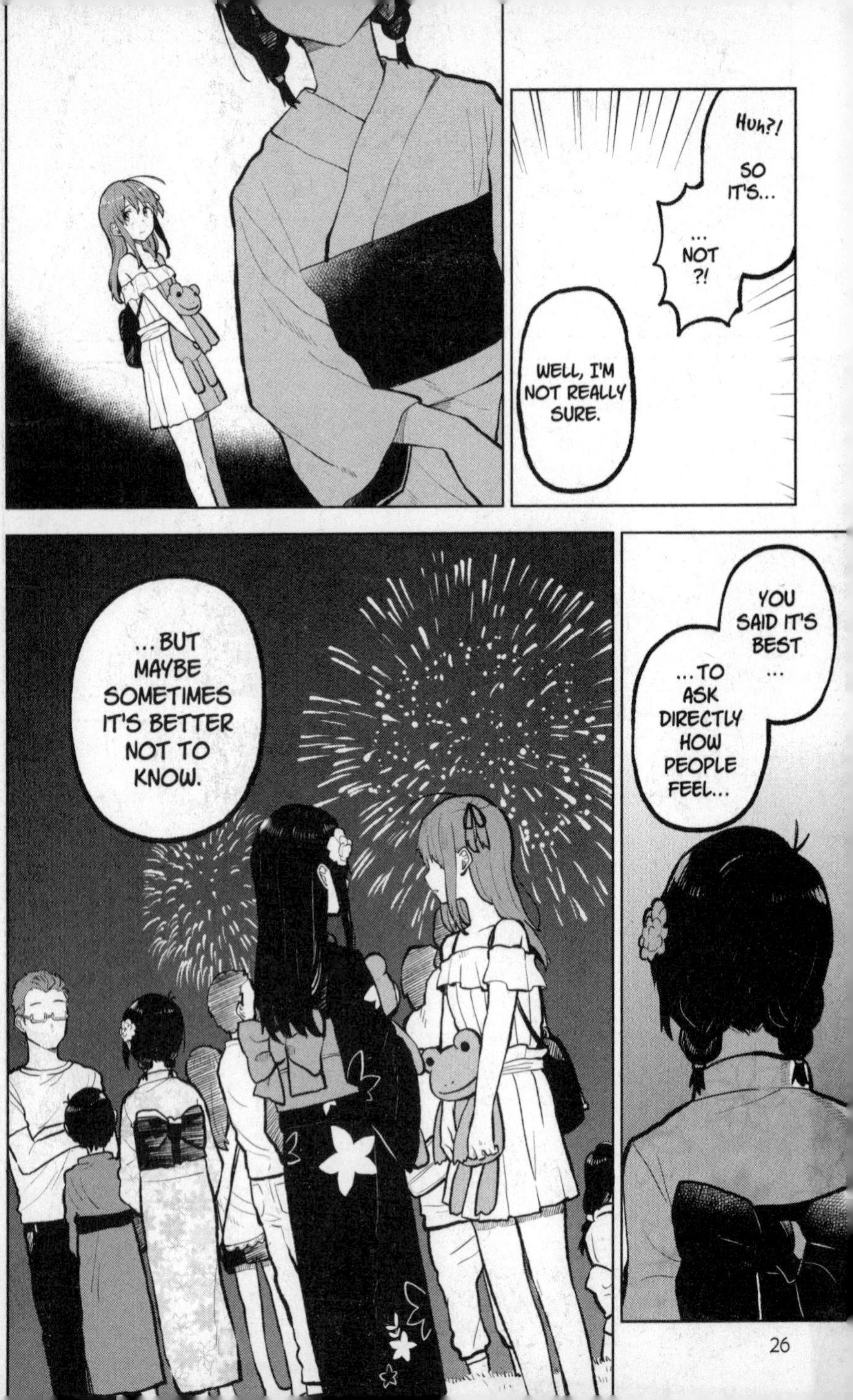
Huh?! SO IT'S... ... NOT ?!
WELL, I'M NOT REALLY SURE.
YOU SAID IT'S BEST ...
...TO ASK DIRECTLY HOW PEOPLE FEEL...
...BUT MAYBE SOMETIMES IT'S BETTER NOT TO KNOW.

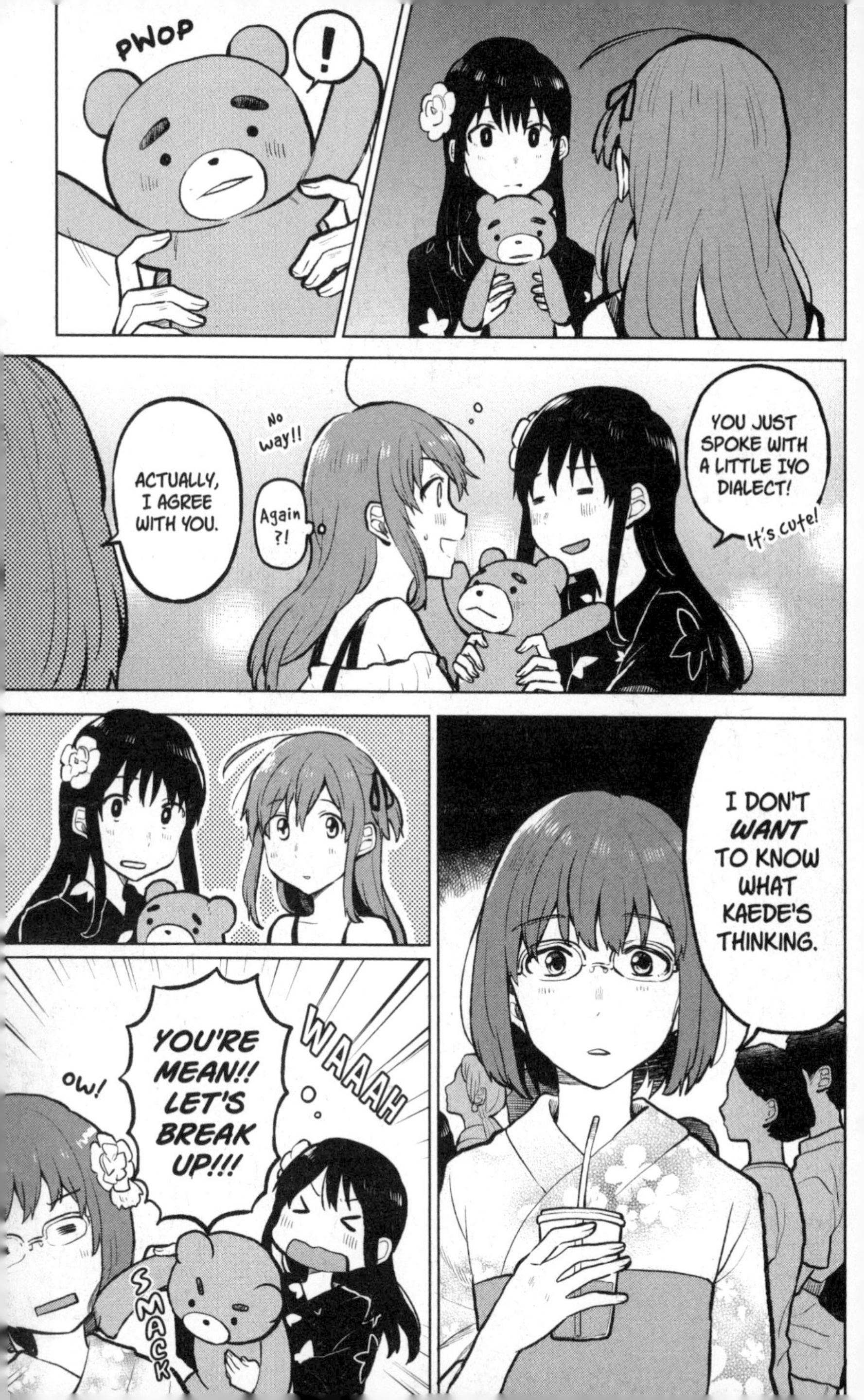

PWOP
!
YOU JUST SPOKE WITH A LITTLE IYO DIALECT!
It's cute!
No way!!
Again ?!
ACTUALLY, I AGREE WITH YOU.
I DON'T *WANT* TO KNOW WHAT KAEDE'S THINKING.
WAAAAH
YOU'RE MEAN!! LET'S BREAK UP!!!
OW!
SMACK

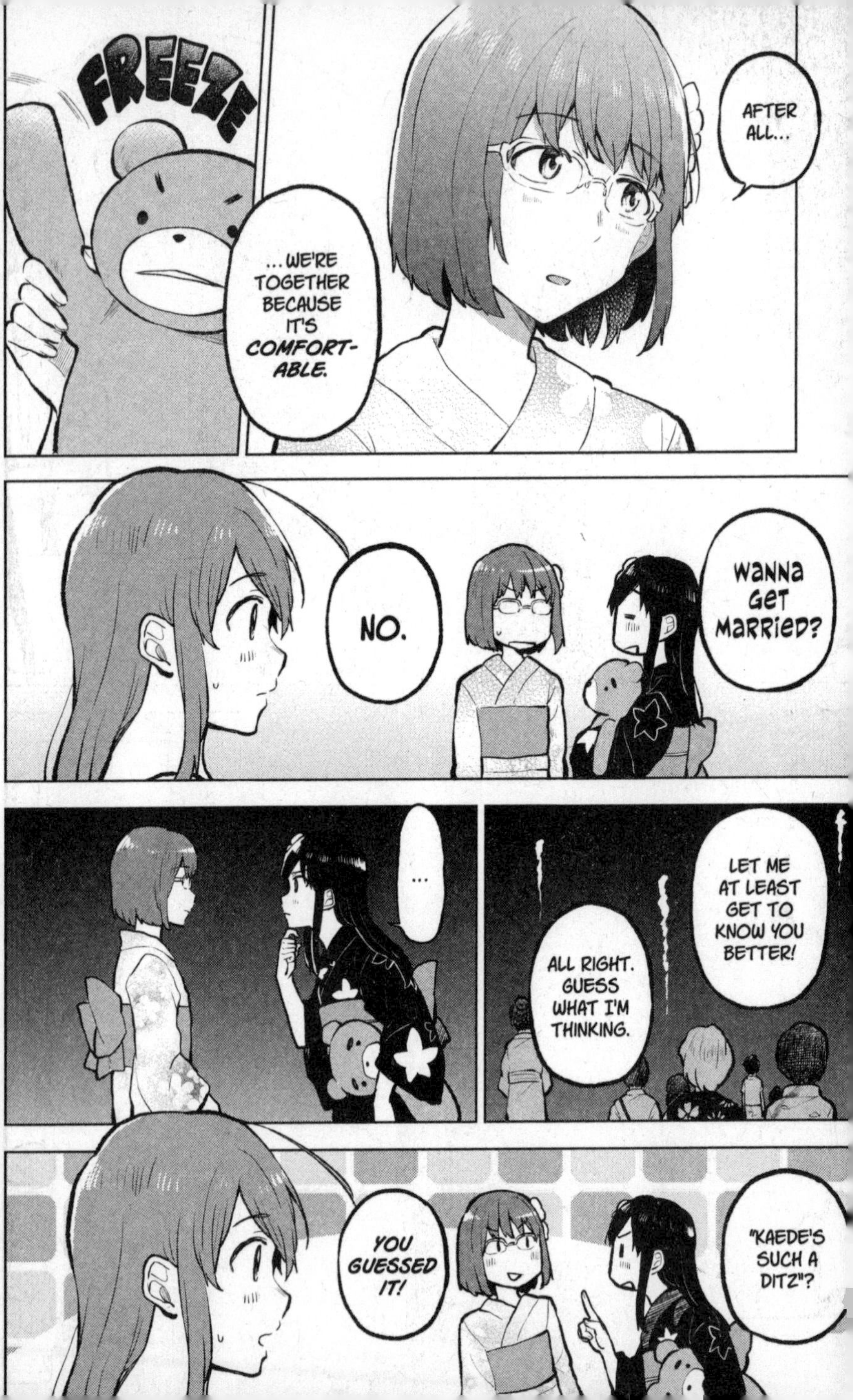
AFTER ALL...
...WE'RE TOGETHER BECAUSE IT'S *COMFORTABLE.*
FREEZE
WANNA GET MARRIED?
NO.
LET ME AT LEAST GET TO KNOW YOU BETTER!
ALL RIGHT. GUESS WHAT I'M THINKING.
...
"KAEDE'S SUCH A DITZ"?
YOU GUESSED IT!

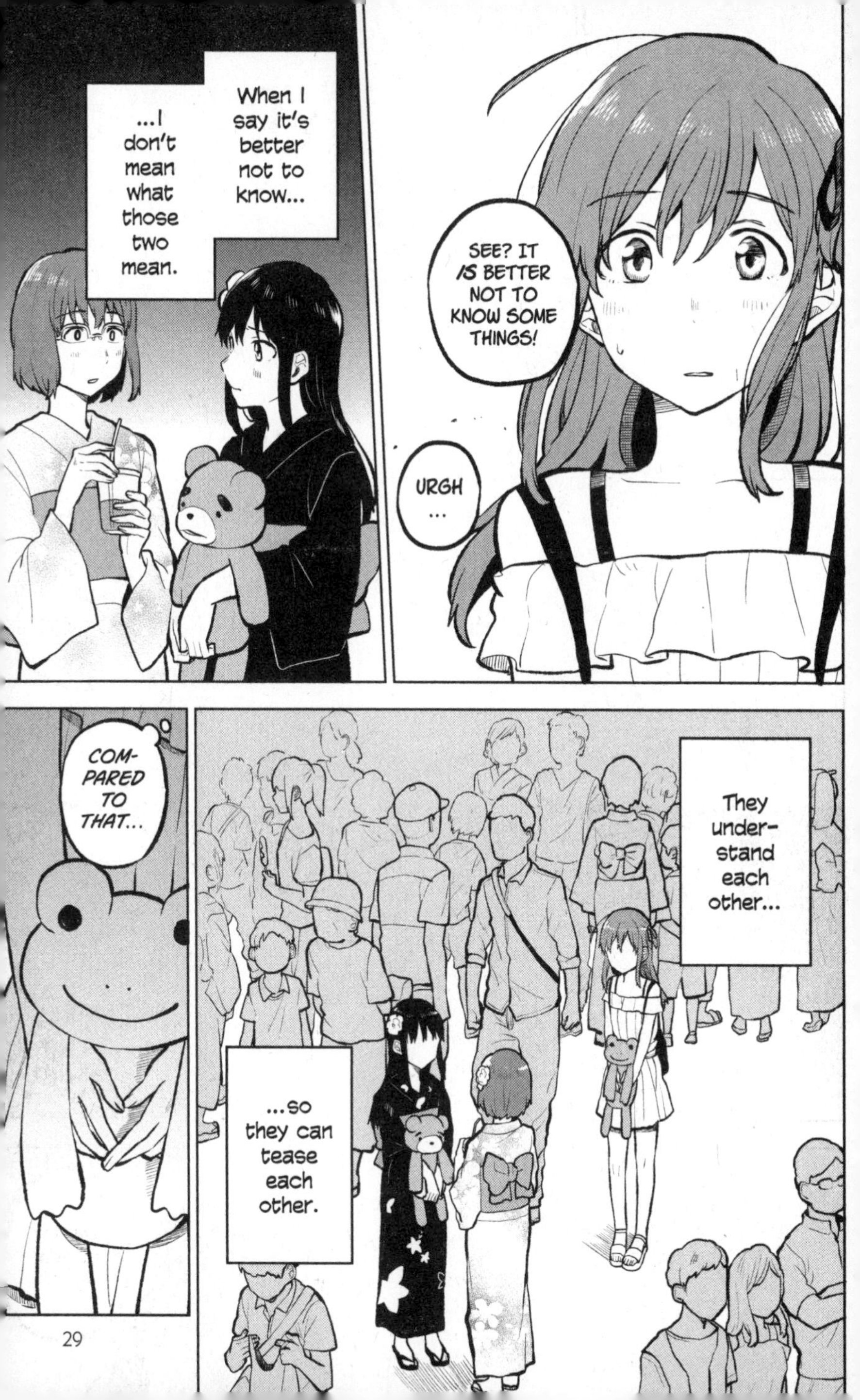
SEE? IT *IS* BETTER NOT TO KNOW SOME THINGS!
URGH ...
When I say it's better not to know...
...I don't mean what those two mean.
They under-stand each other...
...so they can tease each other.
COM-PARED TO THAT...

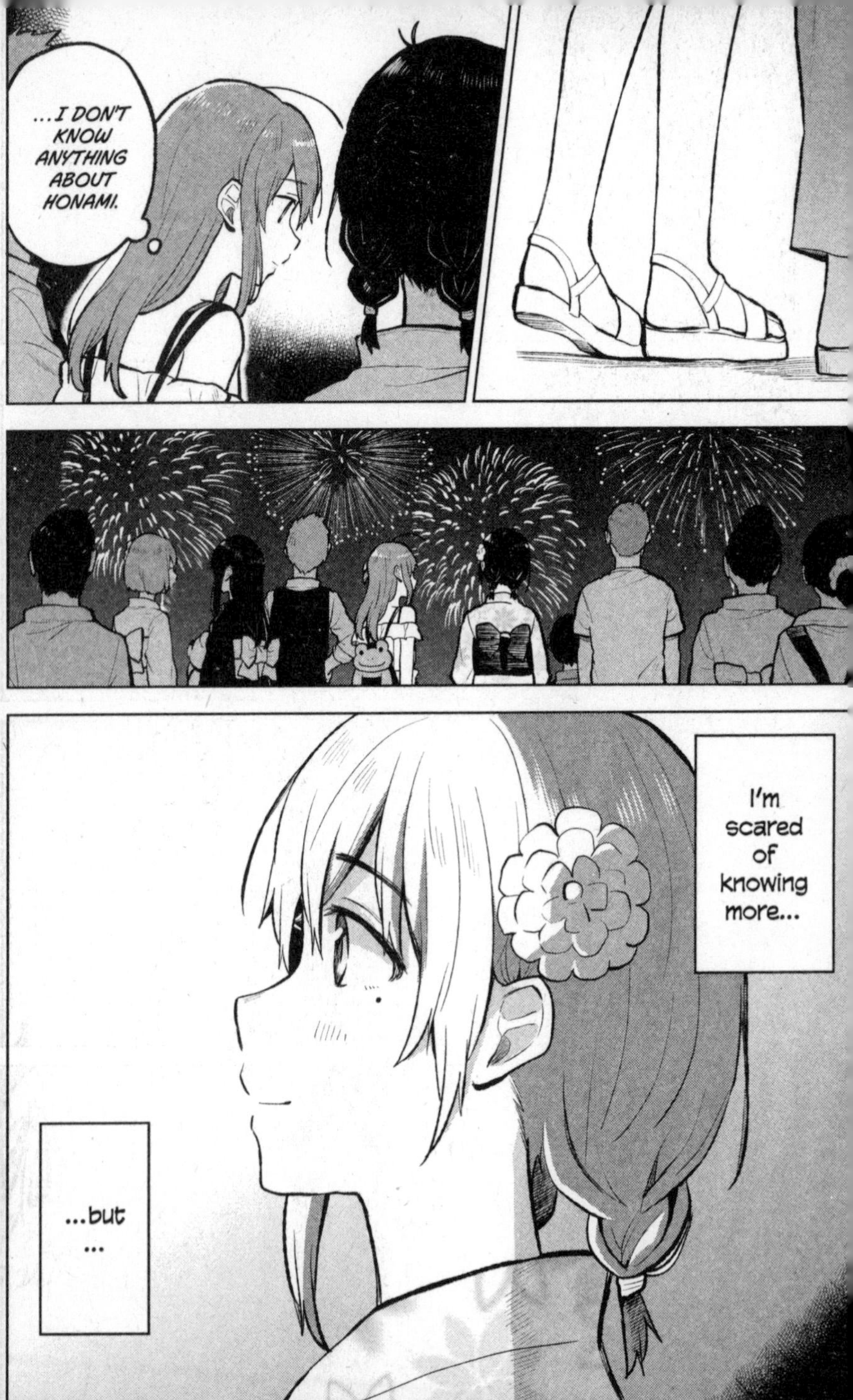
...I DON'T KNOW ANYTHING ABOUT HONAMI.
I'm scared of knowing more...
...but ...

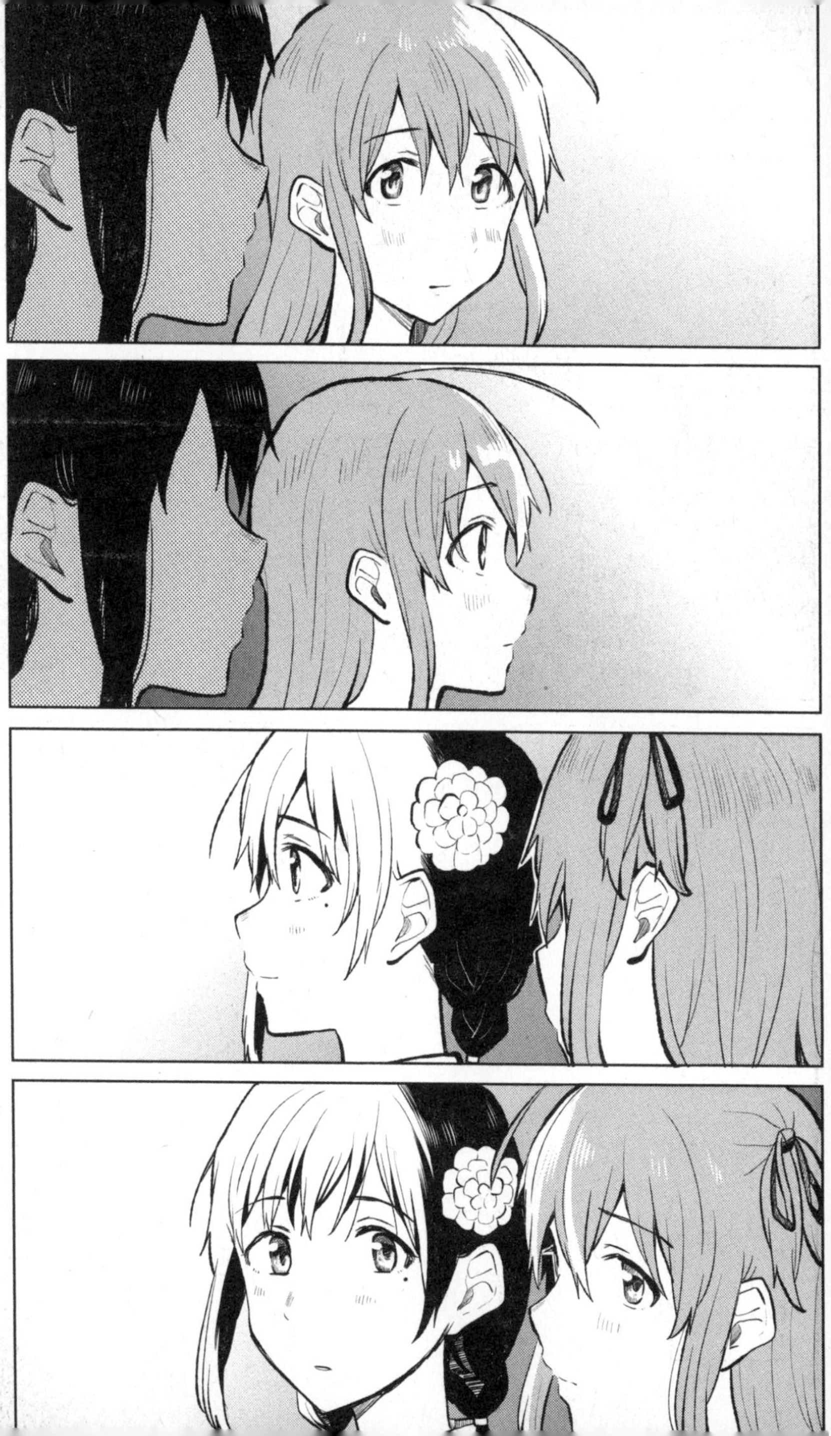

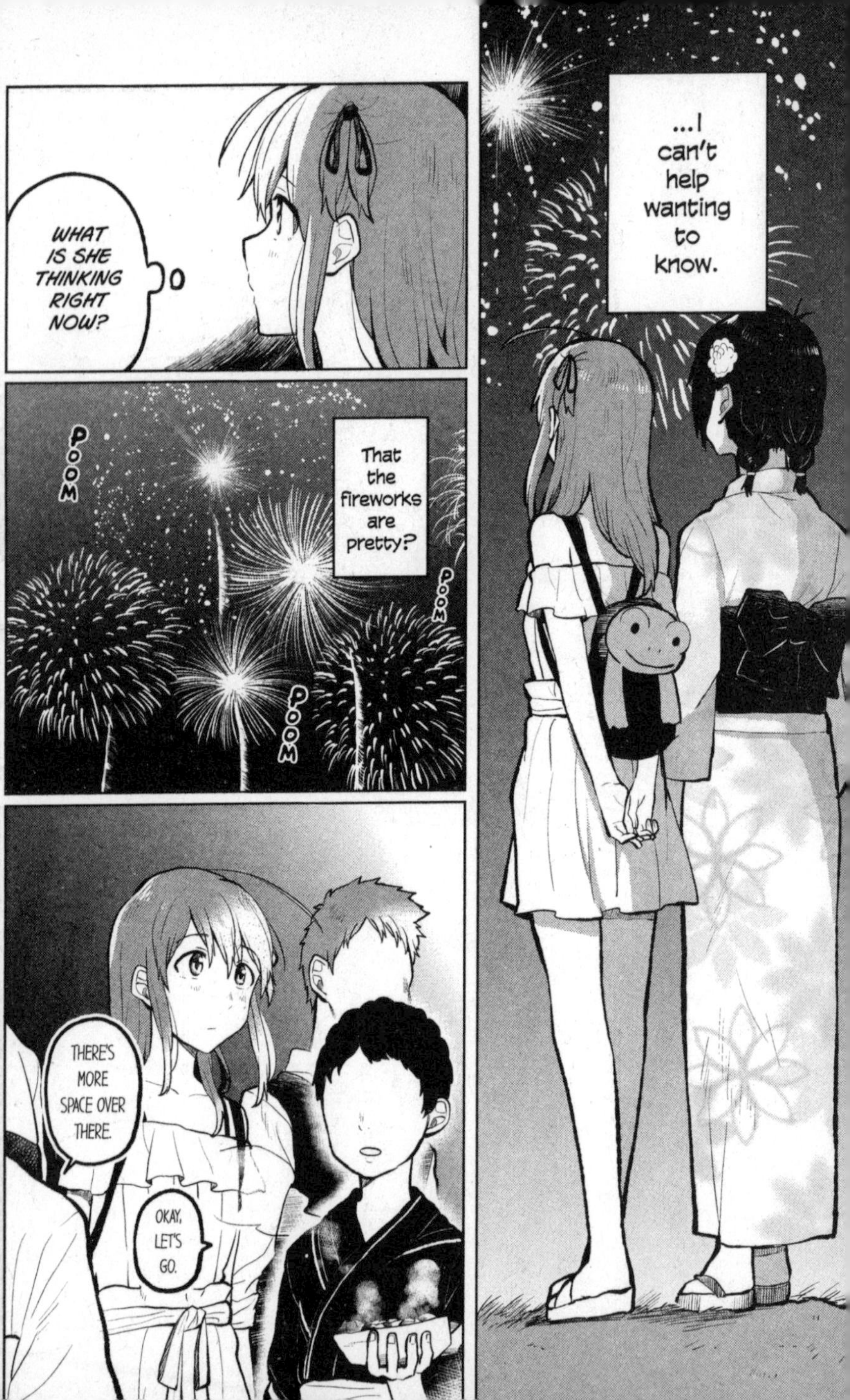
...I can't help wanting to know.
WHAT IS SHE THINKING RIGHT NOW?
That the fireworks are pretty?
POOM
POOM
POOM
THERE'S MORE SPACE OVER THERE.
OKAY, LET'S GO.

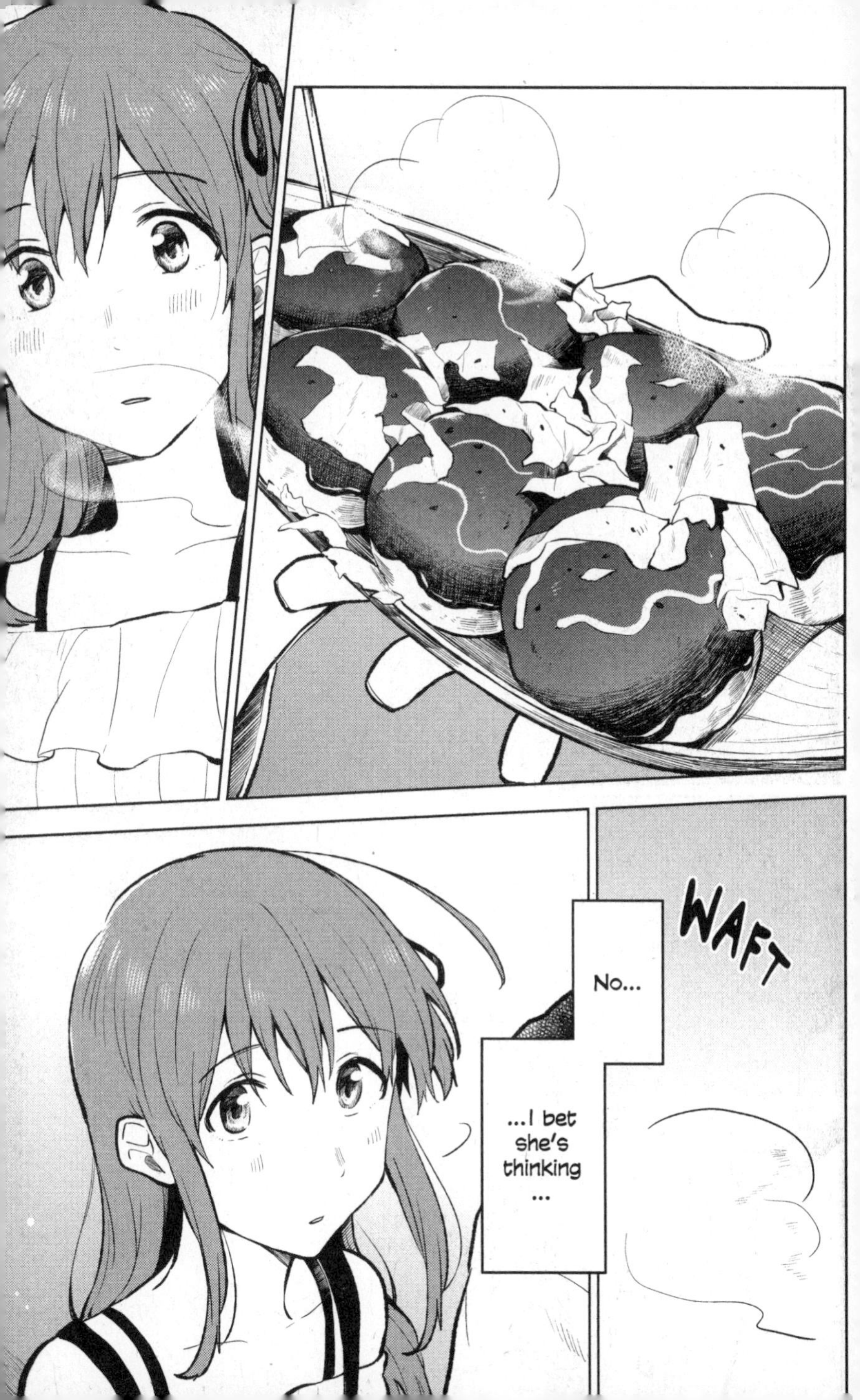
WAFT
No...
...I bet she's thinking ...

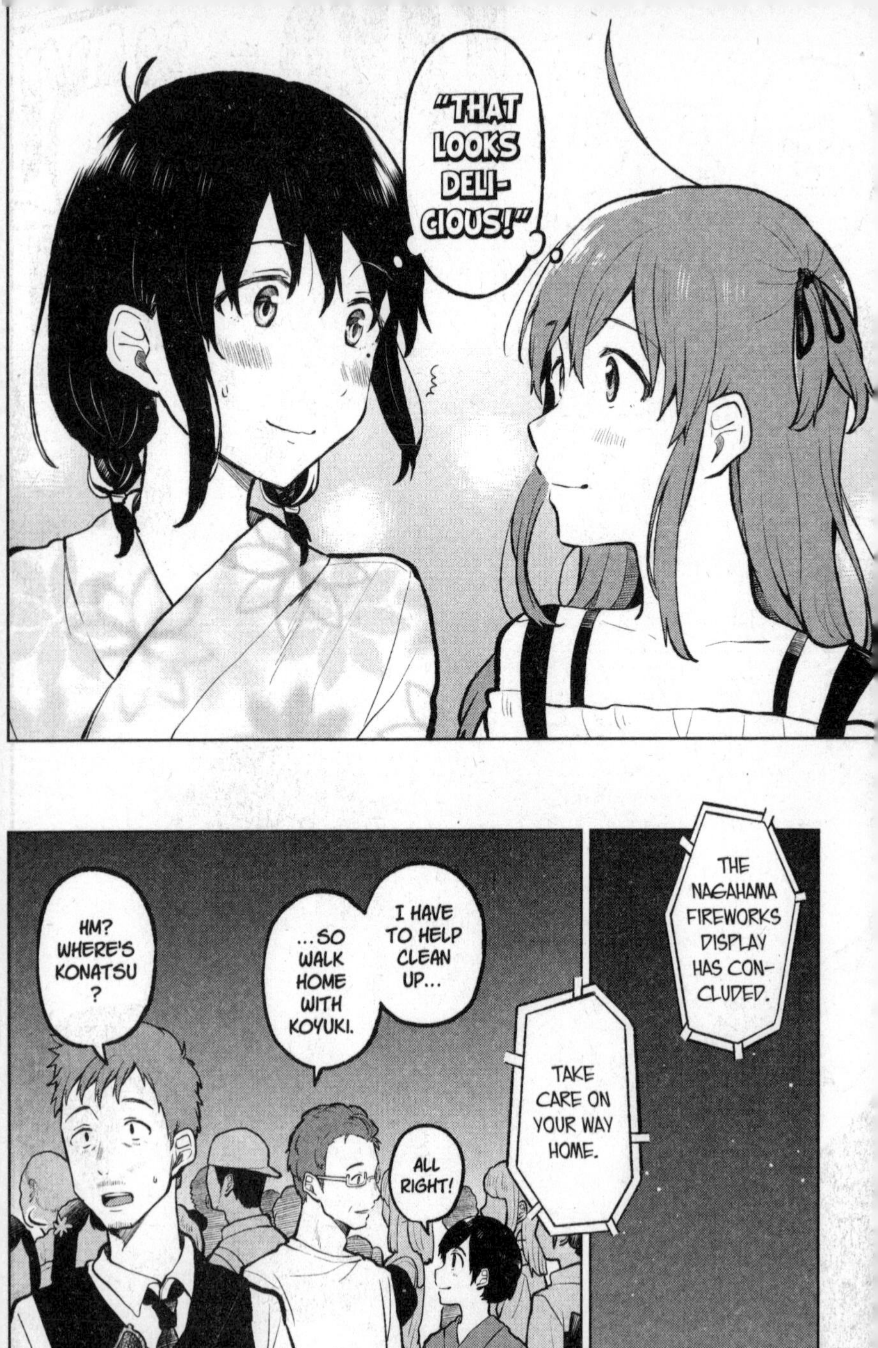
"THAT LOOKS DELI-CIOUS!"
THE NAGAHAMA FIREWORKS DISPLAY HAS CON-CLUDED.
TAKE CARE ON YOUR WAY HOME.
I HAVE TO HELP CLEAN UP...
...SO WALK HOME WITH KOYUKI.
ALL RIGHT!
HM? WHERE'S KONATSU ?

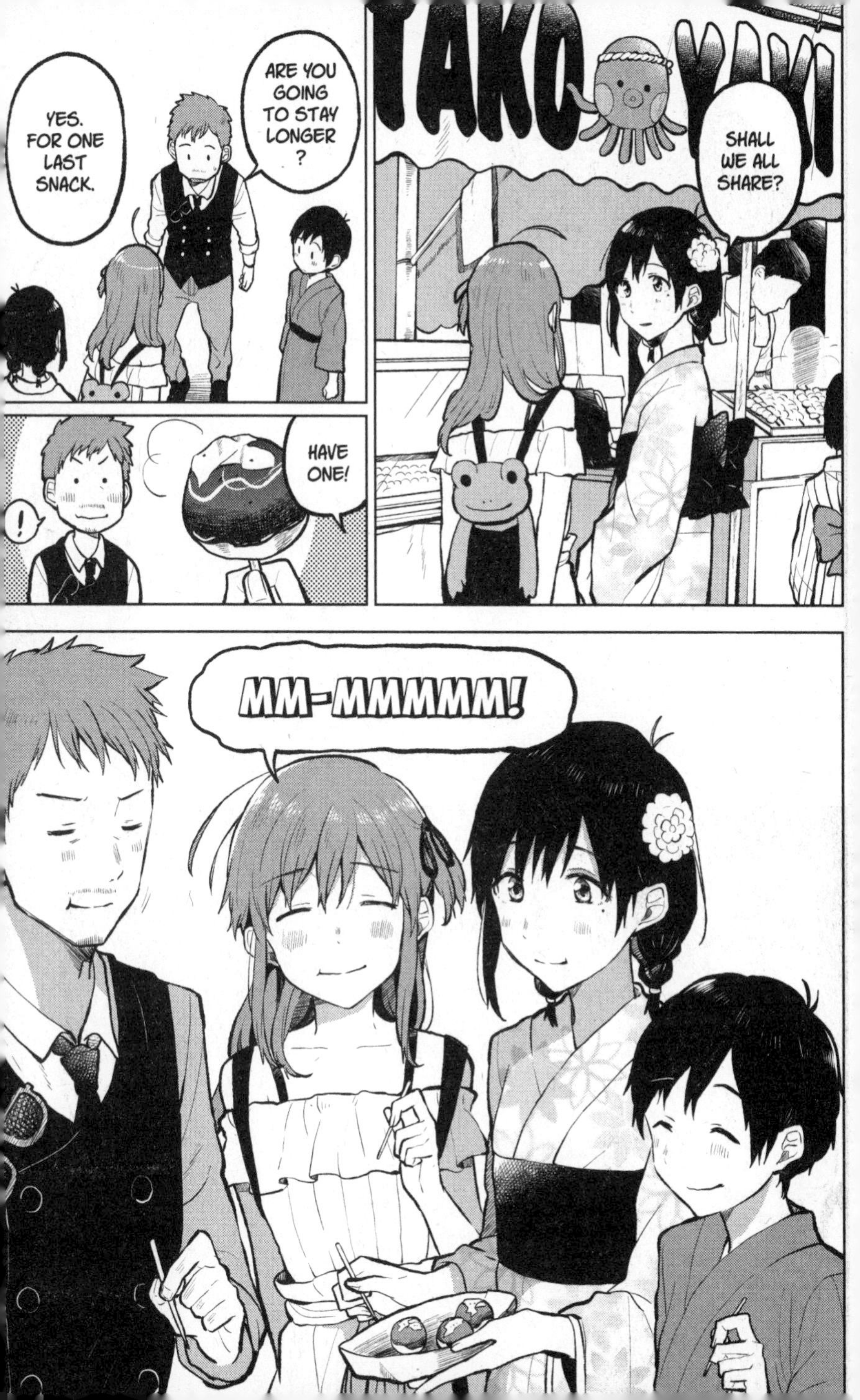
TAKO YAKI
SHALL WE ALL SHARE?
ARE YOU GOING TO STAY LONGER ?
YES. FOR ONE LAST SNACK.
HAVE ONE!
!
MM-MMMMM!

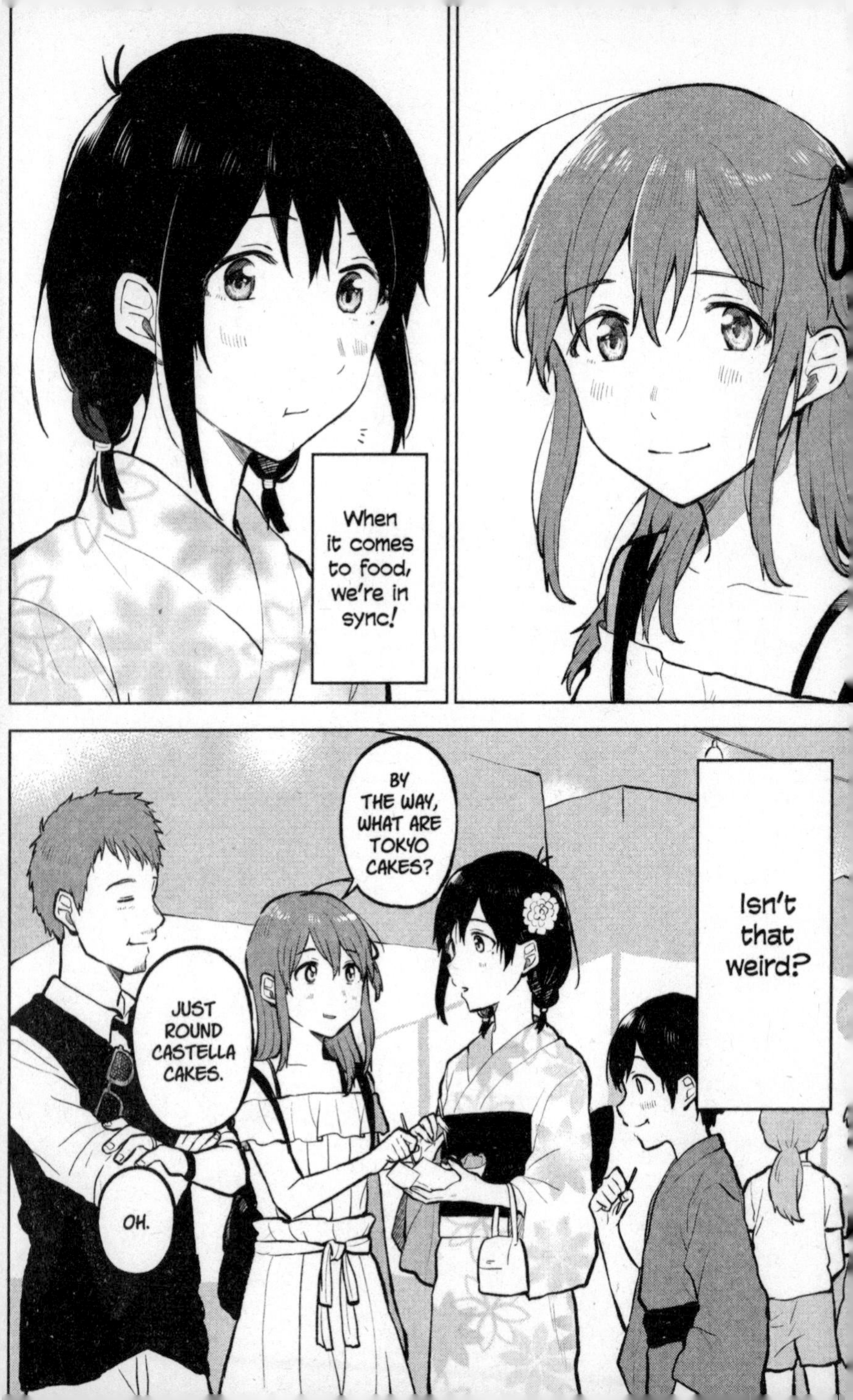
When it comes to food, we're in sync!
Isn't that weird?
BY THE WAY, WHAT ARE TOKYO CAKES?
JUST ROUND CASTELLA CAKES.
OH.

A Tropical Fish
Yearns for Snow

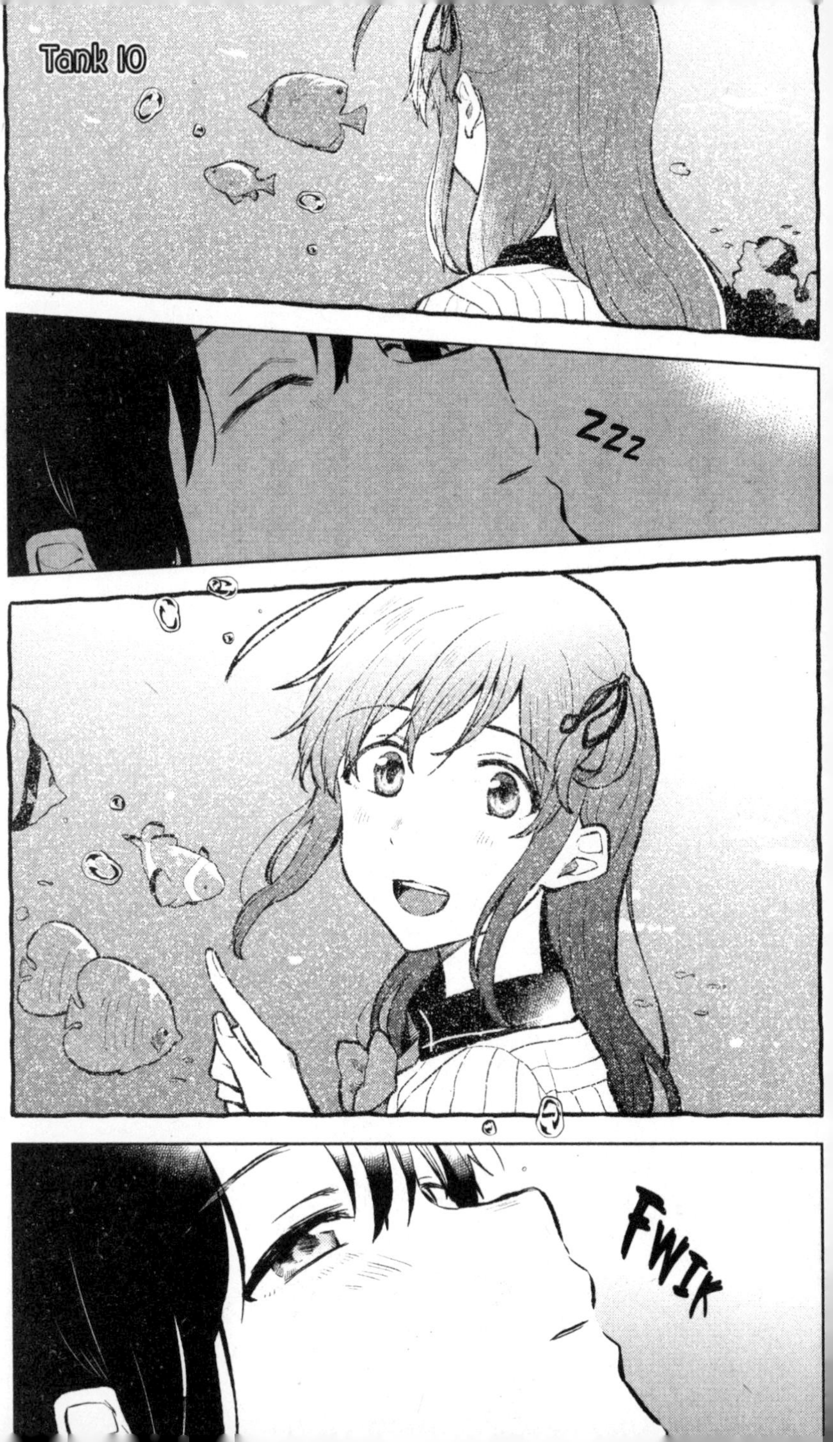
Tank 10
Zzz
FWIK

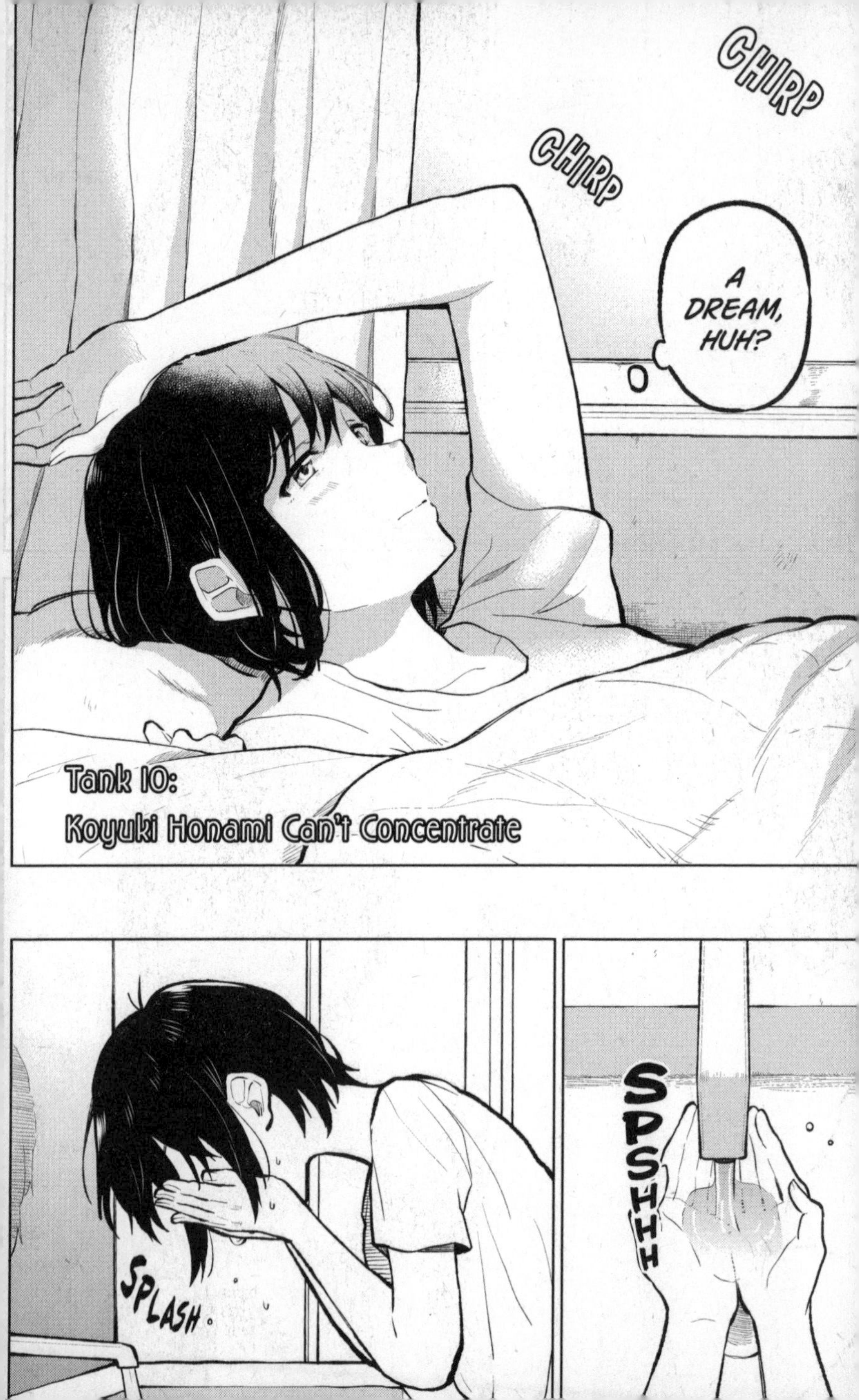
CHIRP
CHIRP
A DREAM, HUH?
Tank 10:
Koyuki Honami Can't Concentrate
SPSHHH
SPLASH

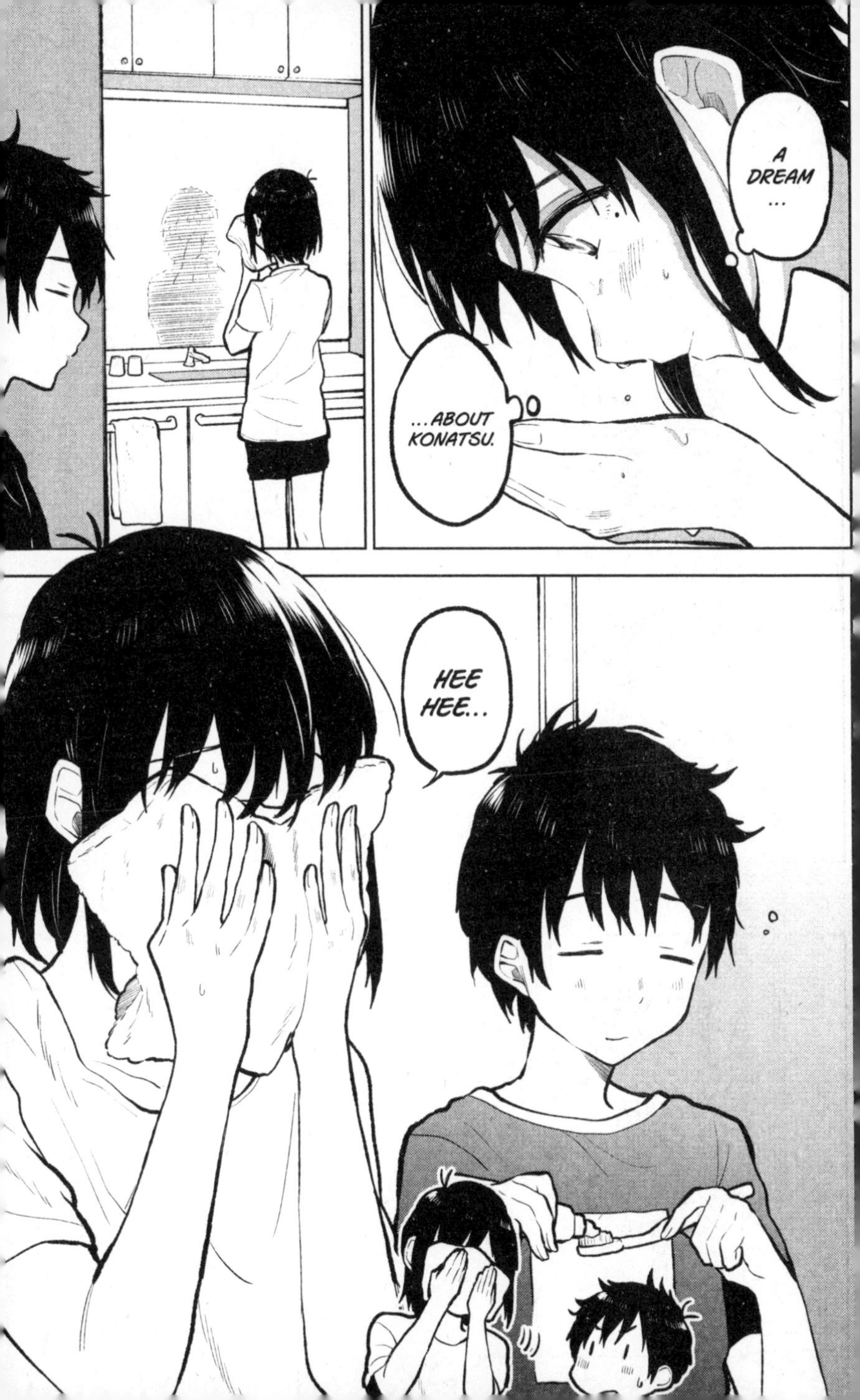
A DREAM ...
...ABOUT KONATSU.
HEE HEE...

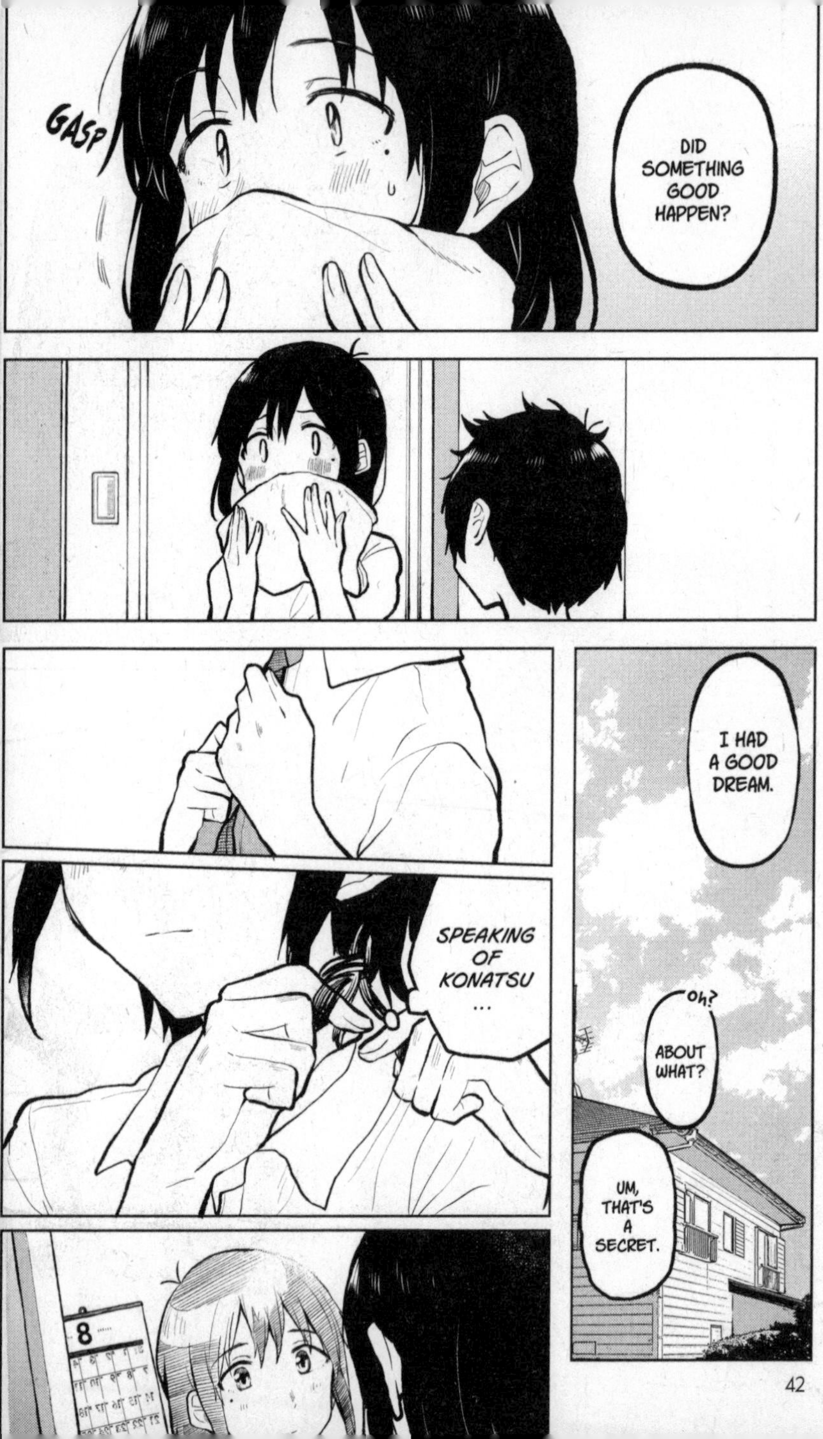
DID SOMETHING GOOD HAPPEN?
GASP
I HAD A GOOD DREAM.
Oh?
ABOUT WHAT?
UM, THAT'S A SECRET.
SPEAKING OF KONATSU ...
8

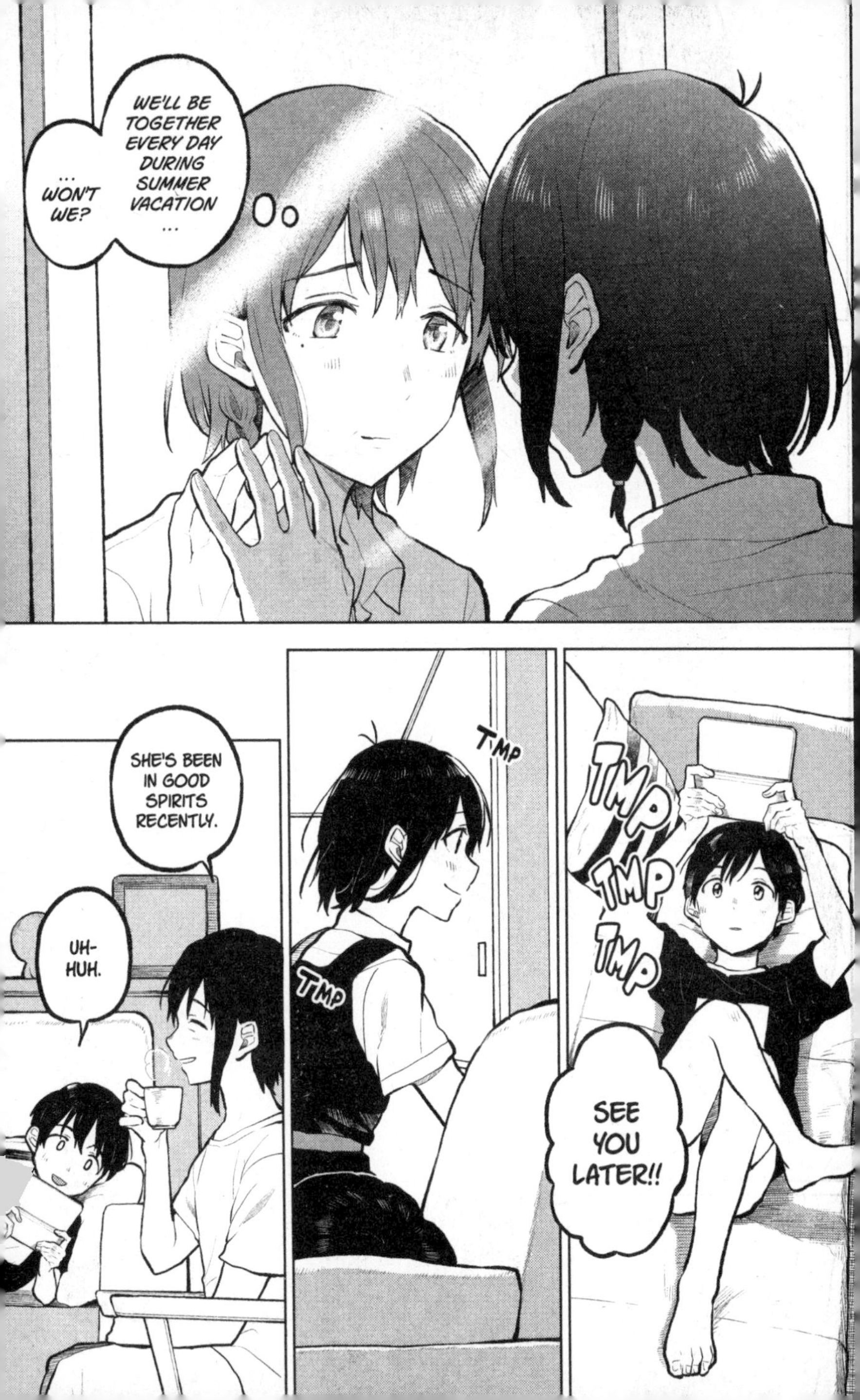
WE'LL BE TOGETHER EVERY DAY DURING SUMMER VACATION ...
... WON'T WE?
TMP
TMP
TMP
SEE YOU LATER!!
TMP
TMP
SHE'S BEEN IN GOOD SPIRITS RECENTLY.
UH-HUH.

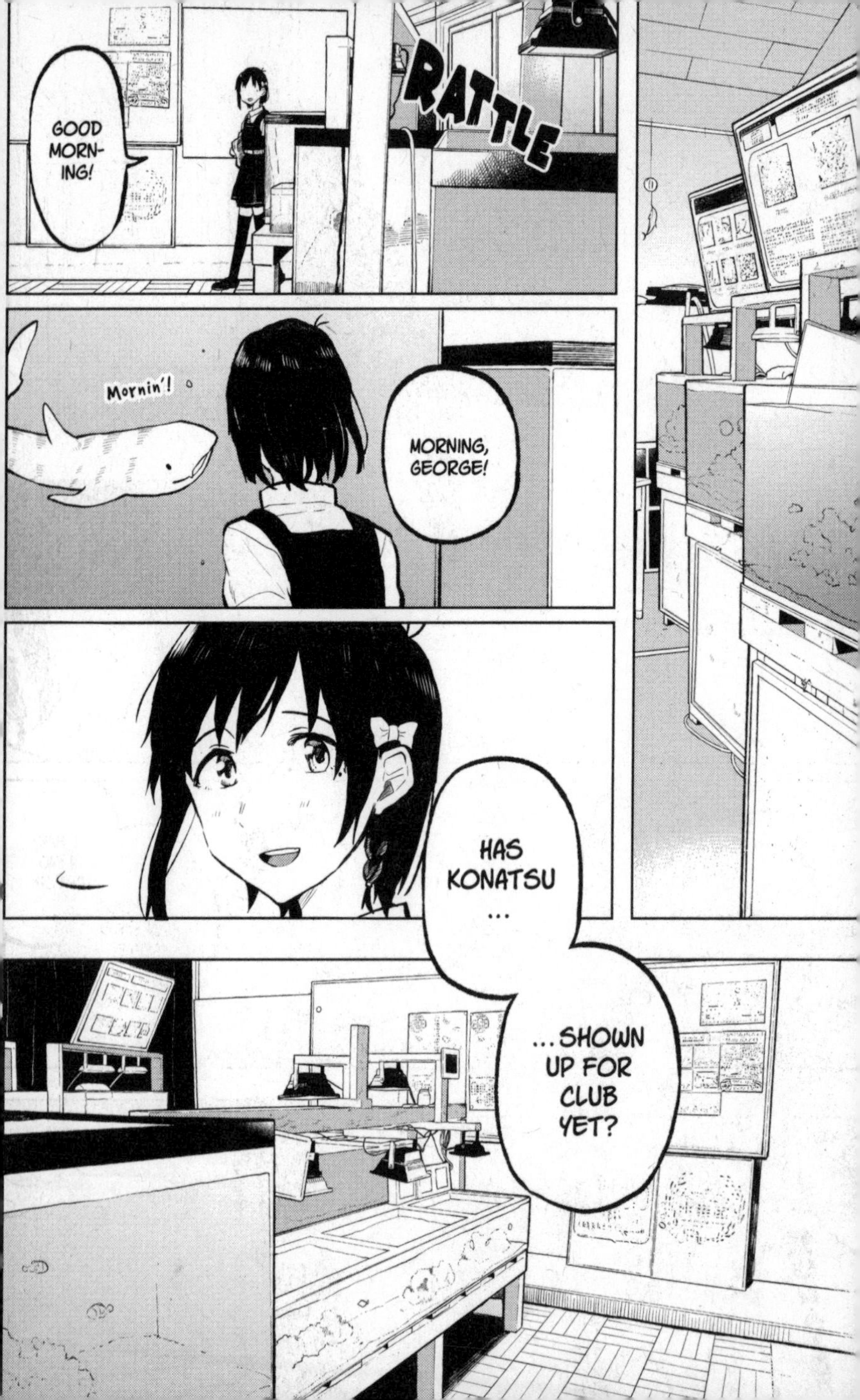
RATTLE
GOOD MORNING!
MORNING, GEORGE!
Mornin'!
HAS KONATSU ...
...SHOWN UP FOR CLUB YET?

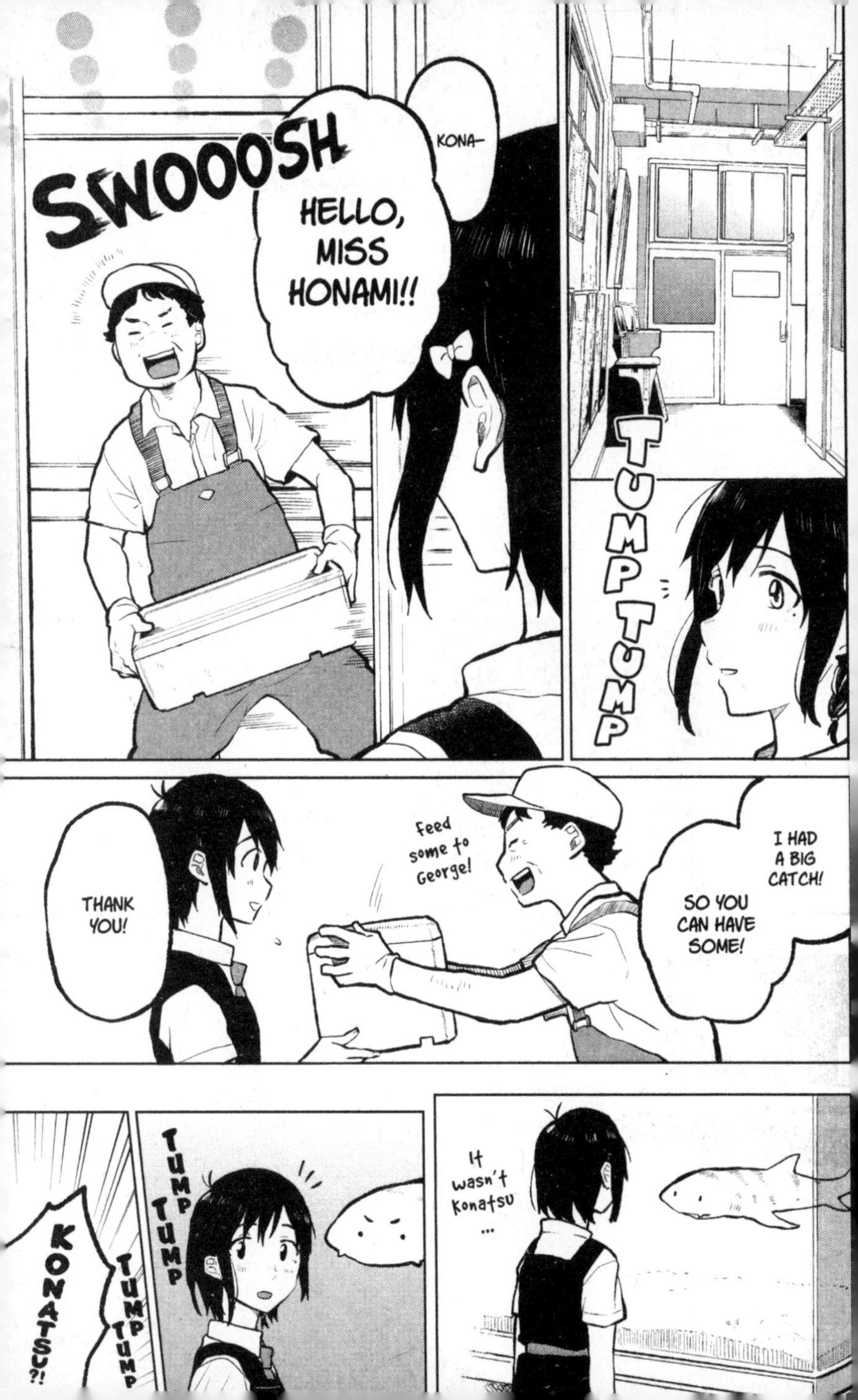
TUMPTUMP
KONA—
SWOOOSH
HELLO, MISS HONAMI!!
I HAD A BIG CATCH!
SO YOU CAN HAVE SOME!
Feed some to George!
THANK YOU!
It wasn't Konatsu ...
TUMP TUMP
TUMP TUMP
KONATSU?!

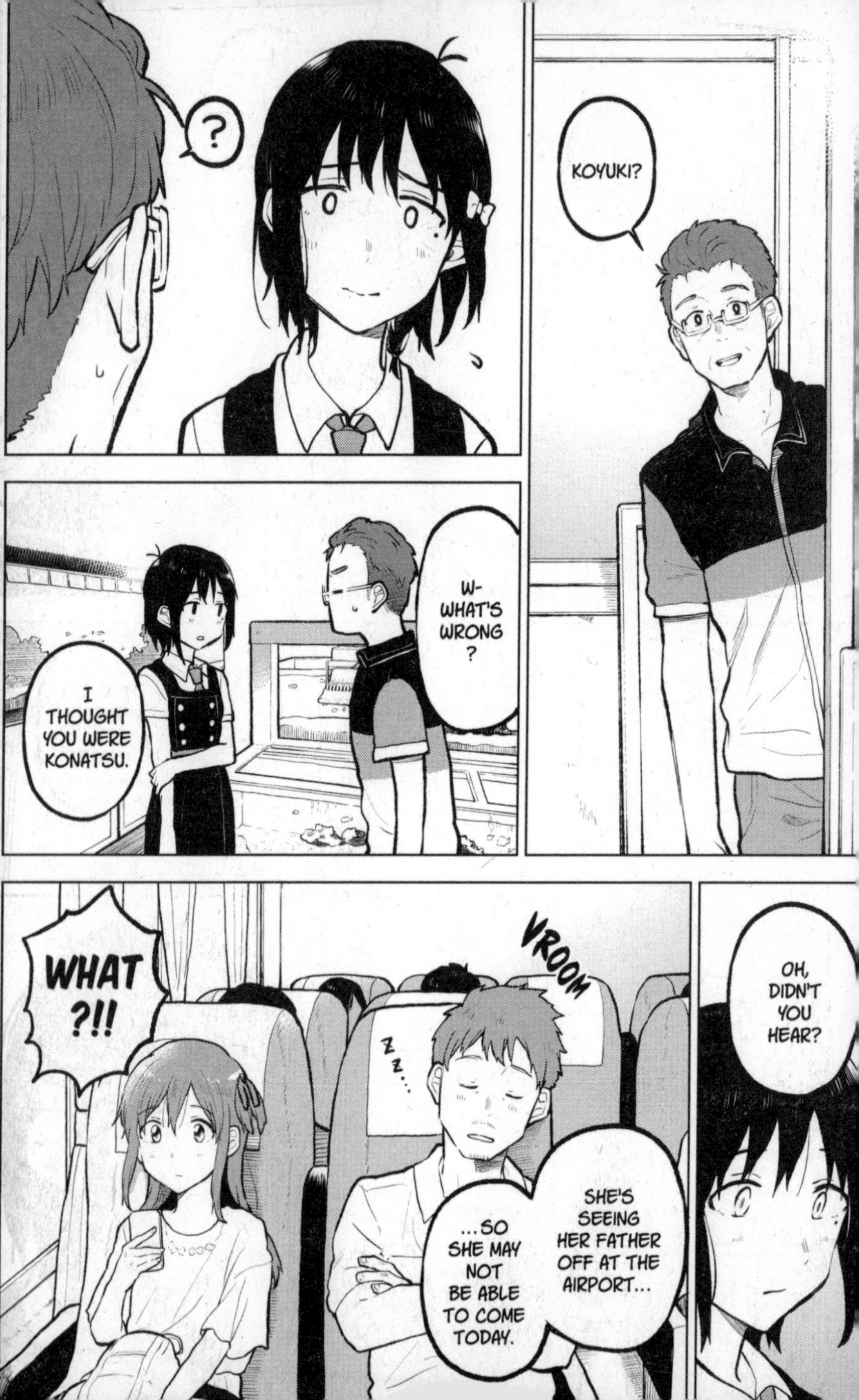
KOYUKI?
?
W-WHAT'S WRONG?
I THOUGHT YOU WERE KONATSU.
OH, DIDN'T YOU HEAR?
SHE'S SEEING HER FATHER OFF AT THE AIRPORT...
...SO SHE MAY NOT BE ABLE TO COME TODAY.
VROOM
Z Z...
WHAT?!!

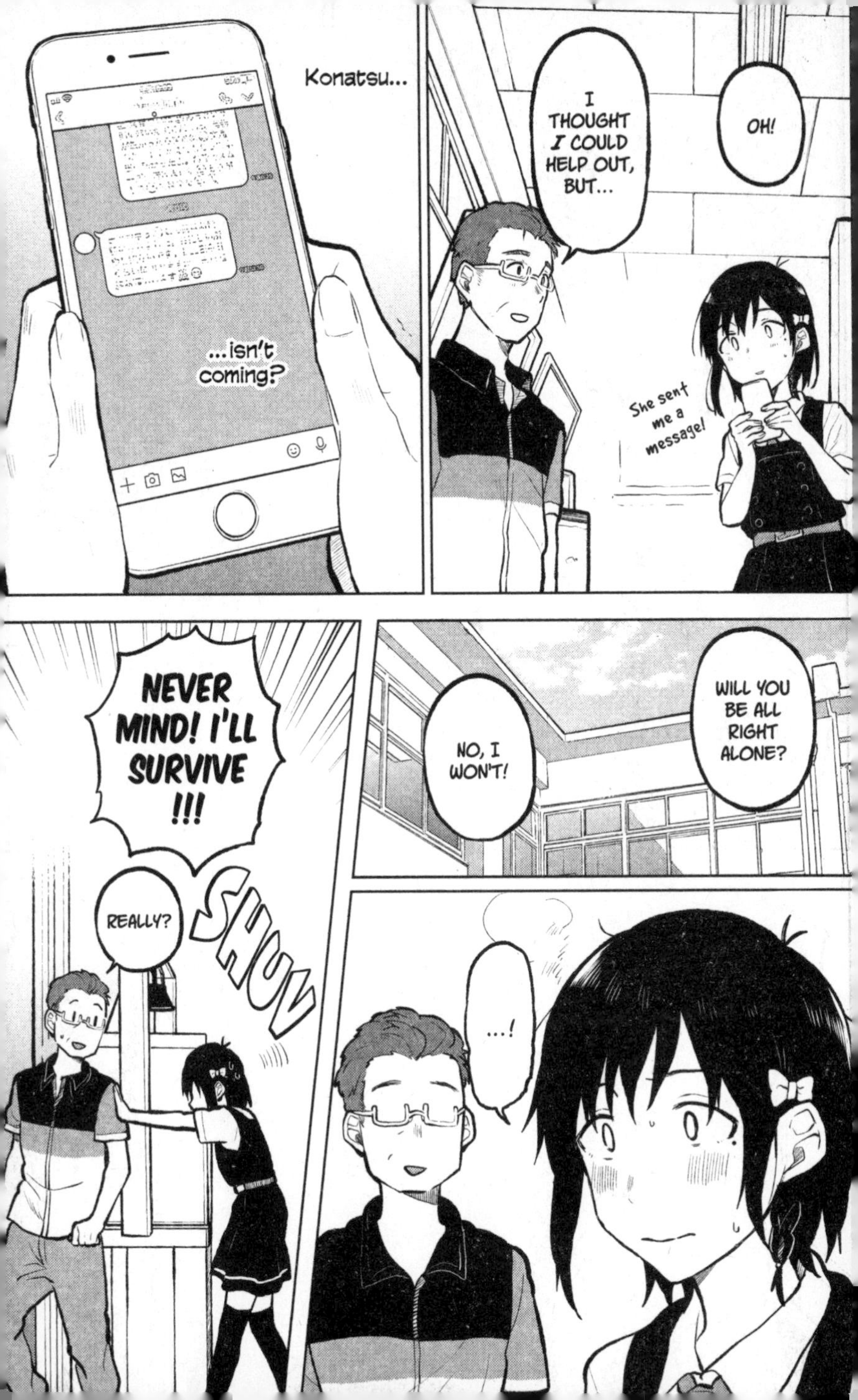
OH!
I THOUGHT I COULD HELP OUT, BUT...
She sent me a message!
Konatsu...
...isn't coming?
WILL YOU BE ALL RIGHT ALONE?
NO, I WON'T!
...!
NEVER MIND! I'LL SURVIVE !!!
SHUV
REALLY?

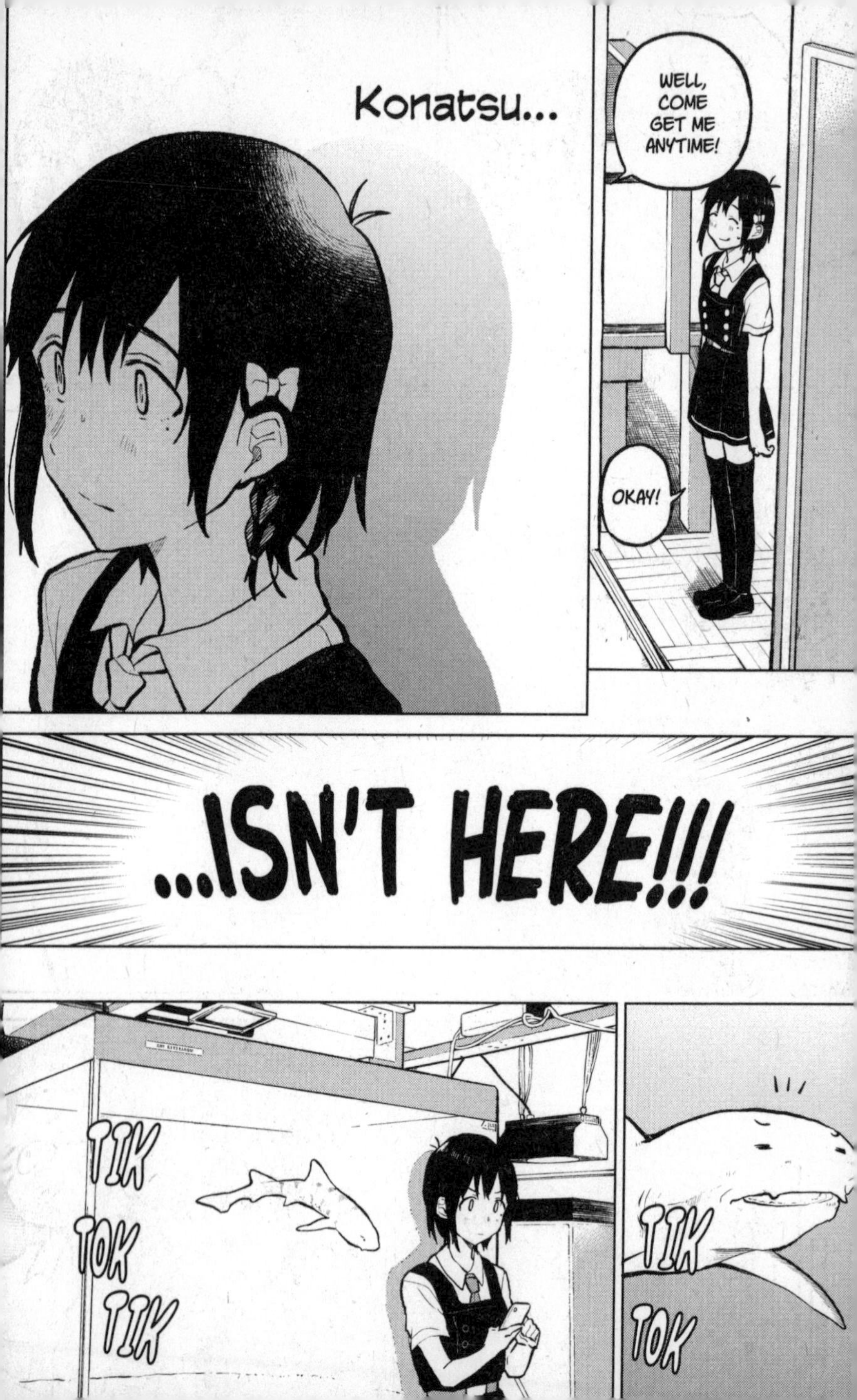
WELL, COME GET ME ANYTIME!
OKAY!
Konatsu...
...ISN'T HERE!!!
TIK
TOK
TIK
TOK
TIK

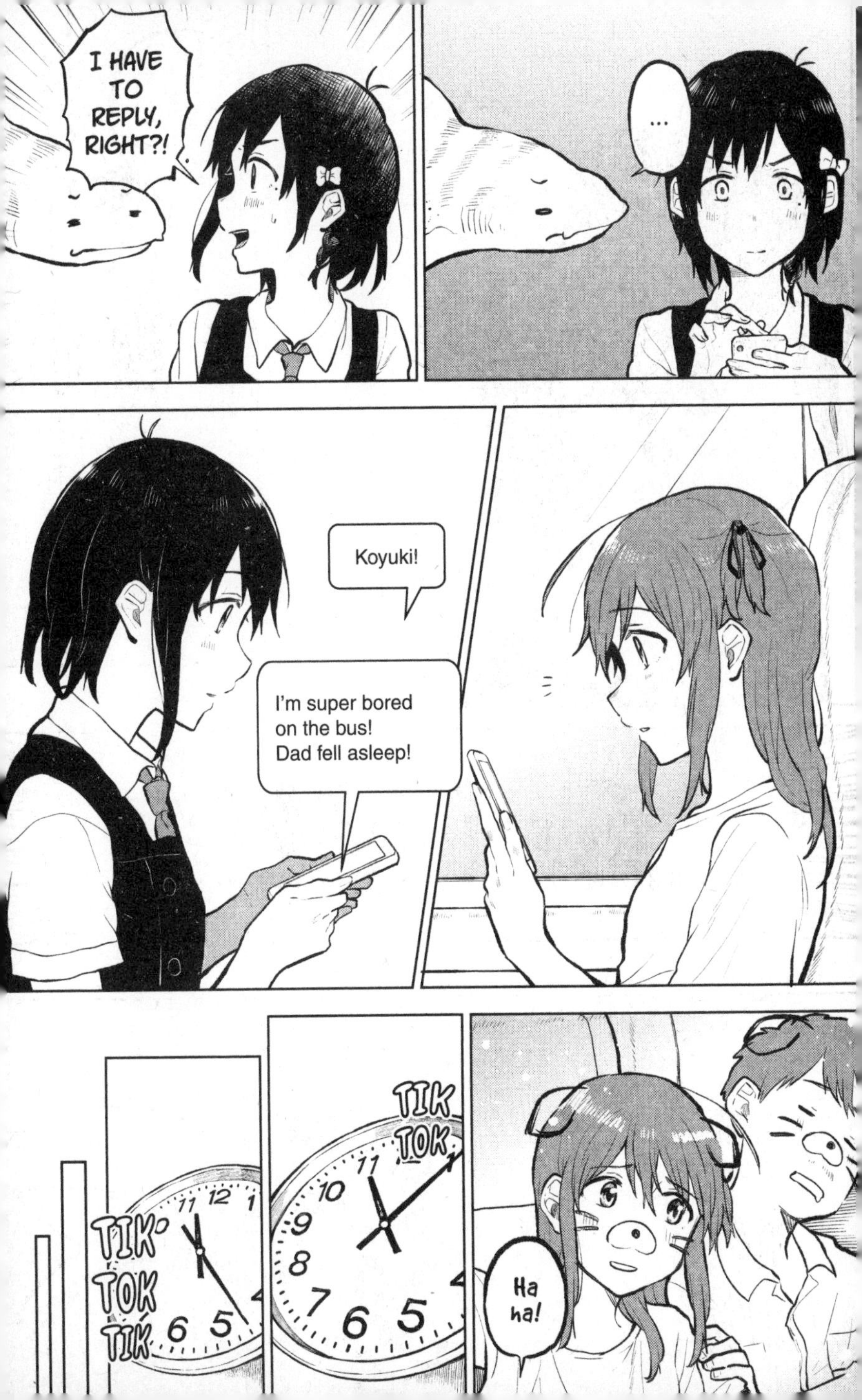
...
I HAVE TO REPLY, RIGHT?!
Koyuki!
I'm super bored on the bus! Dad fell asleep!
Ha ha!
TIK TOK
TIK TOK TIK

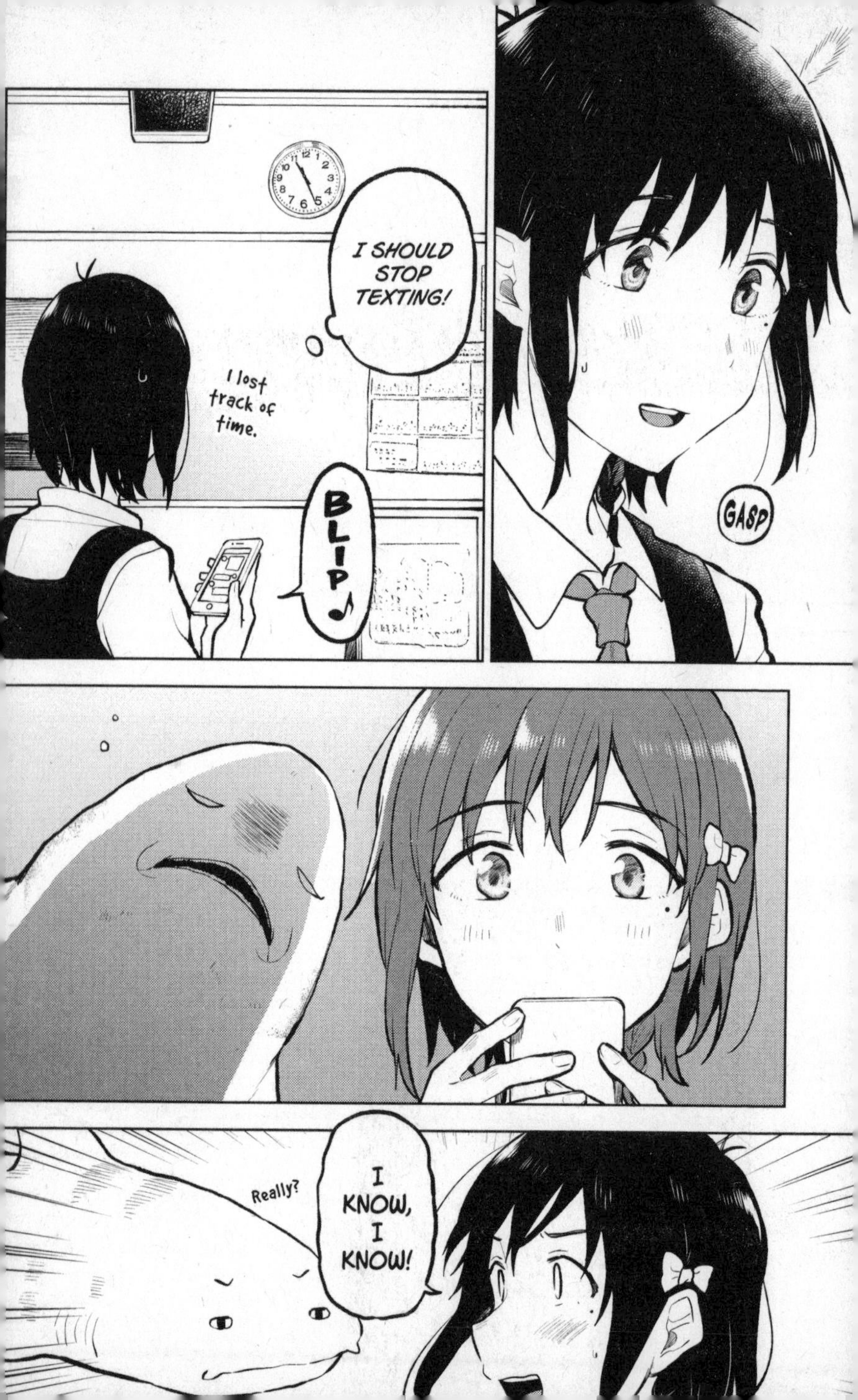
GASP
I SHOULD STOP TEXTING!
I lost track of time.
BLIP♪
I KNOW, I KNOW!
Really?

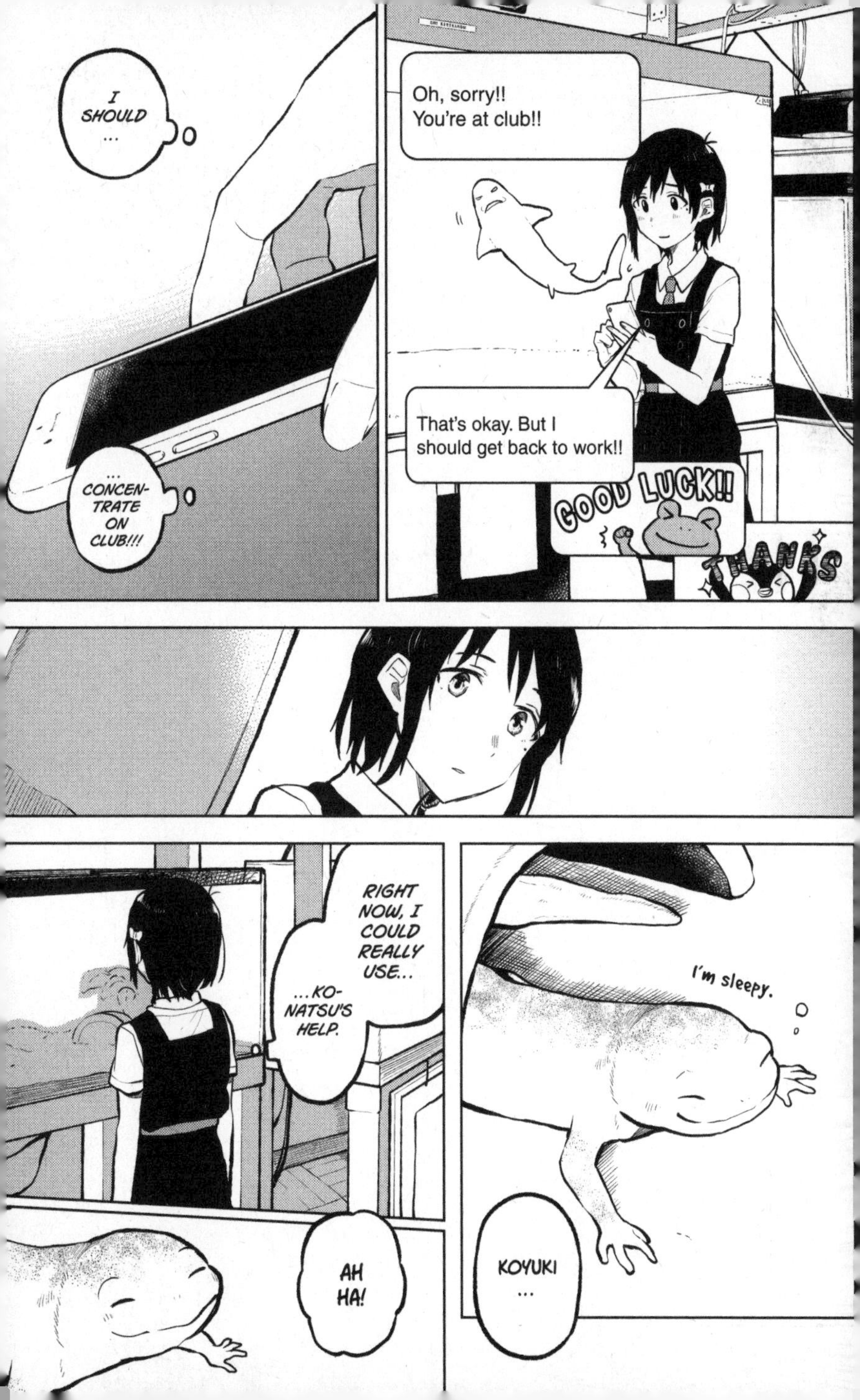
Oh, sorry!! You're at club!!
That's okay. But I should get back to work!!
GOOD LUCK!!
THANKS
I SHOULD ...
... CONCEN-TRATE ON CLUB!!!
I'm sleepy.
KOYUKI ...
RIGHT NOW, I COULD REALLY USE...
...KO-NATSU'S HELP.
AH HA!

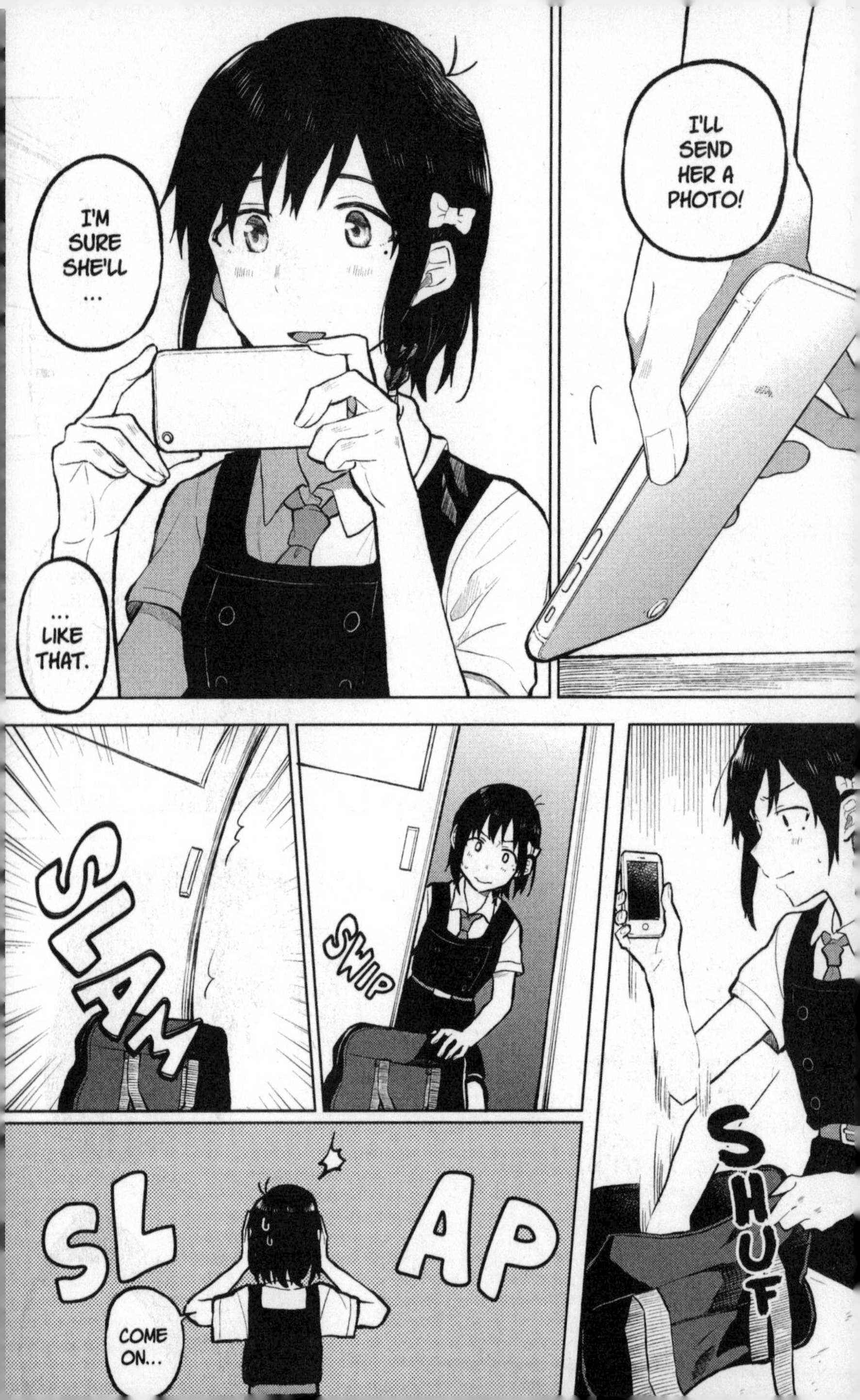
I'LL SEND HER A PHOTO!
I'M SURE SHE'LL ...
... LIKE THAT.
SHUT
SWIP
SLAM
SLAP
COME ON...

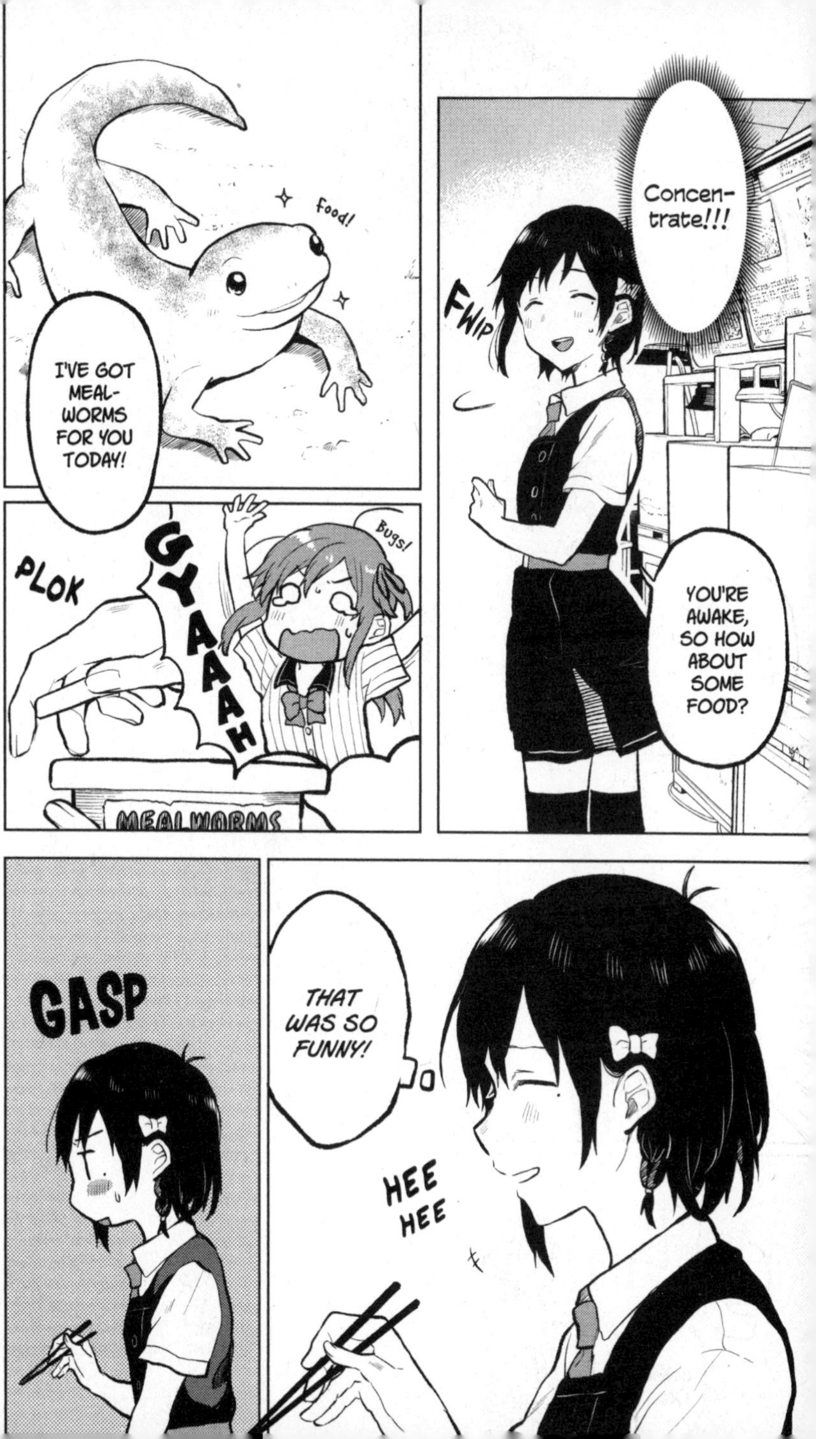
Concentrate!!!
FWIP
YOU'RE AWAKE, SO HOW ABOUT SOME FOOD?
Food!
I'VE GOT MEALWORMS FOR YOU TODAY!
Bugs!
GYAAAAH
PLOK
MEALWORMS
THAT WAS SO FUNNY!
HEE HEE
GASP

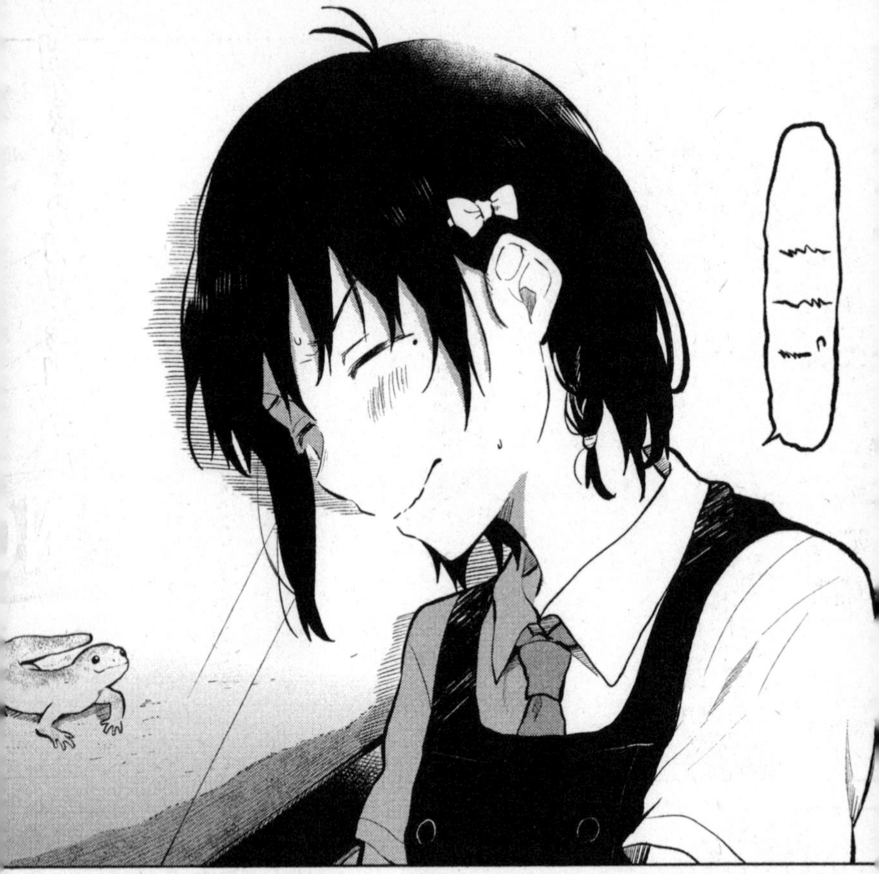

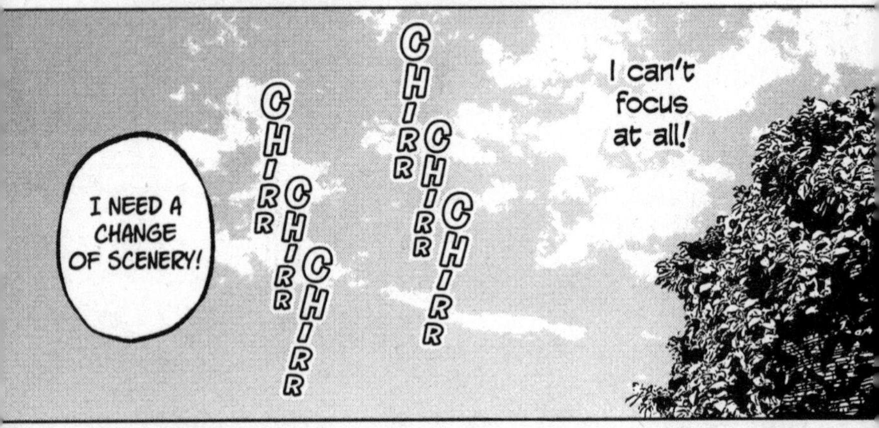

I can't focus at all!
CHIRR CHIRR CHIRR
CHIRR CHIRR CHIRR
I NEED A CHANGE OF SCENERY!

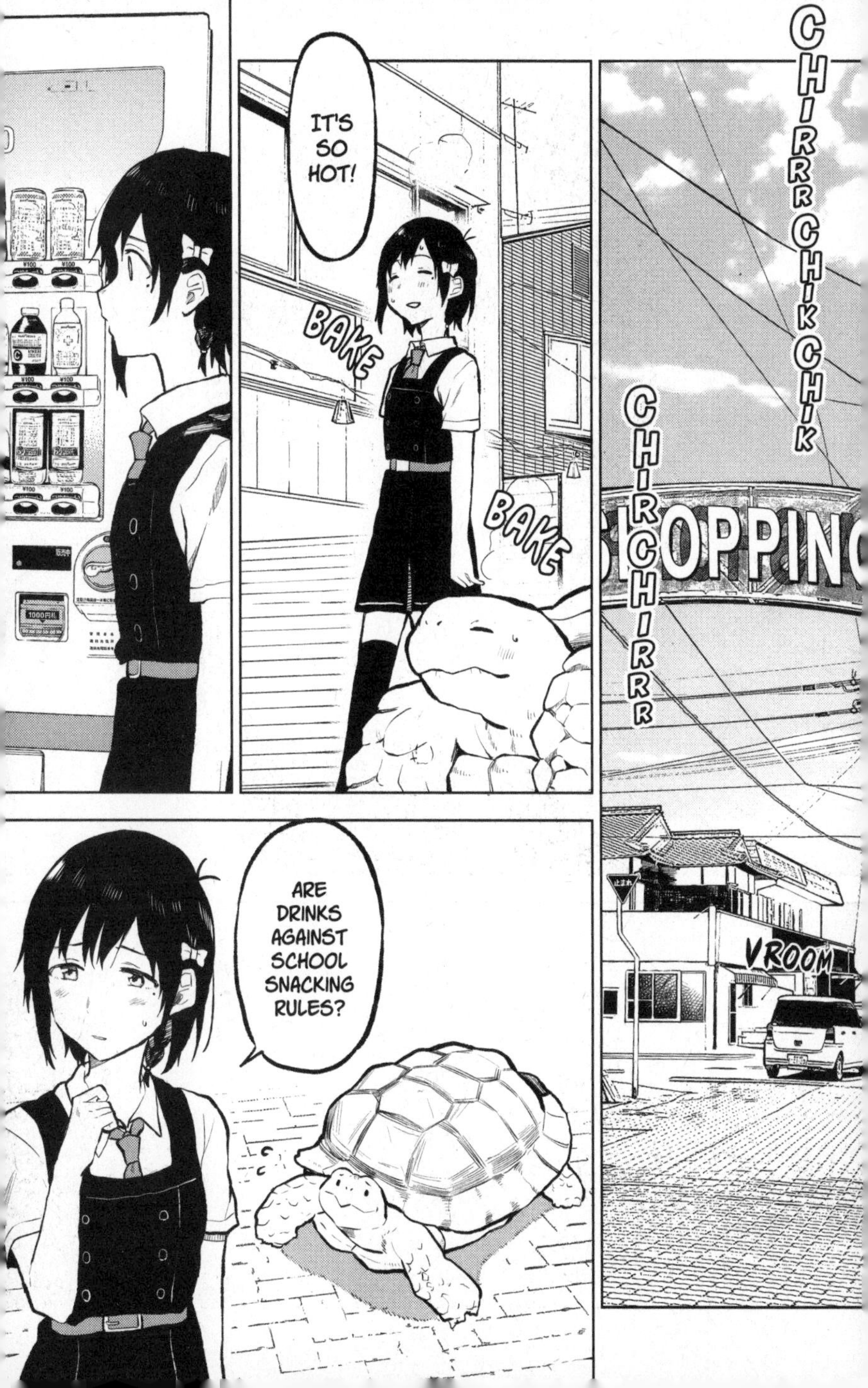
CHIRRRCHIKCHIK
CHIRRCHIRRR
IT'S SO HOT!
BAKE
BAKE
VROOM
ARE DRINKS AGAINST SCHOOL SNACKING RULES?

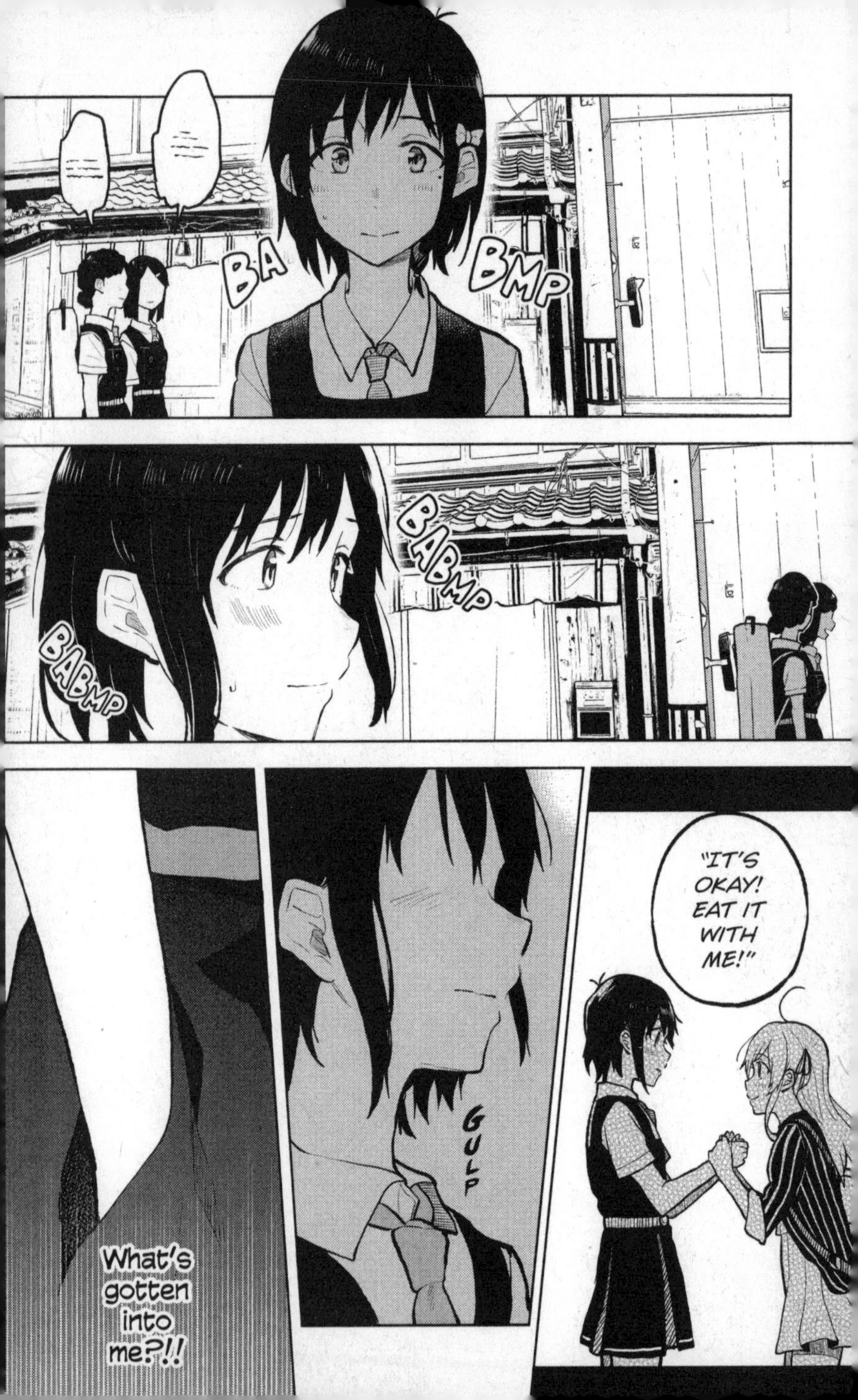

BA BMP
BABMP
BABMP
"IT'S OKAY! EAT IT WITH ME!"
GULP
What's gotten into me?!!

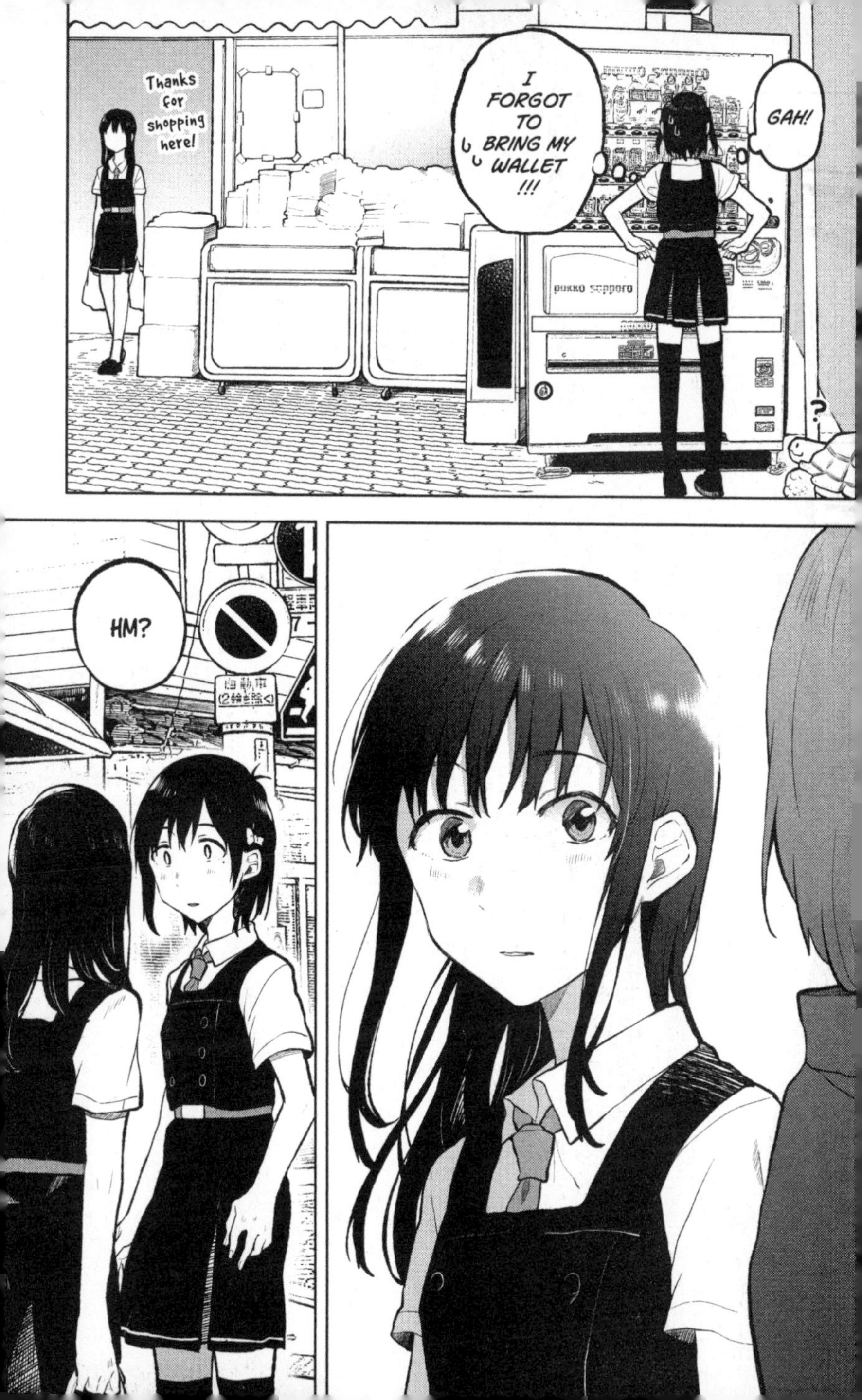
GAH!
I FORGOT TO BRING MY WALLET !!!
pokko sapporo
Thanks for shopping here!
HM?
自動車
(2輪を除く)

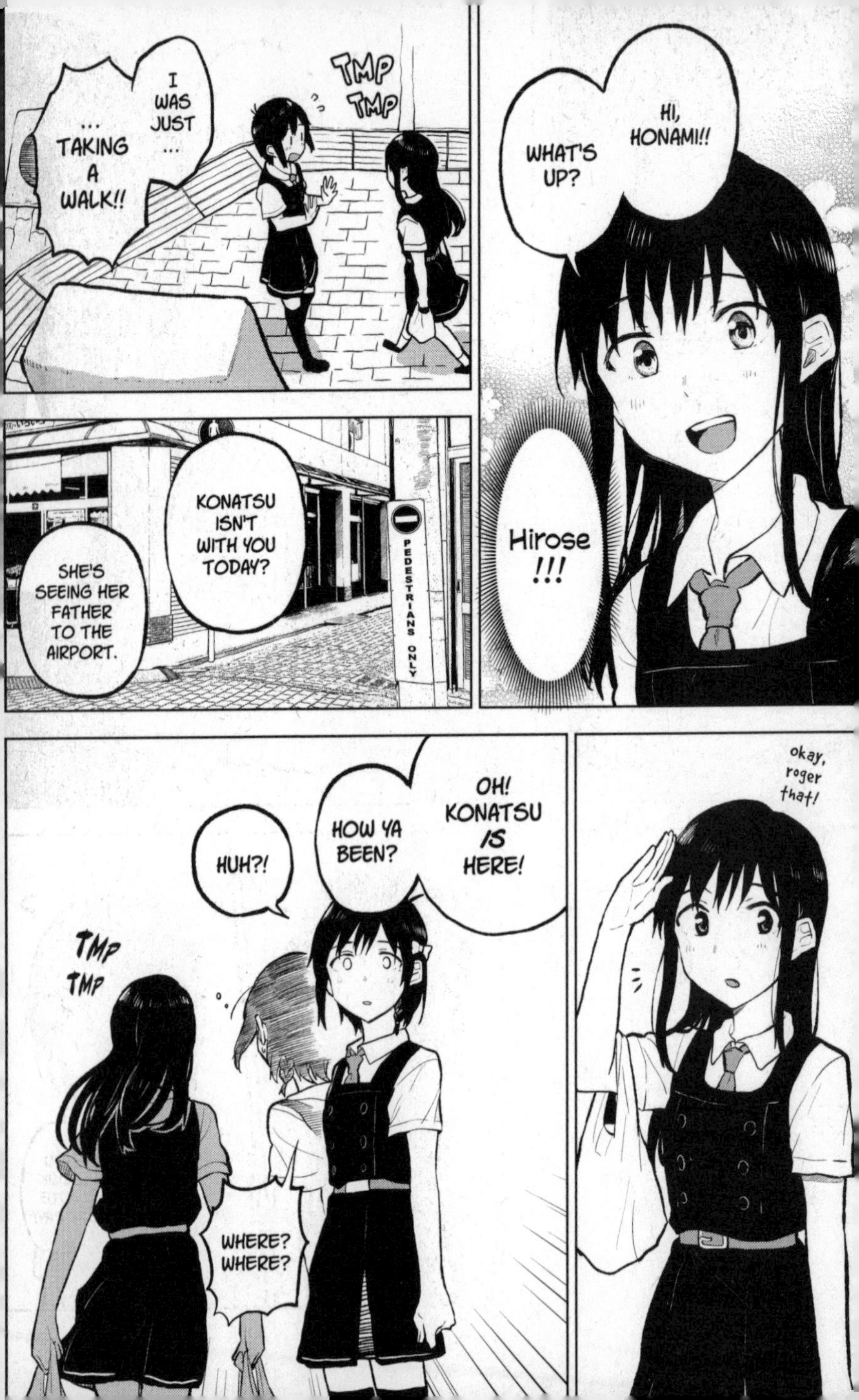
HI, HONAMI!!
WHAT'S UP?
Hirose !!!
TMP TMP
I WAS JUST ...
... TAKING A WALK!!
KONATSU ISN'T WITH YOU TODAY?
PEDESTRIANS ONLY
SHE'S SEEING HER FATHER TO THE AIRPORT.
okay, roger that!
OH! KONATSU IS HERE!
HOW YA BEEN?
HUH?!
TMP TMP
WHERE? WHERE?

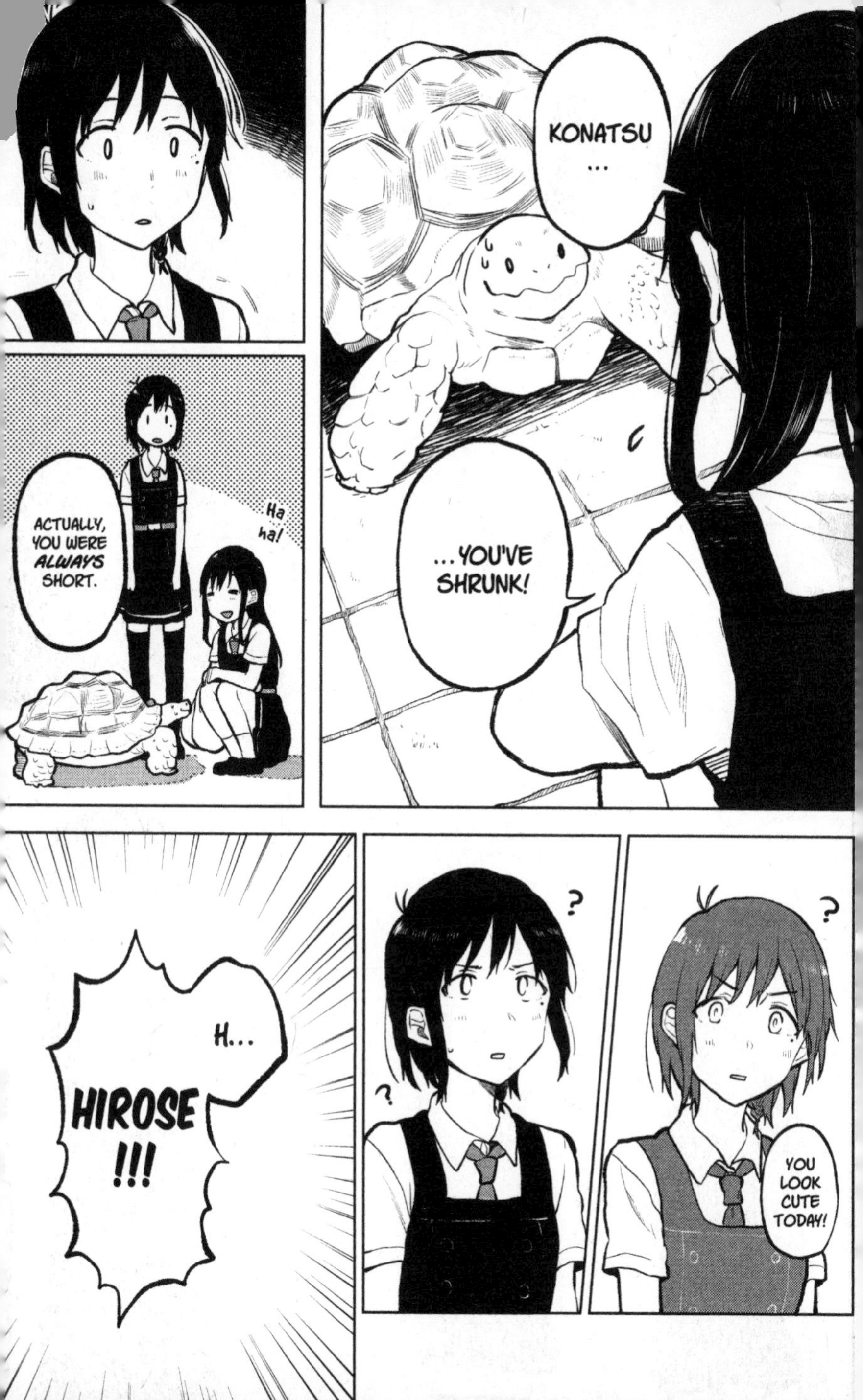
KONATSU
...
...YOU'VE SHRUNK!
ACTUALLY, YOU WERE *ALWAYS* SHORT.
Ha ha!
?
YOU LOOK CUTE TODAY!
?
?
H...
HIROSE !!!

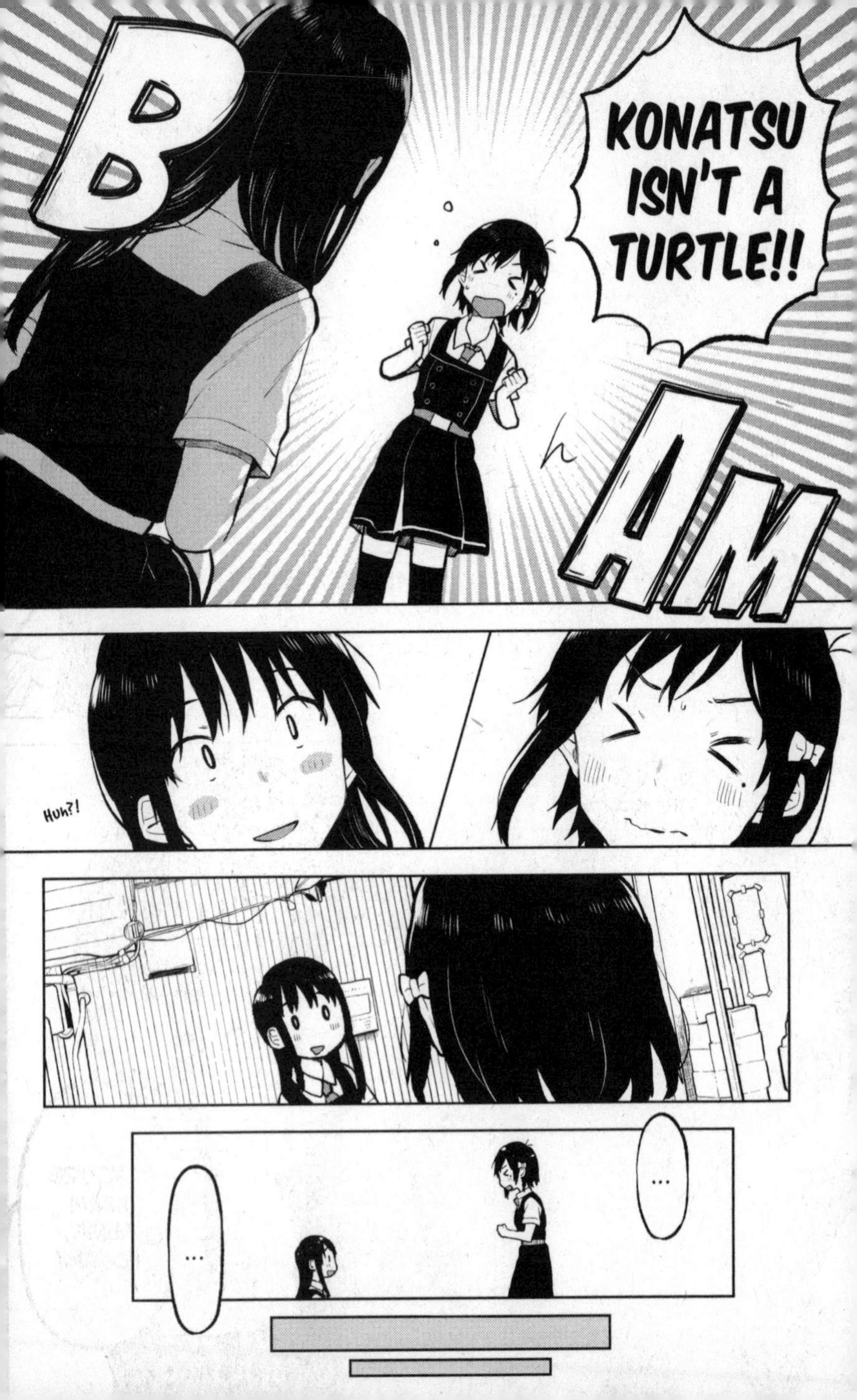
KONATSU ISN'T A TURTLE!!
BAM
Huh?!
...
...

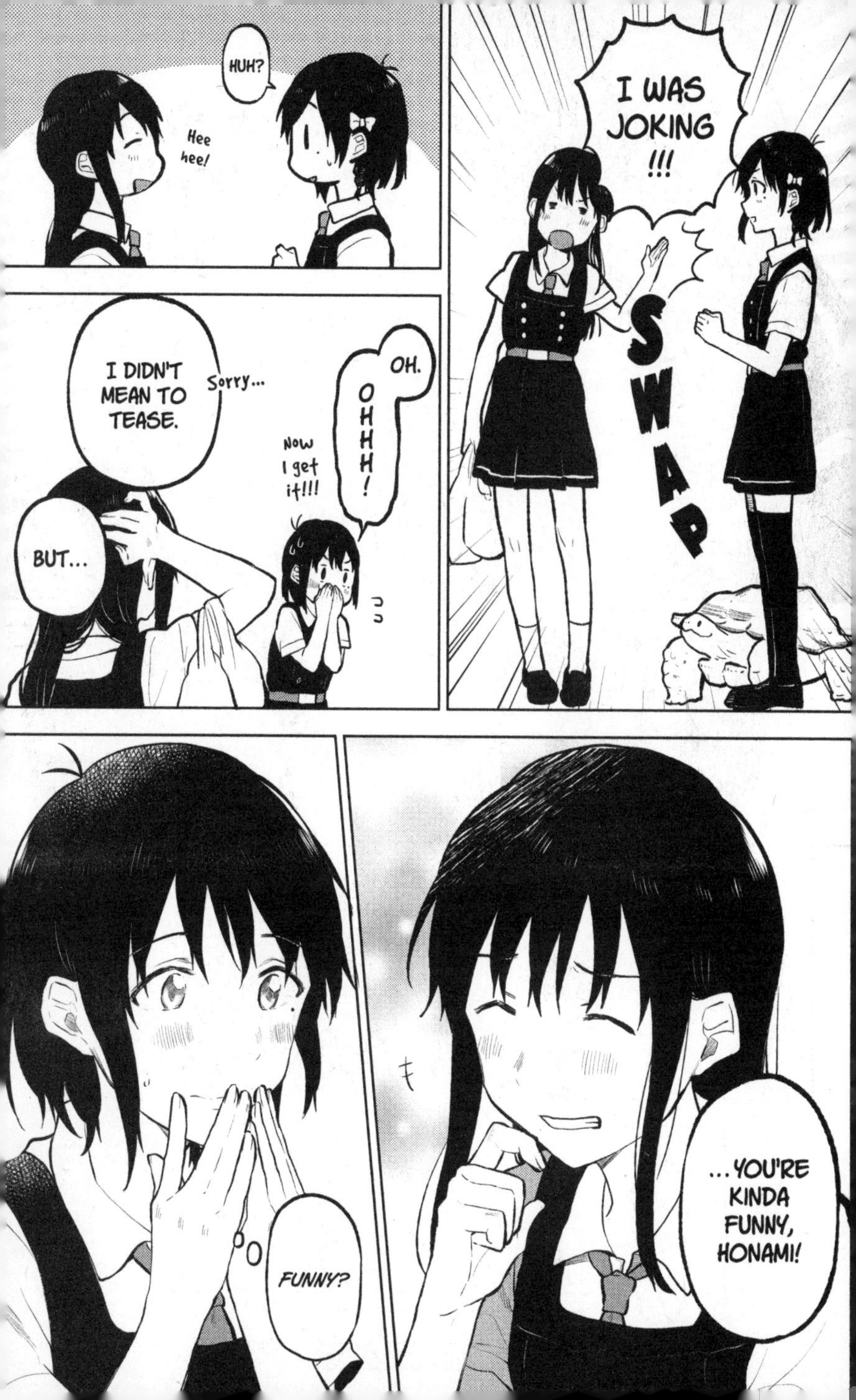

I WAS JOKING !!!
SWAP
HUH?
Hee hee!
OH.
OHHH!
Now I get it!!!
Sorry...
I DIDN'T MEAN TO TEASE.
BUT...
...YOU'RE KINDA FUNNY, HONAMI!
FUNNY?

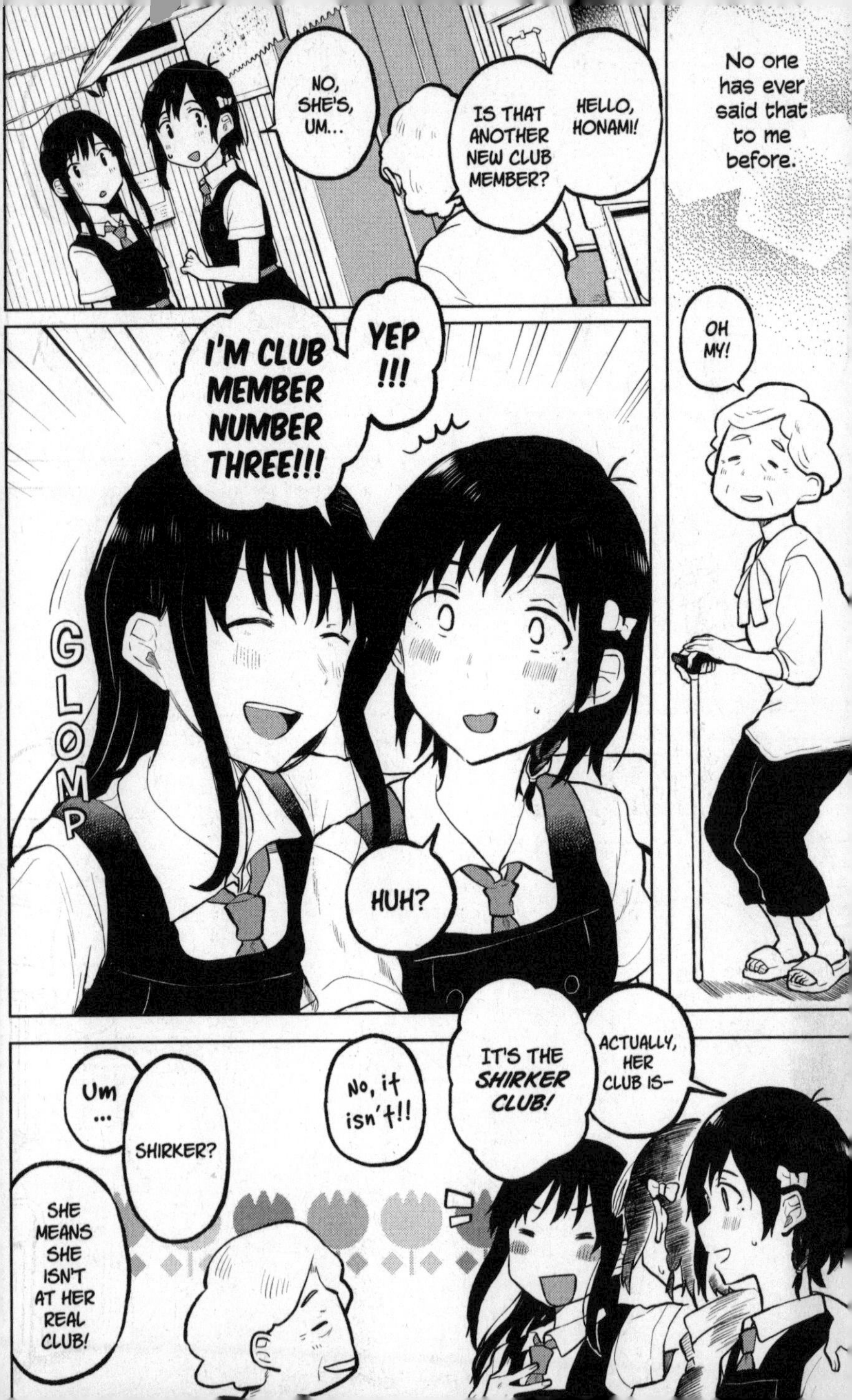

No one has ever said that to me before.
OH MY!
HELLO, HONAMI!
IS THAT ANOTHER NEW CLUB MEMBER?
NO, SHE'S, UM...
YEP !!!
I'M CLUB MEMBER NUMBER THREE!!!
GLOMP
HUH?
ACTUALLY, HER CLUB IS—
IT'S THE SHIRKER CLUB!
No, it isn't!!
SHIRKER?
Um ...
SHE MEANS SHE ISN'T AT HER REAL CLUB!

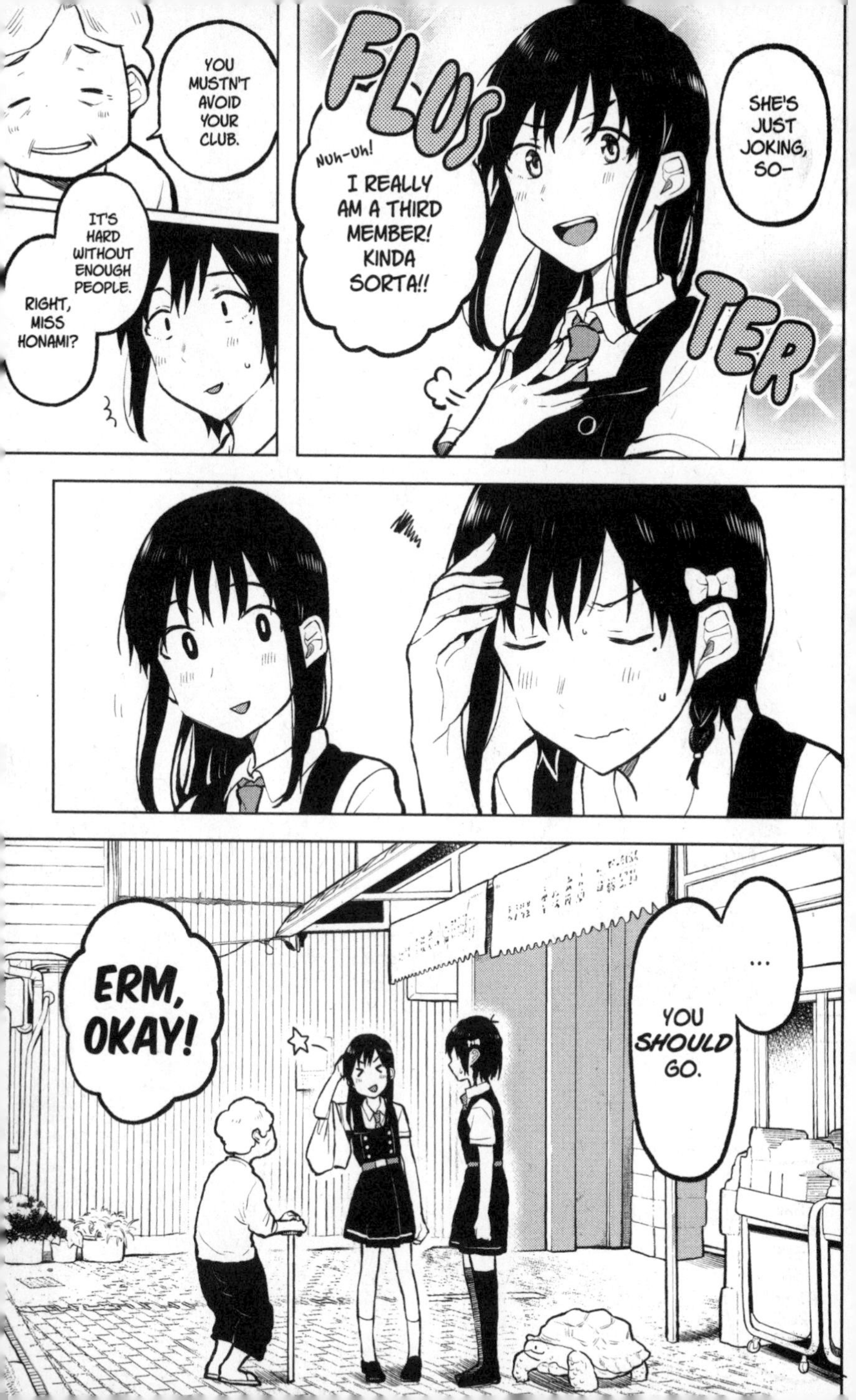
SHE'S JUST JOKING, SO-
FLUSTER
Nuh-uh! I REALLY AM A THIRD MEMBER! KINDA SORTA!!
YOU MUSTN'T AVOID YOUR CLUB.
IT'S HARD WITHOUT ENOUGH PEOPLE. RIGHT, MISS HONAMI?
... YOU SHOULD GO.
ERM, OKAY!

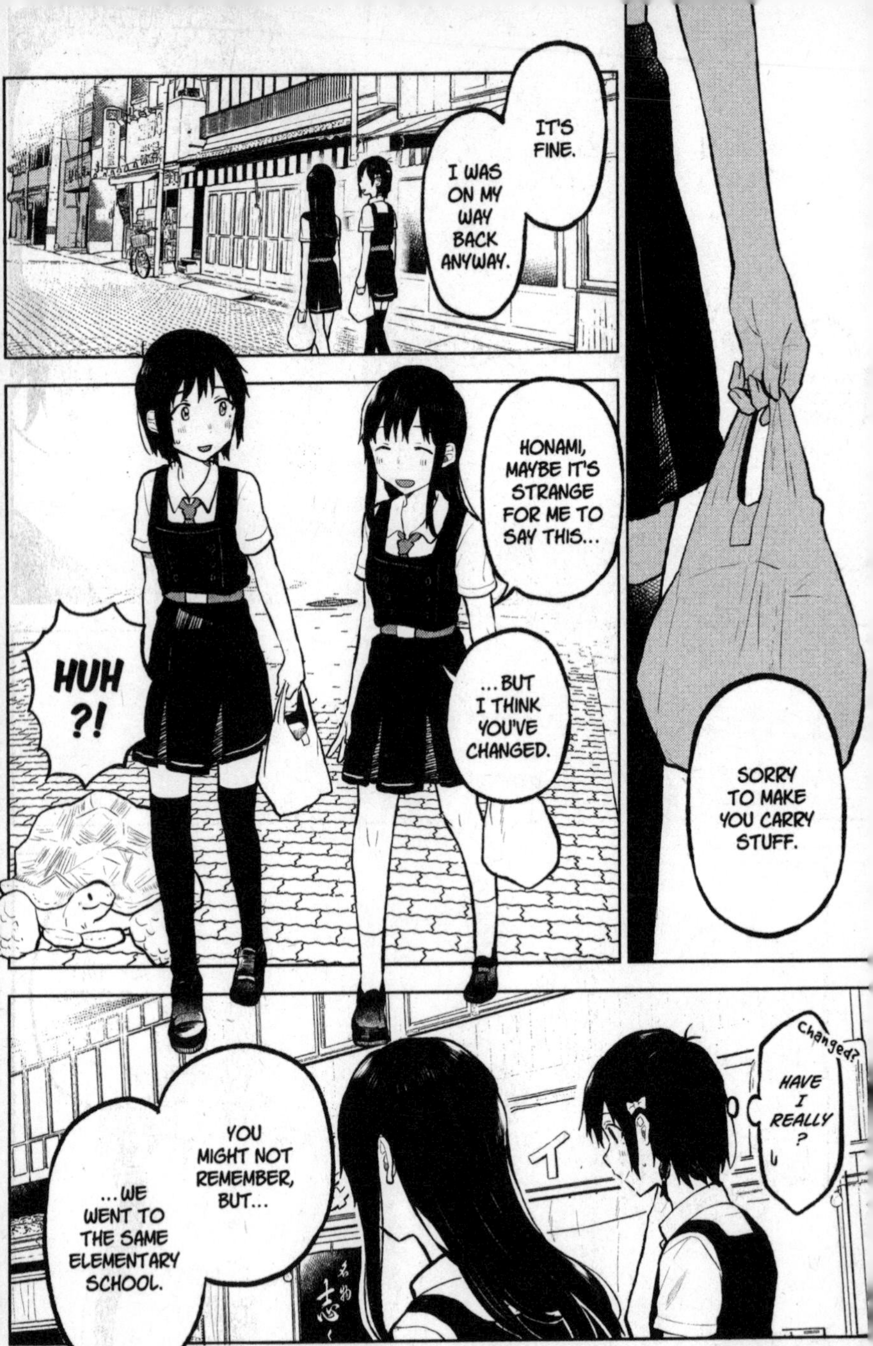
SORRY TO MAKE YOU CARRY STUFF.
IT'S FINE.
I WAS ON MY WAY BACK ANYWAY.
HONAMI, MAYBE IT'S STRANGE FOR ME TO SAY THIS...
...BUT I THINK YOU'VE CHANGED.
HUH ?!
Changed?
HAVE I REALLY ?
YOU MIGHT NOT REMEMBER, BUT...
...WE WENT TO THE SAME ELEMENTARY SCHOOL.

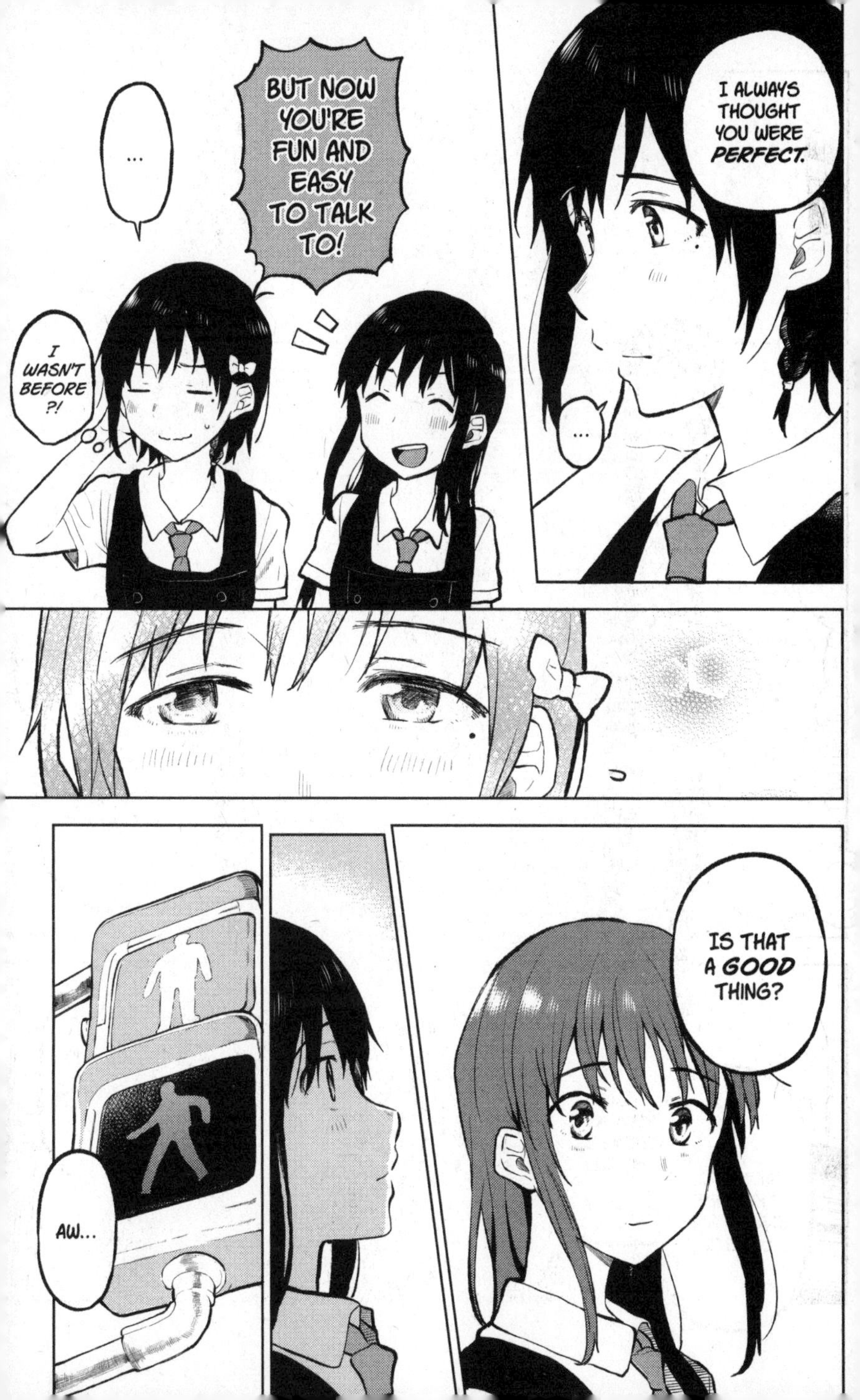
I ALWAYS THOUGHT YOU WERE *PERFECT.*
...
BUT NOW YOU'RE FUN AND EASY TO TALK TO!
...
I WASN'T BEFORE ?!
IS THAT A *GOOD* THING?
AW...

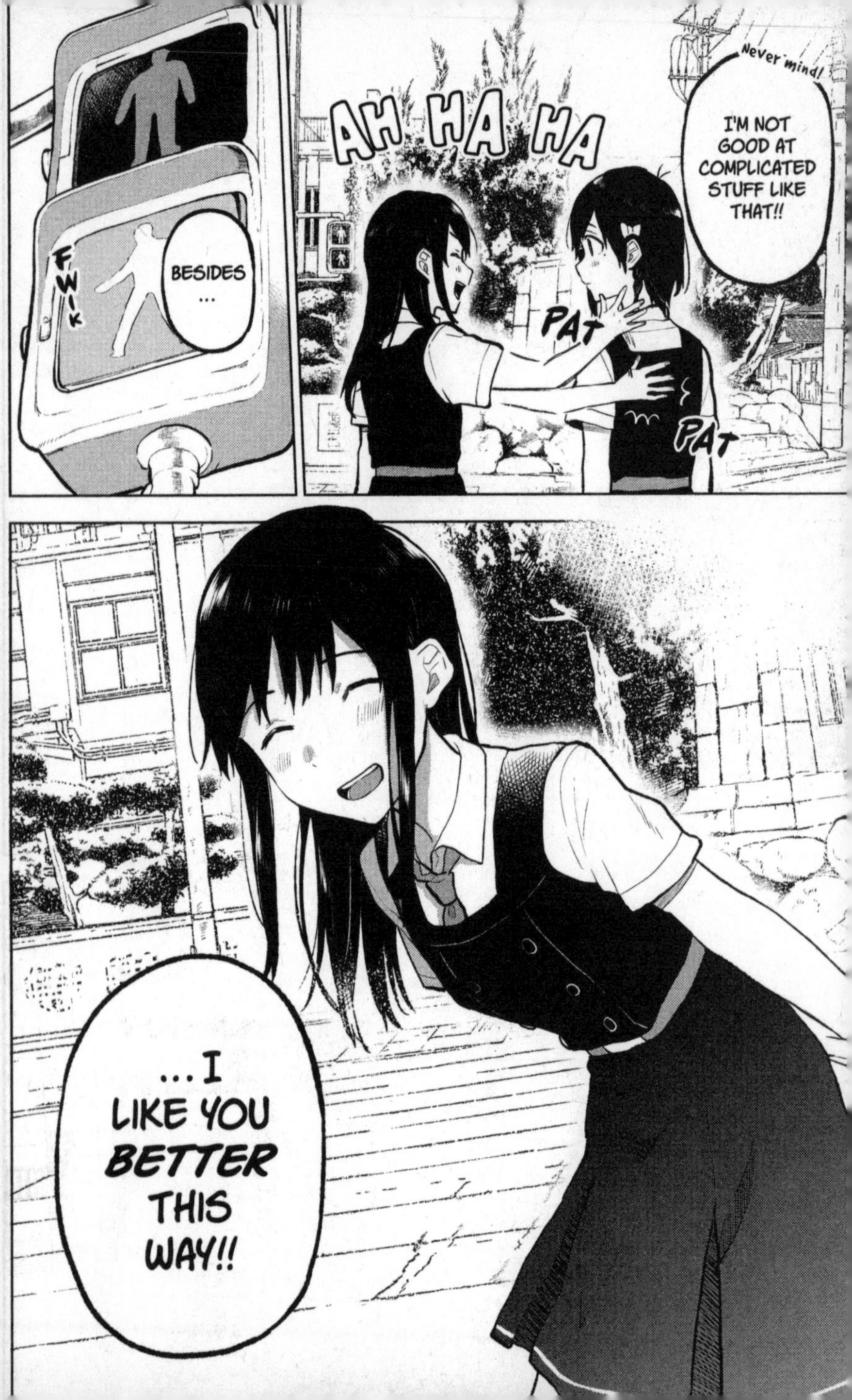
Never mind!
I'M NOT GOOD AT COMPLICATED STUFF LIKE THAT!!
AH HA HA
PAT
PAT
FWIK
BESIDES ...
... I LIKE YOU BETTER THIS WAY!!

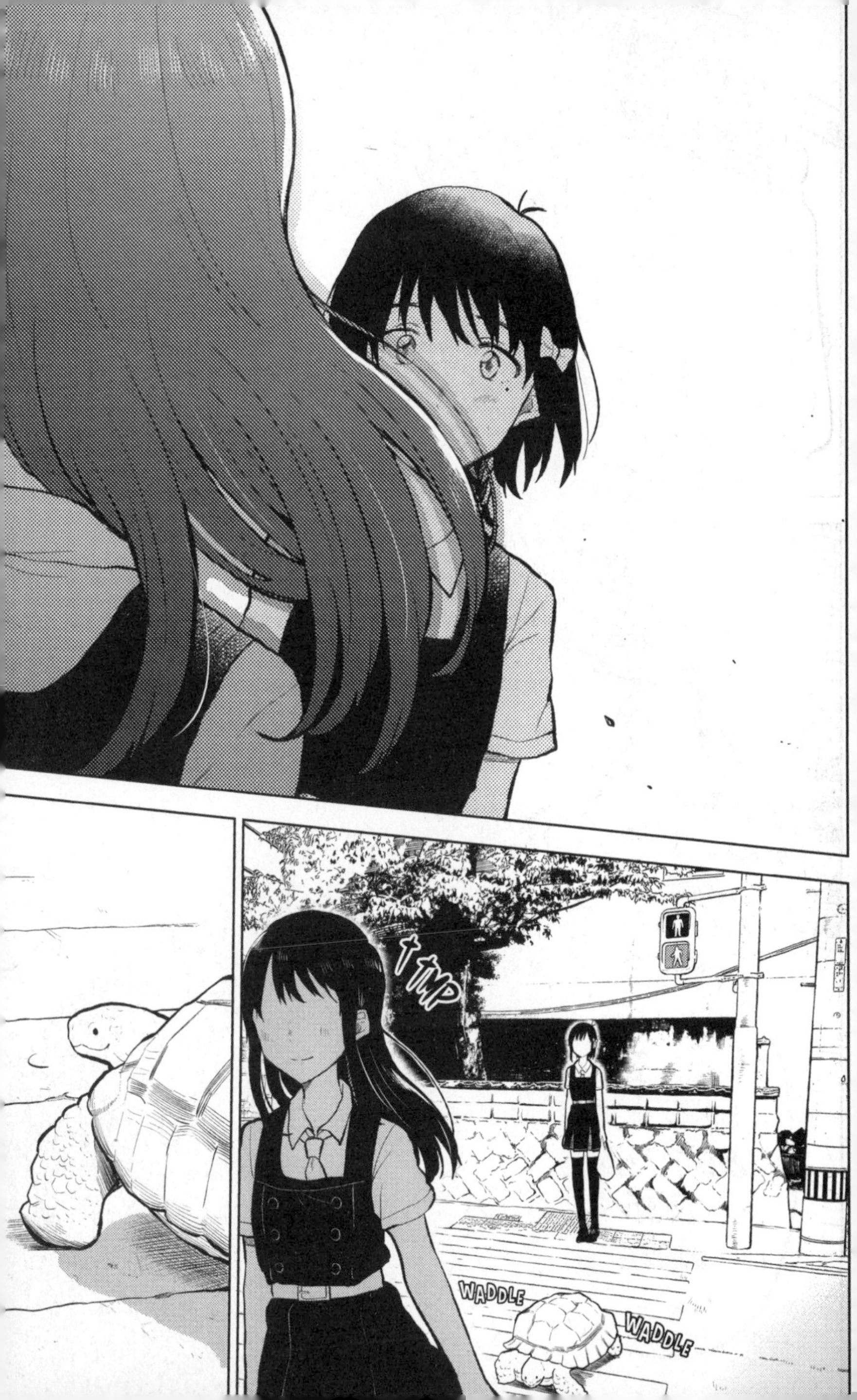
T TMP
WADDLE
WADDLE

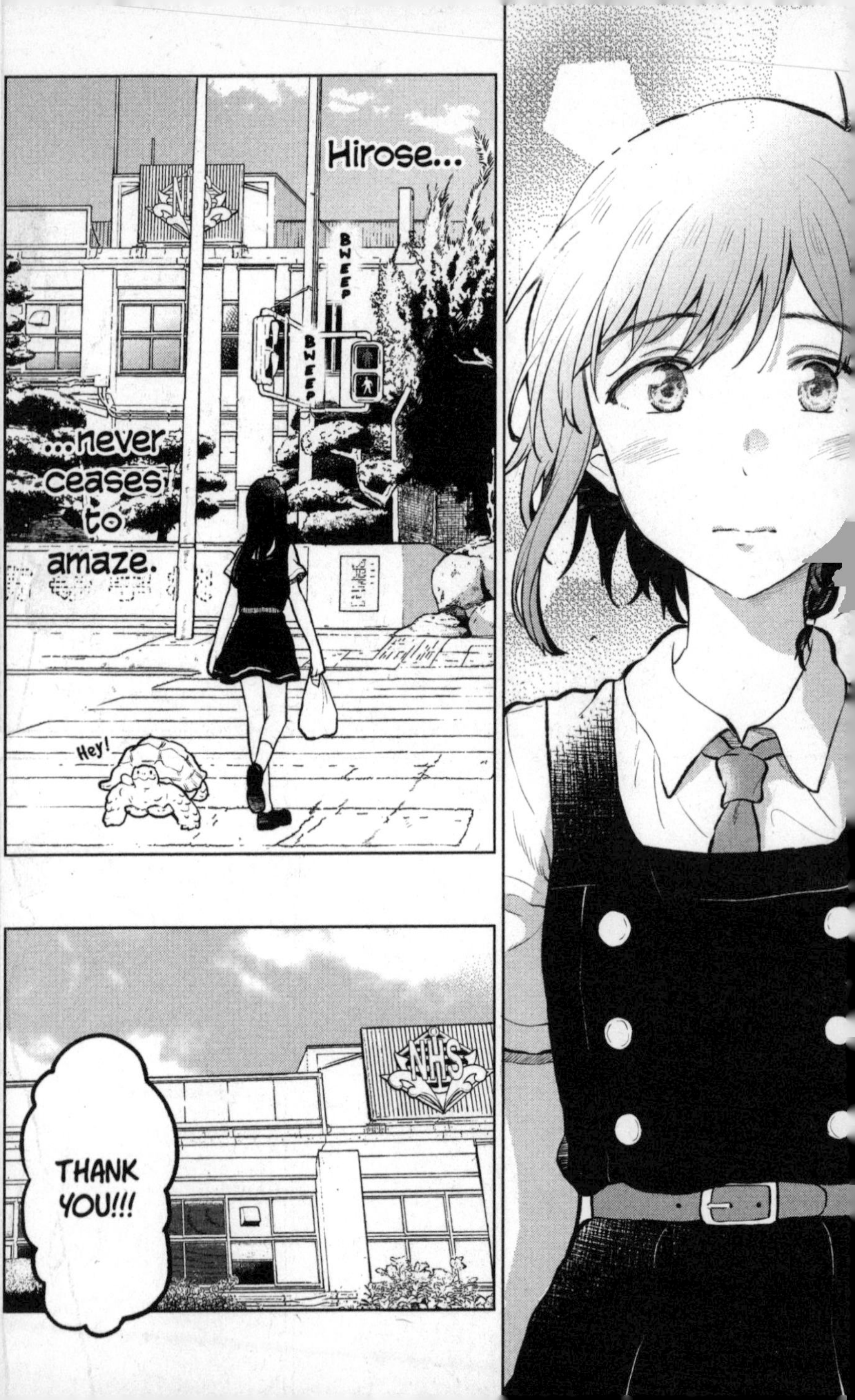
Hirose...
BWEEP
BWEEP
...never ceases to amaze.
Hey!
THANK YOU!!!

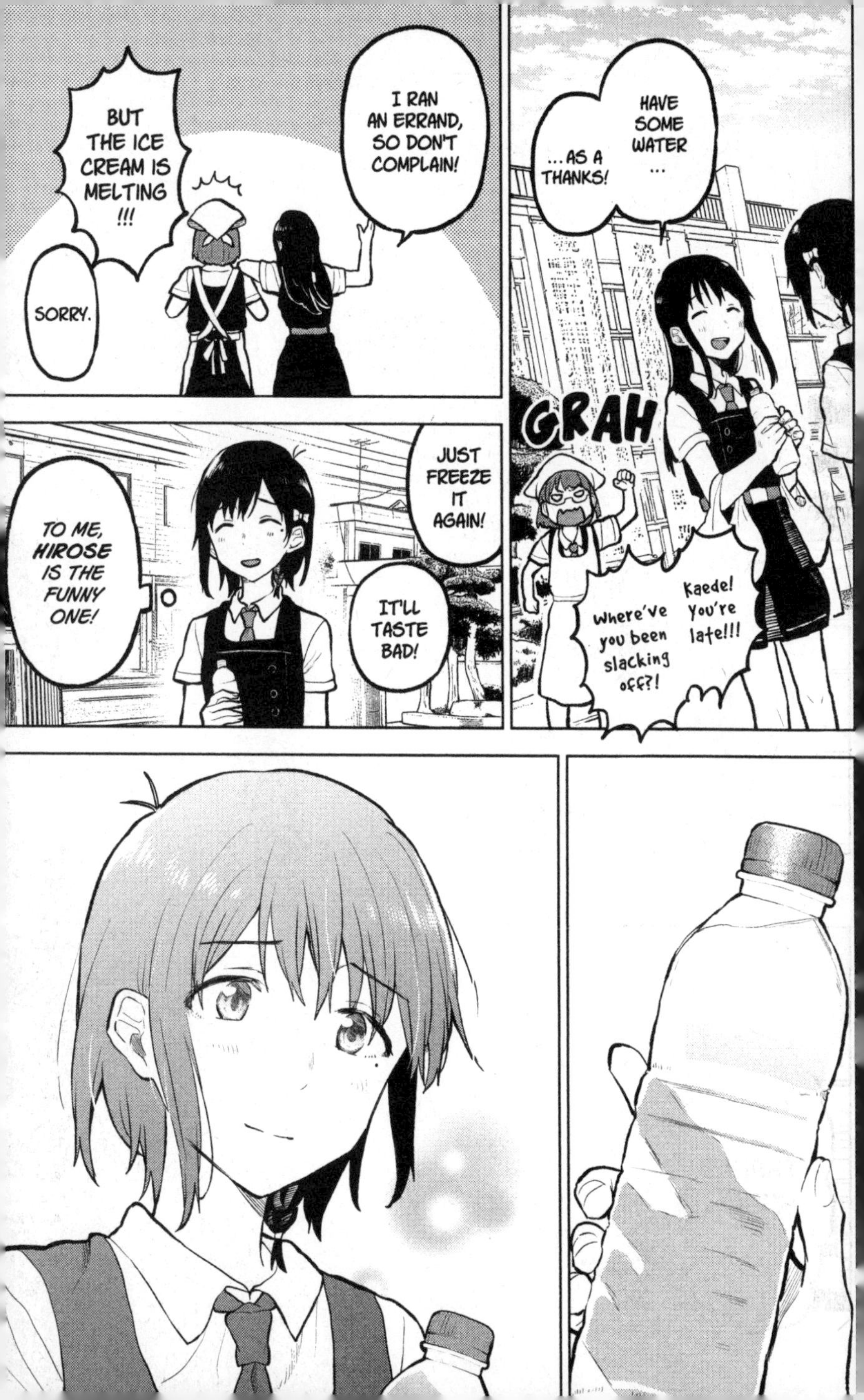
HAVE SOME WATER ...
...AS A THANKS!
GRAH
Kaede! You're late!!!
Where've you been slacking off?!
I RAN AN ERRAND, SO DON'T COMPLAIN!
BUT THE ICE CREAM IS MELTING!!!
SORRY.
JUST FREEZE IT AGAIN!
IT'LL TASTE BAD!
TO ME, HIROSE IS THE FUNNY ONE!

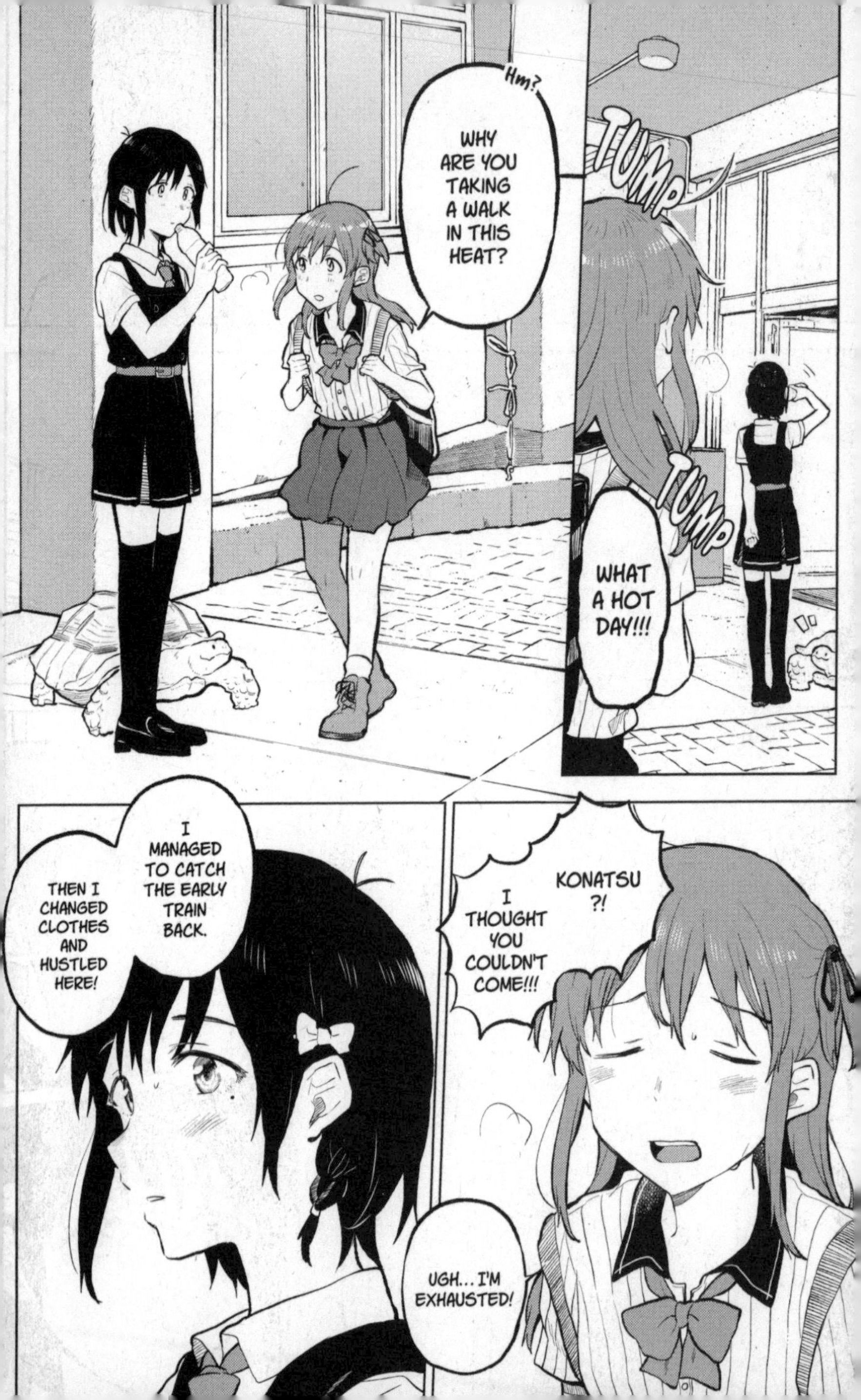
TUMP
TUMP
WHAT A HOT DAY!!!
Hm?
WHY ARE YOU TAKING A WALK IN THIS HEAT?
KONATSU ?!
I THOUGHT YOU COULDN'T COME!!!
UGH... I'M EXHAUSTED!
I MANAGED TO CATCH THE EARLY TRAIN BACK.
THEN I CHANGED CLOTHES AND HUSTLED HERE!

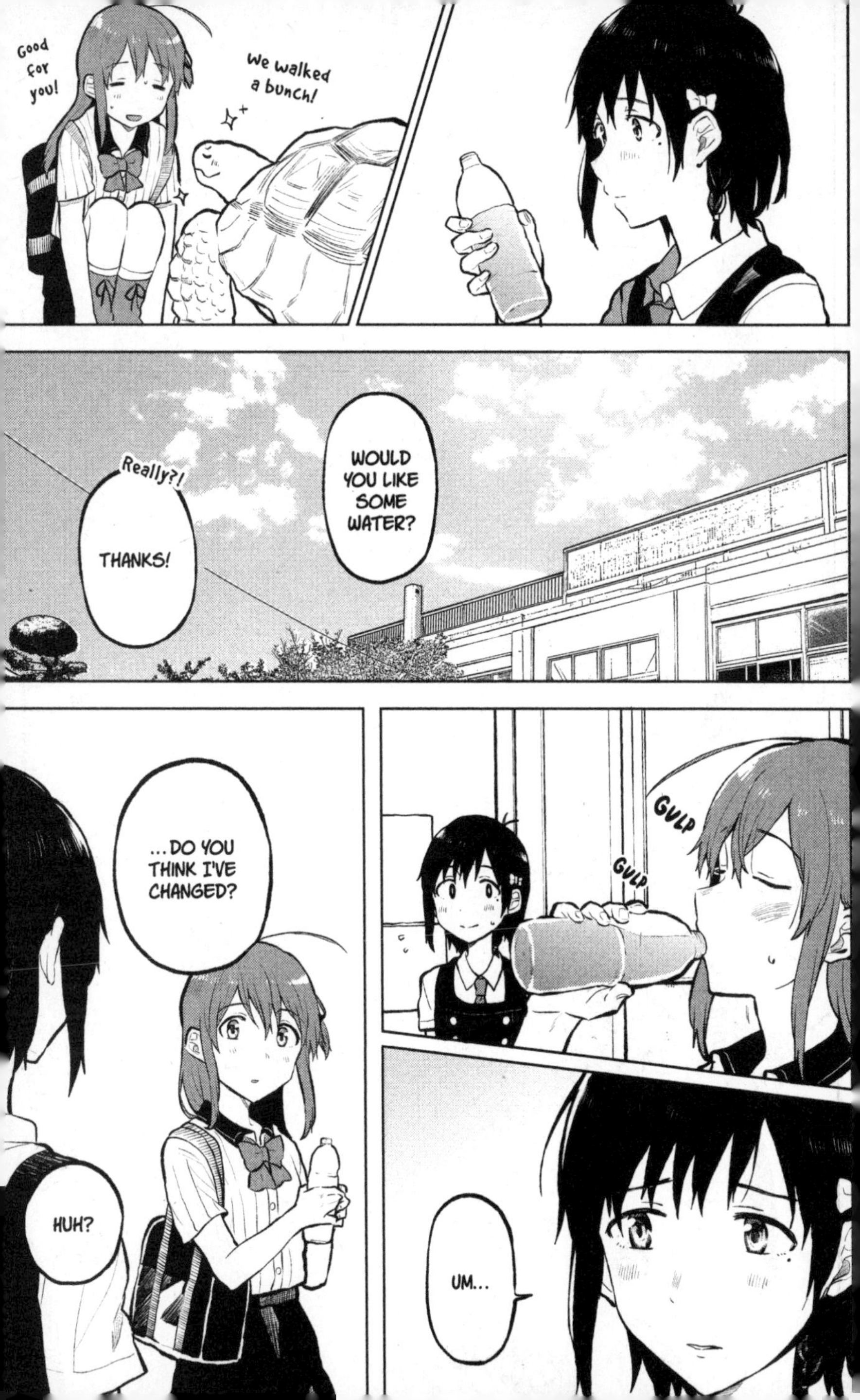
We walked a bunch!
Good for you!
WOULD YOU LIKE SOME WATER?
Really?!
THANKS!
GULP
GULP
UM...
...DO YOU THINK I'VE CHANGED?
HUH?

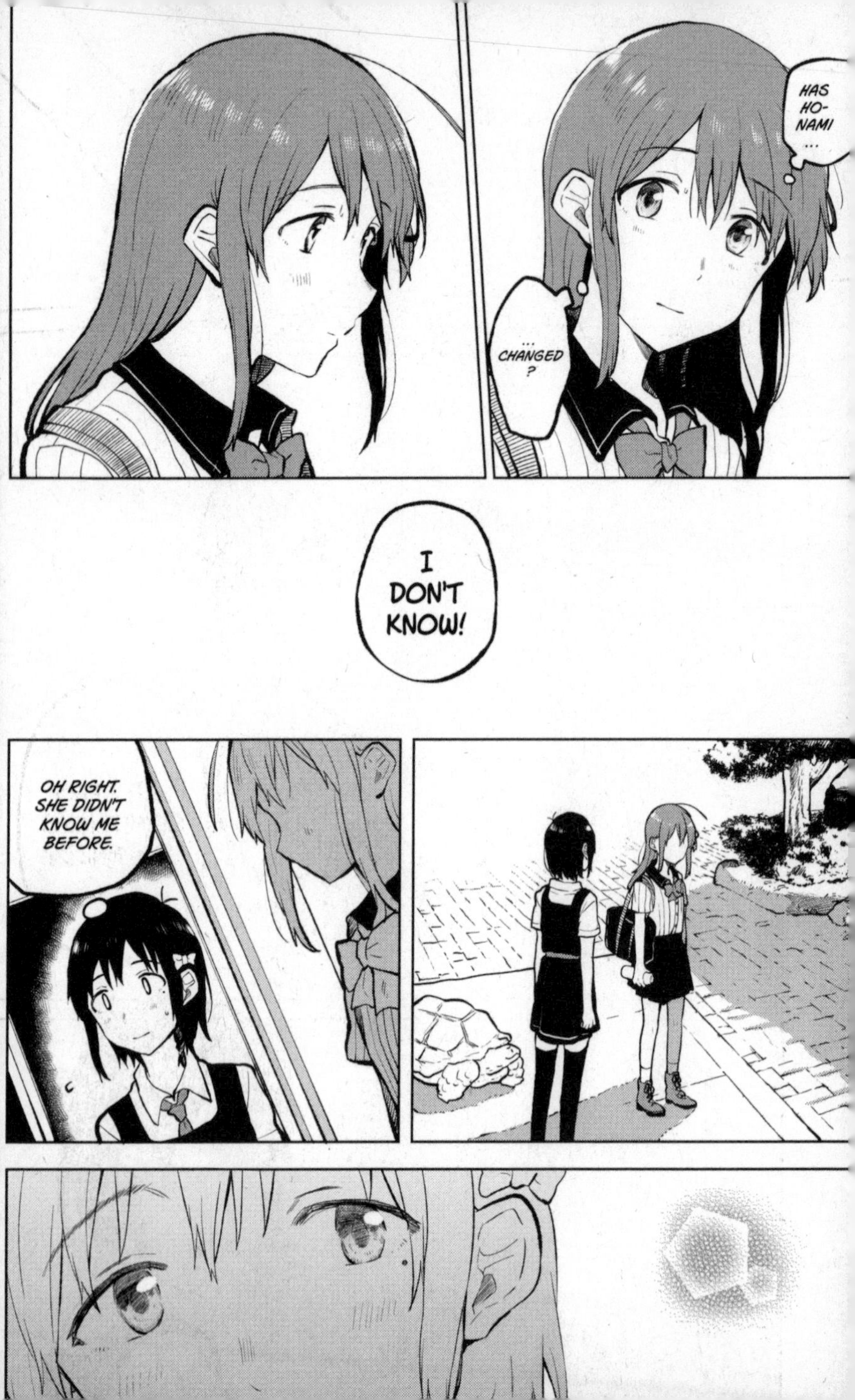
HAS HO-NAMI ...
... CHANGED ?
I DON'T KNOW!
OH RIGHT. SHE DIDN'T KNOW ME BEFORE.

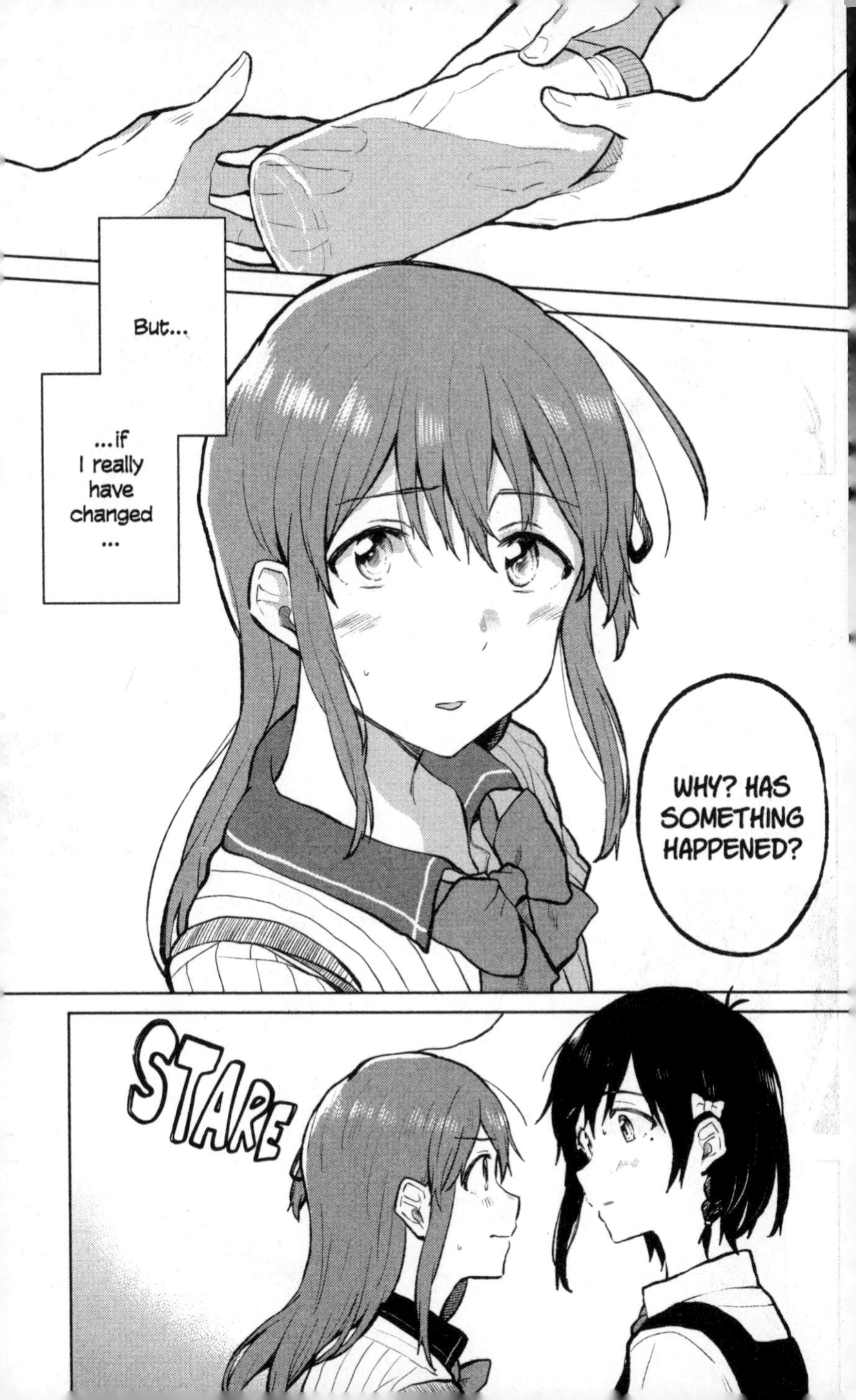
But...
...if I really have changed ...
WHY? HAS SOMETHING HAPPENED?
STARE

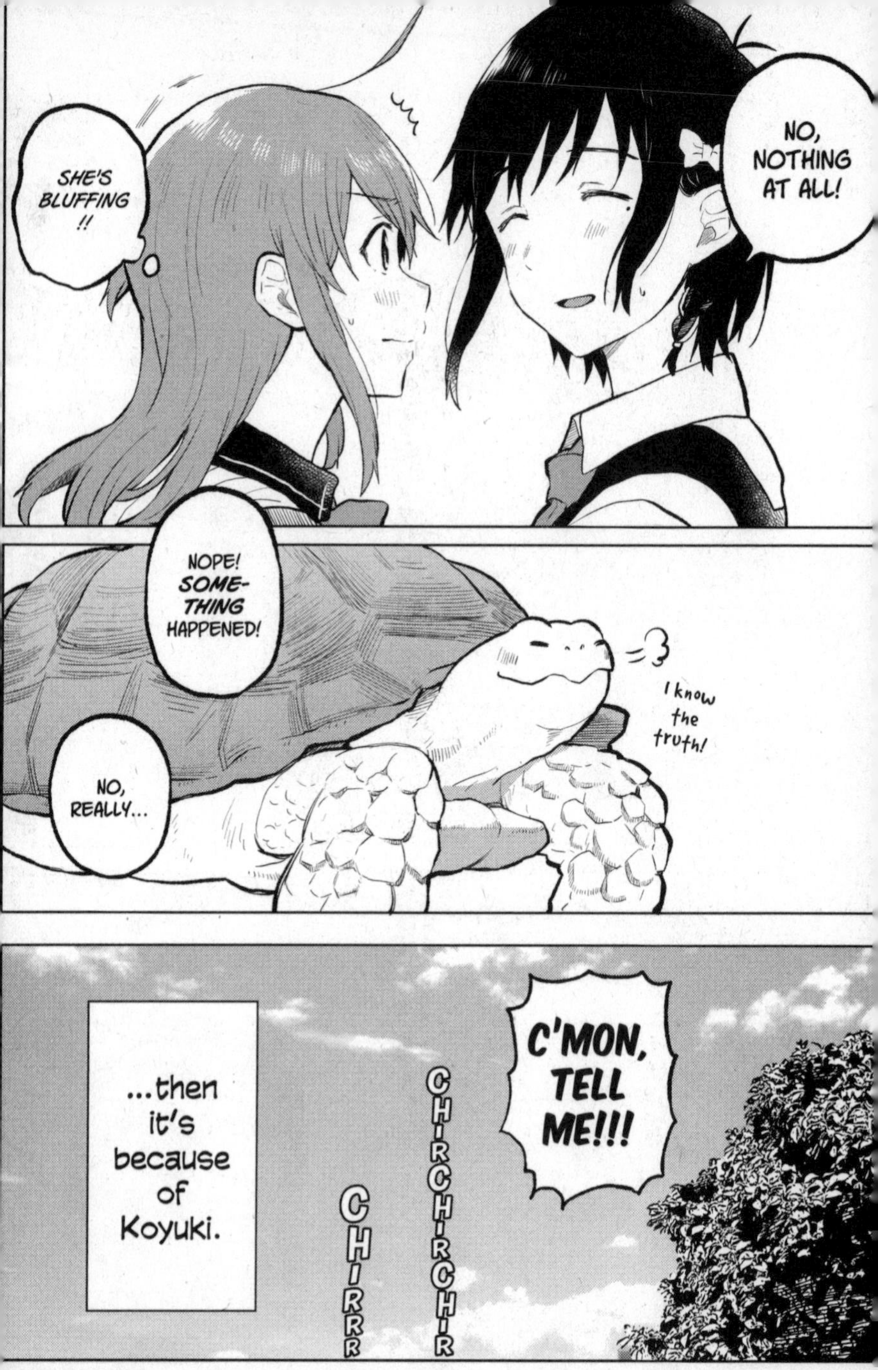
NO, NOTHING AT ALL!
SHE'S BLUFFING!!
NOPE! SOMETHING HAPPENED!
NO, REALLY...
I know the truth!
C'MON, TELL ME!!!
CHIRCHIRCHIR
CHIRRR
...then it's because of Koyuki.

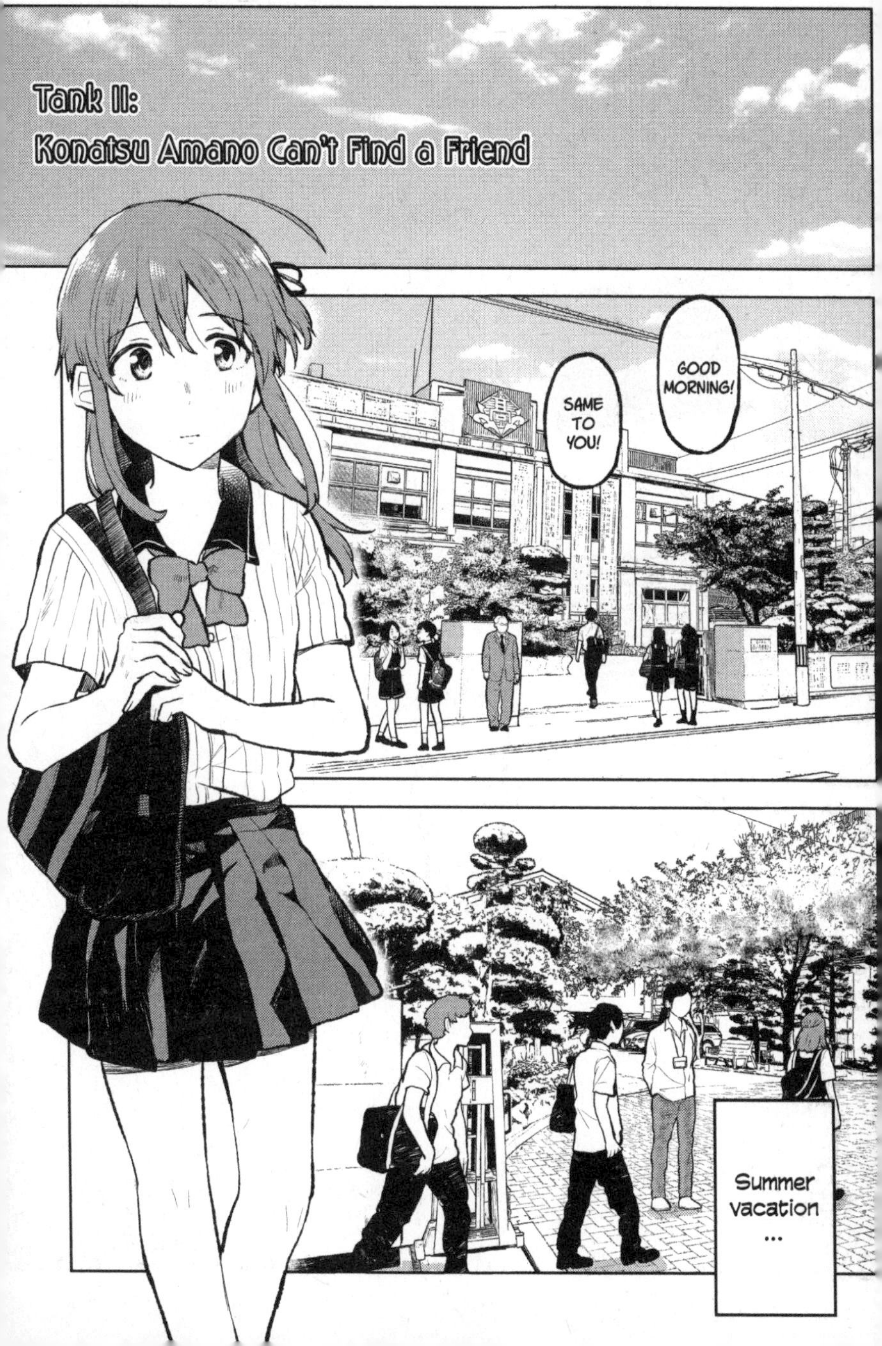
Tank 11:
Konatsu Amano Can't Find a Friend
GOOD MORNING!
SAME TO YOU!
Summer vacation ...

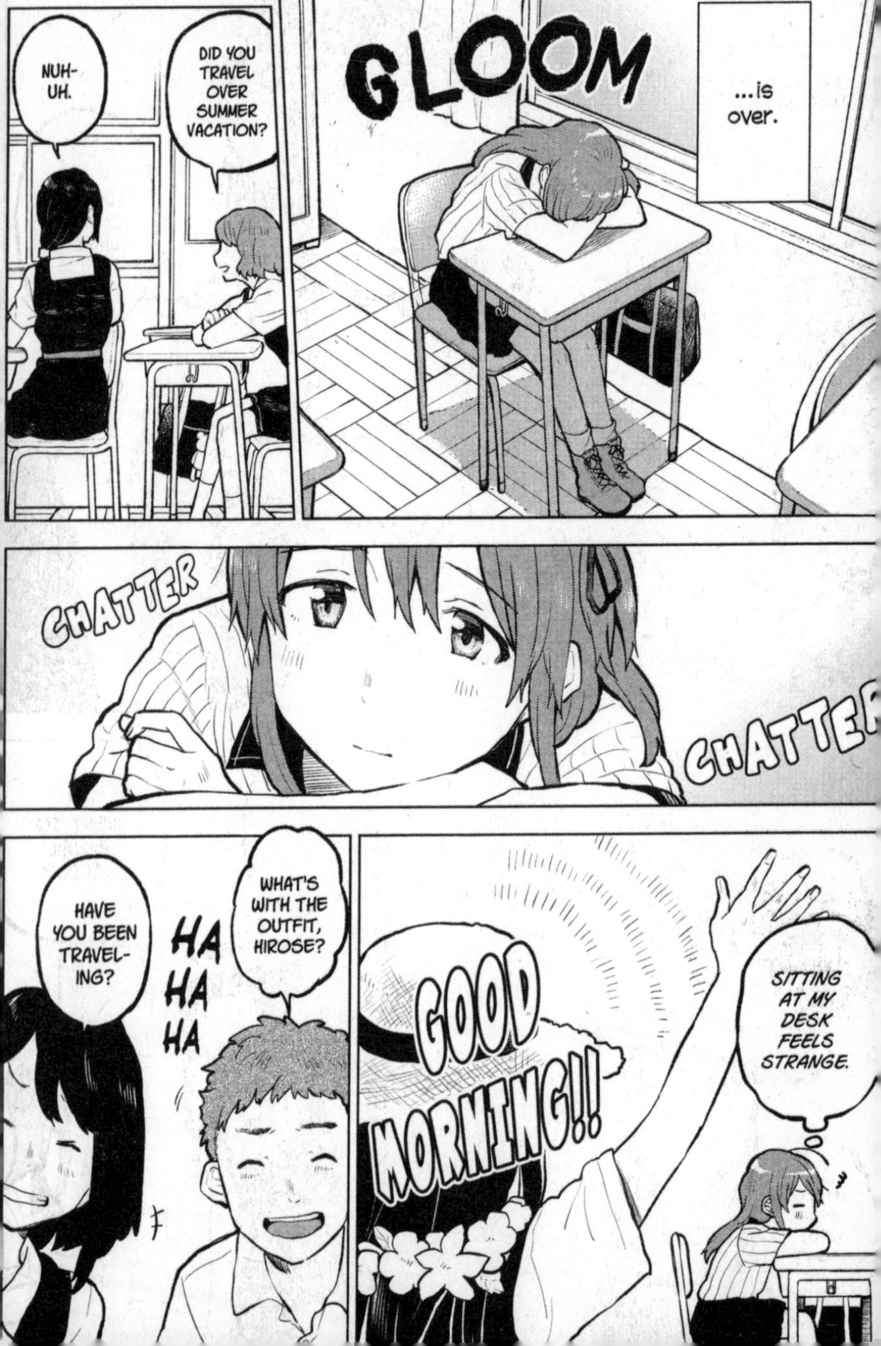
...is over.
GLOOM
DID YOU TRAVEL OVER SUMMER VACATION?
NUH-UH.
CHATTER
CHATTER
SITTING AT MY DESK FEELS STRANGE.
GOOD MORNING!!
WHAT'S WITH THE OUTFIT, HIROSE?
HA HA HA
HAVE YOU BEEN TRAVEL-ING?

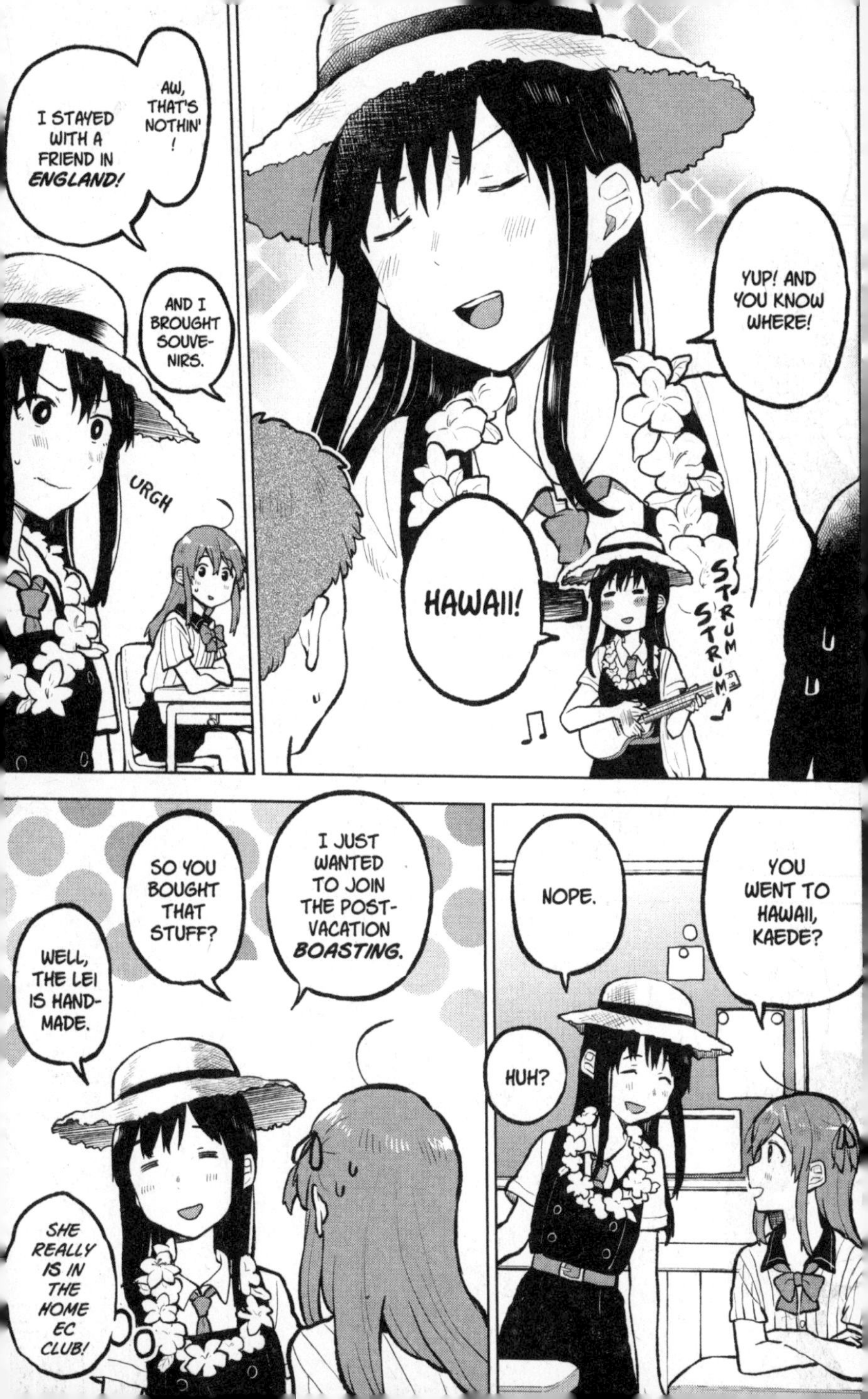
YUP! AND YOU KNOW WHERE!
HAWAII!
STRUM STRUM STRUM
AW, THAT'S NOTHIN'!
I STAYED WITH A FRIEND IN *ENGLAND!*
AND I BROUGHT SOUVE-NIRS.
URGH
YOU WENT TO HAWAII, KAEDE?
NOPE.
HUH?
I JUST WANTED TO JOIN THE POST-VACATION *BOASTING.*
SO YOU BOUGHT THAT STUFF?
WELL, THE LEI IS HAND-MADE.
SHE REALLY IS IN THE HOME EC CLUB!

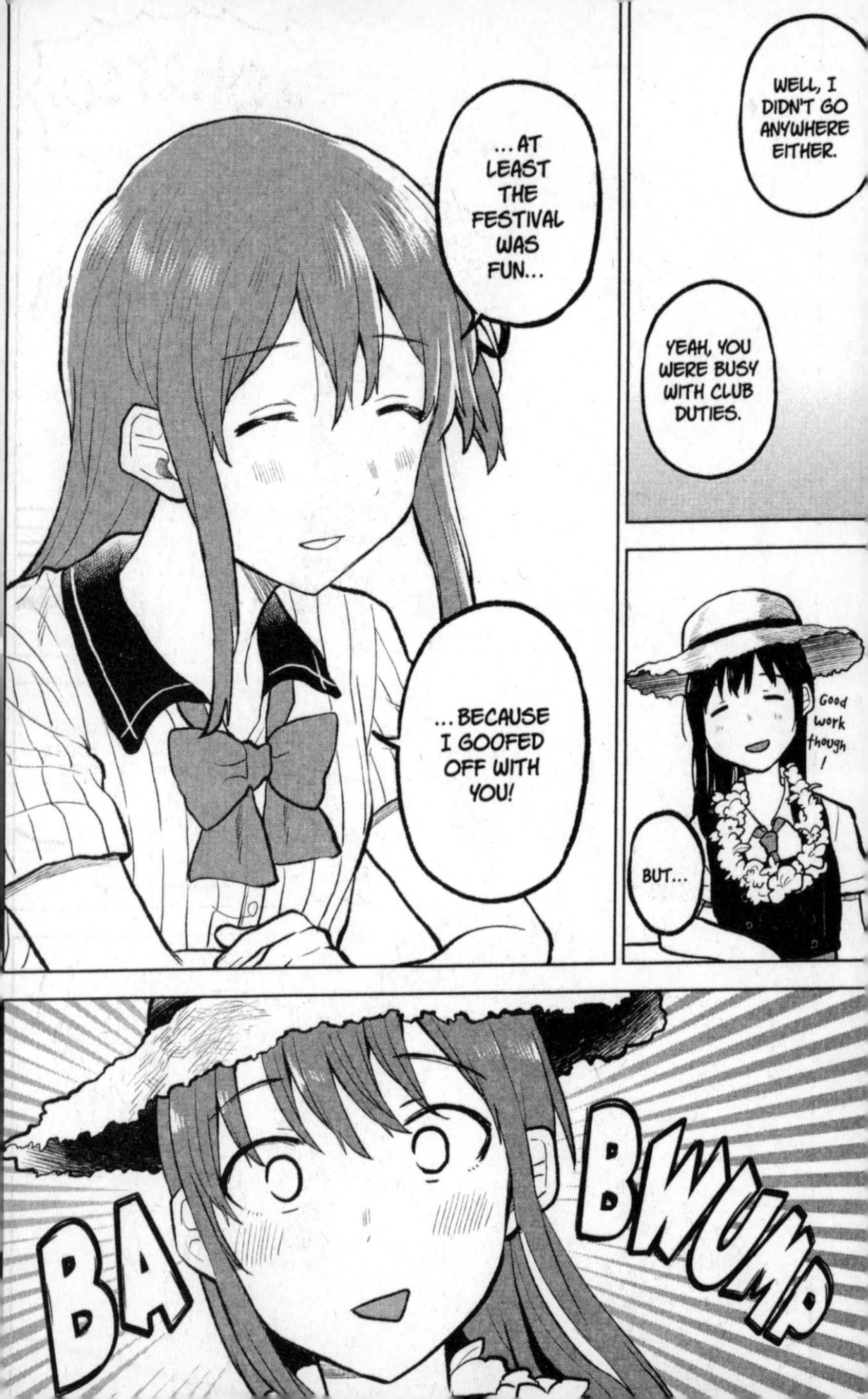
WELL, I DIDN'T GO ANYWHERE EITHER.
YEAH, YOU WERE BUSY WITH CLUB DUTIES.
Good work though!
BUT...
...AT LEAST THE FESTIVAL WAS FUN...
...BECAUSE I GOOFED OFF WITH YOU!
BA BWUMP

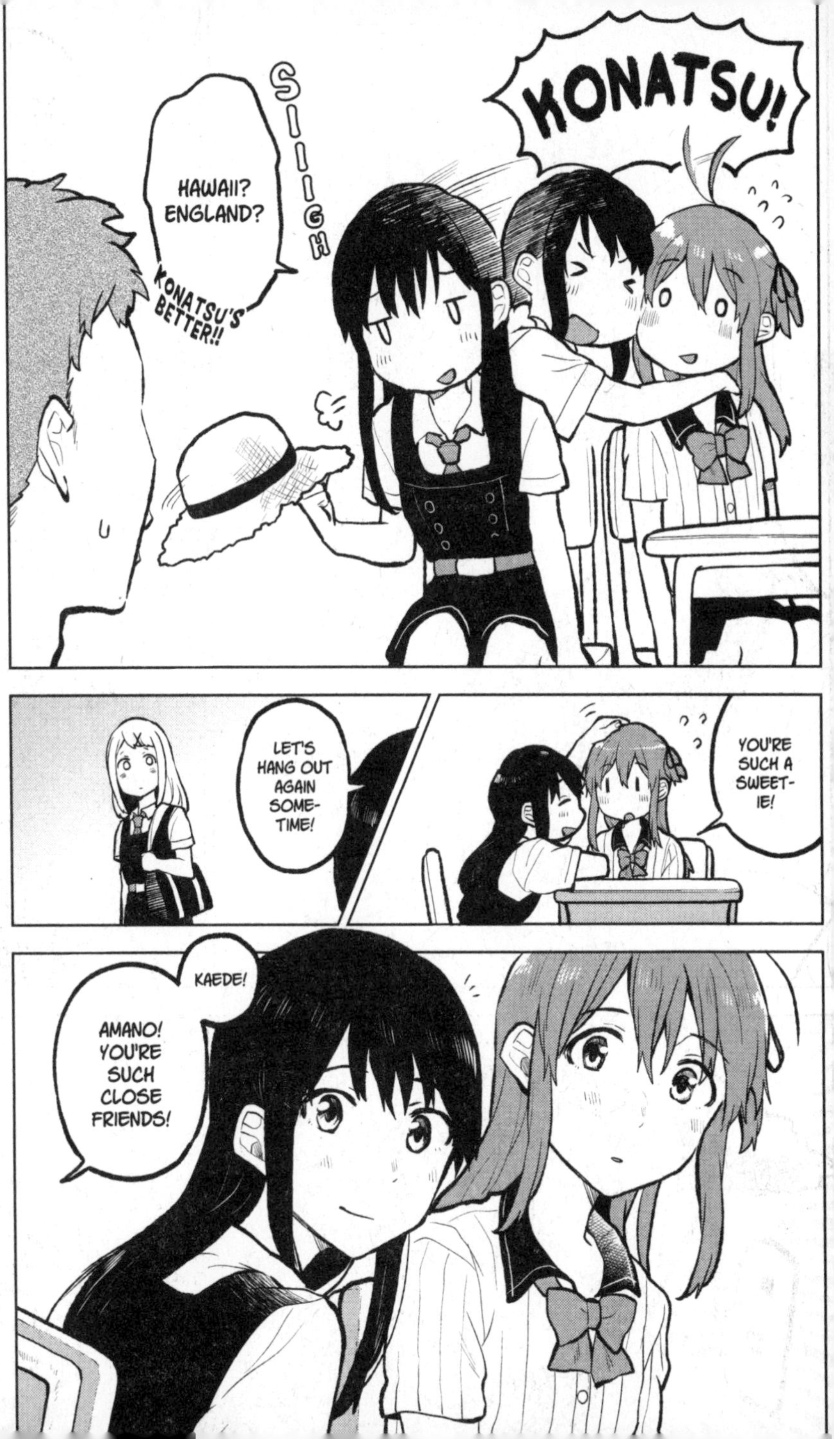
KONATSU!
SIIIIGH
HAWAII? ENGLAND?
KONATSU'S BETTER!!
YOU'RE SUCH A SWEET-IE!
LET'S HANG OUT AGAIN SOME-TIME!
KAEDE!
AMANO! YOU'RE SUCH CLOSE FRIENDS!

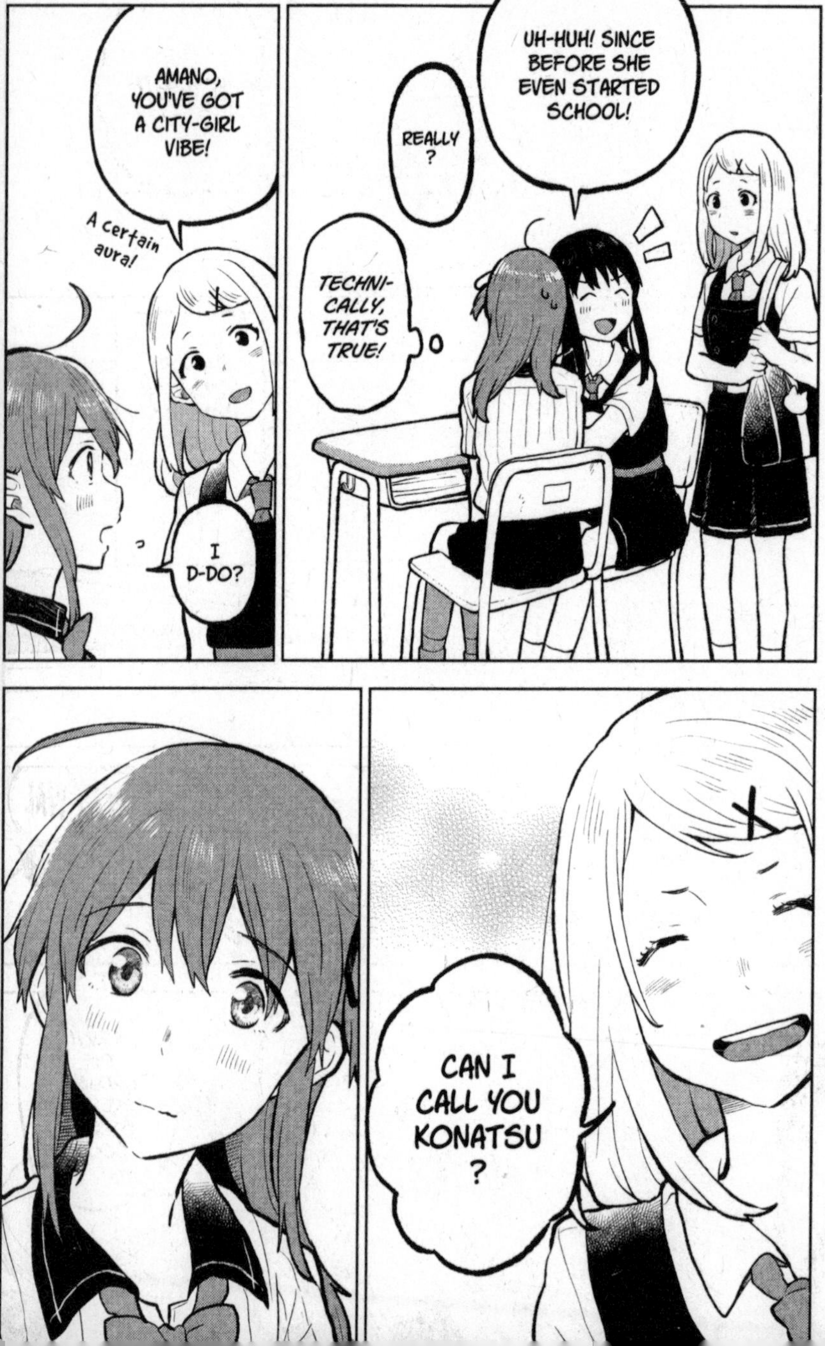
UH-HUH! SINCE BEFORE SHE EVEN STARTED SCHOOL!
REALLY?
TECHNICALLY, THAT'S TRUE!
AMANO, YOU'VE GOT A CITY-GIRL VIBE!
A certain aura!
I D-DO?
CAN I CALL YOU KONATSU?

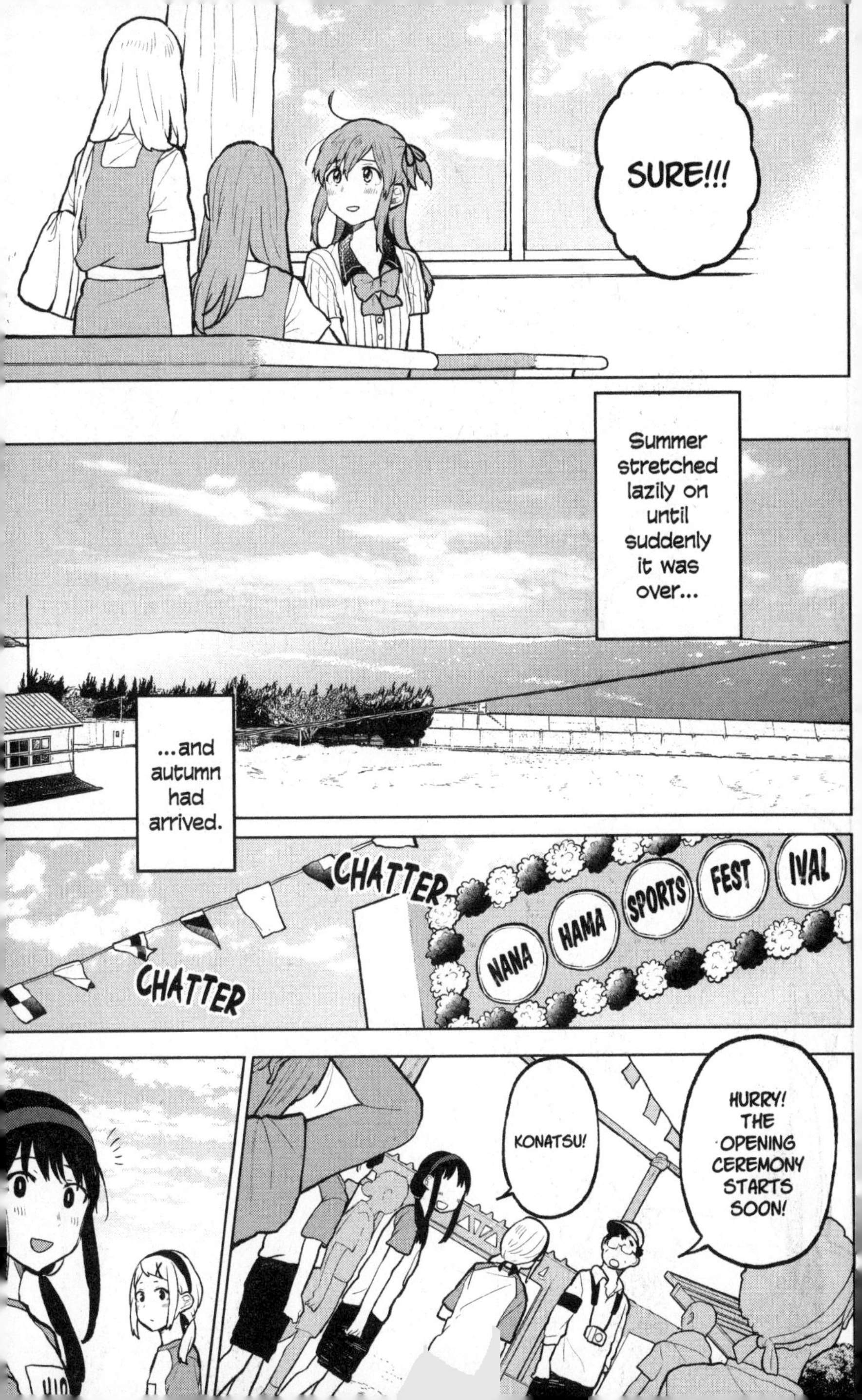
SURE!!!
Summer stretched lazily on until suddenly it was over...
...and autumn had arrived.
NANA HAMA SPORTS FEST IVAL
CHATTER
CHATTER
HURRY! THE OPENING CEREMONY STARTS SOON!
KONATSU!

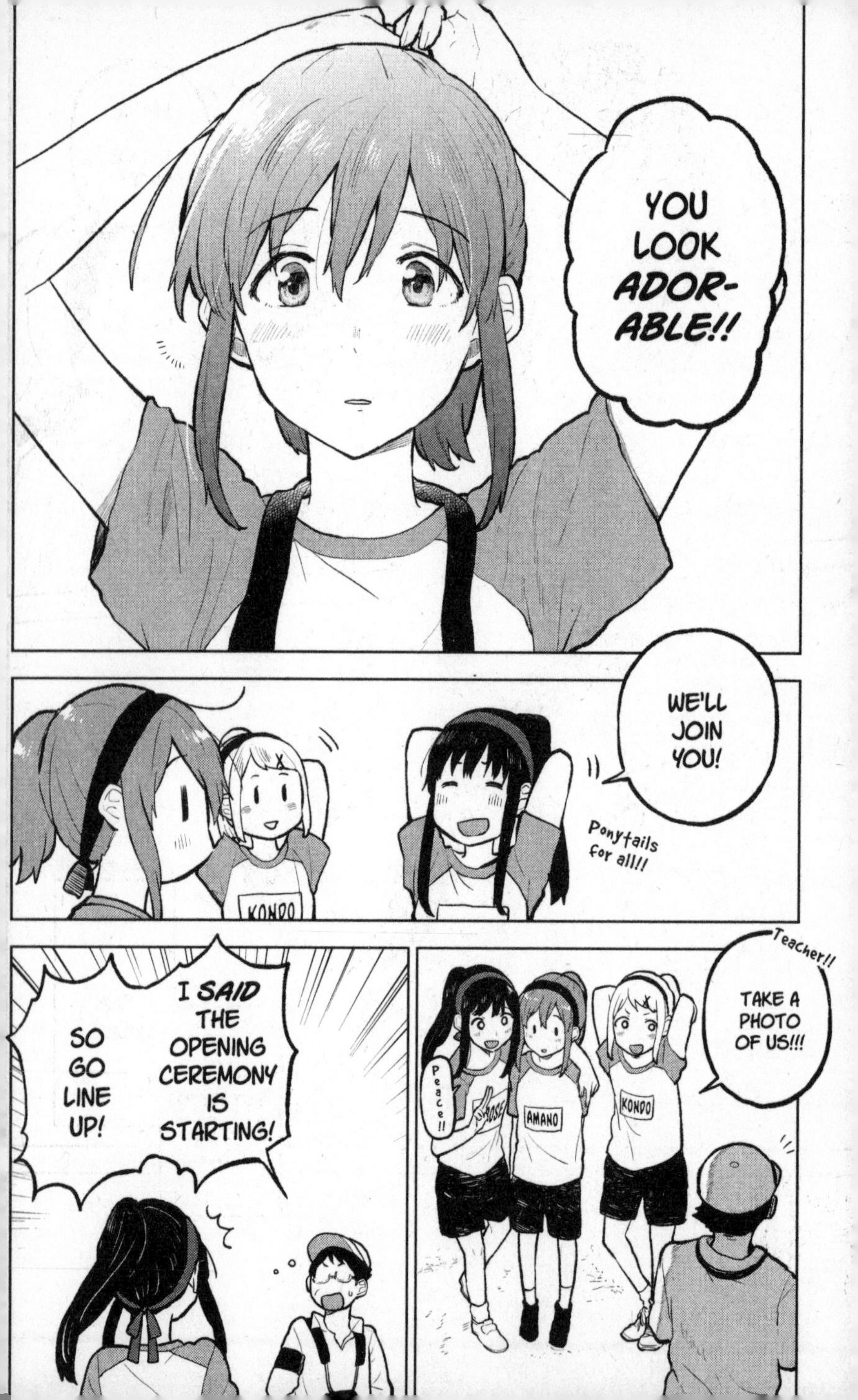
YOU LOOK ADOR-ABLE!!
WE'LL JOIN YOU!
Ponytails for all!!
KONDO
Teacher!!
TAKE A PHOTO OF US!!!
Peace!!
AMANO
KONDO
I SAID THE OPENING CEREMONY IS STARTING!
SO GO LINE UP!

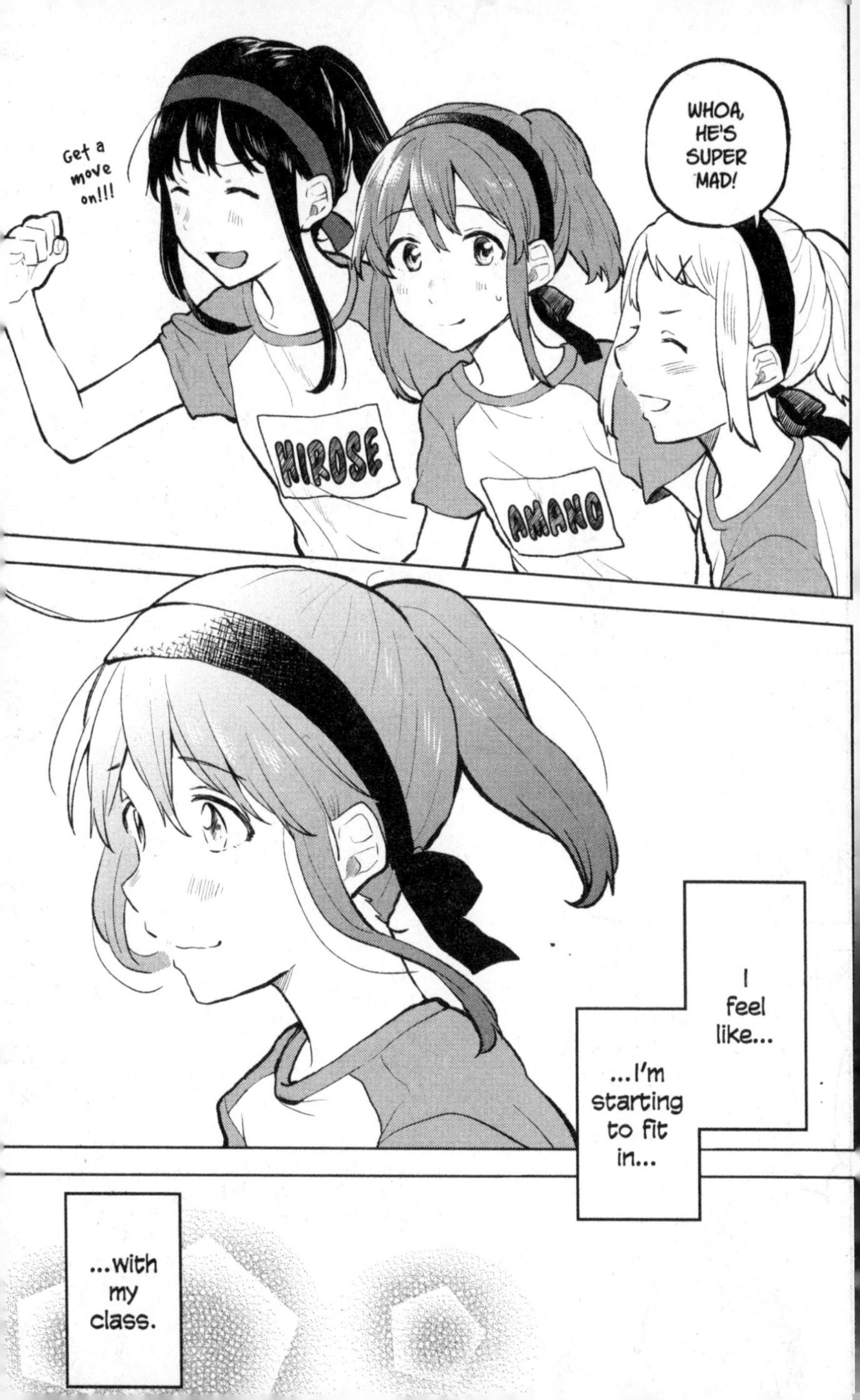
WHOA, HE'S SUPER MAD!
Get a move on!!!
HIROSE
AMANO
I feel like...
...I'm starting to fit in...
...with my class.

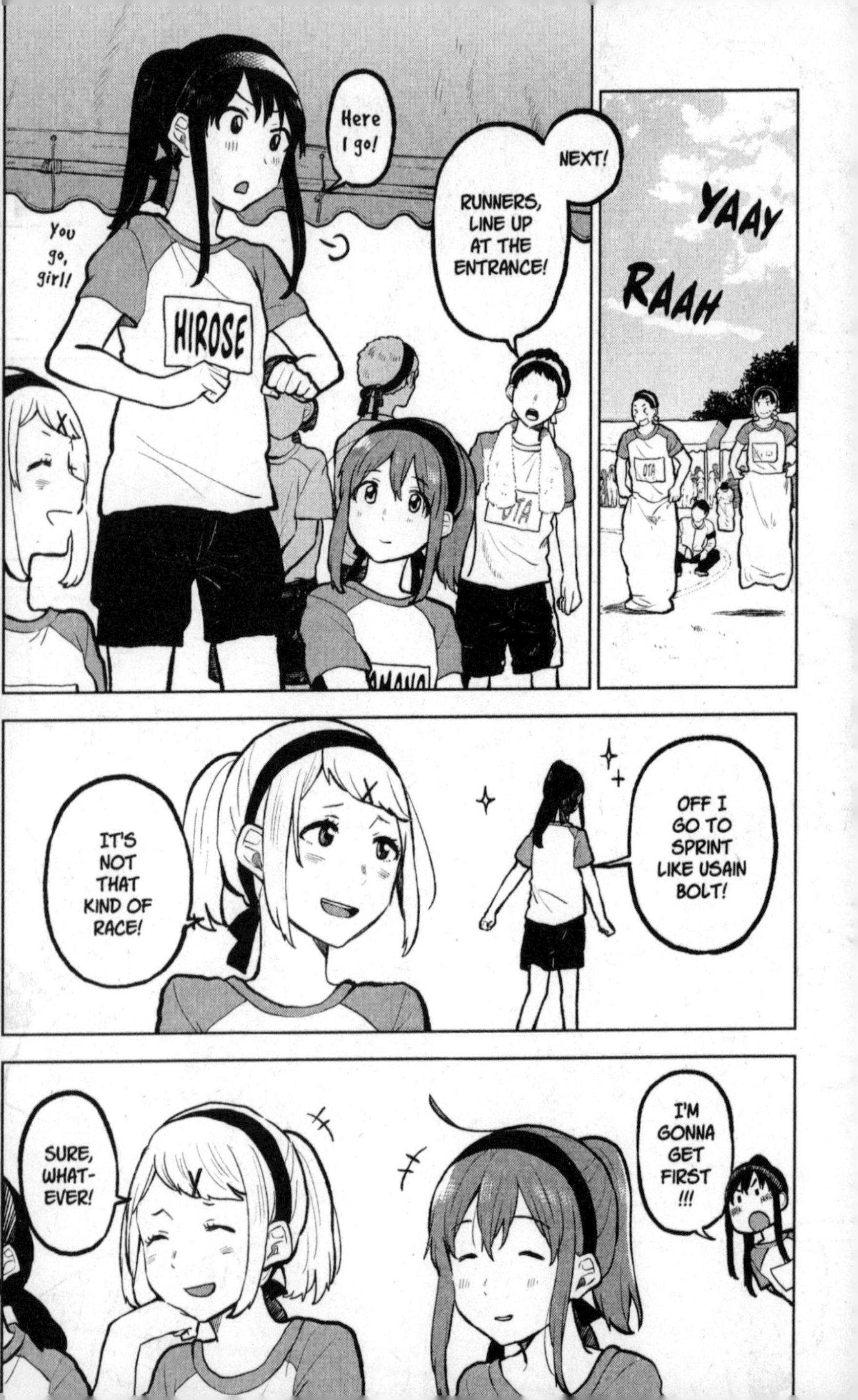
YAAY
RAAH
NEXT!
RUNNERS, LINE UP AT THE ENTRANCE!
Here I go!
HIROSE
You go, girl!
OFF I GO TO SPRINT LIKE USAIN BOLT!
IT'S NOT THAT KIND OF RACE!
I'M GONNA GET FIRST!!!
SURE, WHAT-EVER!

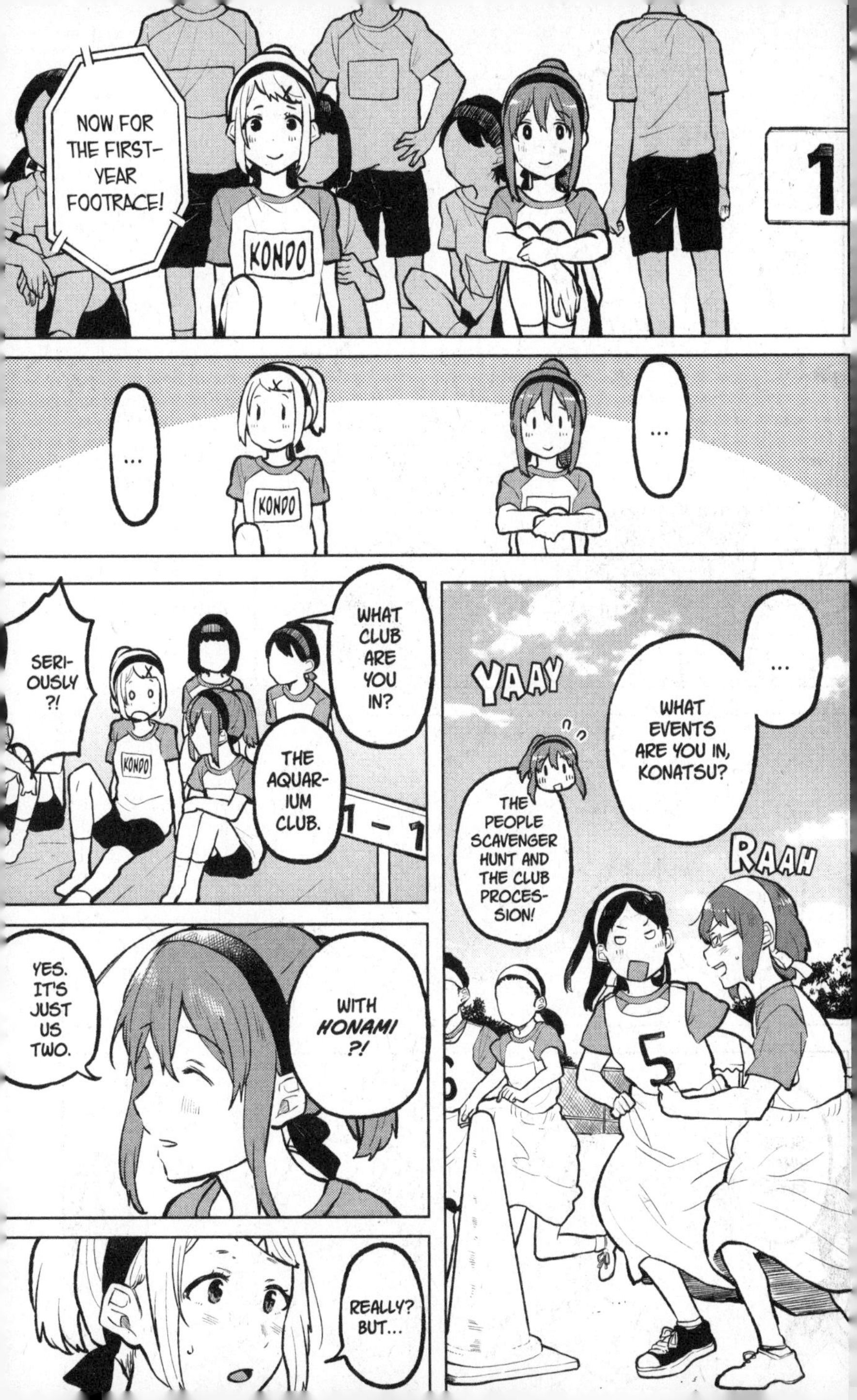
1
NOW FOR THE FIRST-YEAR FOOTRACE!
...
...
...
WHAT EVENTS ARE YOU IN, KONATSU?
YAAY
THE PEOPLE SCAVENGER HUNT AND THE CLUB PROCESSION!
RAAH
5
WHAT CLUB ARE YOU IN?
THE AQUARIUM CLUB.
SERIOUSLY?!
KONDO
WITH HONAMI?!
YES. IT'S JUST US TWO.
REALLY? BUT...

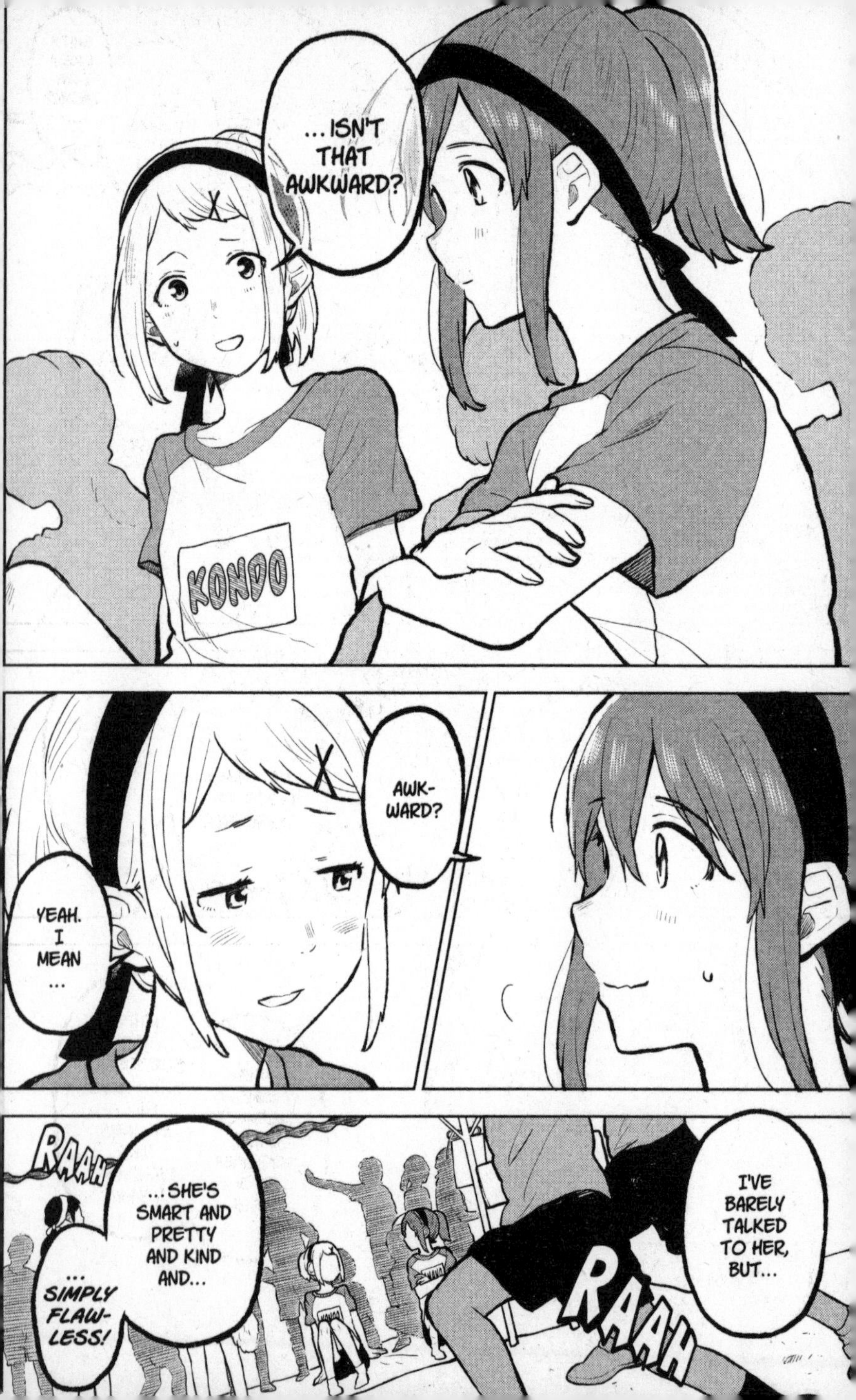
...ISN'T THAT AWKWARD?
AWK-WARD?
YEAH. I MEAN ...
I'VE BARELY TALKED TO HER, BUT...
RAAH
...SHE'S SMART AND PRETTY AND KIND AND...
...SIMPLY FLAW-LESS!
RAAH
KONDO

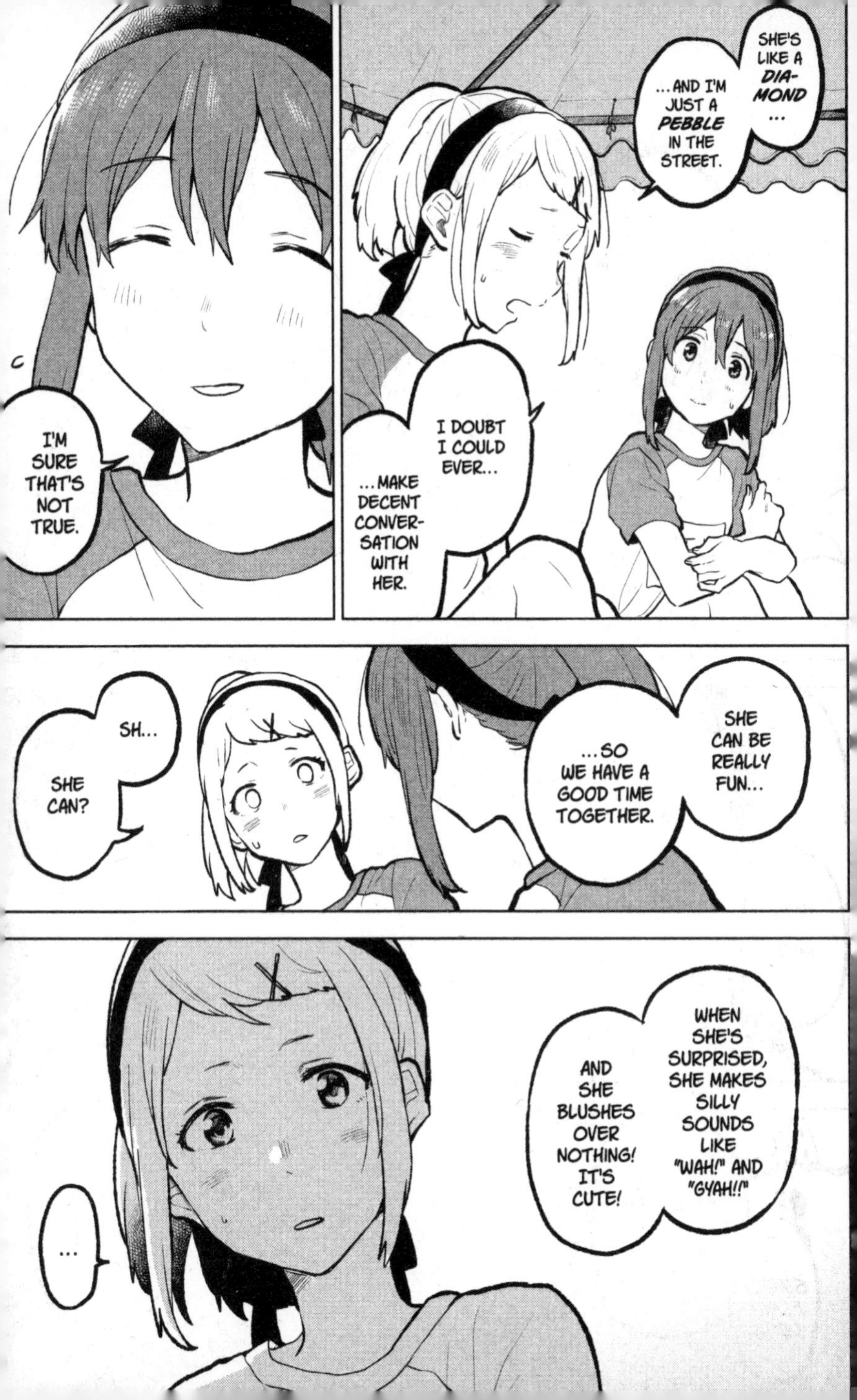
SHE'S LIKE A DIAMOND...
...AND I'M JUST A PEBBLE IN THE STREET.
I DOUBT I COULD EVER...
...MAKE DECENT CONVERSATION WITH HER.
I'M SURE THAT'S NOT TRUE.
SHE CAN BE REALLY FUN...
...SO WE HAVE A GOOD TIME TOGETHER.
SH...
SHE CAN?
WHEN SHE'S SURPRISED, SHE MAKES SILLY SOUNDS LIKE "WAH!" AND "GYAH!!"
AND SHE BLUSHES OVER NOTHING! IT'S CUTE!
...

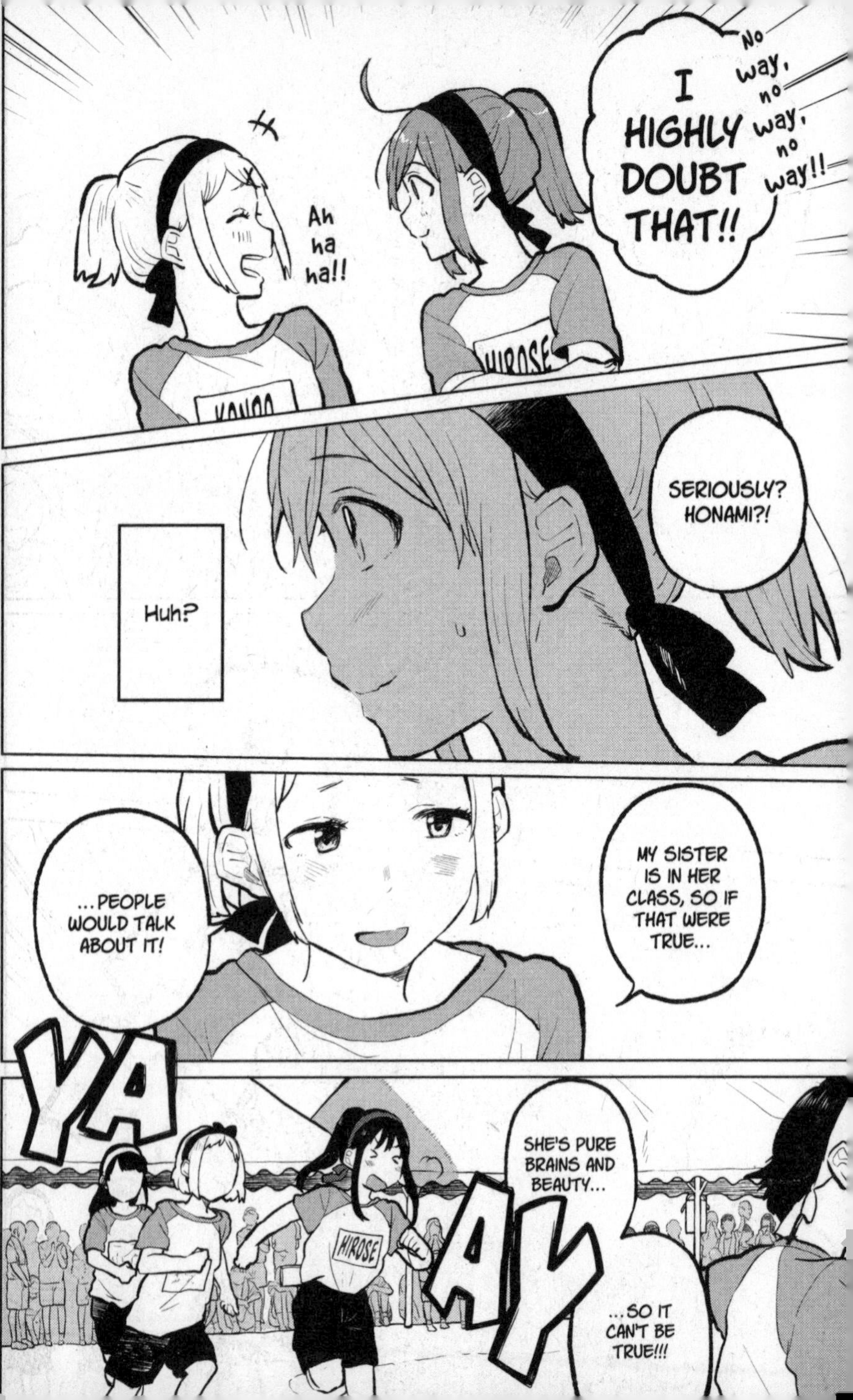
I HIGHLY DOUBT THAT!!
No way, no way, no way!!
Ah ha ha!!
HIROSE
SERIOUSLY? HONAMI?!
Huh?
MY SISTER IS IN HER CLASS, SO IF THAT WERE TRUE...
...PEOPLE WOULD TALK ABOUT IT!
SHE'S PURE BRAINS AND BEAUTY...
...SO IT CAN'T BE TRUE!!!
YA
AY
HIROSE

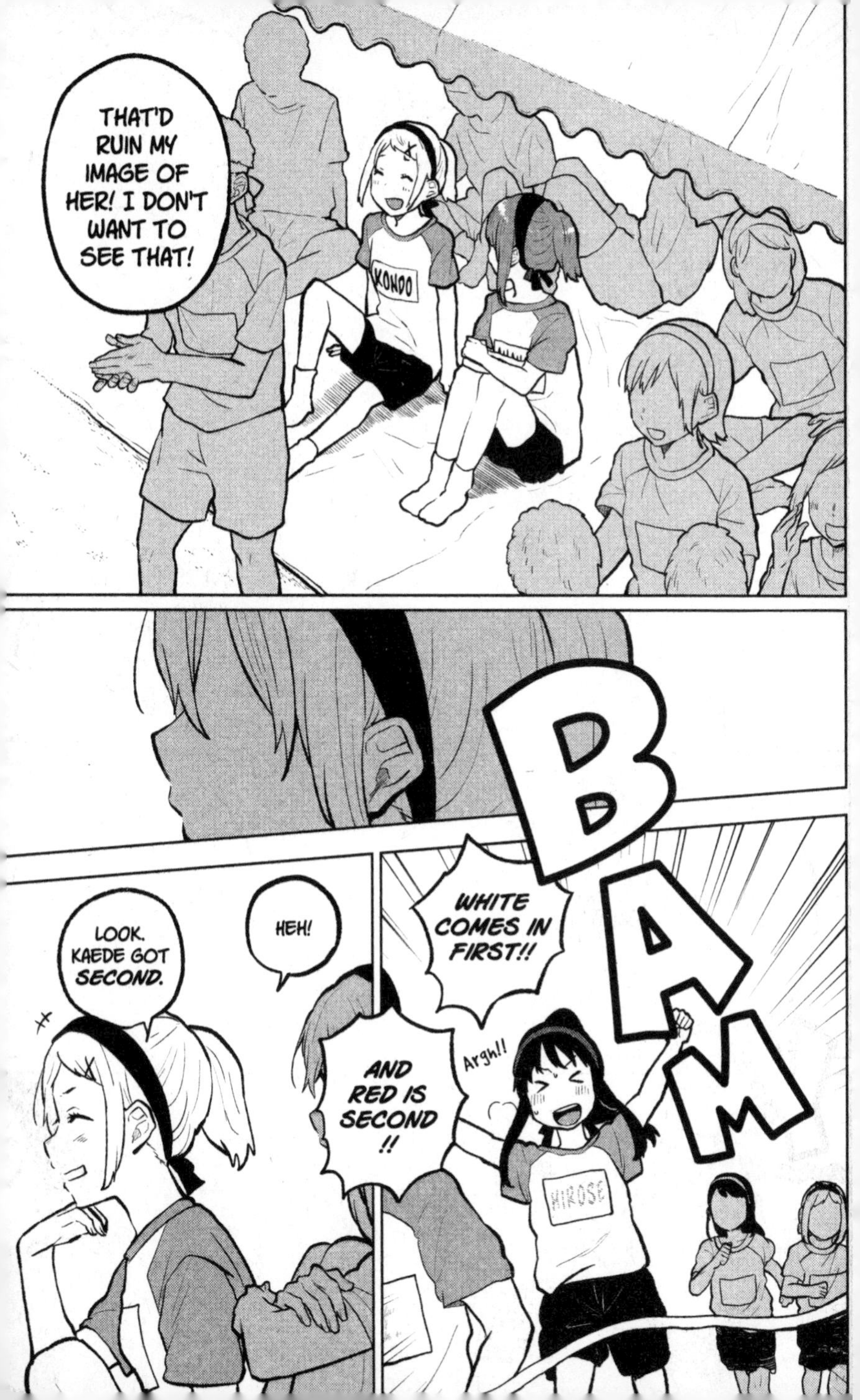
THAT'D RUIN MY IMAGE OF HER! I DON'T WANT TO SEE THAT!
KONDO
BAM
WHITE COMES IN FIRST!!
Argh!!
AND RED IS SECOND !!
HEH!
LOOK. KAEDE GOT SECOND.

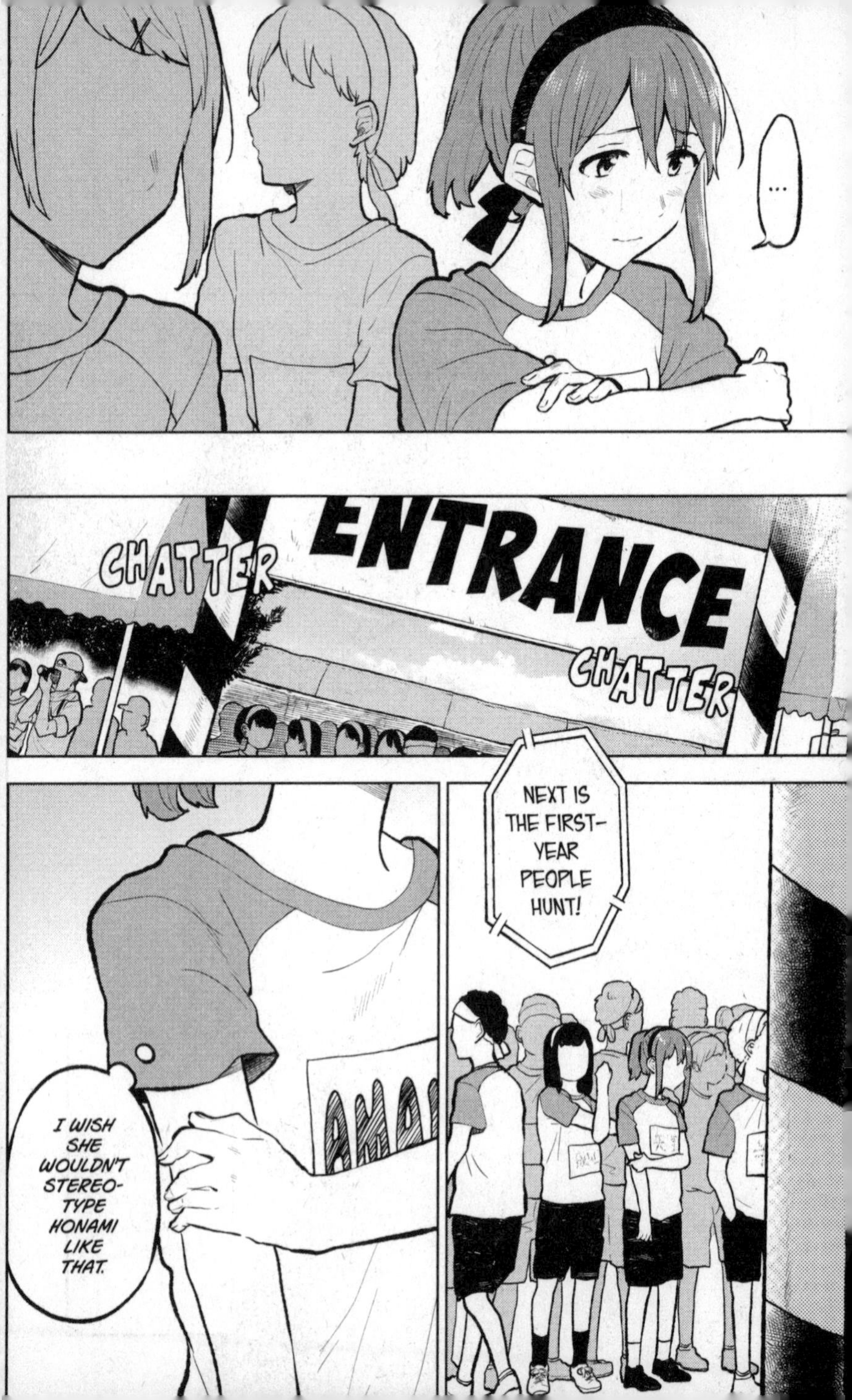
...
ENTRANCE
CHATTER
CHATTER
NEXT IS THE FIRST-YEAR PEOPLE HUNT!
I WISH SHE WOULDN'T STEREOTYPE HONAMI LIKE THAT.

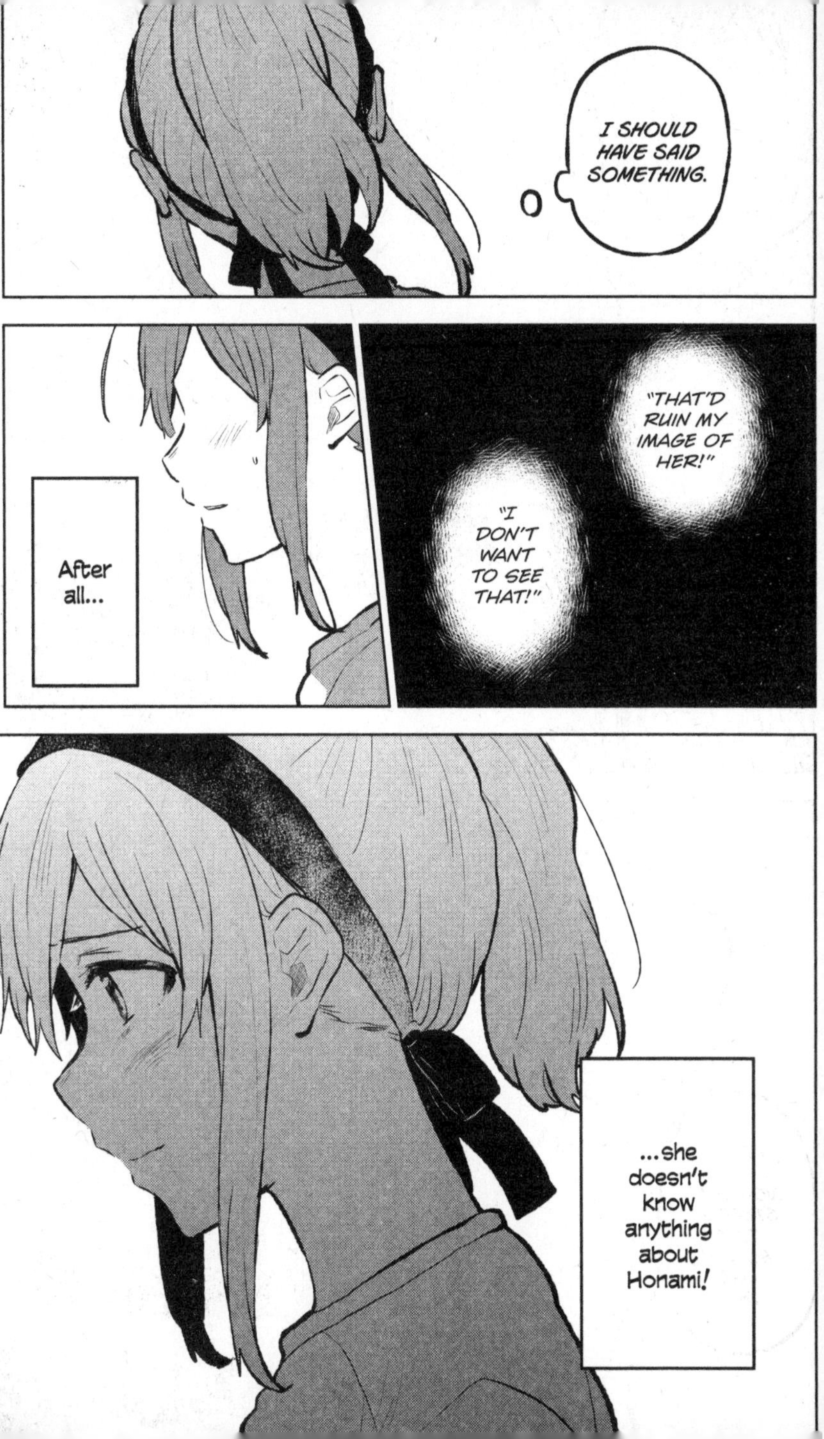
I SHOULD HAVE SAID SOMETHING.
"THAT'D RUIN MY IMAGE OF HER!"
"I DON'T WANT TO SEE THAT!"
After all...
...she doesn't know anything about Honami!

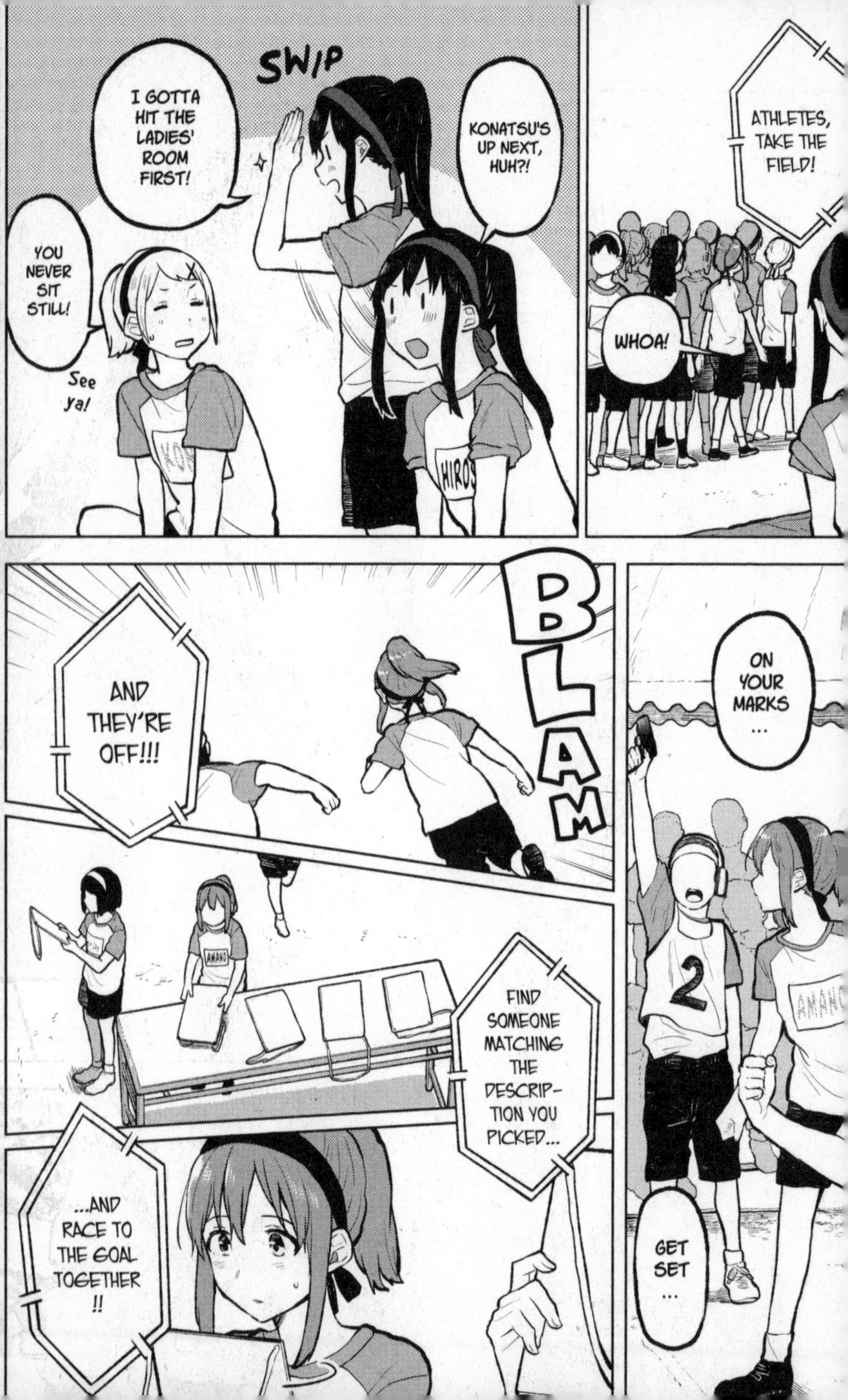
ATHLETES, TAKE THE FIELD!
WHOA!
SWIP
KONATSU'S UP NEXT, HUH?!
I GOTTA HIT THE LADIES' ROOM FIRST!
YOU NEVER SIT STILL!
See ya!
ON YOUR MARKS ...
GET SET ...
BLAM
AND THEY'RE OFF!!!
AMANO
FIND SOMEONE MATCHING THE DESCRIP-TION YOU PICKED...
...AND RACE TO THE GOAL TOGETHER !!

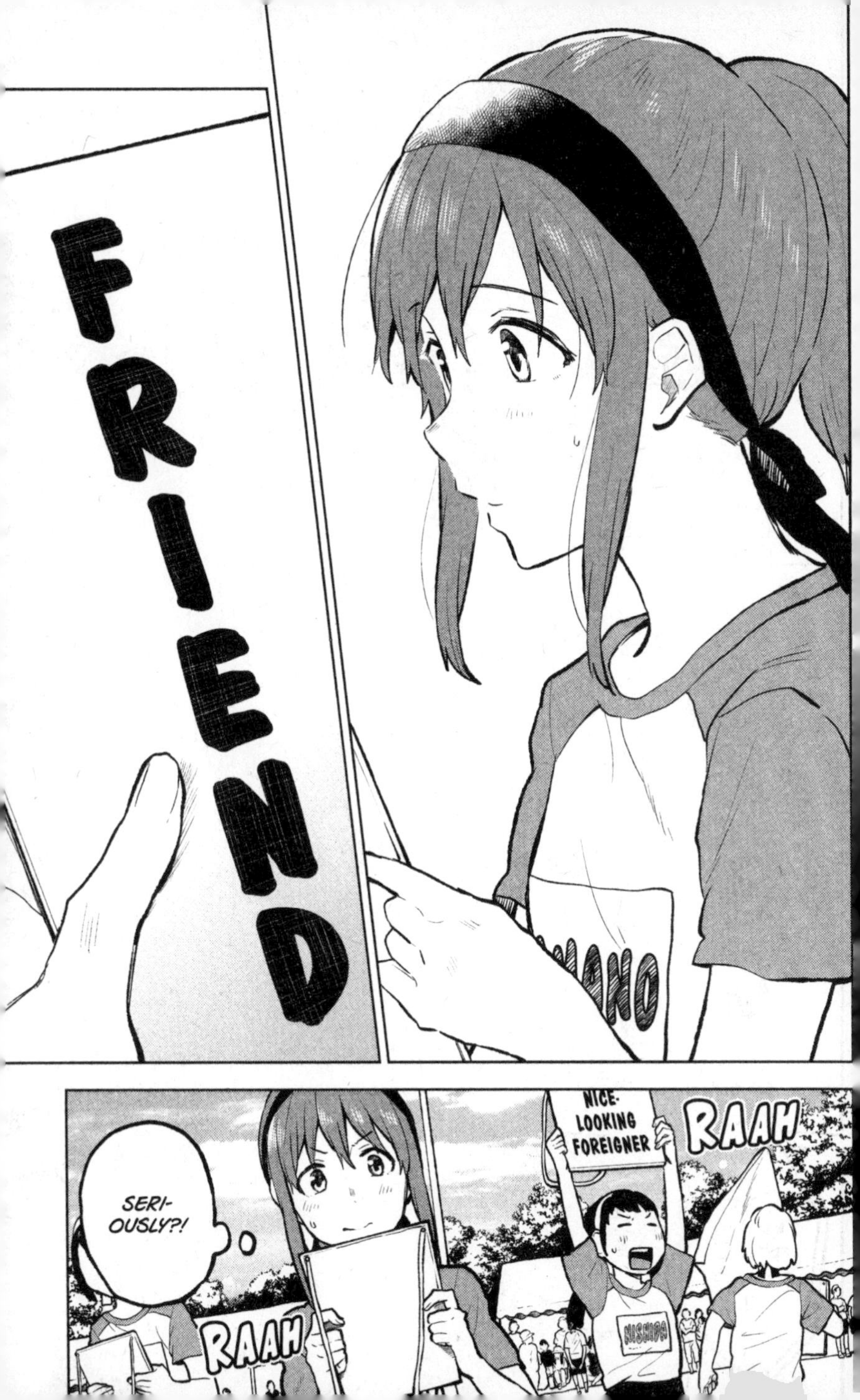
FRIEND
RAAH
NICE-LOOKING FOREIGNER
SERI-OUSLY?!
NISHIDA
RAAH

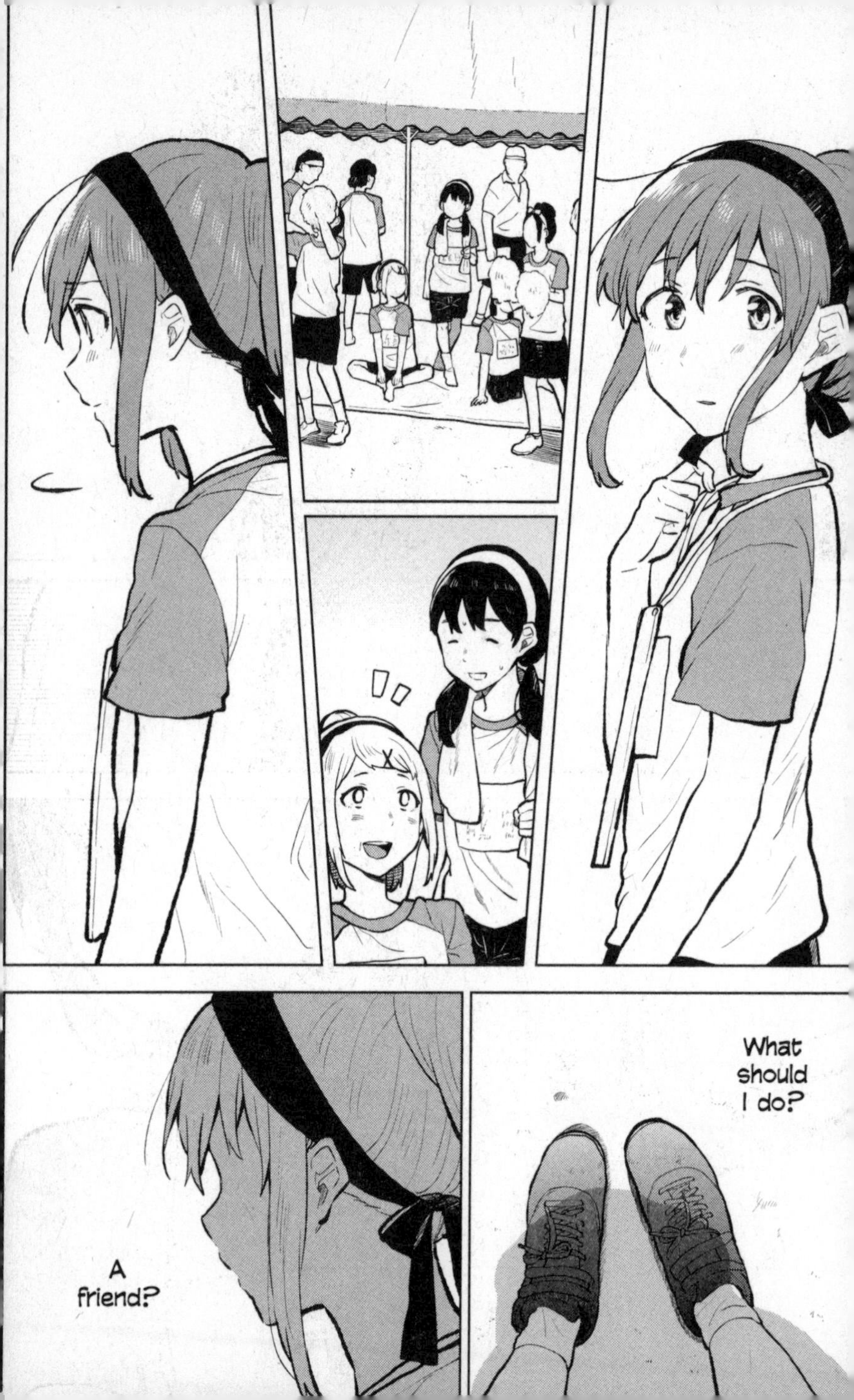
What should I do?
A friend?

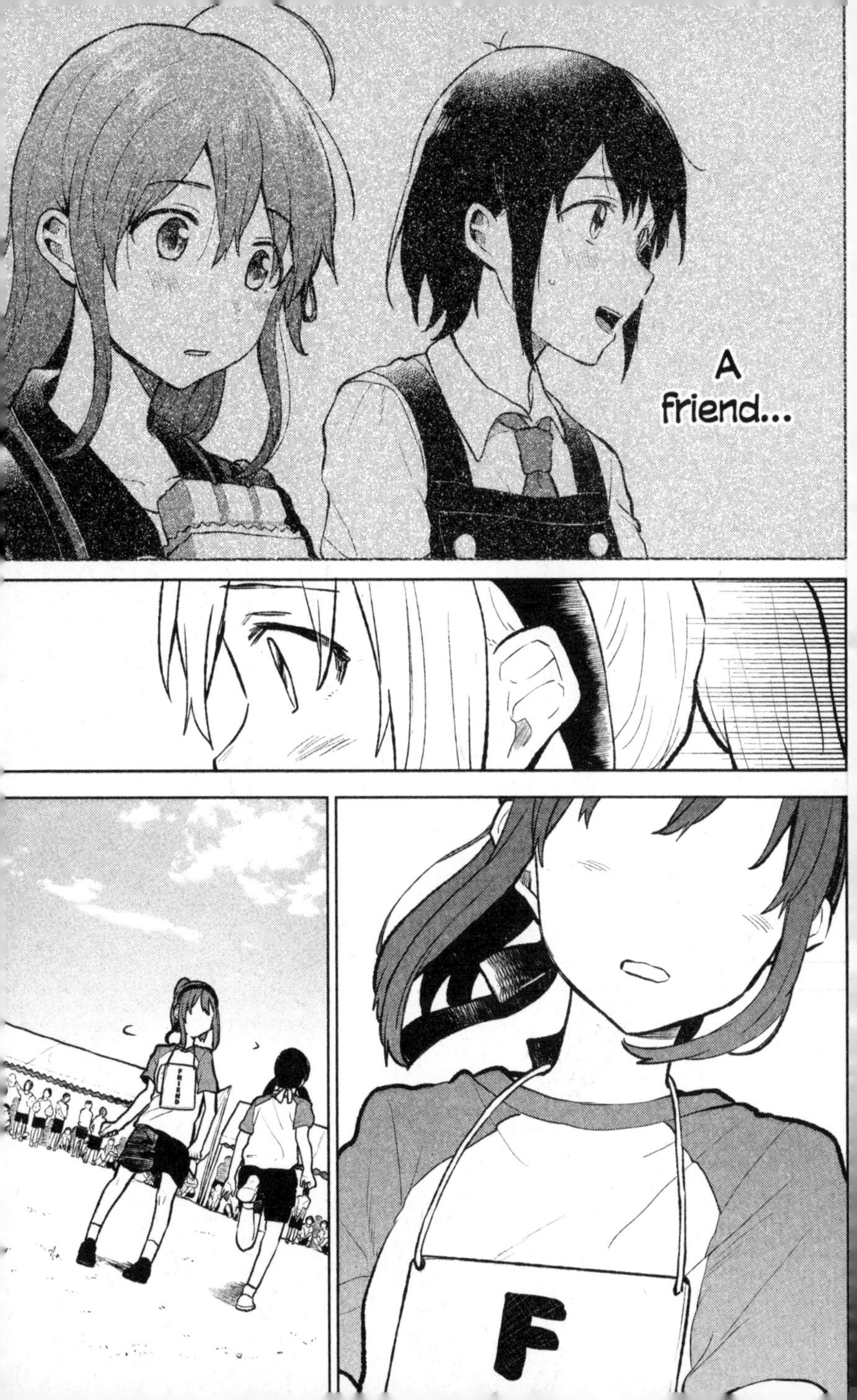
A friend...
FRIEND
F

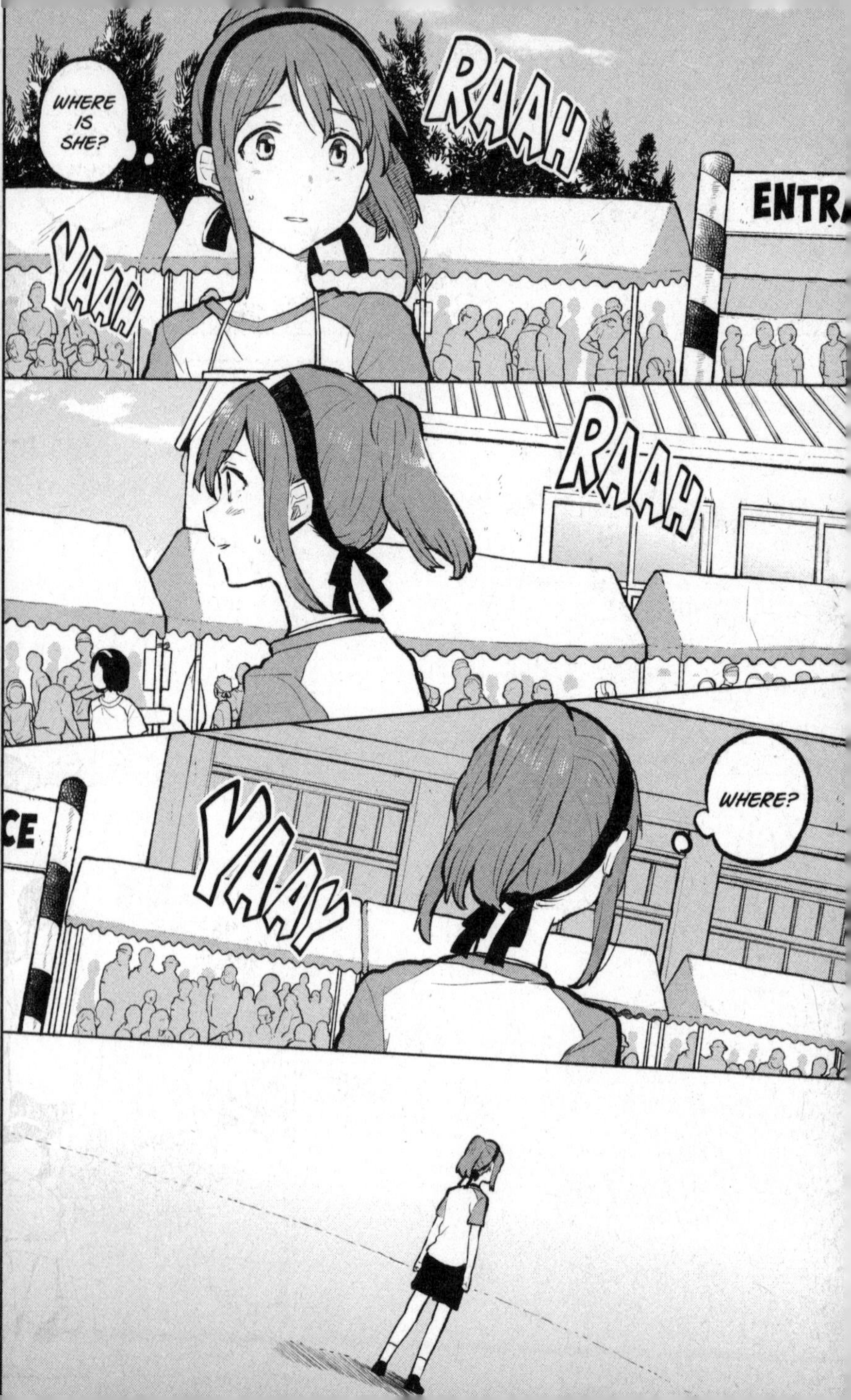
ENTRA
RAAH
WHERE IS SHE?
YAAH
RAAH
WHERE?
YAAY
CE

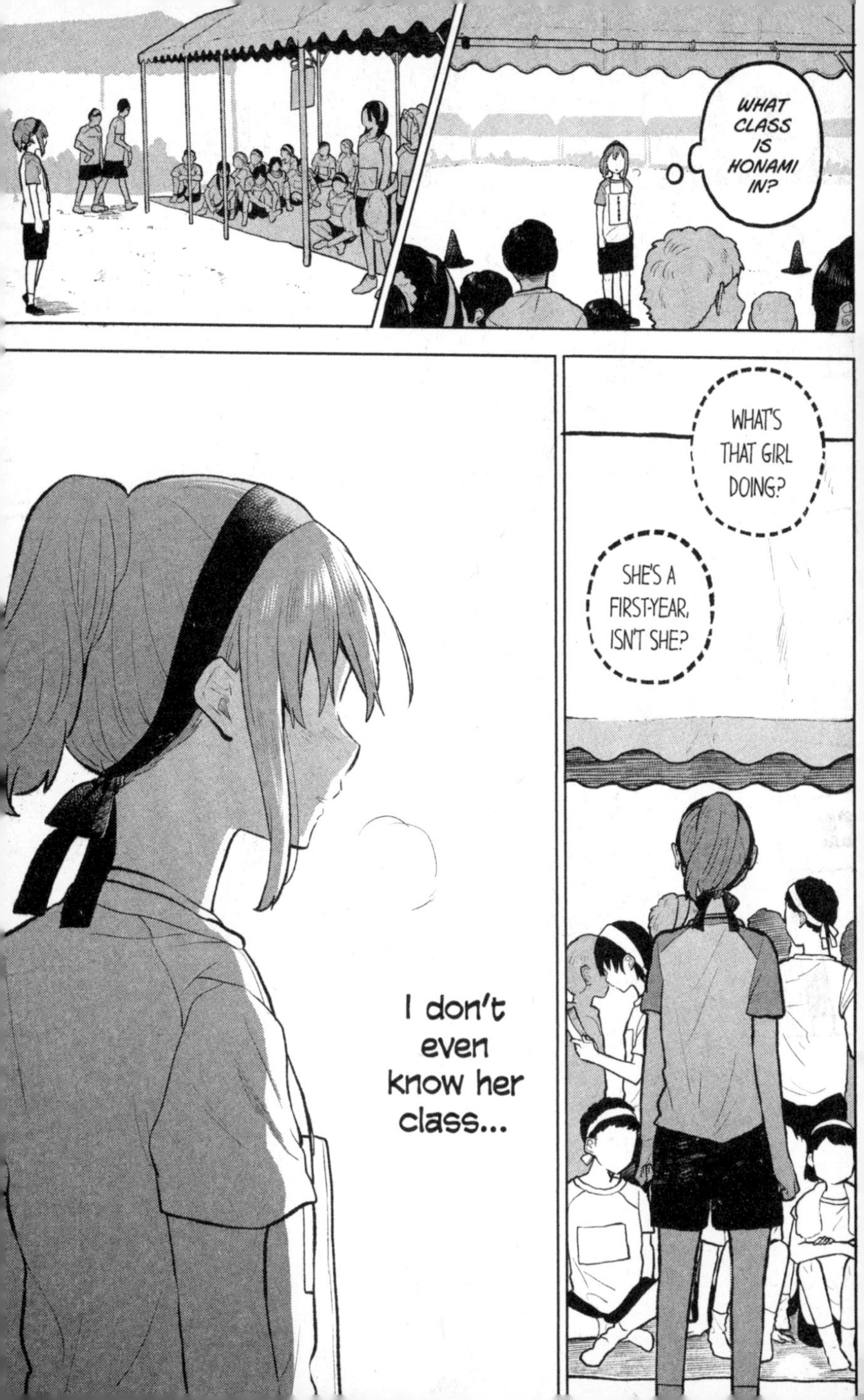
WHAT CLASS IS HONAMI IN?
WHAT'S THAT GIRL DOING?
SHE'S A FIRST-YEAR, ISN'T SHE?
I don't even know her class...

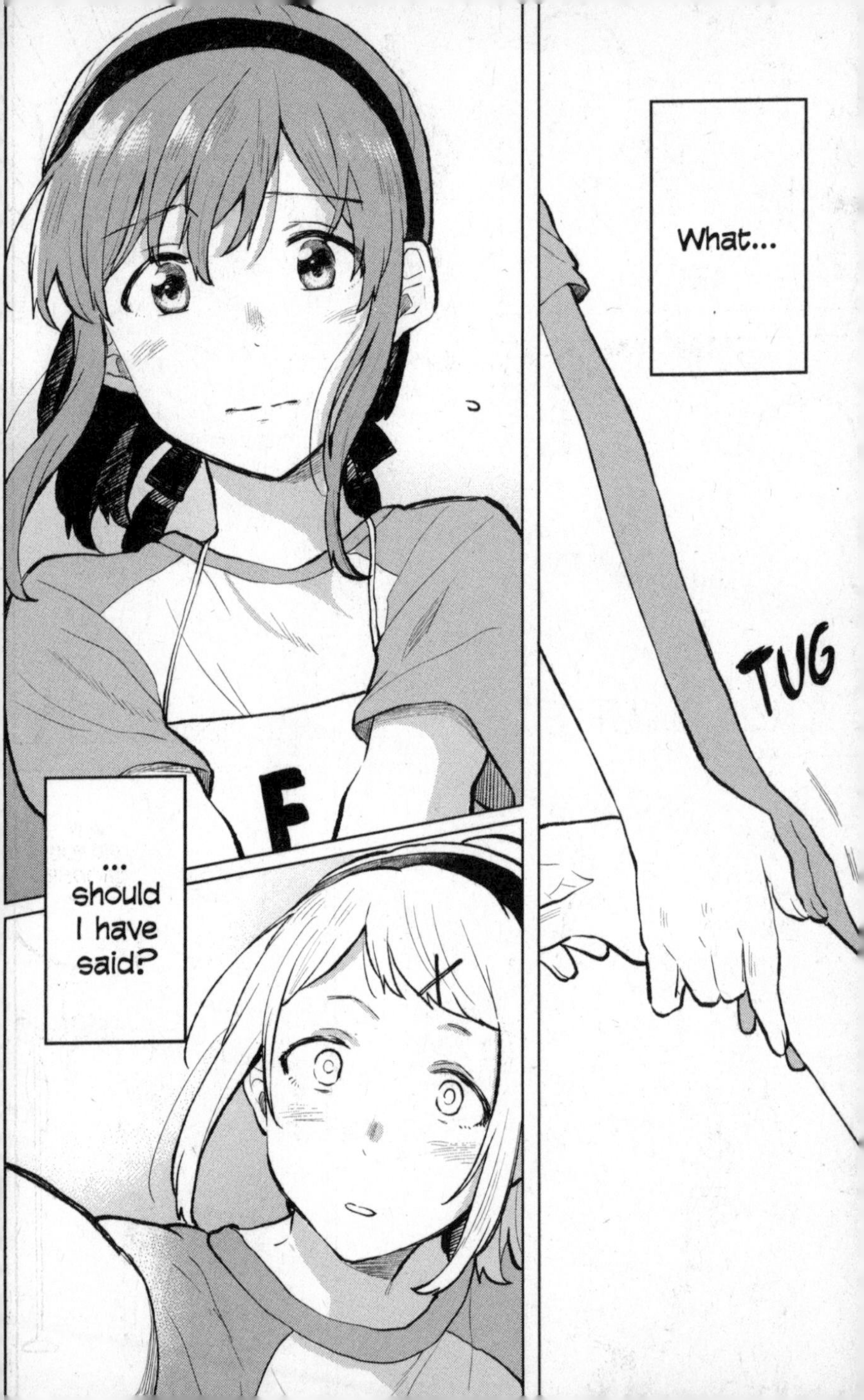
What...
TUG
... should I have said?

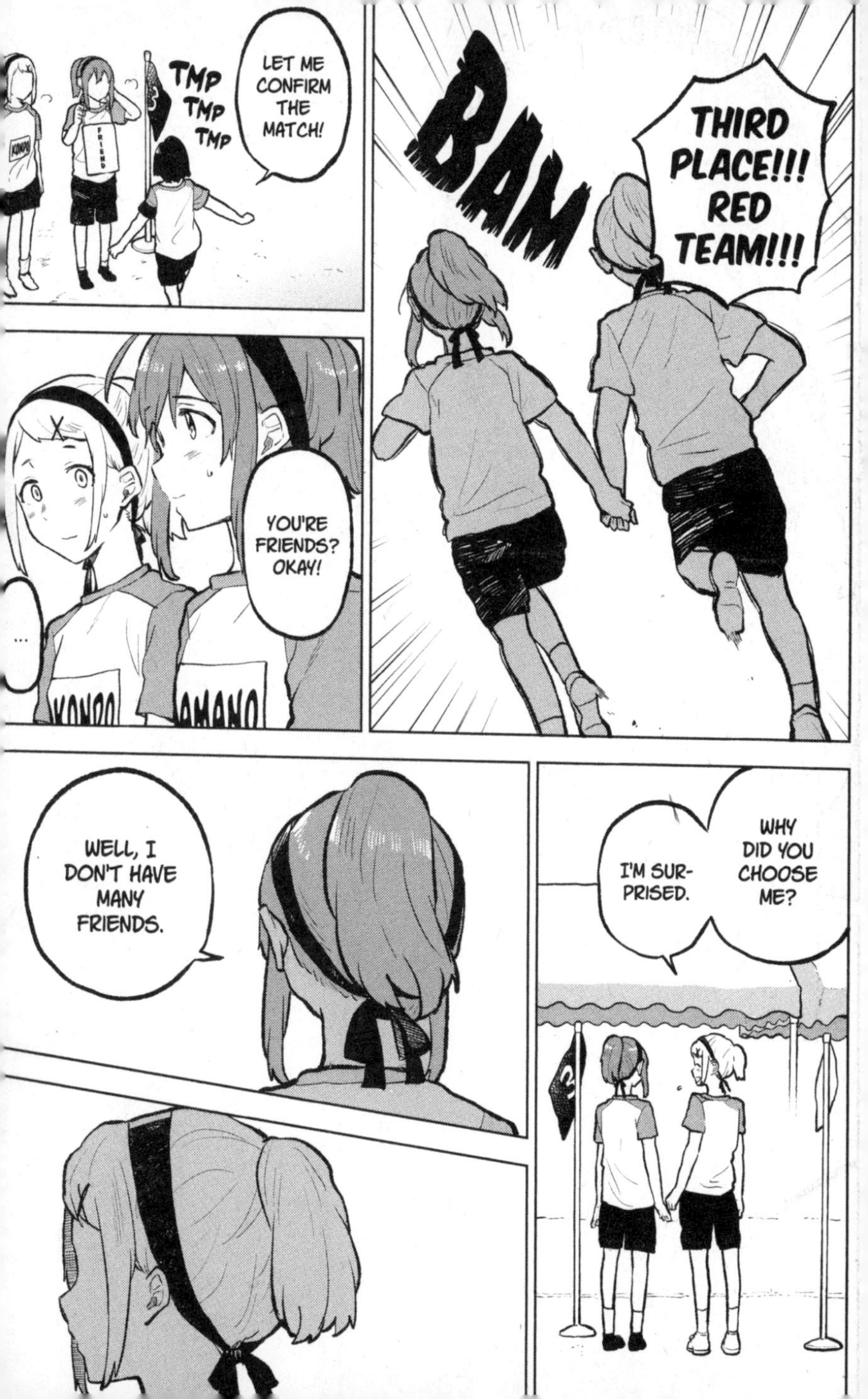
BAM
THIRD PLACE!!! RED TEAM!!!
LET ME CONFIRM THE MATCH!
TMP TMP TMP
YOU'RE FRIENDS? OKAY!
...
WHY DID YOU CHOOSE ME?
I'M SURPRISED.
WELL, I DON'T HAVE MANY FRIENDS.

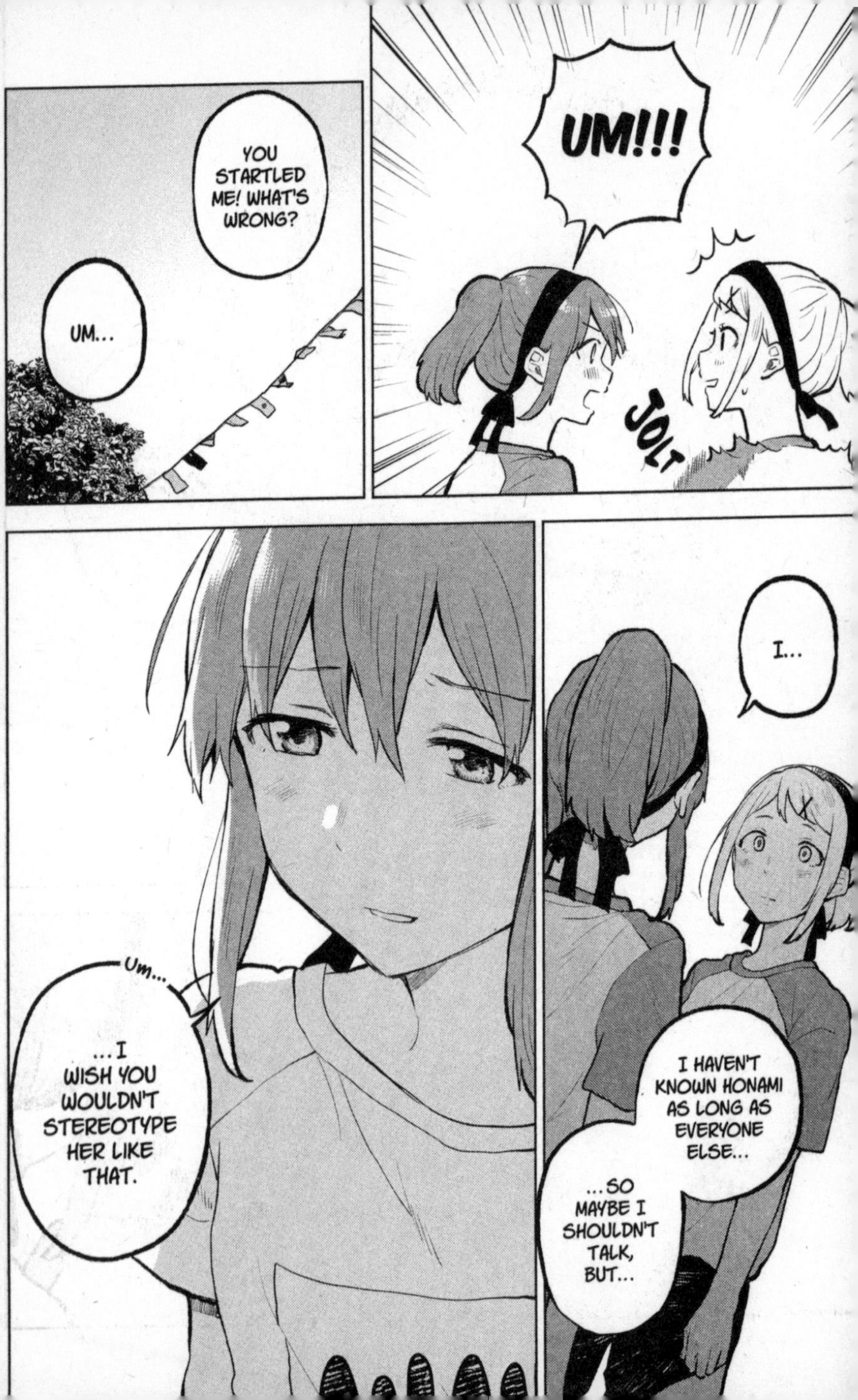
UM!!!
JOLT
YOU STARTLED ME! WHAT'S WRONG?
UM...
I...
I HAVEN'T KNOWN HONAMI AS LONG AS EVERYONE ELSE...
...SO MAYBE I SHOULDN'T TALK, BUT...
Um...
...I WISH YOU WOULDN'T STEREOTYPE HER LIKE THAT.

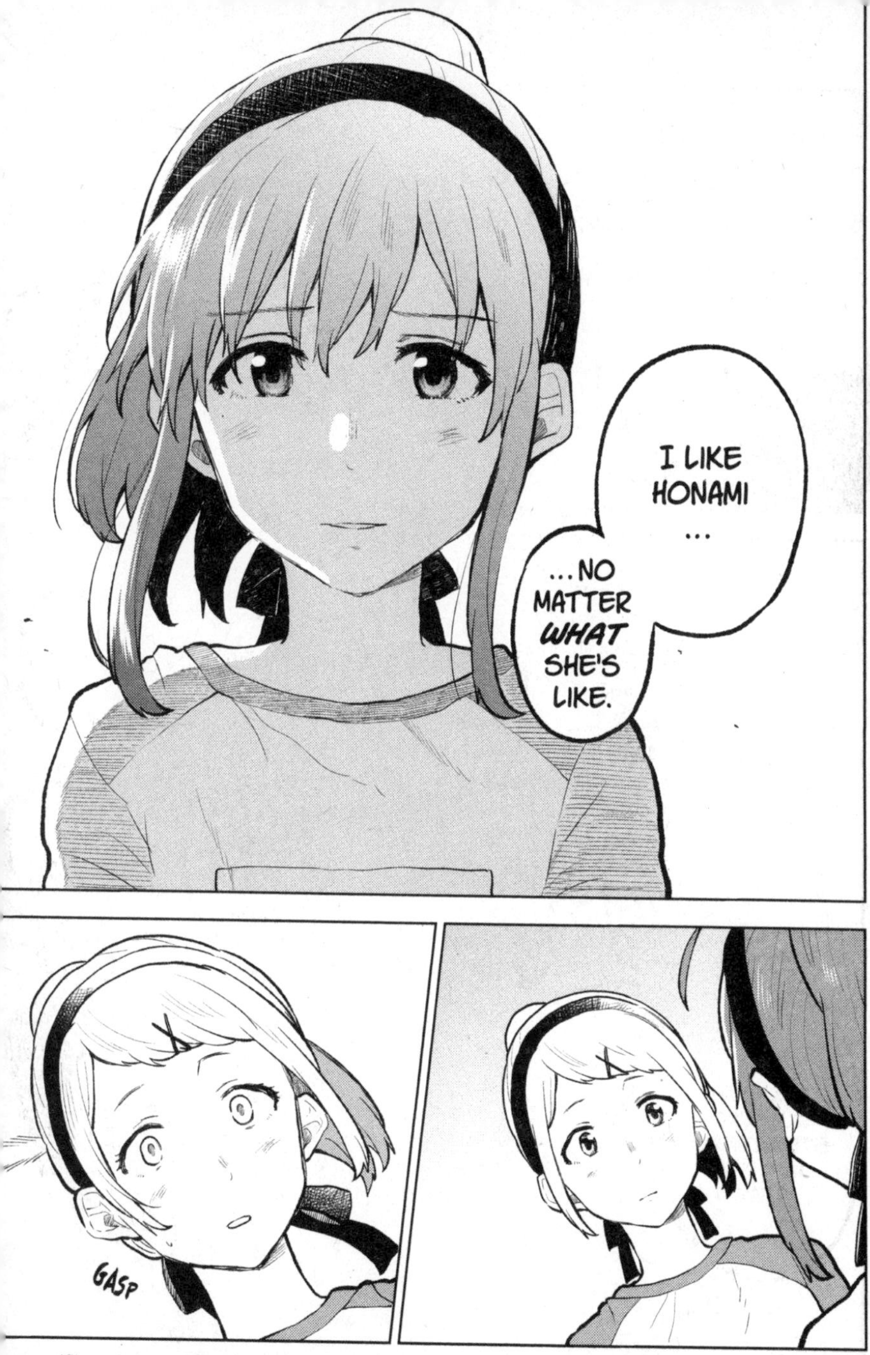
I LIKE HONAMI ...
...NO MATTER *WHAT* SHE'S LIKE.
GASP

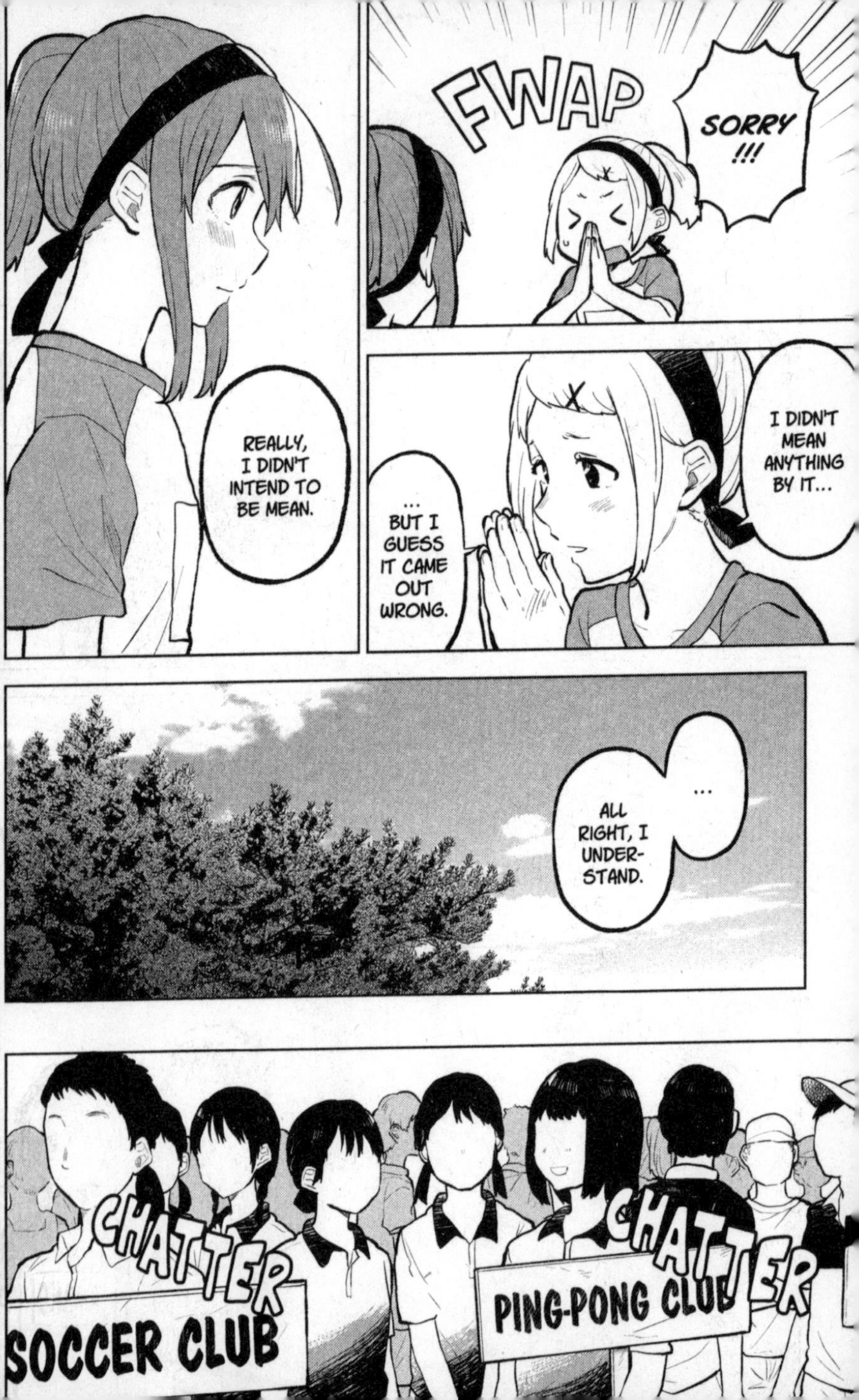
FWAP
SORRY !!!
I DIDN'T MEAN ANYTHING BY IT...
... BUT I GUESS IT CAME OUT WRONG.
REALLY, I DIDN'T INTEND TO BE MEAN.
...
ALL RIGHT, I UNDER-STAND.
CHATTER
CHATTER
PING-PONG CLUB
SOCCER CLUB

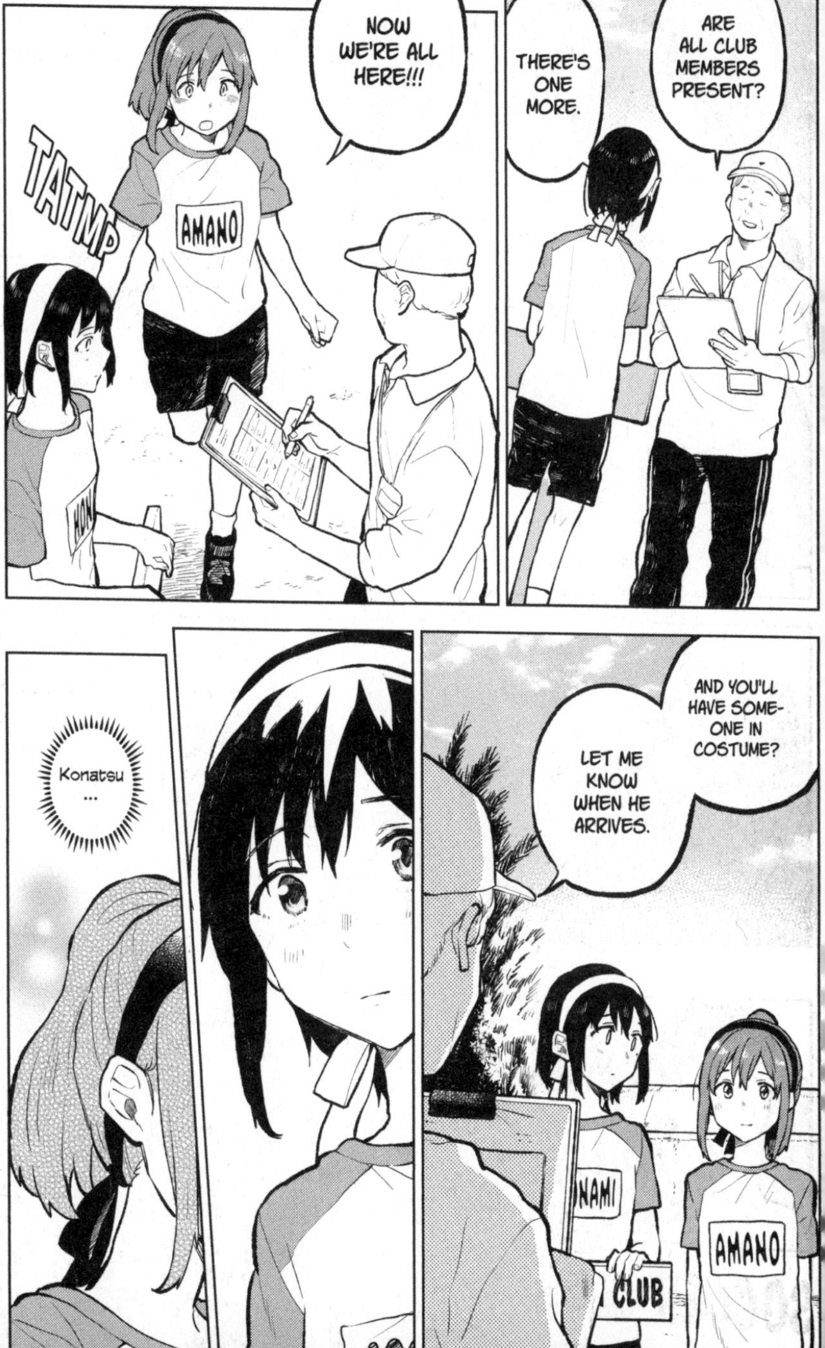
ARE ALL CLUB MEMBERS PRESENT?
THERE'S ONE MORE.
NOW WE'RE ALL HERE!!!
TATMP
AMANO
AND YOU'LL HAVE SOME-ONE IN COSTUME?
LET ME KNOW WHEN HE ARRIVES.
AMANO
Konatsu ...

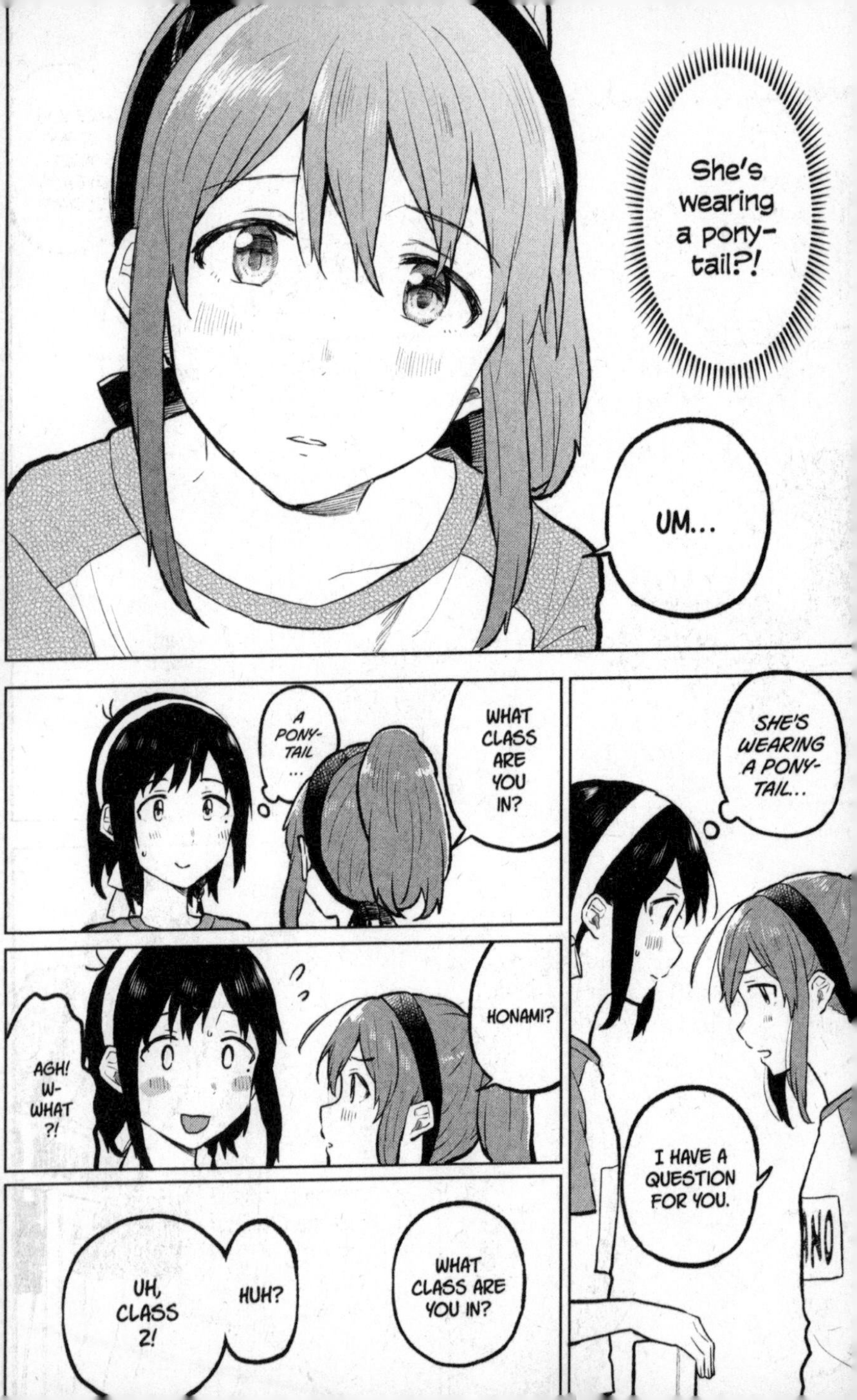
She's wearing a pony-tail?!
UM...
SHE'S WEARING A PONY-TAIL...
I HAVE A QUESTION FOR YOU.
WHAT CLASS ARE YOU IN?
A PONY-TAIL...
HONAMI?
AGH! W-WHAT?!
WHAT CLASS ARE YOU IN?
HUH?
UH, CLASS 2!

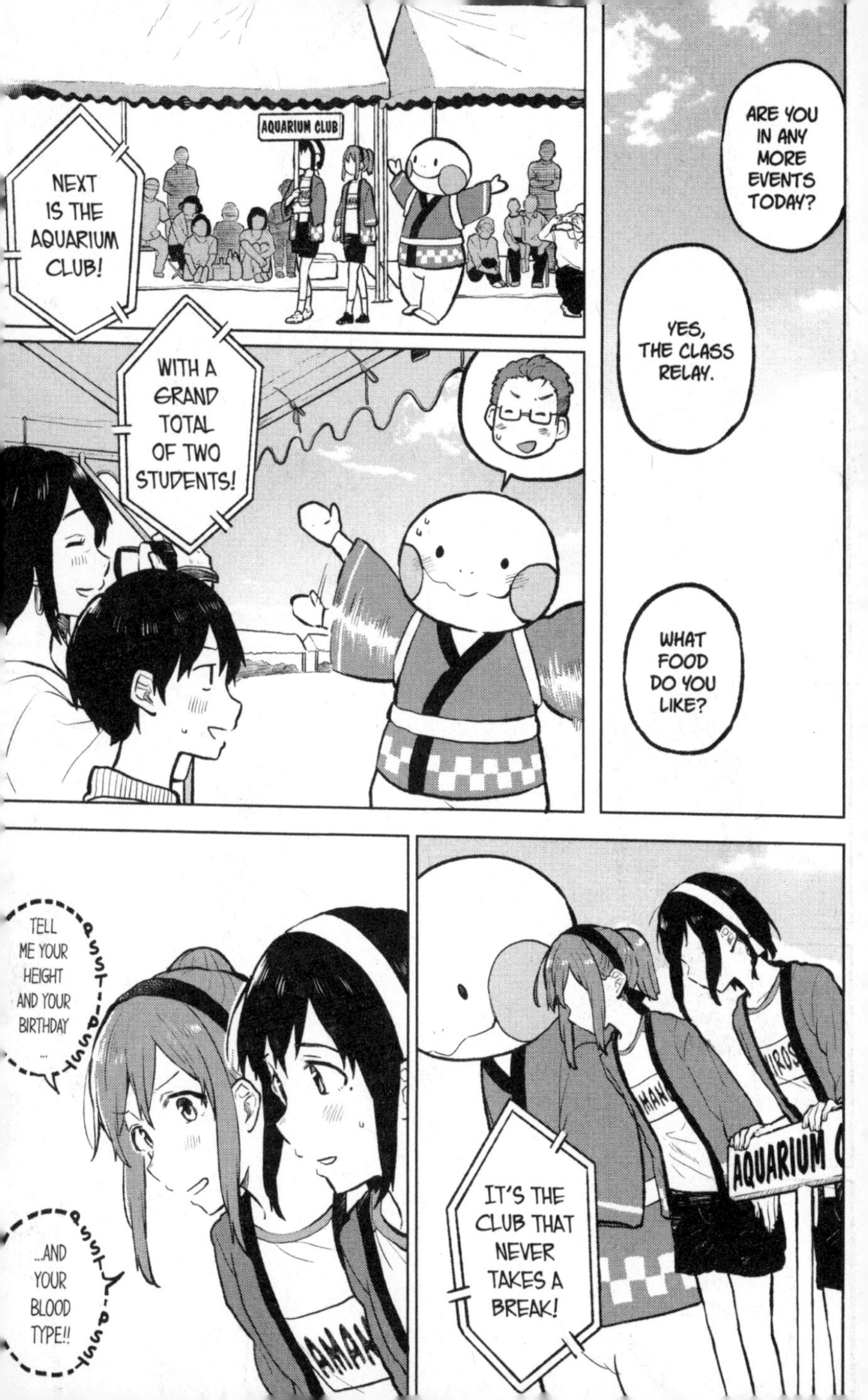
ARE YOU IN ANY MORE EVENTS TODAY?
YES, THE CLASS RELAY.
WHAT FOOD DO YOU LIKE?
AQUARIUM CLUB
NEXT IS THE AQUARIUM CLUB!
WITH A GRAND TOTAL OF TWO STUDENTS!
IT'S THE CLUB THAT NEVER TAKES A BREAK!
TELL ME YOUR HEIGHT AND YOUR BIRTHDAY...
...AND YOUR BLOOD TYPE!!

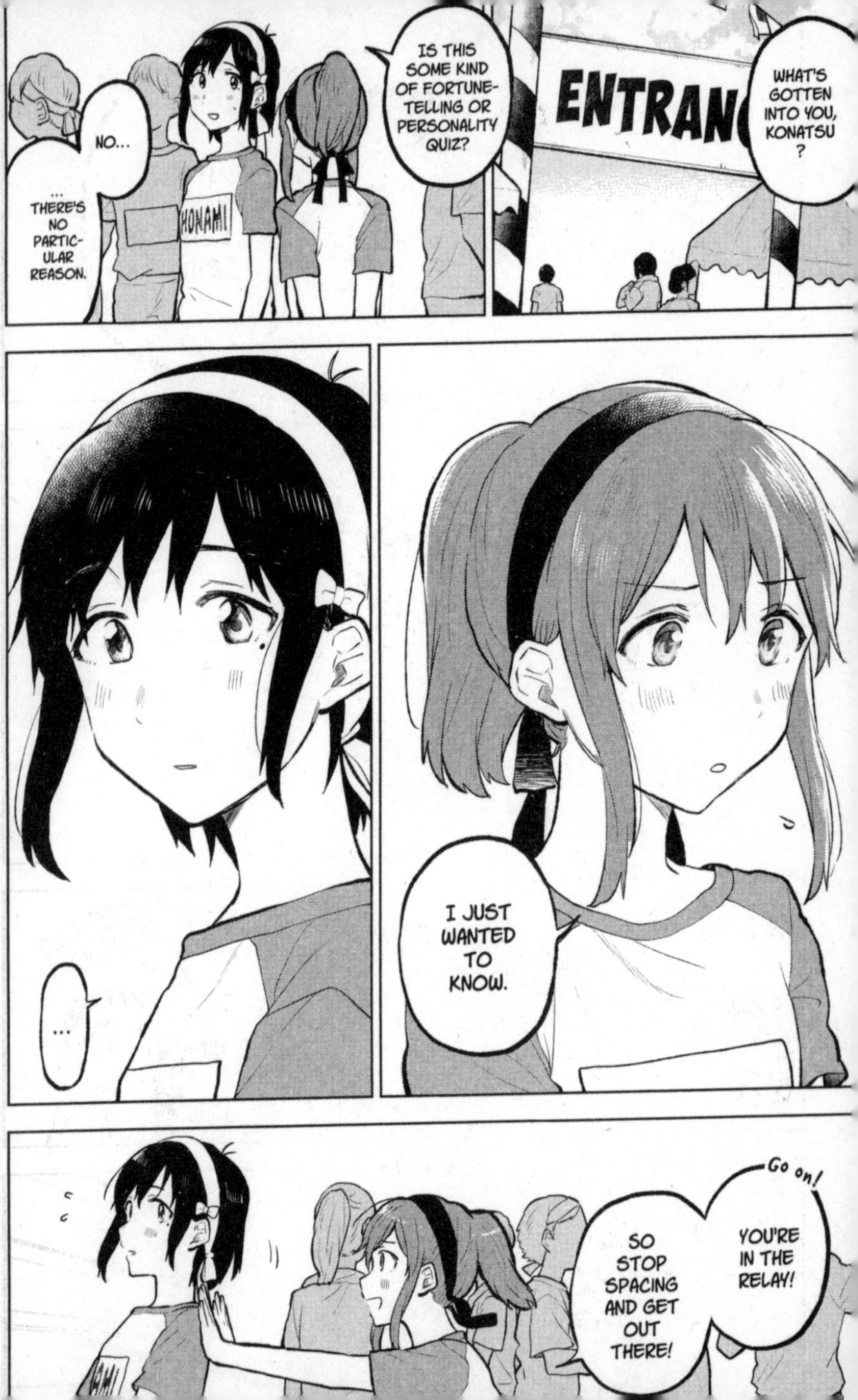
WHAT'S GOTTEN INTO YOU, KONATSU?
ENTRANC
IS THIS SOME KIND OF FORTUNE-TELLING OR PERSONALITY QUIZ?
NO...
... THERE'S NO PARTICULAR REASON.
HONAMI
I JUST WANTED TO KNOW.
...
Go on!
YOU'RE IN THE RELAY!
SO STOP SPACING AND GET OUT THERE!

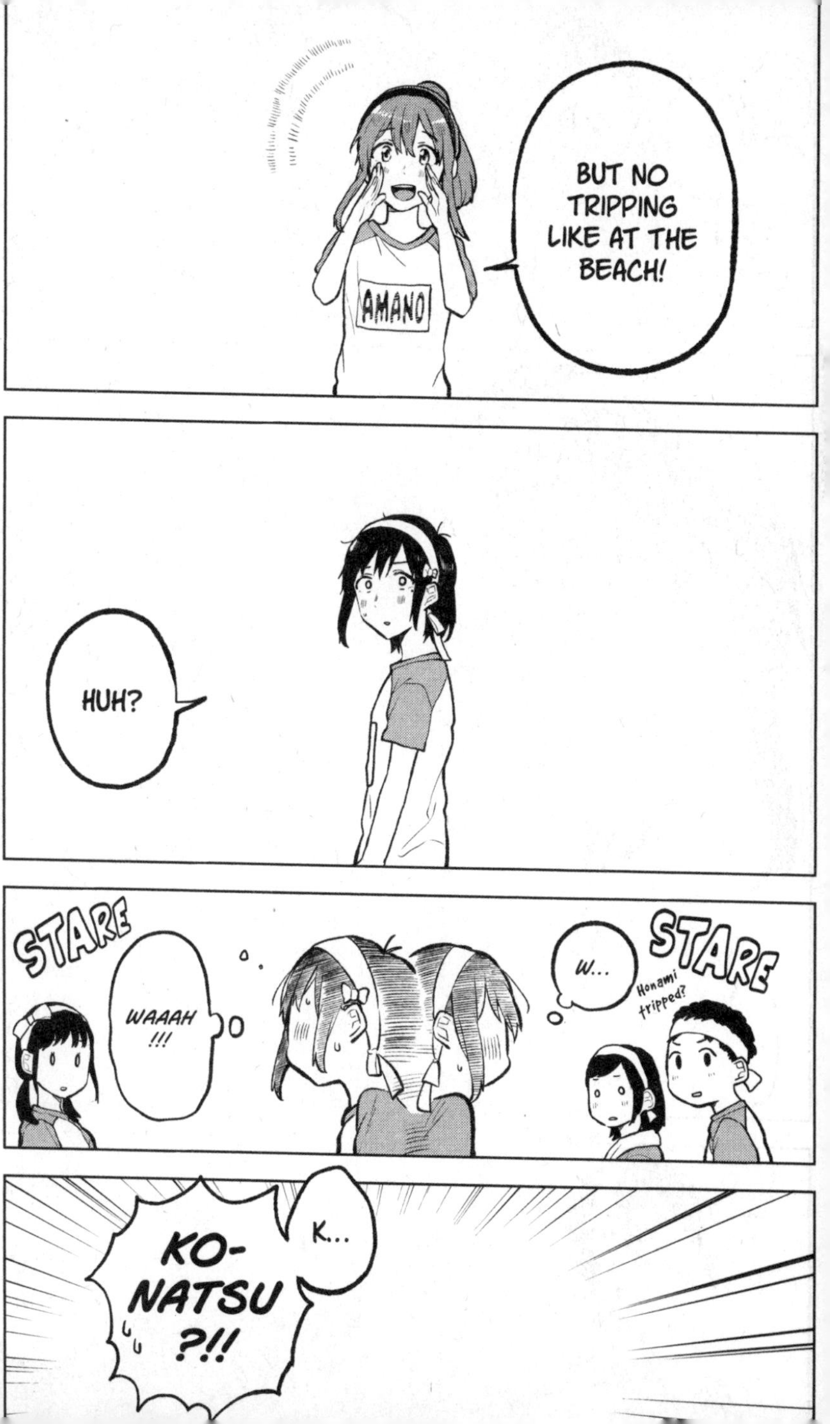
BUT NO TRIPPING LIKE AT THE BEACH!
AMANO
HUH?
STARE
W...
Honami tripped?
STARE
WAAAH!!!
K...
KO-NATSU?!!

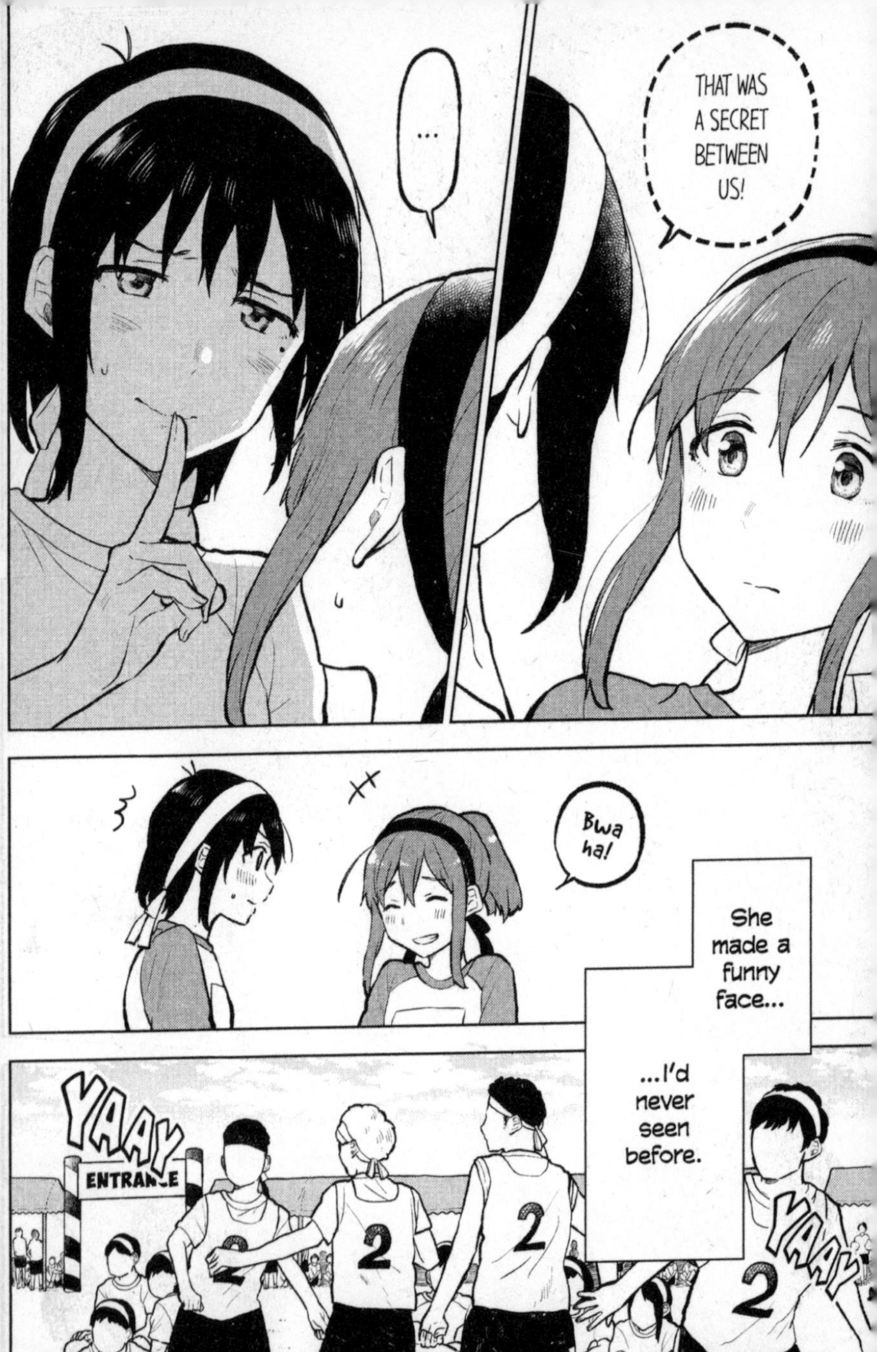
THAT WAS A SECRET BETWEEN US!
...
Bwa ha!
She made a funny face...
...I'd never seen before.
YAAY
YAAY
ENTRAN_E

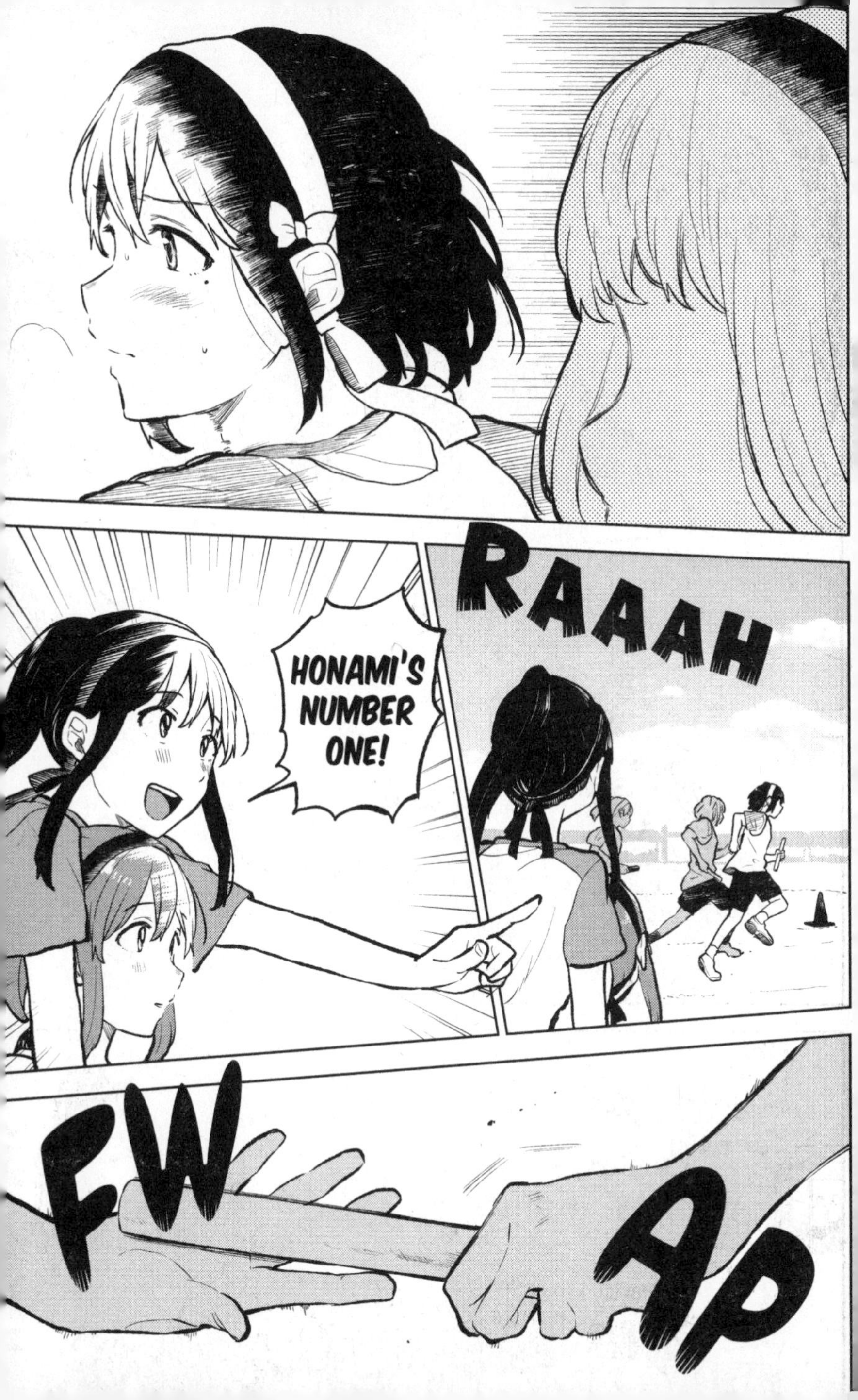
RAAAH
HONAMI'S NUMBER ONE!
FWAP

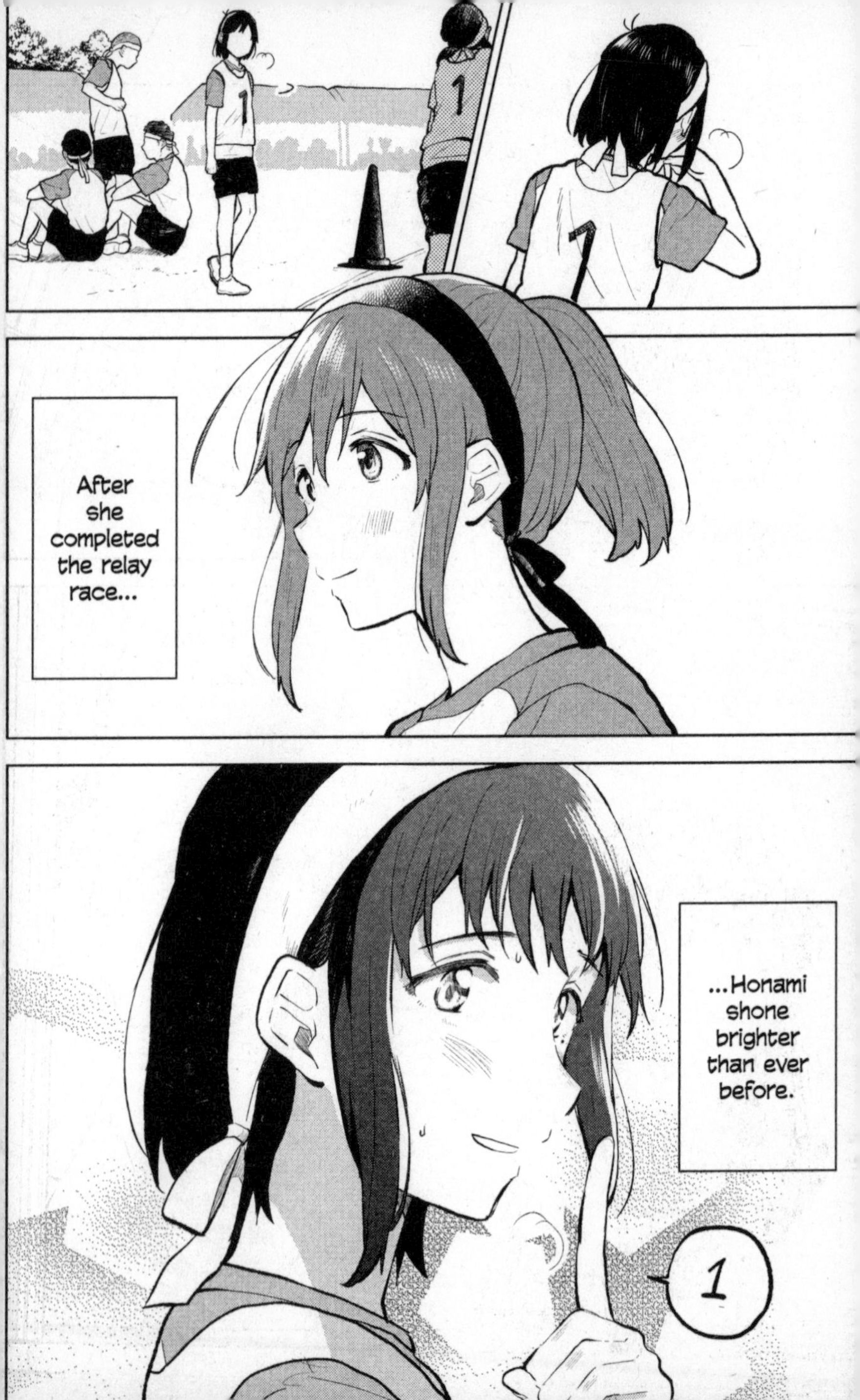
After she completed the relay race...
...Honami shone brighter than ever before.
1

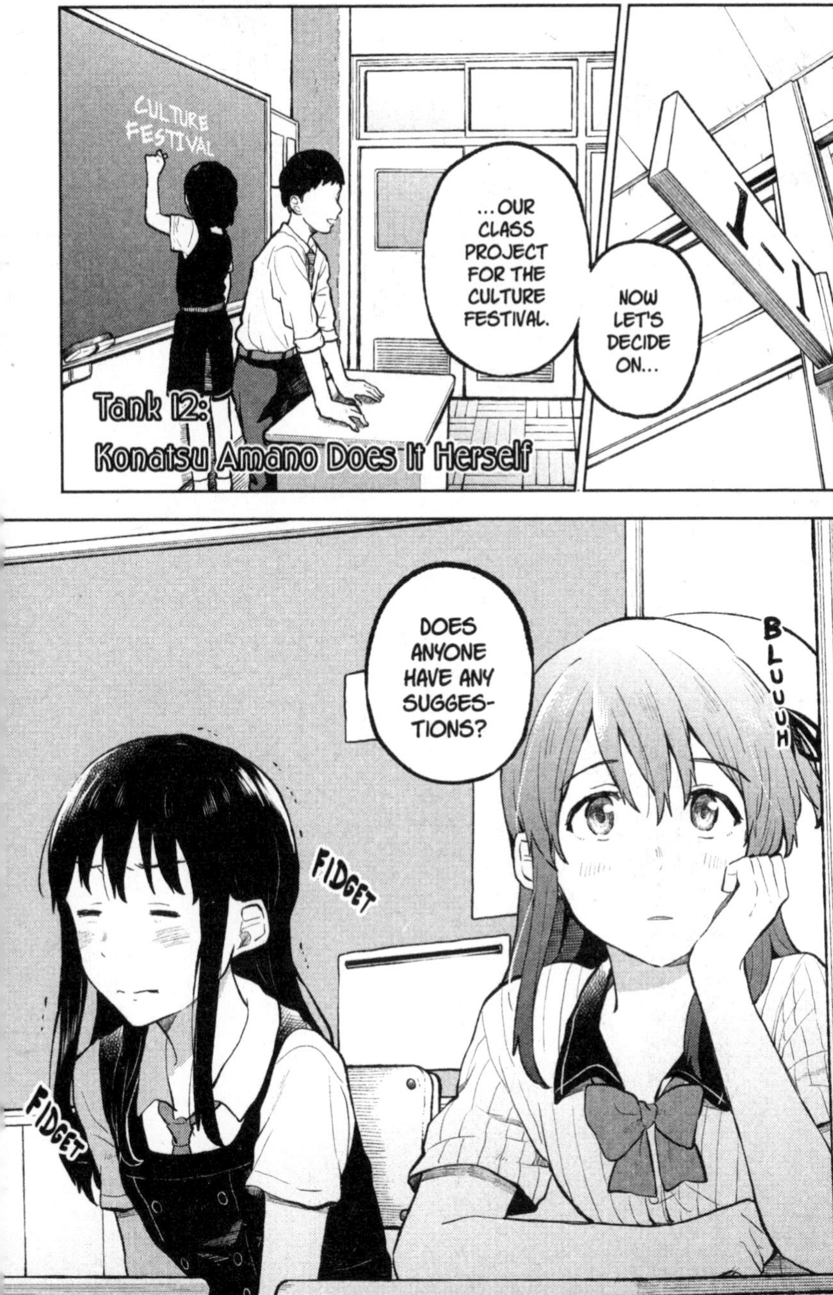
NOW LET'S DECIDE ON...
...OUR CLASS PROJECT FOR THE CULTURE FESTIVAL.
CULTURE FESTIVAL
Tank 12: Konatsu Amano Does It Herself
DOES ANYONE HAVE ANY SUGGES-TIONS?
BLUUUH
FIDGET
FIDGET

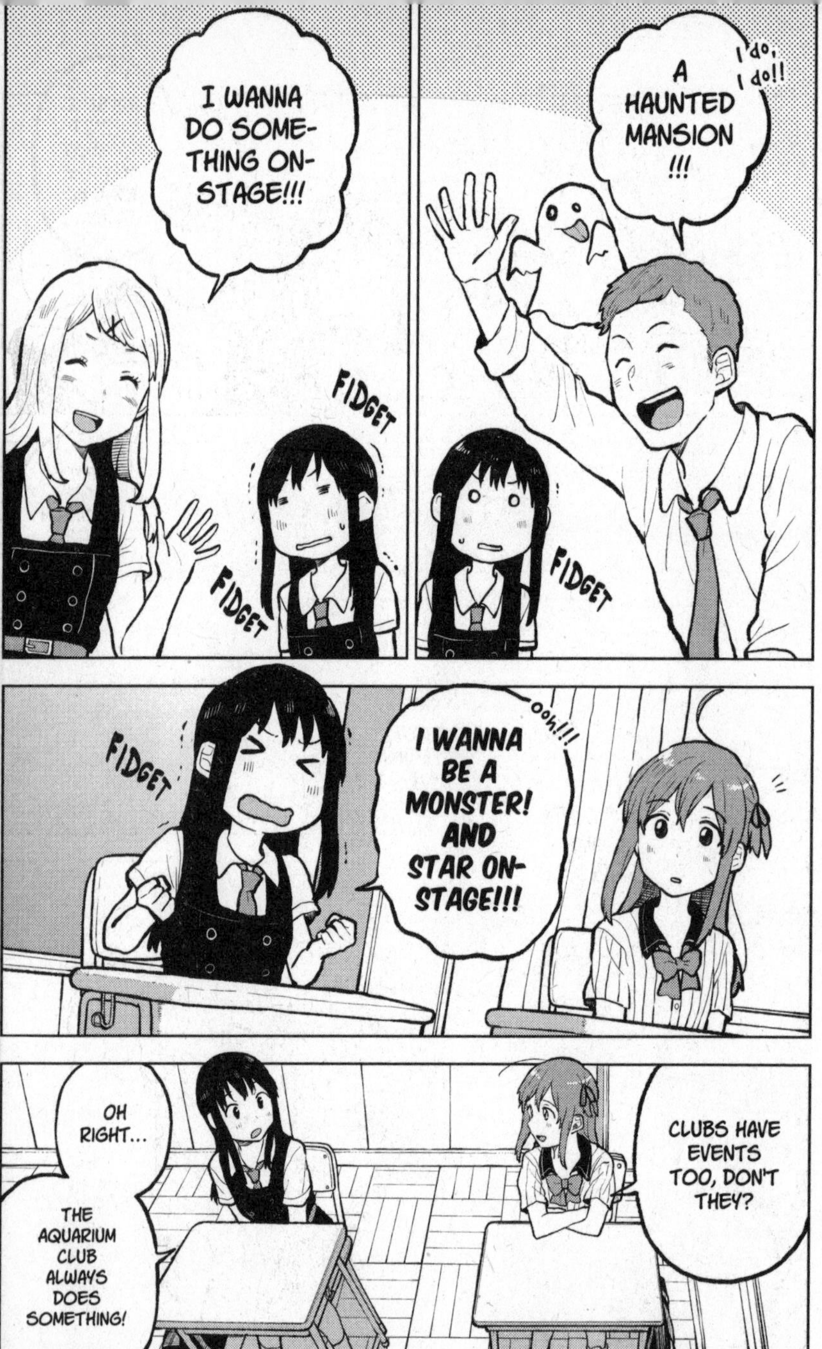
A HAUNTED MANSION!!!
I do, I do!!
FIDGET
I WANNA DO SOMETHING ON-STAGE!!!
FIDGET
FIDGET
ooh!!!
I WANNA BE A MONSTER! AND STAR ON-STAGE!!!
FIDGET
CLUBS HAVE EVENTS TOO, DON'T THEY?
OH RIGHT...
THE AQUARIUM CLUB ALWAYS DOES SOMETHING!

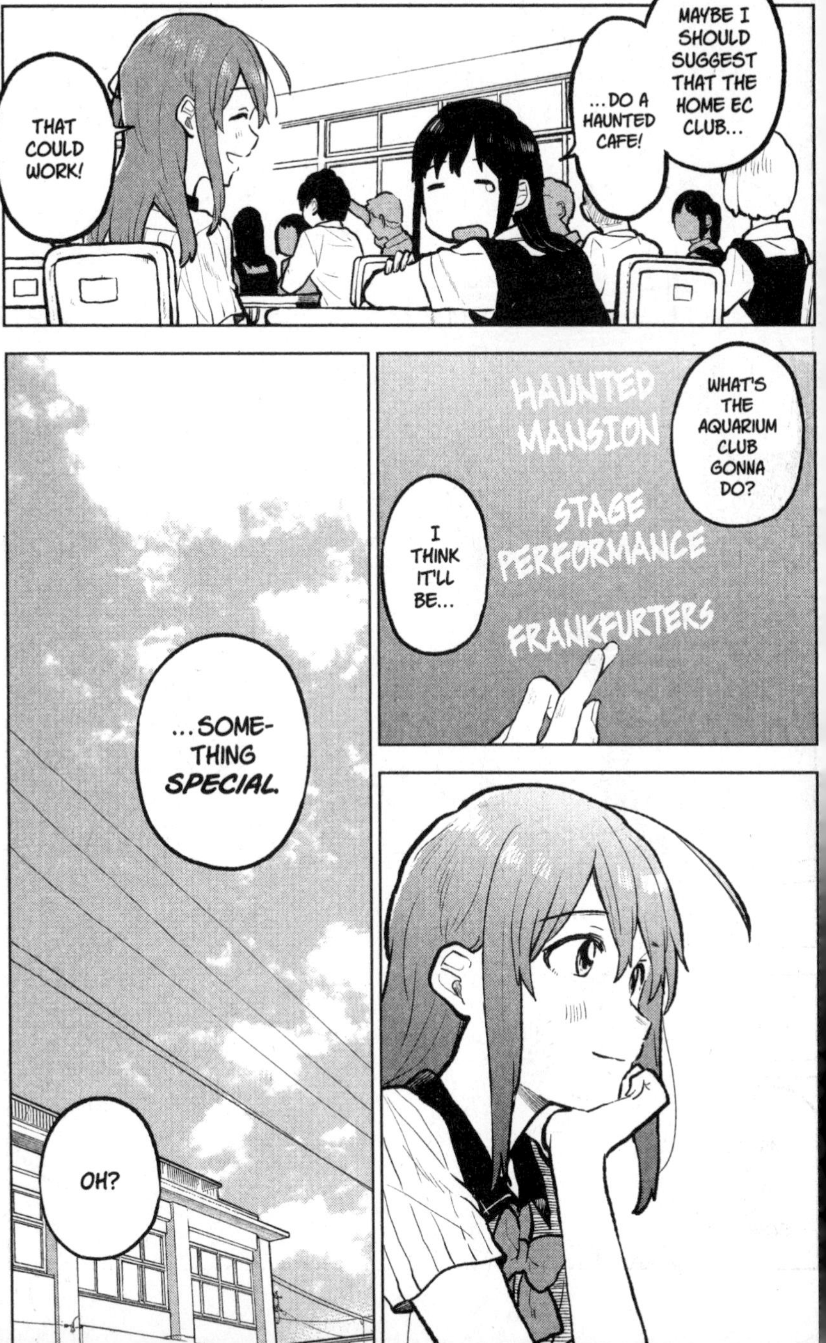
MAYBE I SHOULD SUGGEST THAT THE HOME EC CLUB...
...DO A HAUNTED CAFE!
THAT COULD WORK!
WHAT'S THE AQUARIUM CLUB GONNA DO?
HAUNTED MANSION
STAGE PERFORMANCE
FRANKFURTERS
I THINK IT'LL BE...
...SOME-THING *SPECIAL.*
OH?

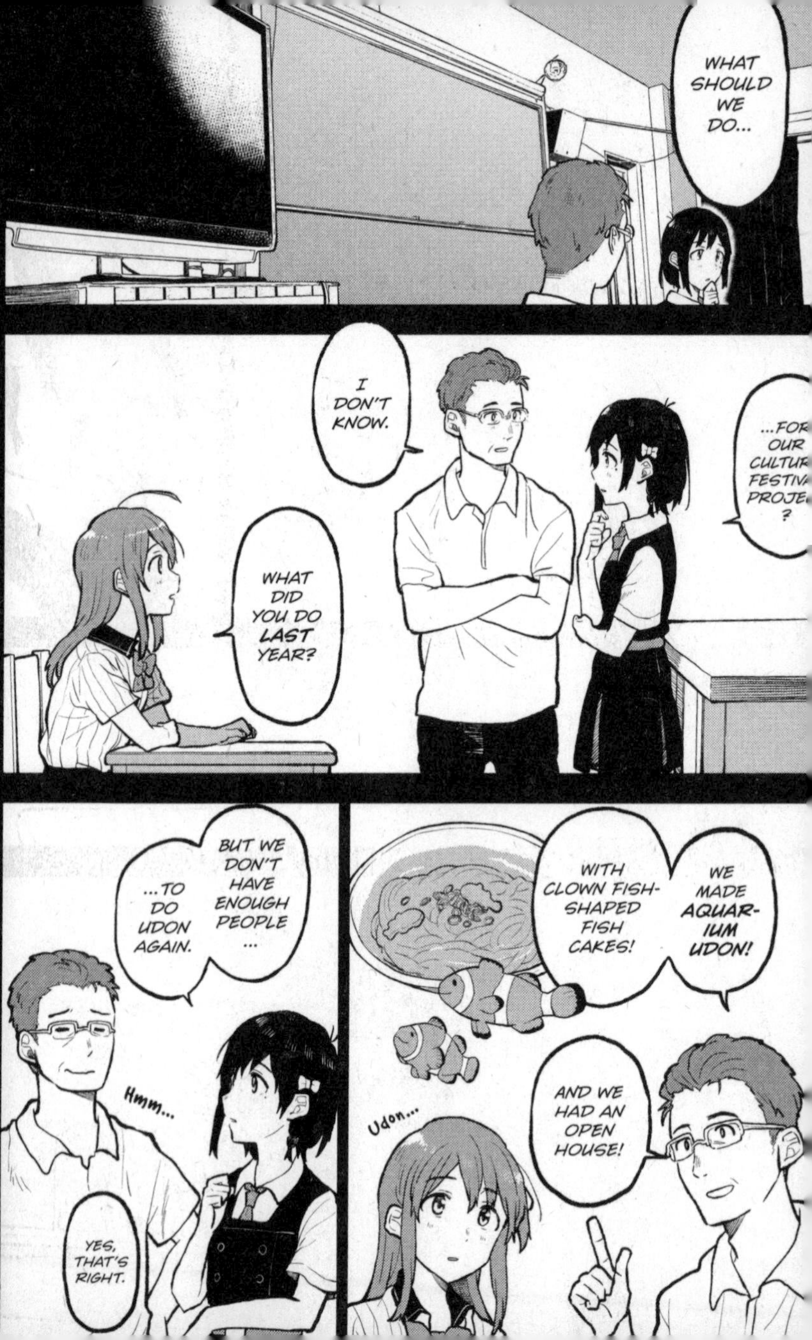
WHAT SHOULD WE DO...
...FOR OUR CULTUR FESTIVA PROJE ?
I DON'T KNOW.
WHAT DID YOU DO LAST YEAR?
WE MADE AQUARIUM UDON!
WITH CLOWN FISH-SHAPED FISH CAKES!
AND WE HAD AN OPEN HOUSE!
Udon...
BUT WE DON'T HAVE ENOUGH PEOPLE ...
...TO DO UDON AGAIN.
Hmm...
YES, THAT'S RIGHT.

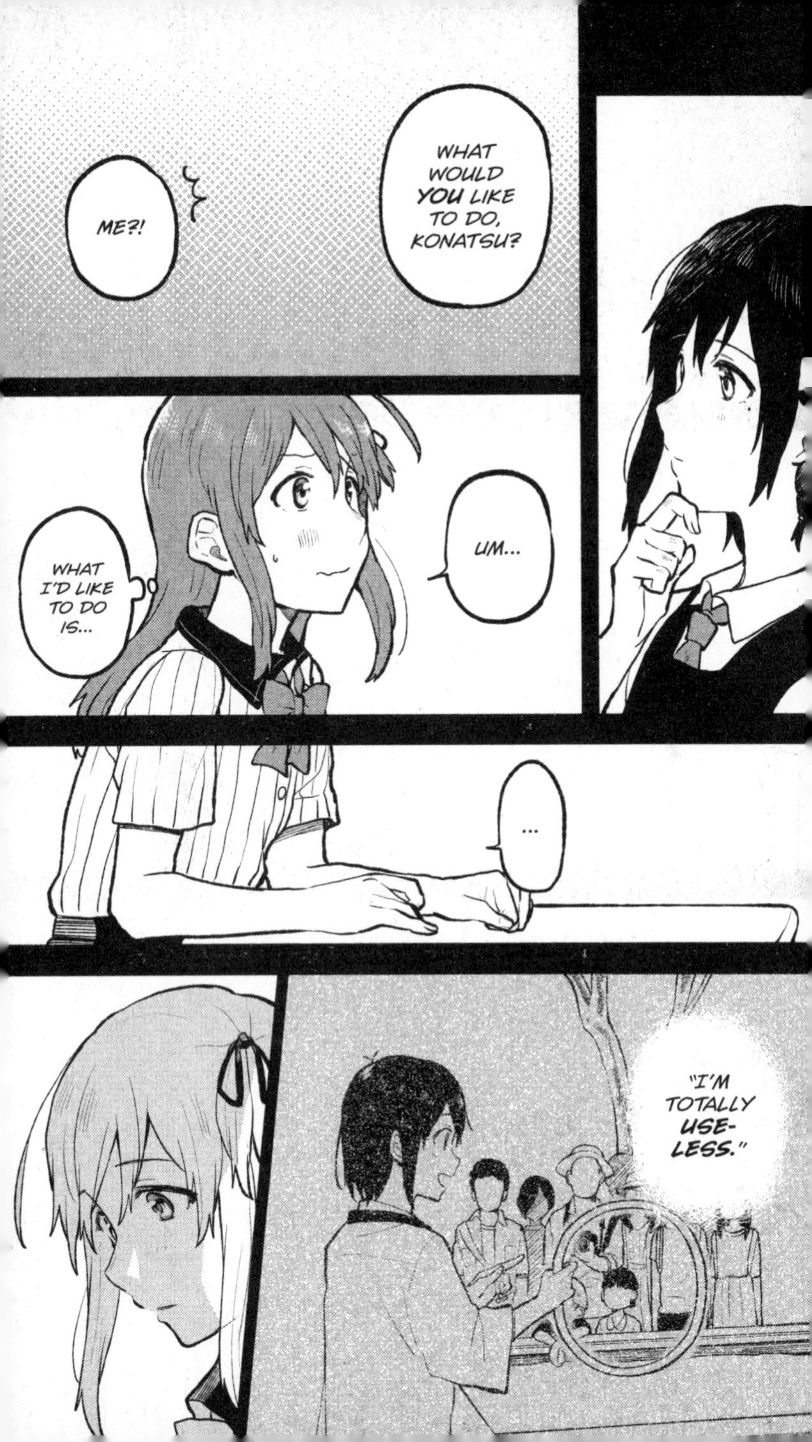
WHAT WOULD YOU LIKE TO DO, KONATSU?
ME?!
UM...
WHAT I'D LIKE TO DO IS...
...
"I'M TOTALLY USE-LESS."

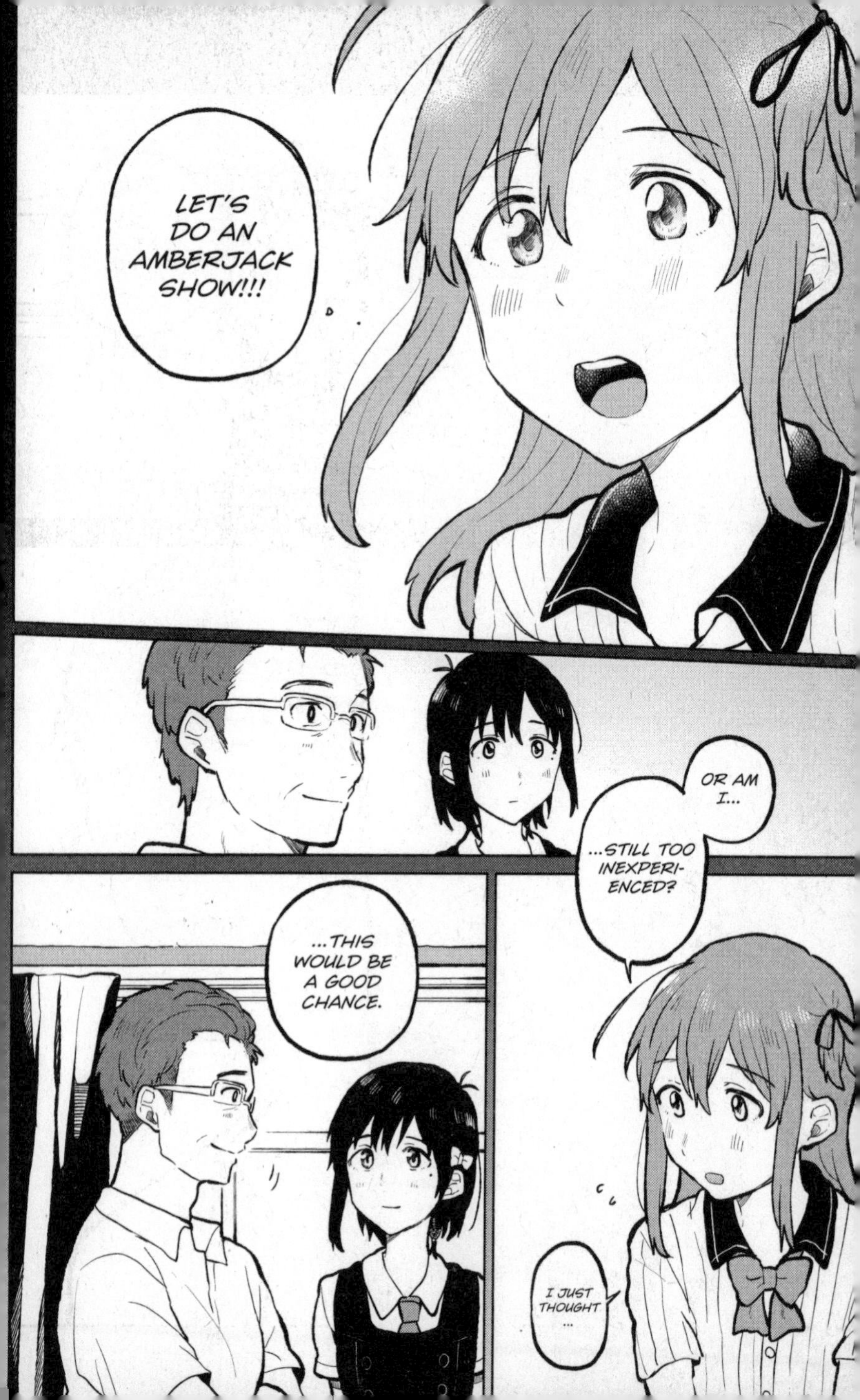
LET'S DO AN AMBERJACK SHOW!!!
OR AM I...
...STILL TOO INEXPERIENCED?
I JUST THOUGHT...
...THIS WOULD BE A GOOD CHANCE.

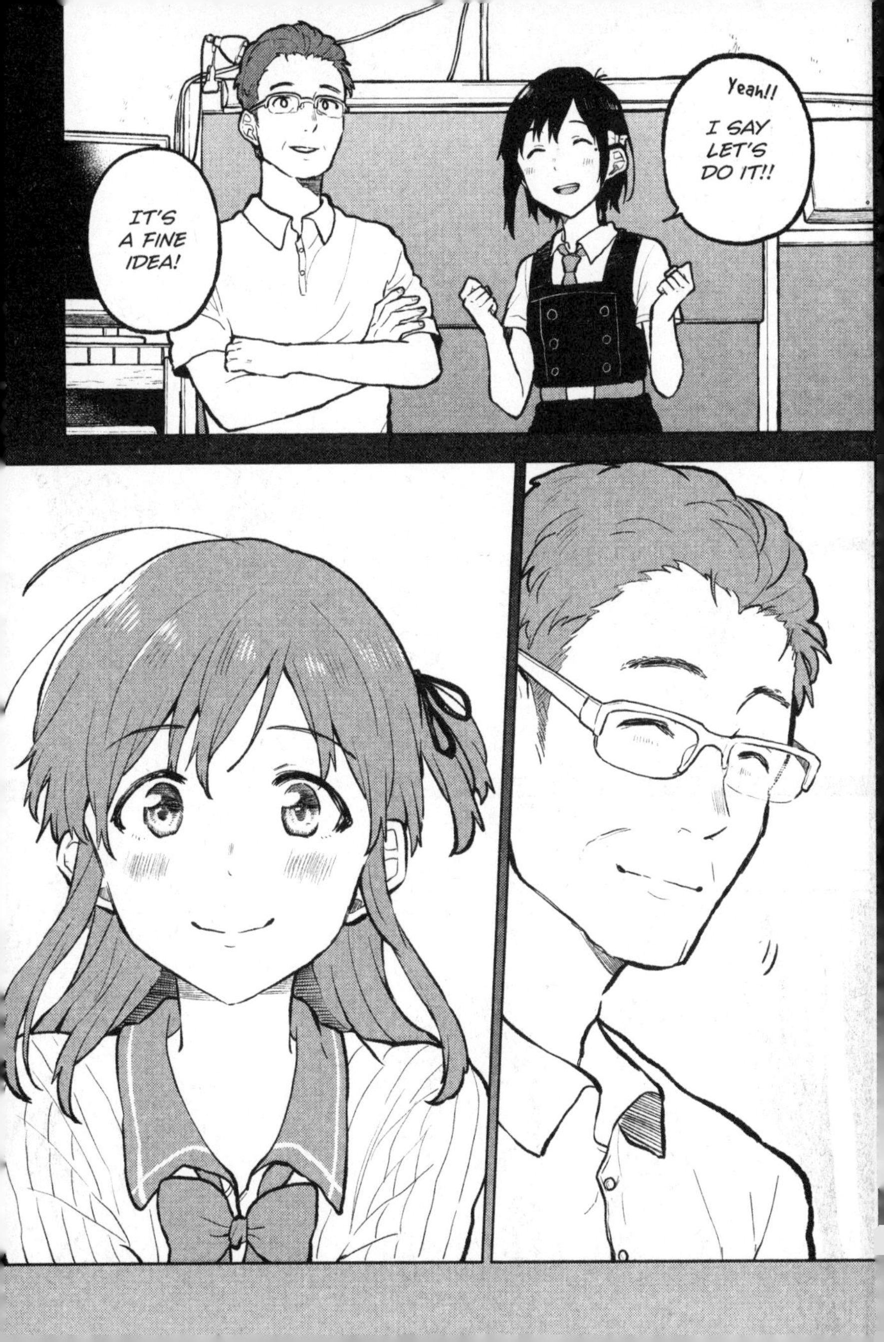
Yeah!! I SAY LET'S DO IT!!
IT'S A FINE IDEA!

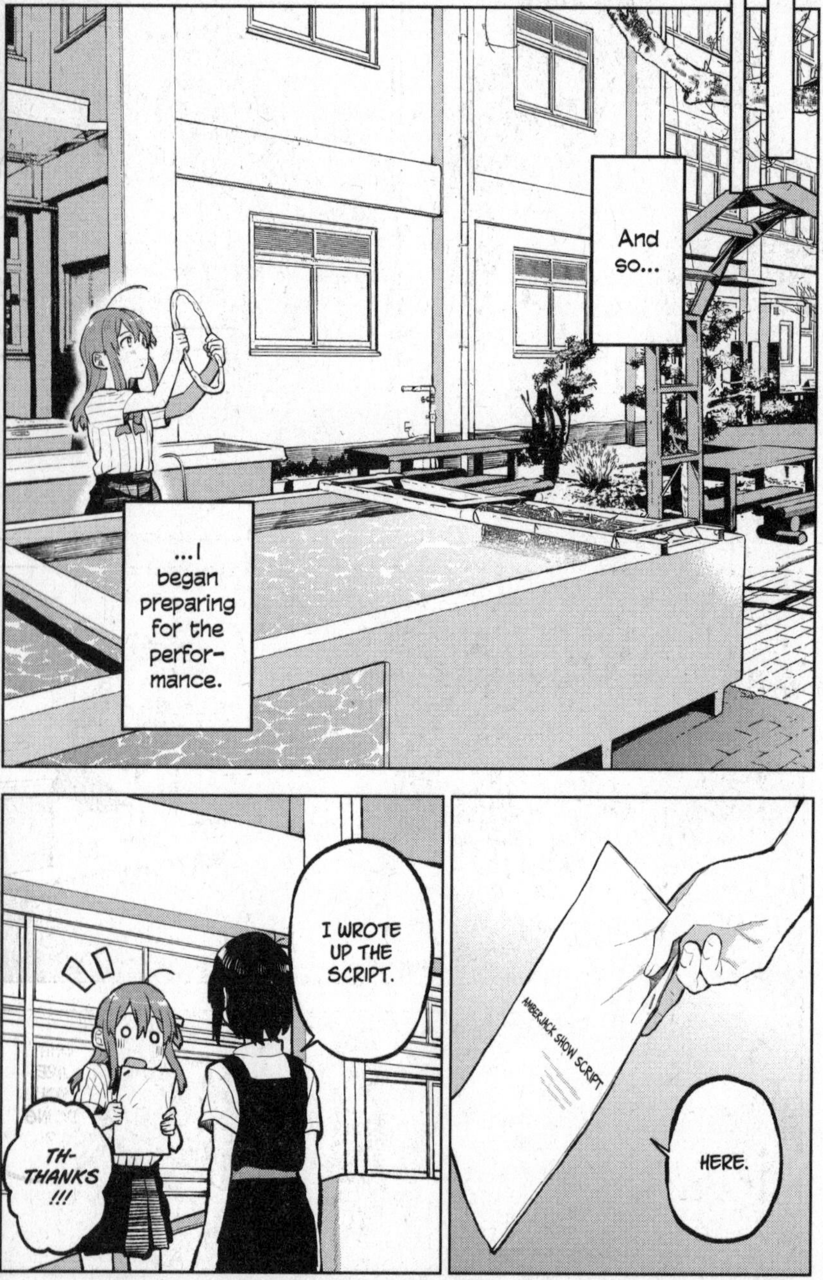
And so...
...I began preparing for the performance.
AMBERJACK SHOW SCRIPT
HERE.
I WROTE UP THE SCRIPT.
TH-THANKS!!!

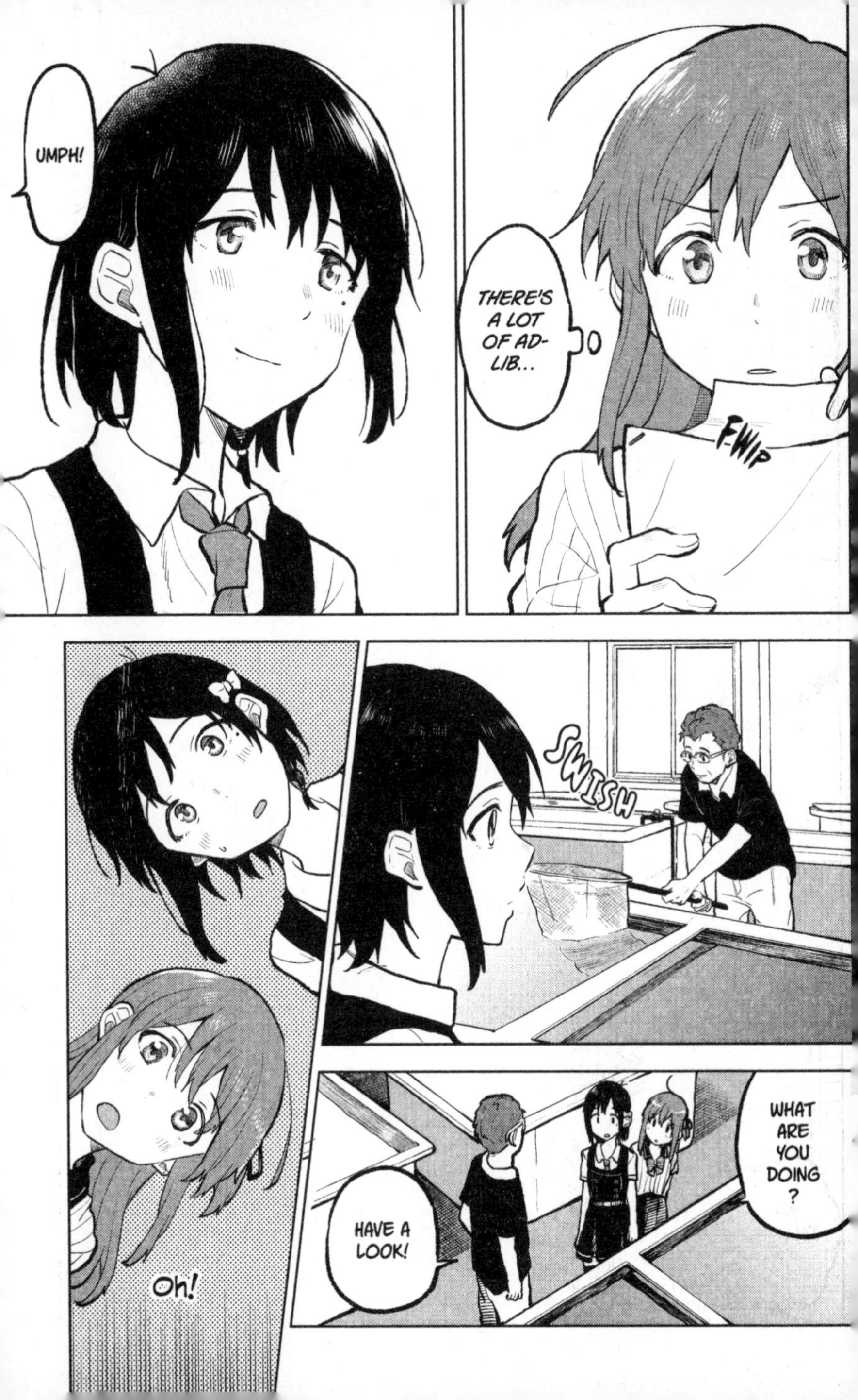
THERE'S A LOT OF AD-LIB...
F-WIP
UMPH!
SWISH
Oh!
WHAT ARE YOU DOING?
HAVE A LOOK!

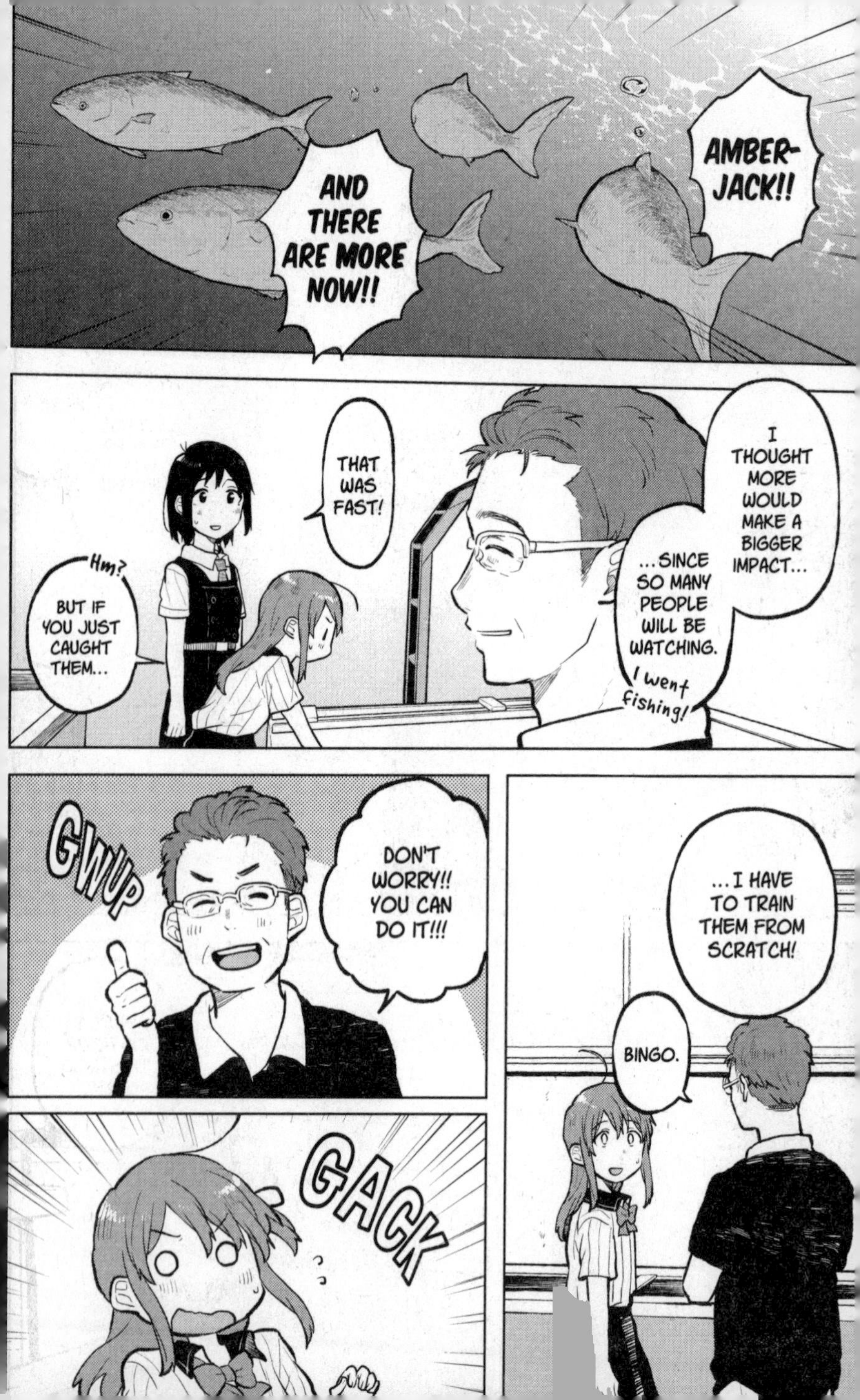
AMBER-JACK!!
AND THERE ARE MORE NOW!!
I THOUGHT MORE WOULD MAKE A BIGGER IMPACT...
...SINCE SO MANY PEOPLE WILL BE WATCHING.
I went fishing!
THAT WAS FAST!
Hm?
BUT IF YOU JUST CAUGHT THEM...
...I HAVE TO TRAIN THEM FROM SCRATCH!
BINGO.
DON'T WORRY!! YOU CAN DO IT!!!
GWUP
GACK

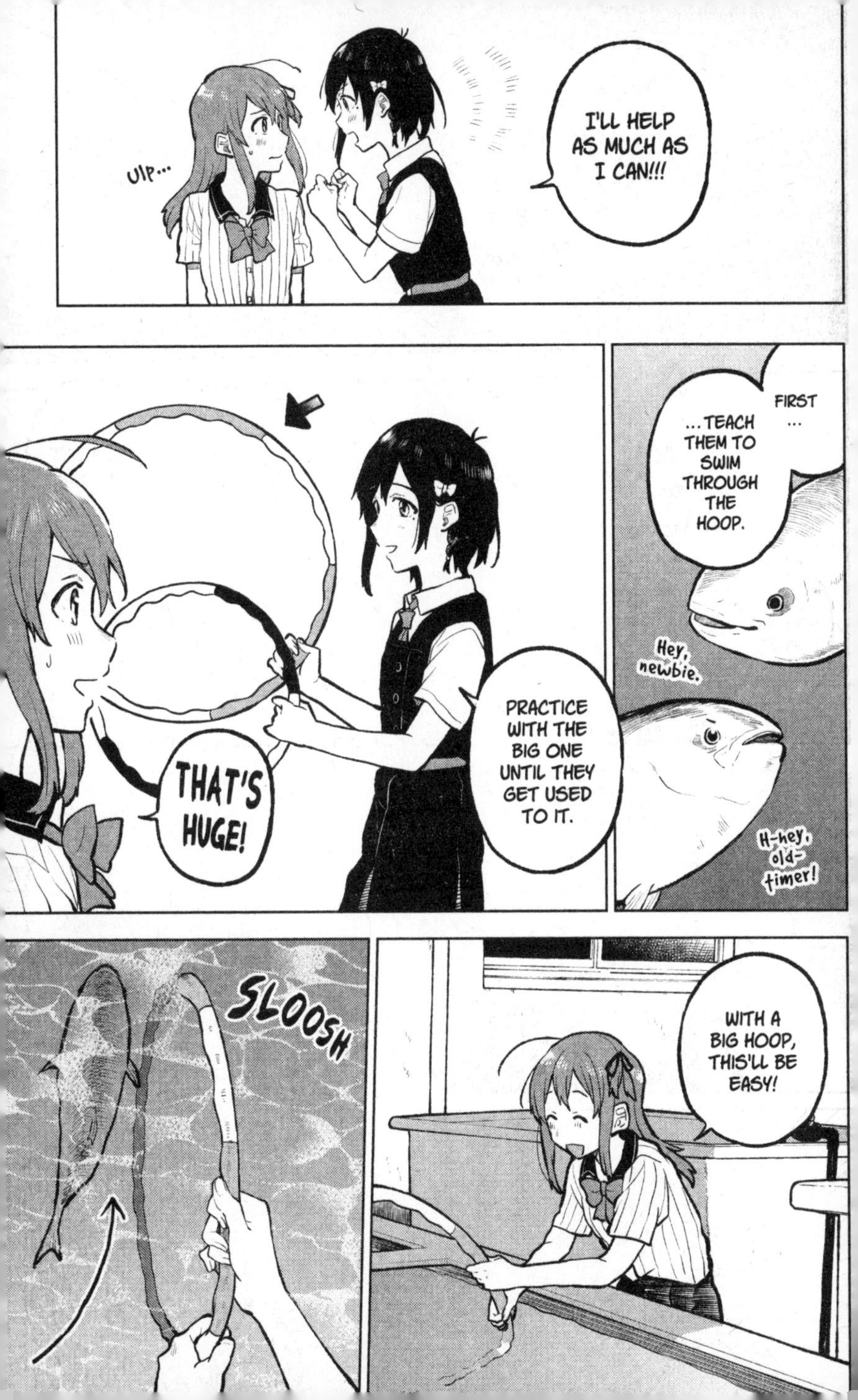
I'LL HELP AS MUCH AS I CAN!!!
ulp...
FIRST ... ...TEACH THEM TO SWIM THROUGH THE HOOP.
Hey, newbie.
H-hey, old-timer!
PRACTICE WITH THE BIG ONE UNTIL THEY GET USED TO IT.
THAT'S HUGE!
WITH A BIG HOOP, THIS'LL BE EASY!
SLOOSH

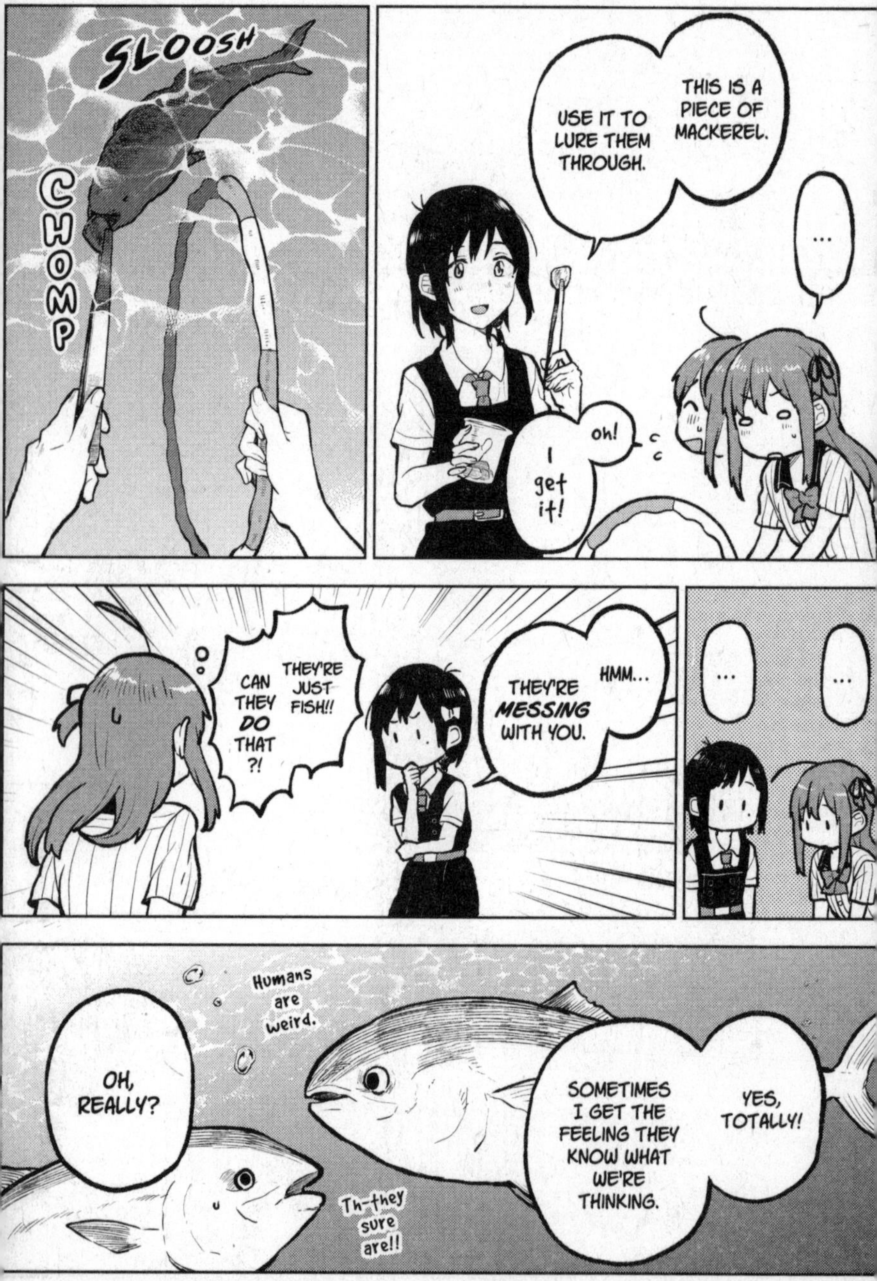
THIS IS A PIECE OF MACKEREL.
USE IT TO LURE THEM THROUGH.
...
Oh!
I get it!
SLOOSH
CHOMP
...
...
HMM...
THEY'RE MESSING WITH YOU.
THEY'RE JUST FISH!!
CAN THEY DO THAT?!
YES, TOTALLY!
SOMETIMES I GET THE FEELING THEY KNOW WHAT WE'RE THINKING.
Humans are weird.
OH, REALLY?
Th-they sure are!!

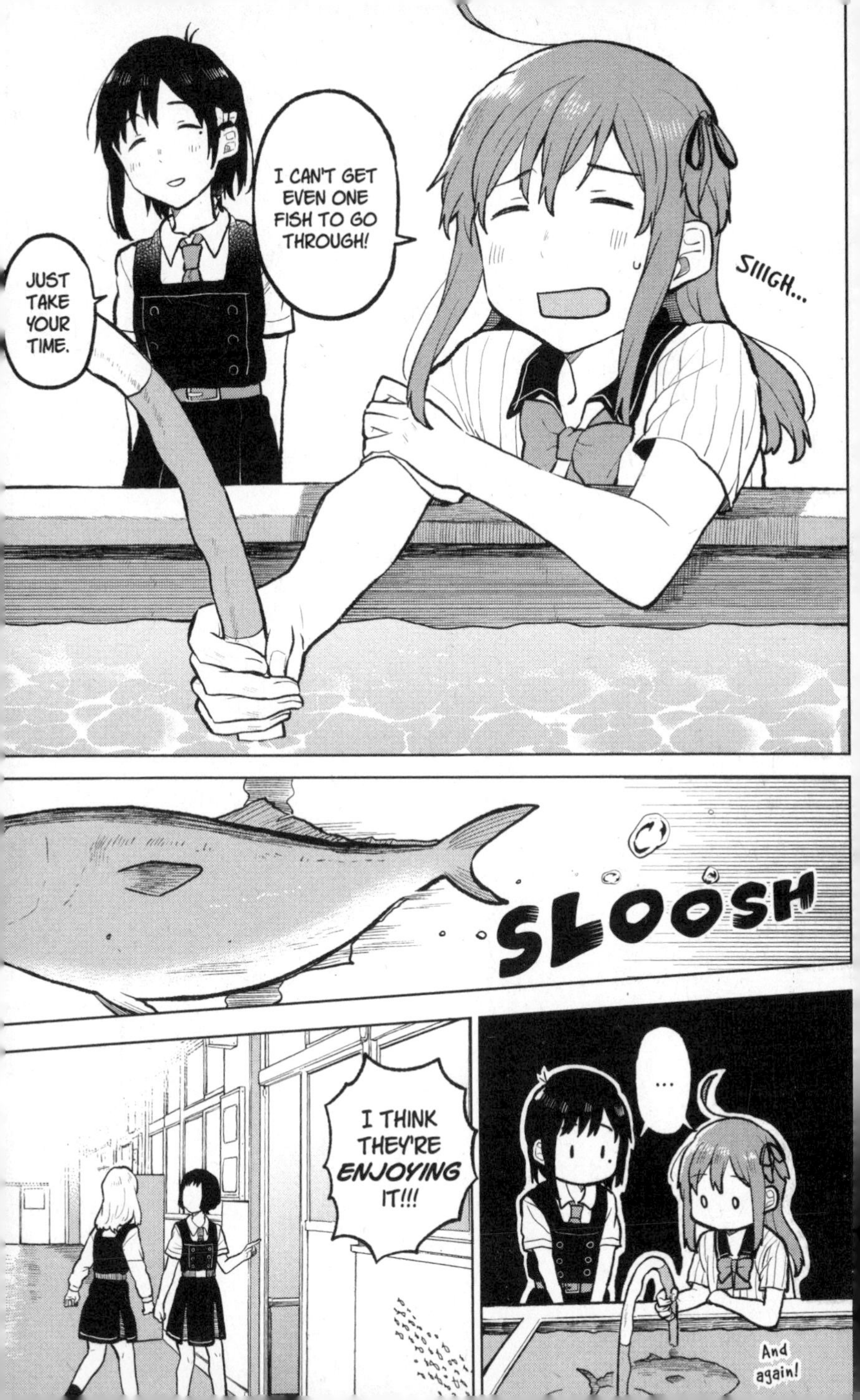
SIIIGH...
I CAN'T GET EVEN ONE FISH TO GO THROUGH!
JUST TAKE YOUR TIME.
SLOOSH
...
And again!
I THINK THEY'RE *ENJOYING* IT!!!

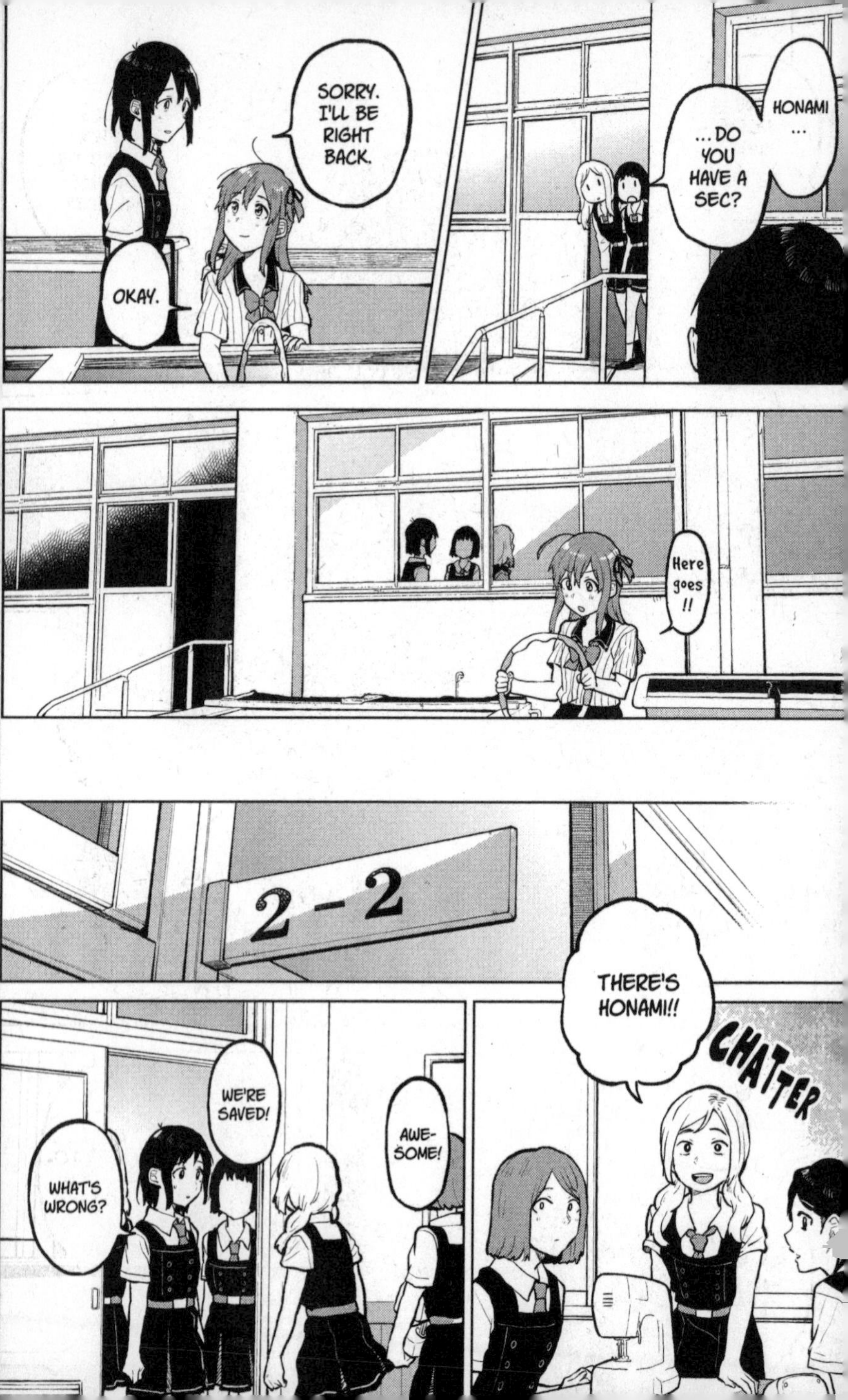
HONAMI ...
...DO YOU HAVE A SEC?
SORRY. I'LL BE RIGHT BACK.
OKAY.
Here goes!!
2-2
THERE'S HONAMI!!
CHATTER
AWE-SOME!
WE'RE SAVED!
WHAT'S WRONG?

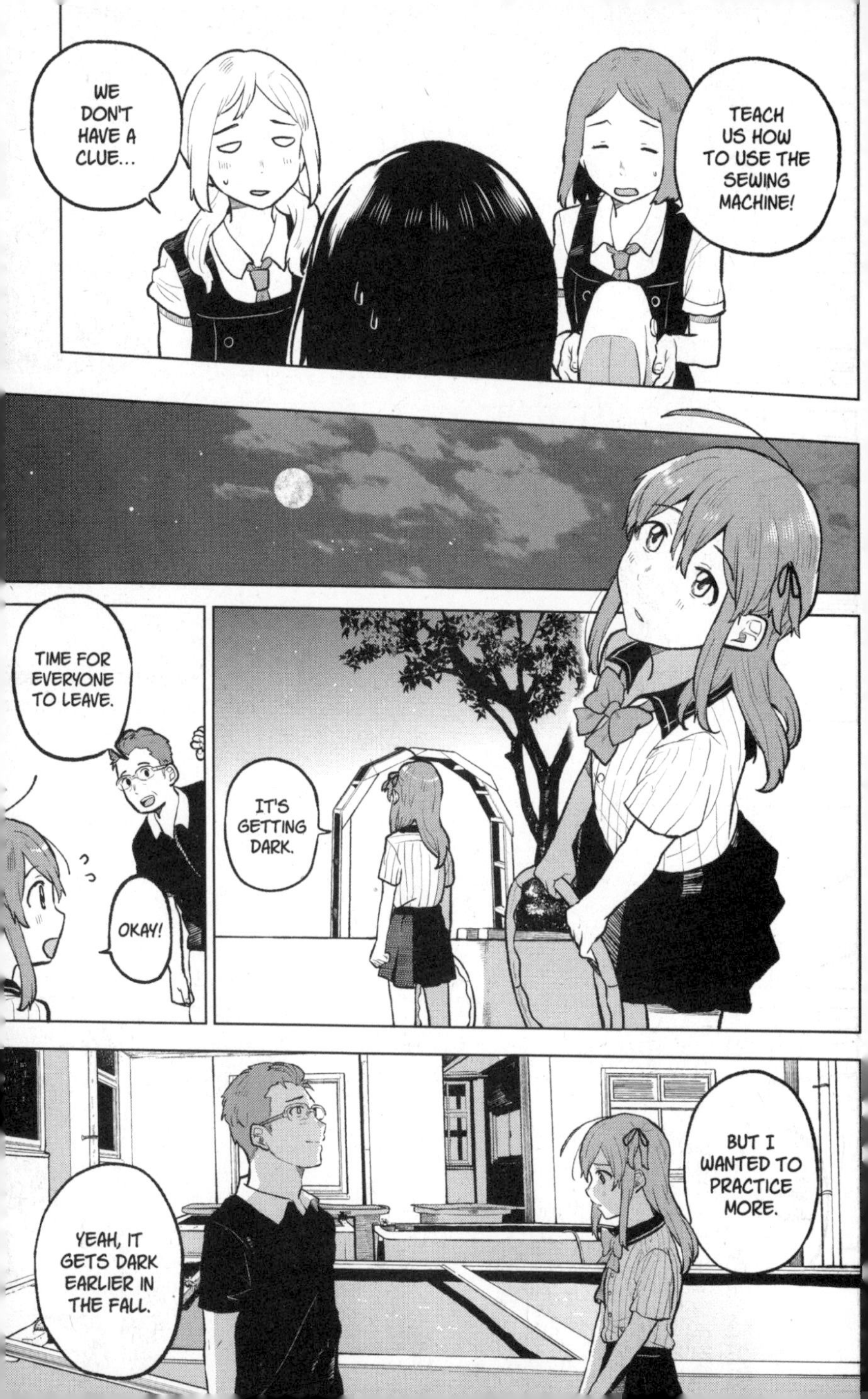
TEACH US HOW TO USE THE SEWING MACHINE!
WE DON'T HAVE A CLUE...
IT'S GETTING DARK.
TIME FOR EVERYONE TO LEAVE.
OKAY!
BUT I WANTED TO PRACTICE MORE.
YEAH, IT GETS DARK EARLIER IN THE FALL.

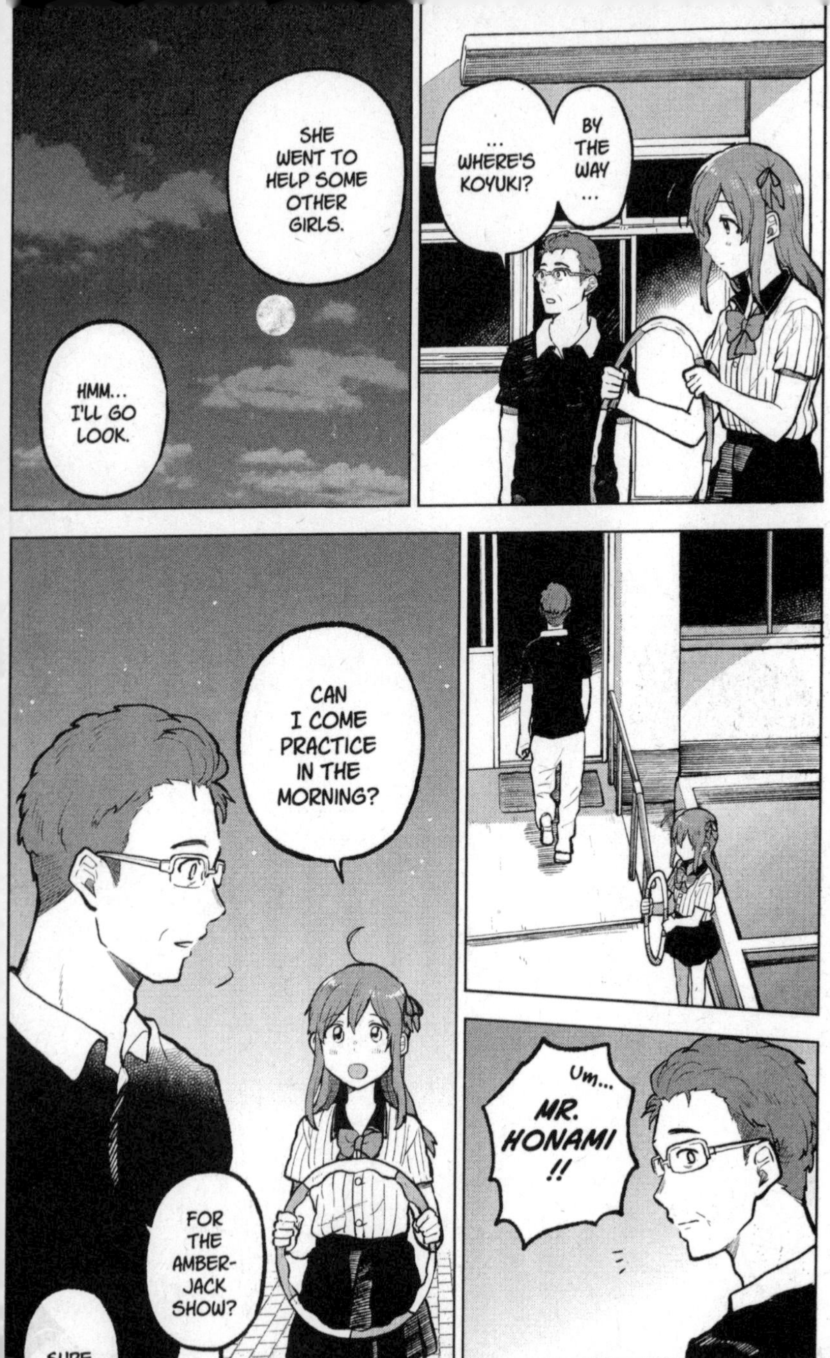
BY THE WAY...
...WHERE'S KOYUKI?
SHE WENT TO HELP SOME OTHER GIRLS.
HMM... I'LL GO LOOK.
Um... MR. HONAMI!!
CAN I COME PRACTICE IN THE MORNING?
FOR THE AMBER-JACK SHOW?
SURE.

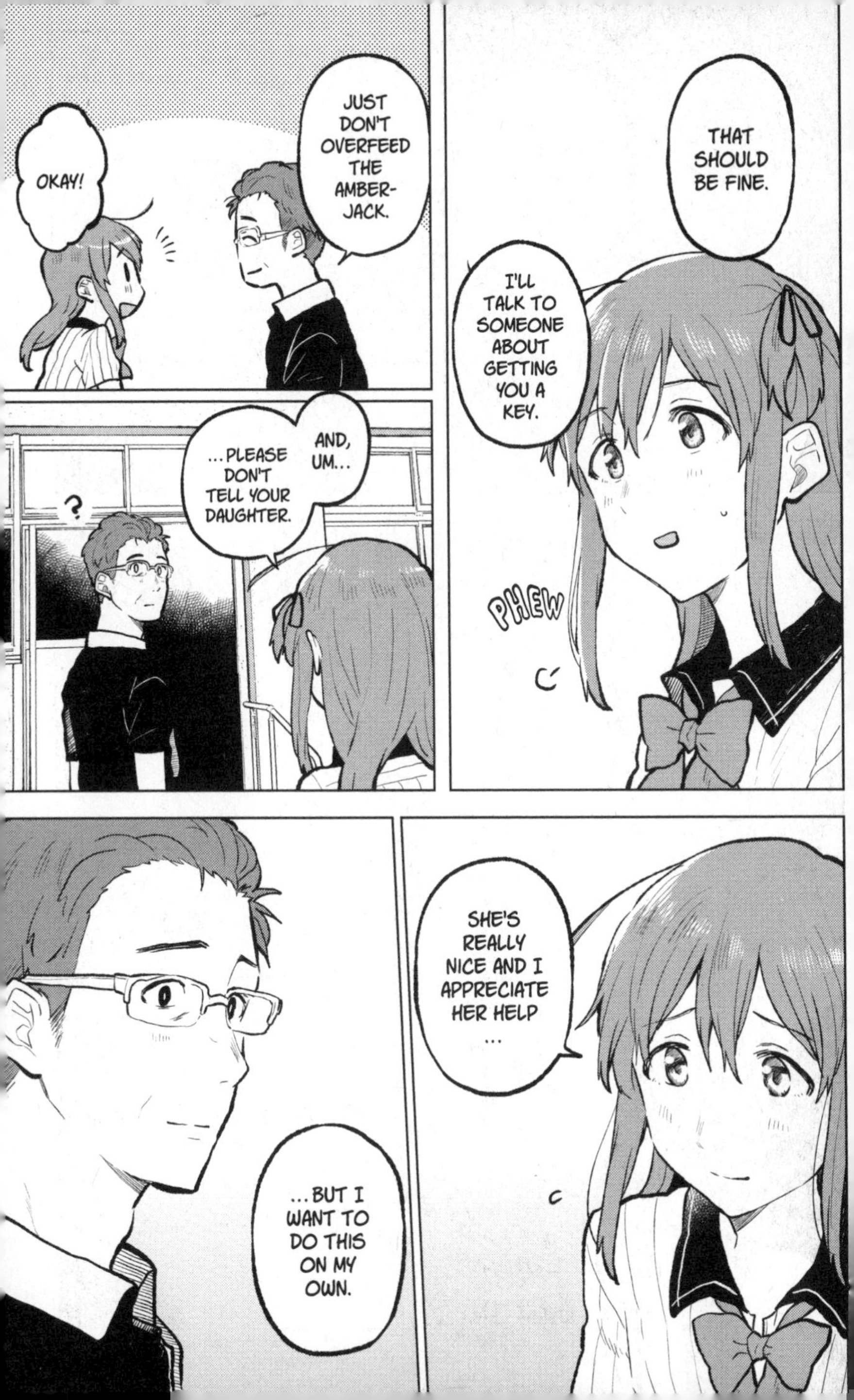
THAT SHOULD BE FINE.
I'LL TALK TO SOMEONE ABOUT GETTING YOU A KEY.
PHEW
JUST DON'T OVERFEED THE AMBER-JACK.
OKAY!
AND, UM...
...PLEASE DON'T TELL YOUR DAUGHTER.
?
SHE'S REALLY NICE AND I APPRECIATE HER HELP ...
...BUT I WANT TO DO THIS ON MY OWN.

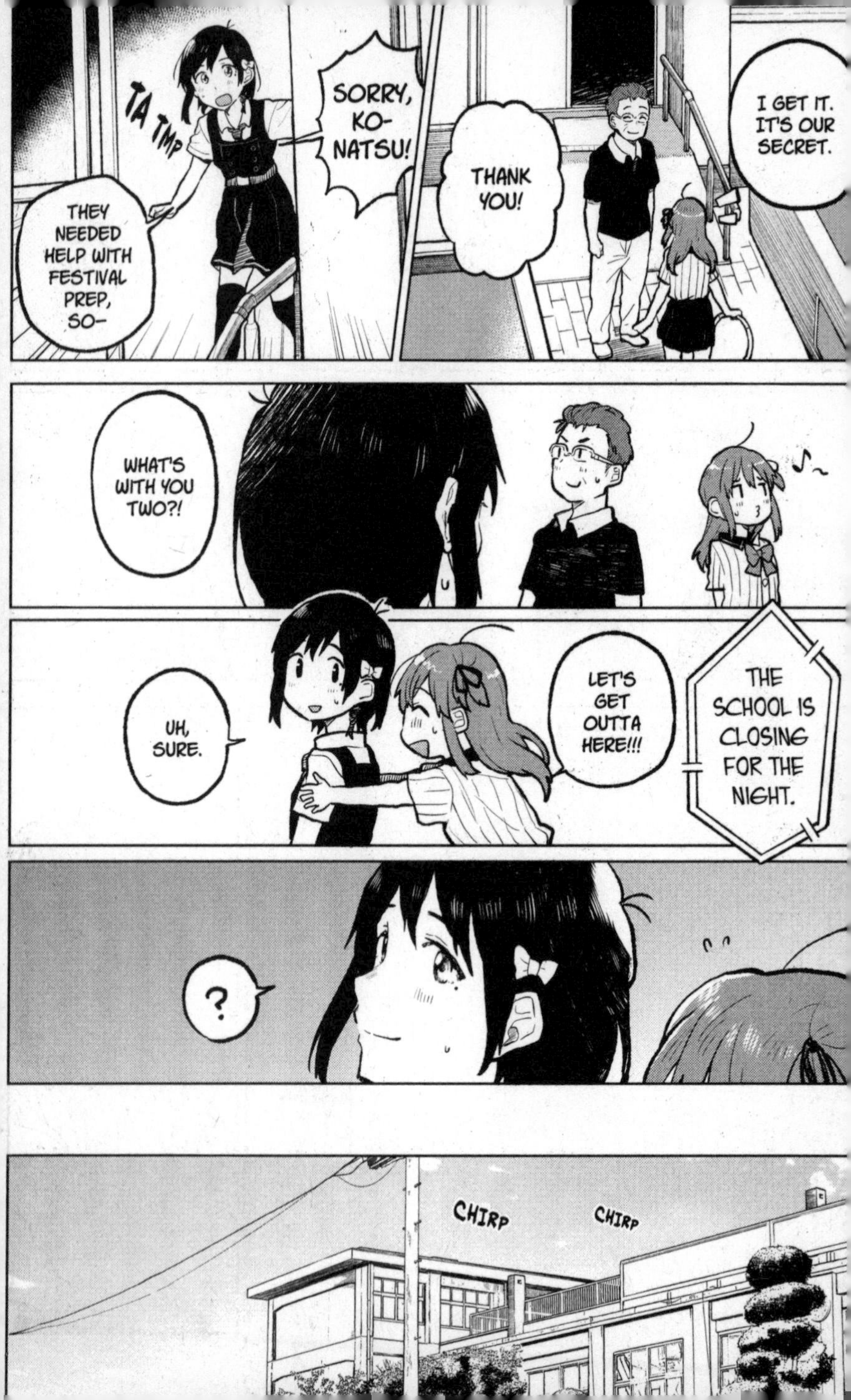
I GET IT. IT'S OUR SECRET.
THANK YOU!
SORRY, KO-NATSU!
TA TMP
THEY NEEDED HELP WITH FESTIVAL PREP, SO-
WHAT'S WITH YOU TWO?!
THE SCHOOL IS CLOSING FOR THE NIGHT.
LET'S GET OUTTA HERE!!!
UH, SURE.
?
CHIRP
CHIRP

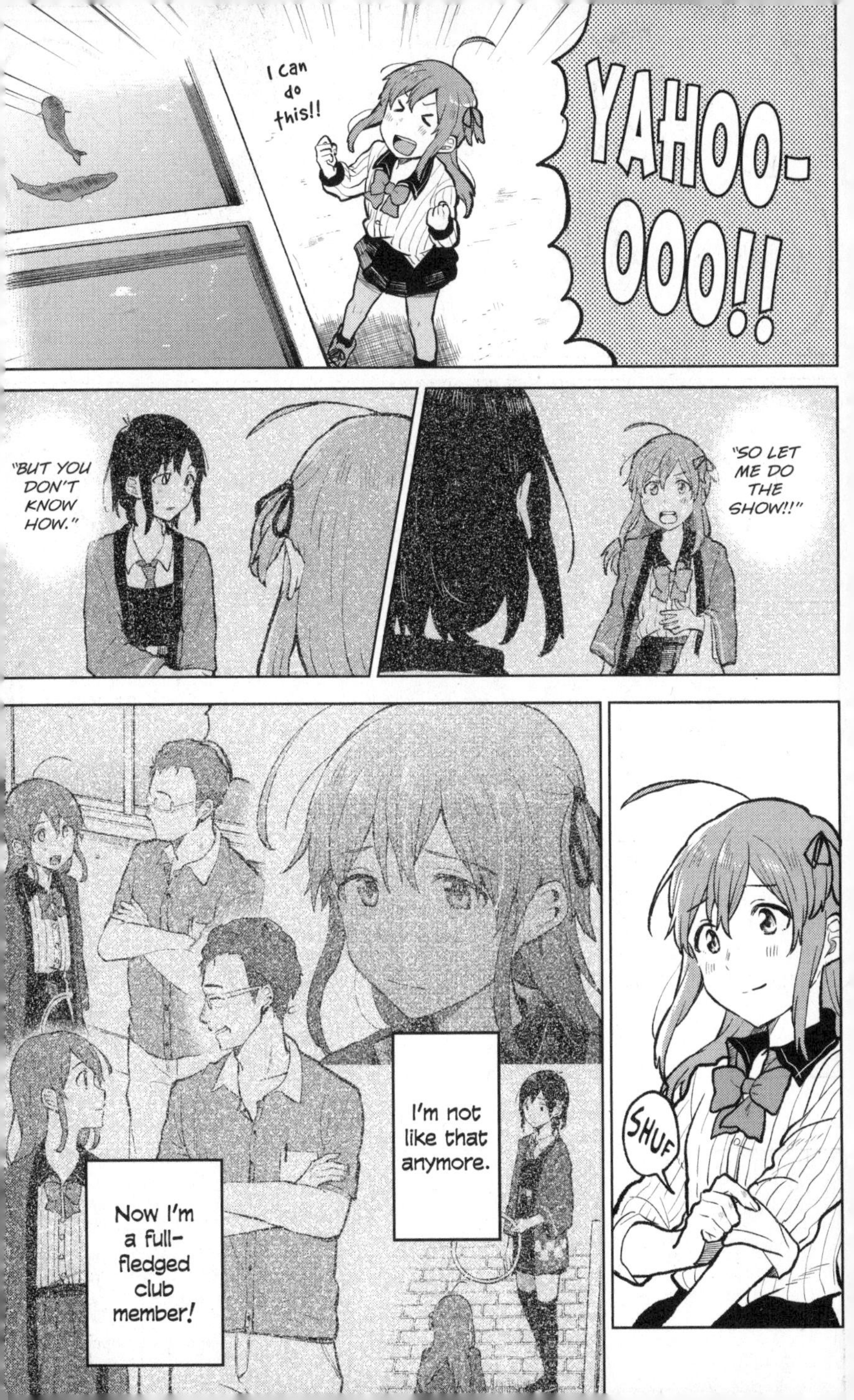
YAHOO-OOO!!
I can do this!!
"SO LET ME DO THE SHOW!!"
"BUT YOU DON'T KNOW HOW."
SHUF
I'm not like that anymore.
Now I'm a full-fledged club member!

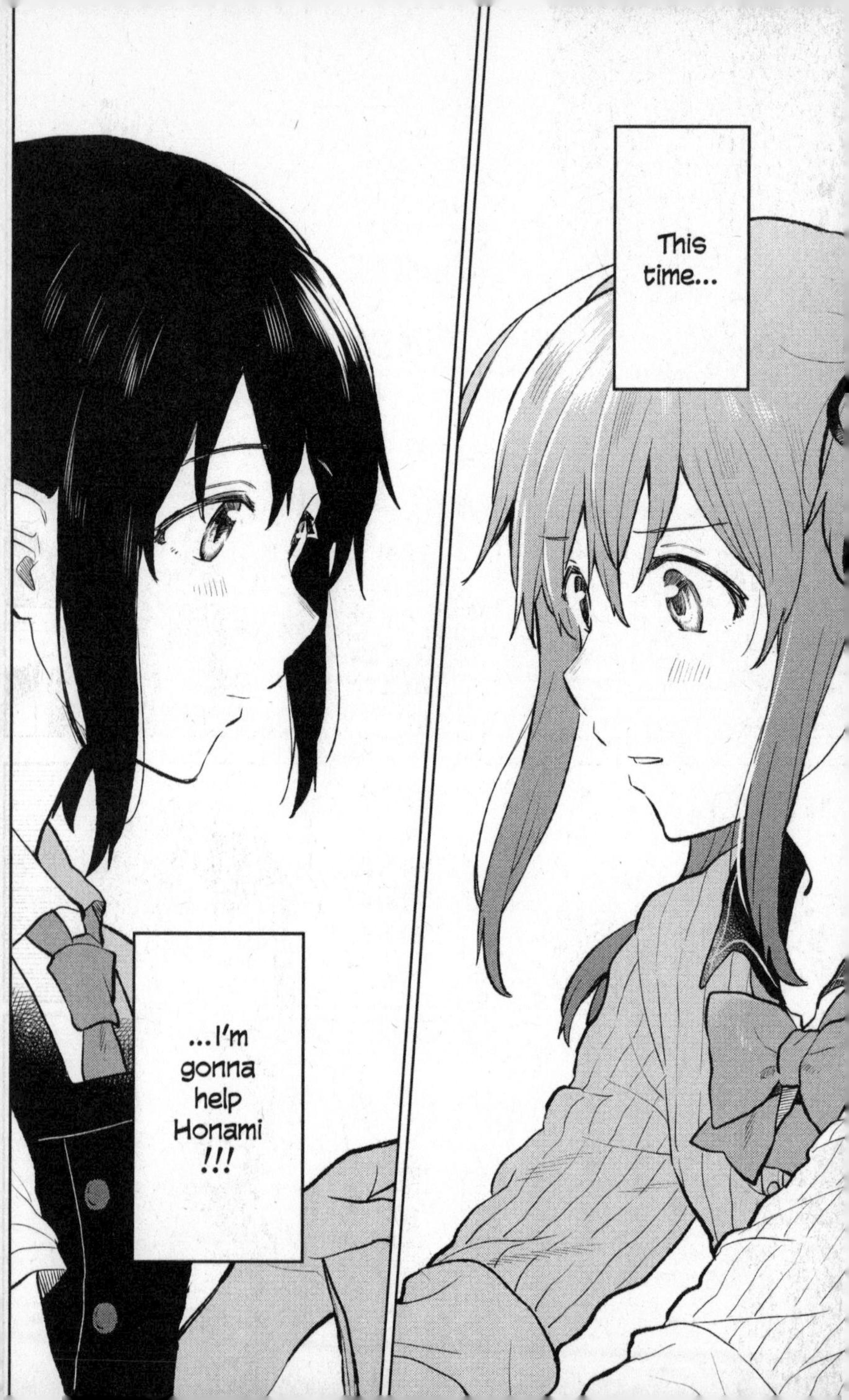
This time...
...I'm gonna help Honami!!!

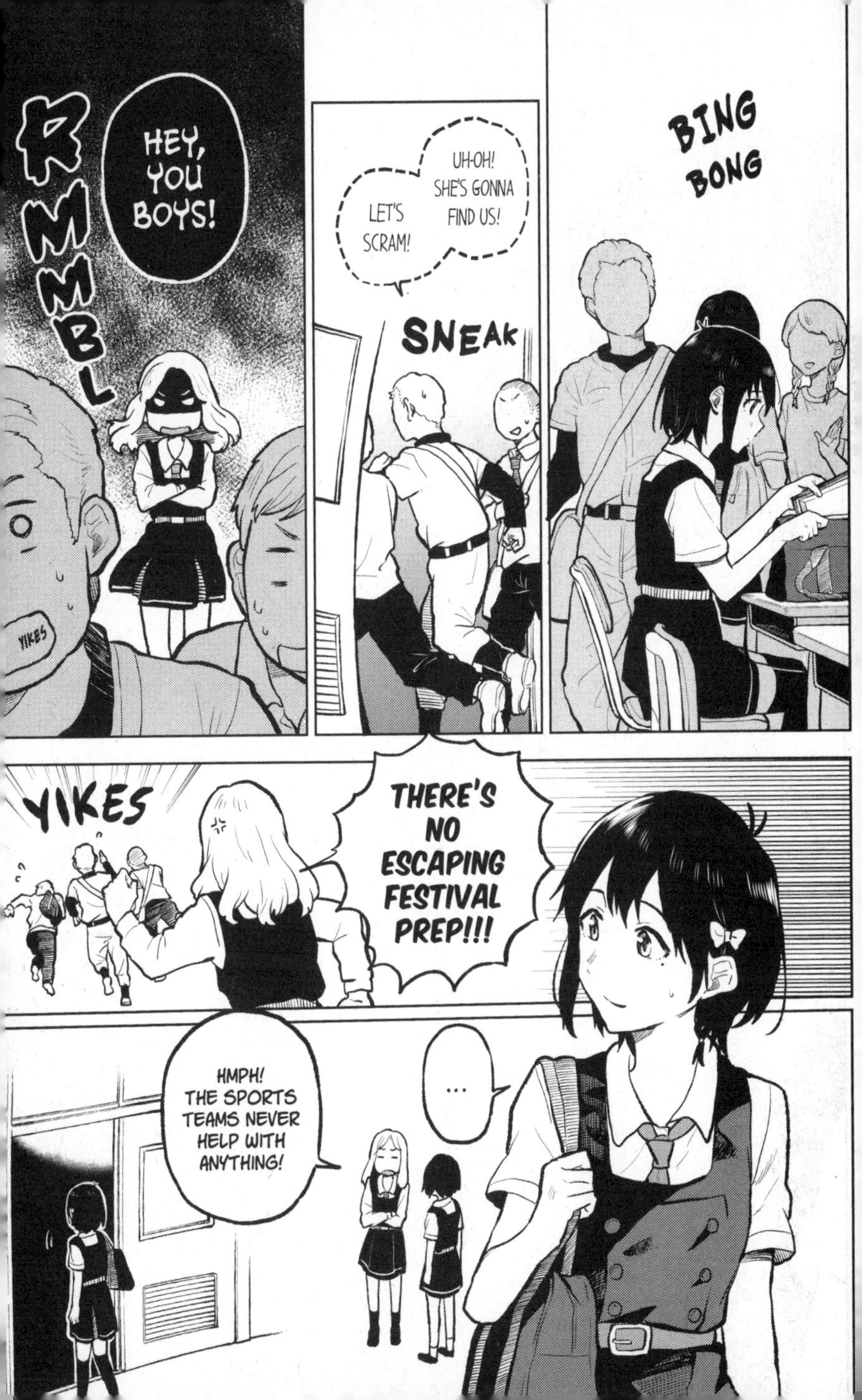
BING BONG
UH-OH! SHE'S GONNA FIND US!
LET'S SCRAM!
SNEAk
HEY, YOU BOYS!
RMMMBL
YIKES
THERE'S NO ESCAPING FESTIVAL PREP!!!
YIKES
...
HMPH! THE SPORTS TEAMS NEVER HELP WITH ANYTHING!

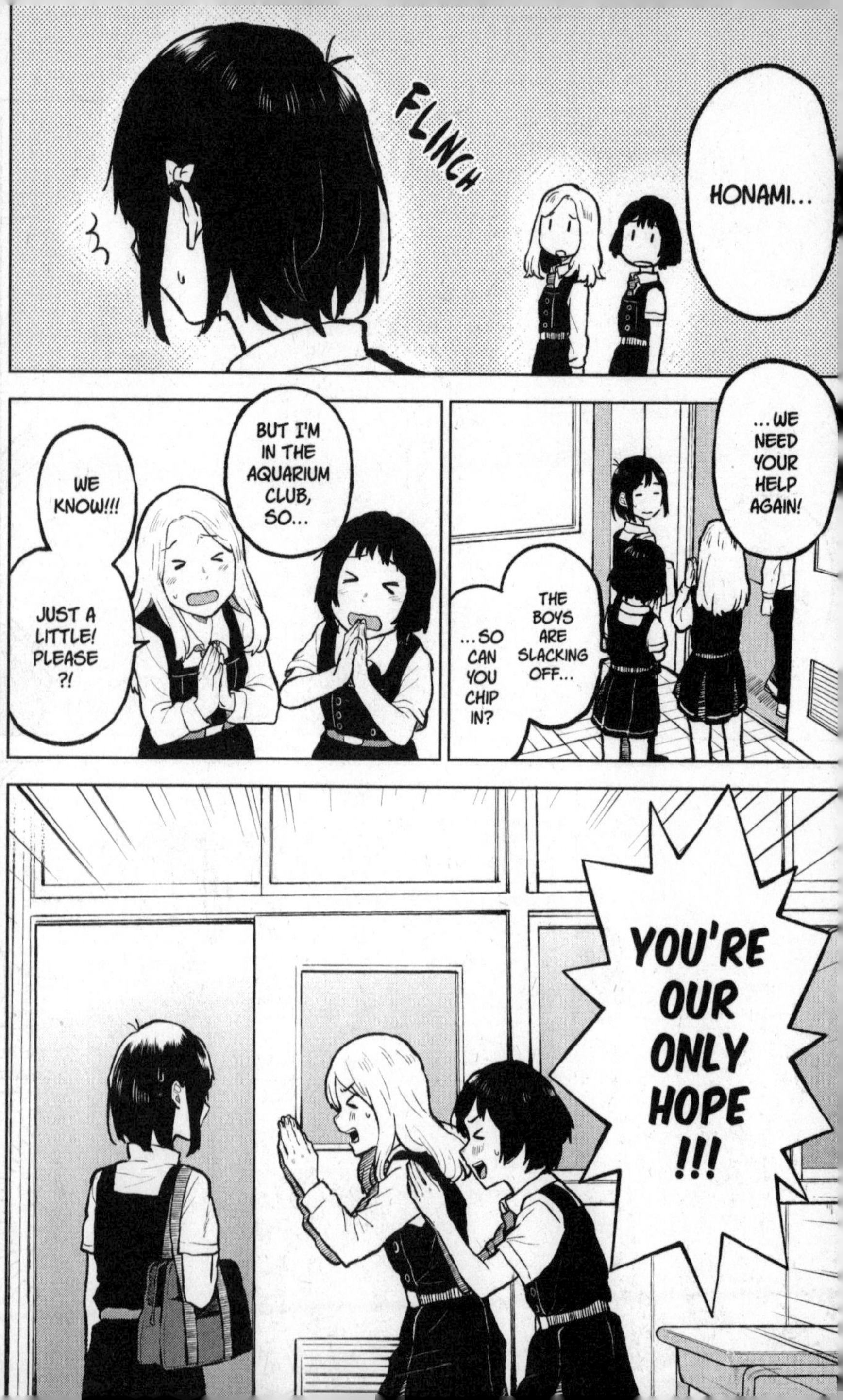
HONAMI...
FLINCH
...WE NEED YOUR HELP AGAIN!
THE BOYS ARE SLACKING OFF...
...SO CAN YOU CHIP IN?
BUT I'M IN THE AQUARIUM CLUB, SO...
WE KNOW!!!
JUST A LITTLE! PLEASE?!
YOU'RE OUR ONLY HOPE!!!

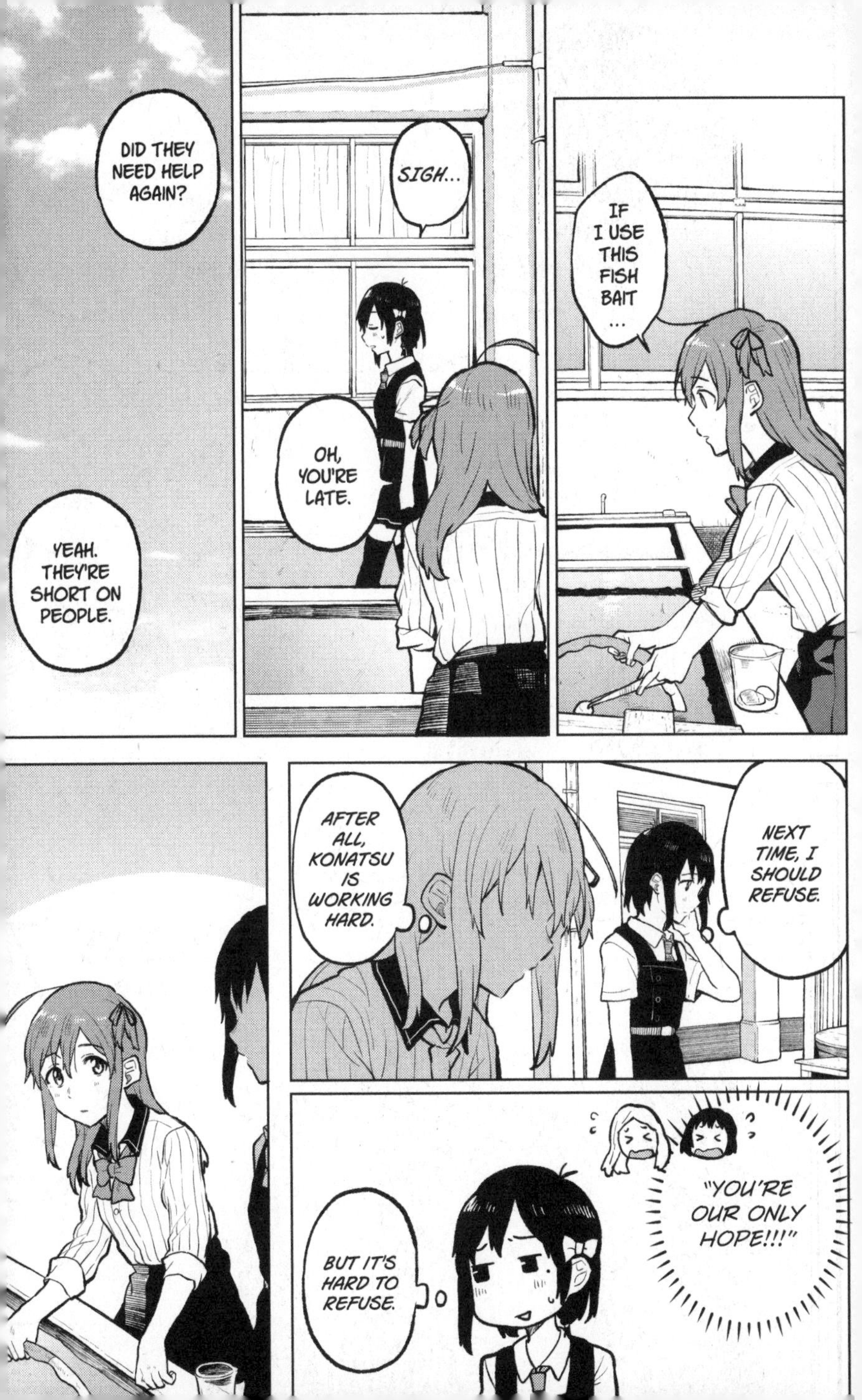
IF I USE THIS FISH BAIT ...
SIGH...
OH, YOU'RE LATE.
DID THEY NEED HELP AGAIN?
YEAH. THEY'RE SHORT ON PEOPLE.
NEXT TIME, I SHOULD REFUSE.
AFTER ALL, KONATSU IS WORKING HARD.
"YOU'RE OUR ONLY HOPE!!!"
BUT IT'S HARD TO REFUSE.

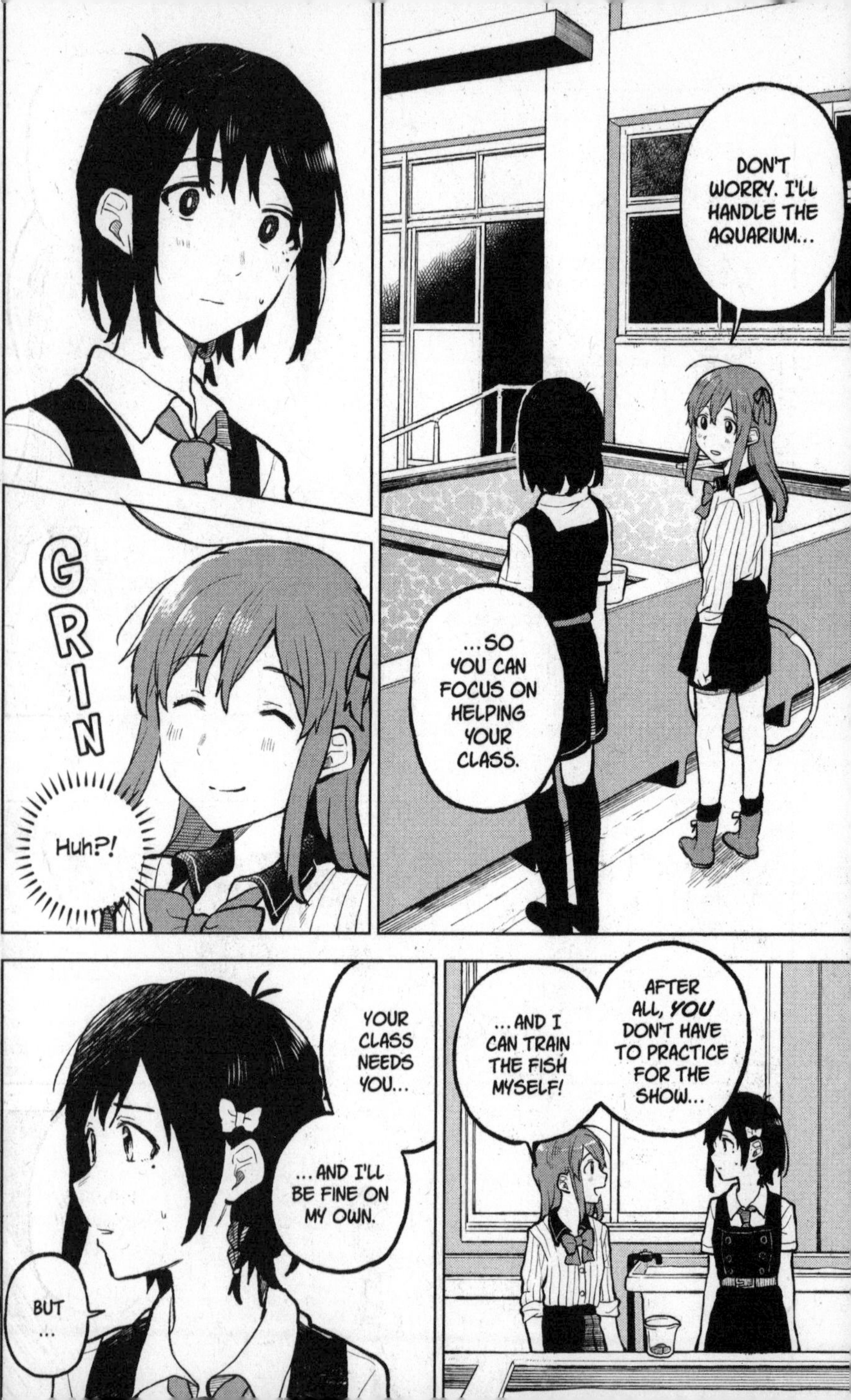
DON'T WORRY. I'LL HANDLE THE AQUARIUM...
...SO YOU CAN FOCUS ON HELPING YOUR CLASS.
GRIN
Huh?!
AFTER ALL, *YOU* DON'T HAVE TO PRACTICE FOR THE SHOW...
...AND I CAN TRAIN THE FISH MYSELF!
YOUR CLASS NEEDS YOU...
...AND I'LL BE FINE ON MY OWN.
BUT ...

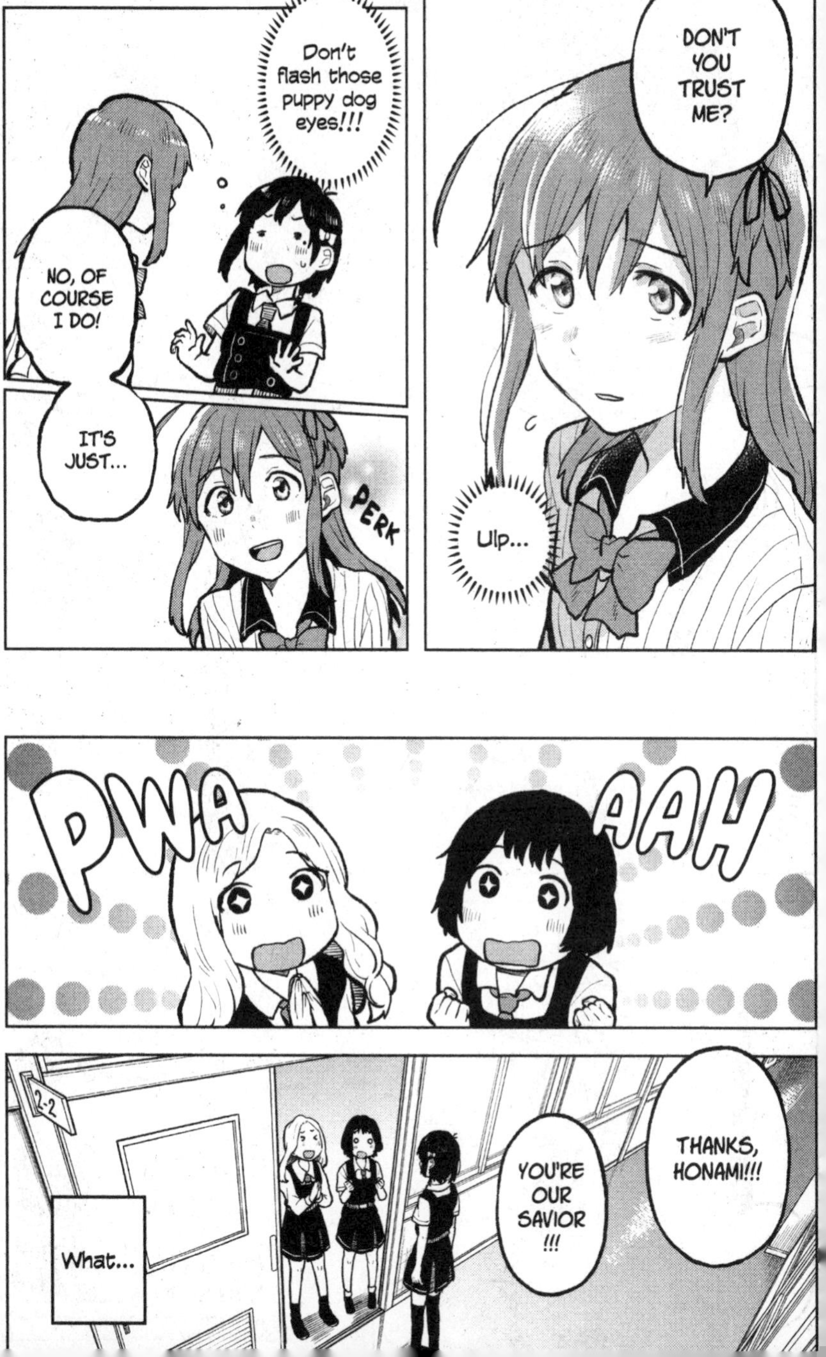
DON'T YOU TRUST ME?
Ulp...
Don't flash those puppy dog eyes!!!
NO, OF COURSE I DO!
IT'S JUST...
PERK
PWAAAH
THANKS, HONAMI!!!
YOU'RE OUR SAVIOR!!!
What...

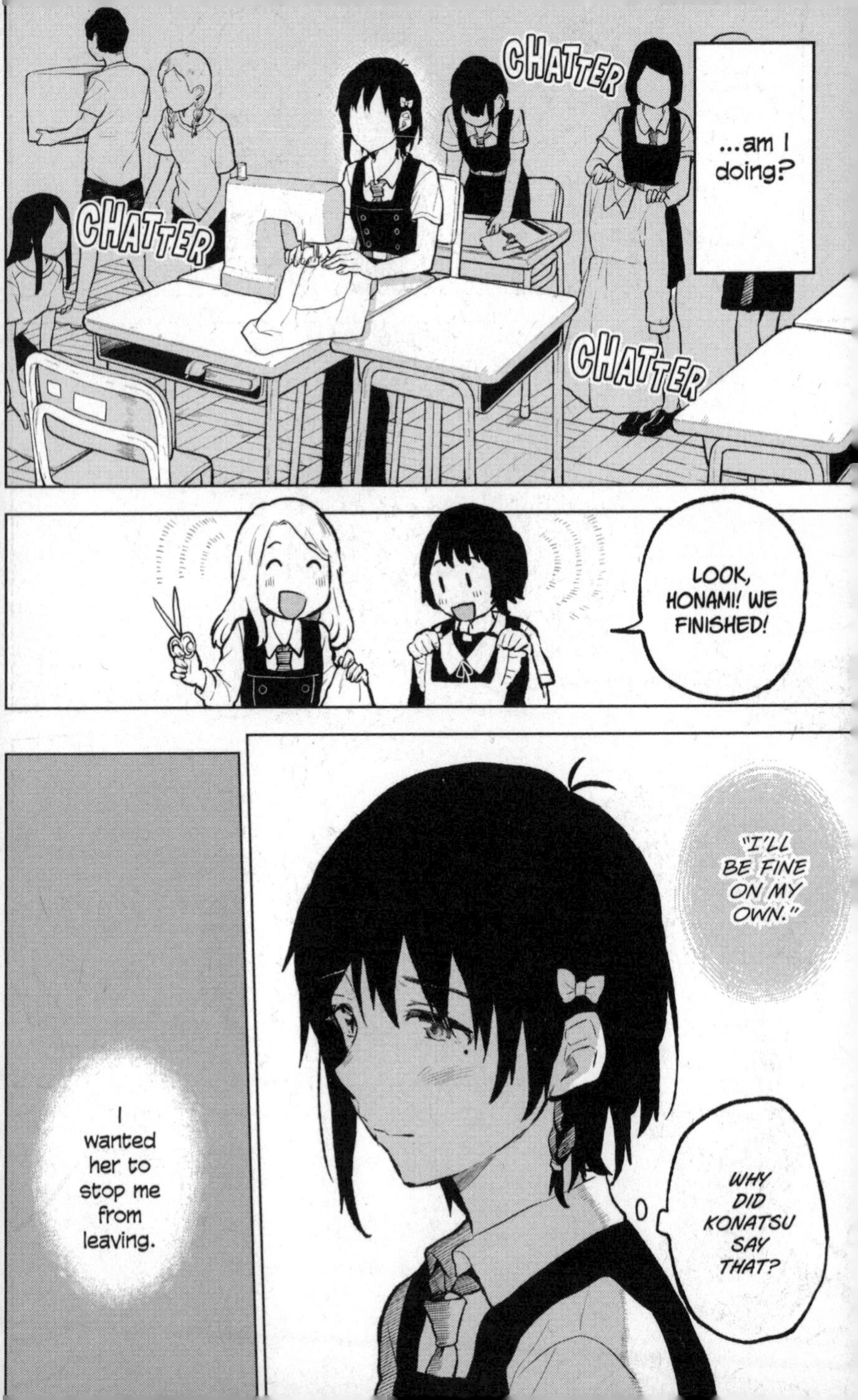
...am I doing?
CHATTER
CHATTER
CHATTER
LOOK, HONAMI! WE FINISHED!
"I'LL BE FINE ON MY OWN."
WHY DID KONATSU SAY THAT?
I wanted her to stop me from leaving.

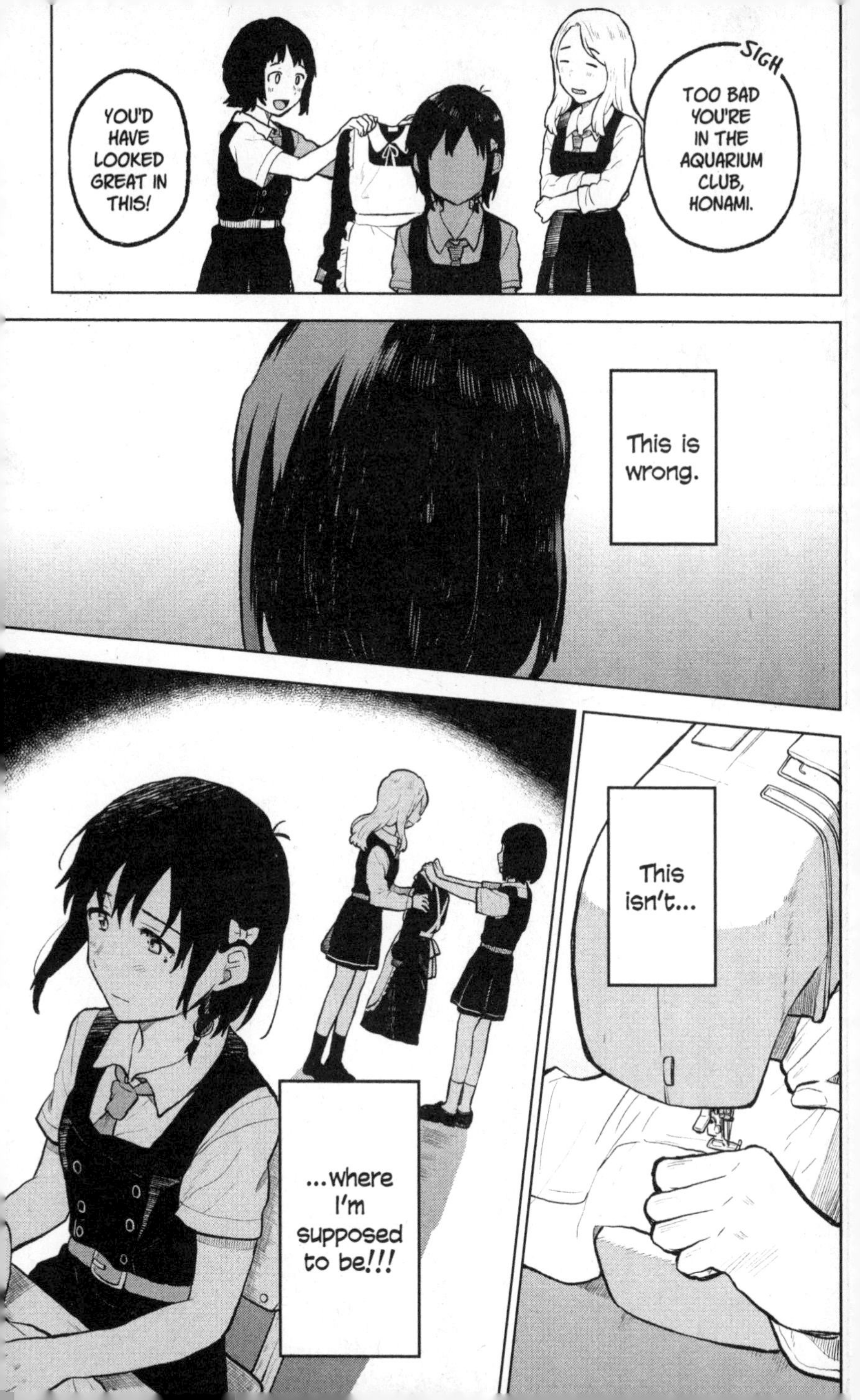
SIGH
TOO BAD YOU'RE IN THE AQUARIUM CLUB, HONAMI.
YOU'D HAVE LOOKED GREAT IN THIS!
This is wrong.
This isn't...
...where I'm supposed to be!!!

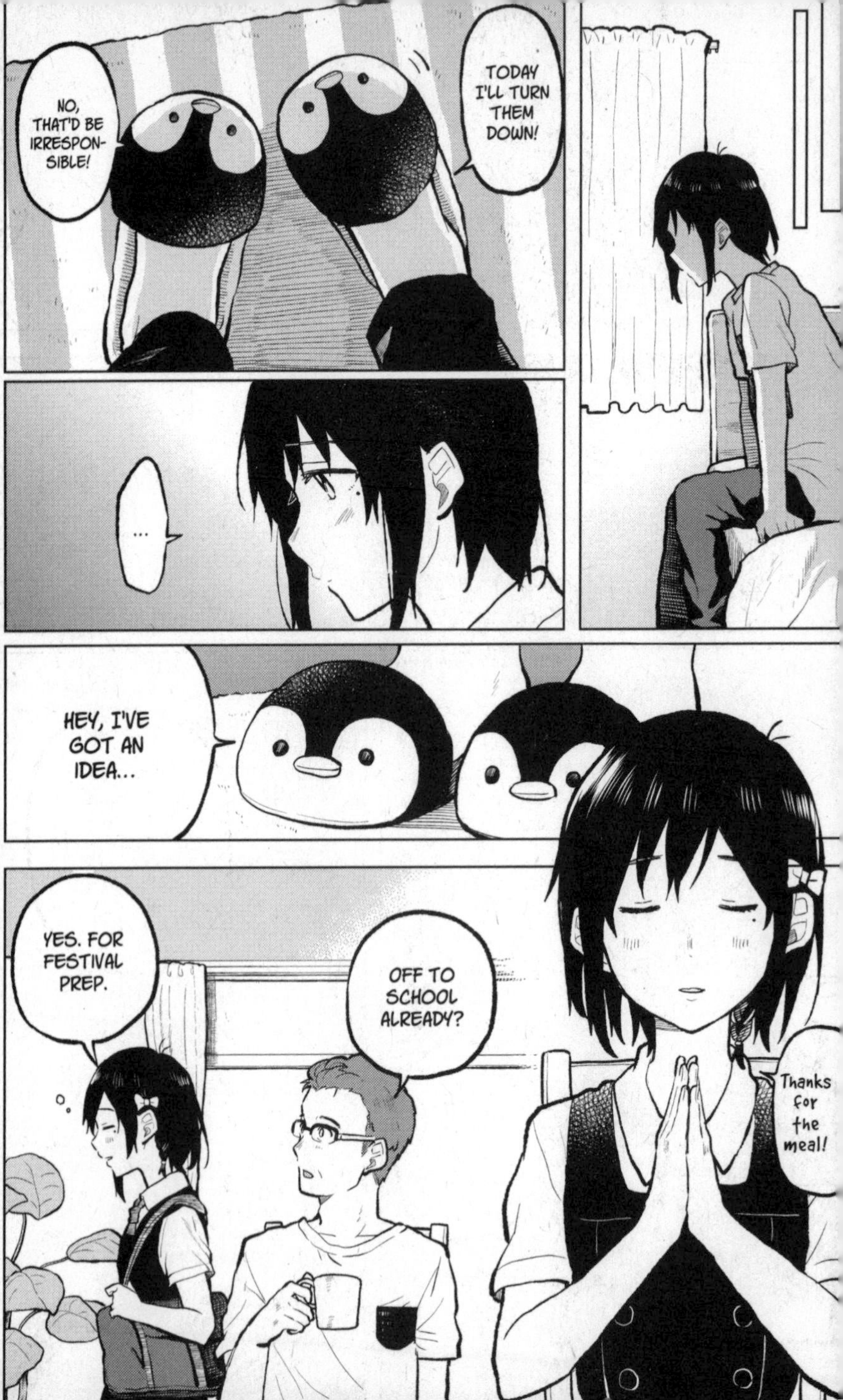
TODAY I'LL TURN THEM DOWN!
NO, THAT'D BE IRRESPON-SIBLE!
...
HEY, I'VE GOT AN IDEA...
Thanks for the meal!
OFF TO SCHOOL ALREADY?
YES. FOR FESTIVAL PREP.

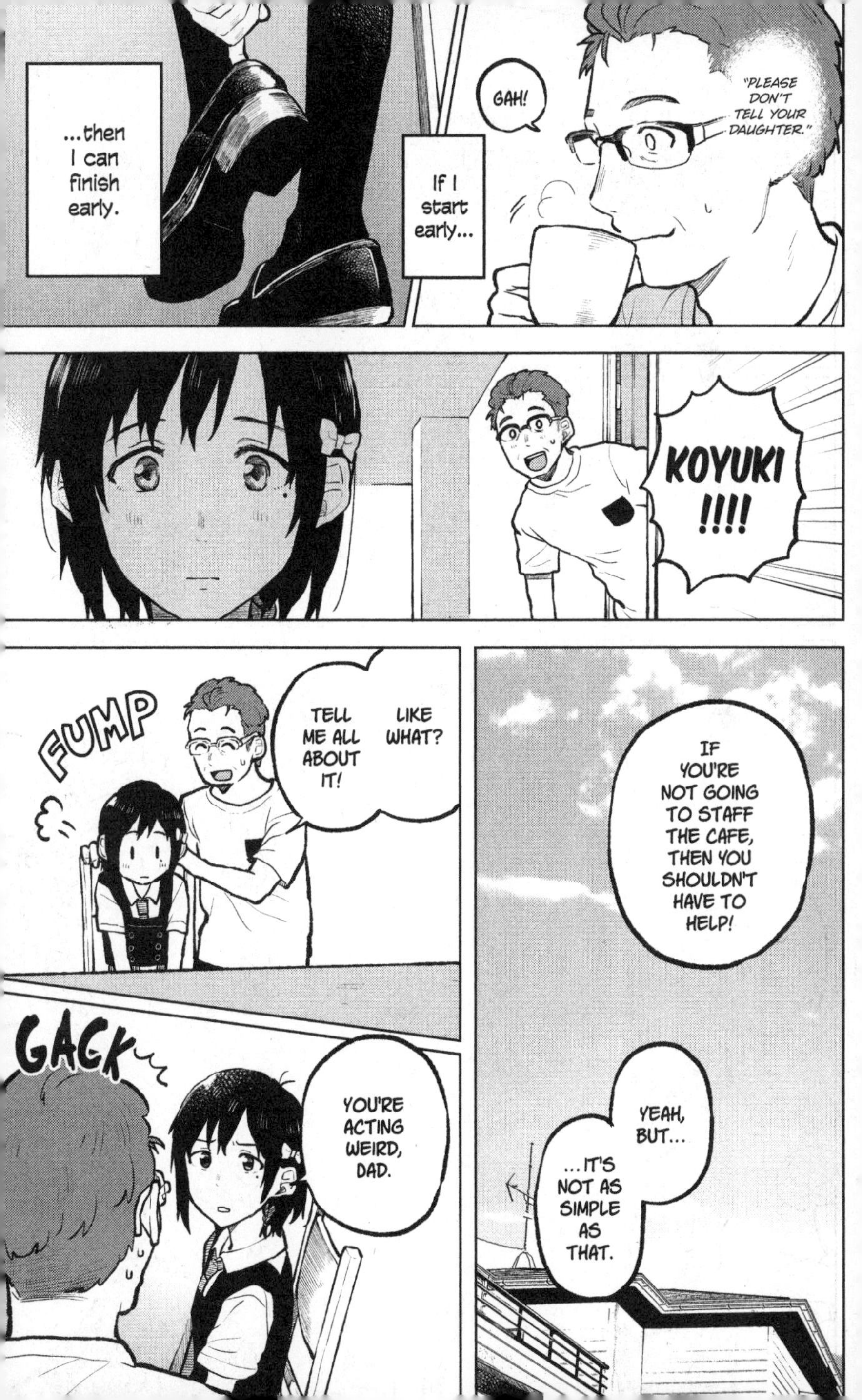
"PLEASE DON'T TELL YOUR DAUGHTER."
GAH!
If I start early...
...then I can finish early.
KOYUKI !!!!
IF YOU'RE NOT GOING TO STAFF THE CAFE, THEN YOU SHOULDN'T HAVE TO HELP!
YEAH, BUT...
...IT'S NOT AS SIMPLE AS THAT.
LIKE WHAT?
TELL ME ALL ABOUT IT!
FUMP
YOU'RE ACTING WEIRD, DAD.
GACK

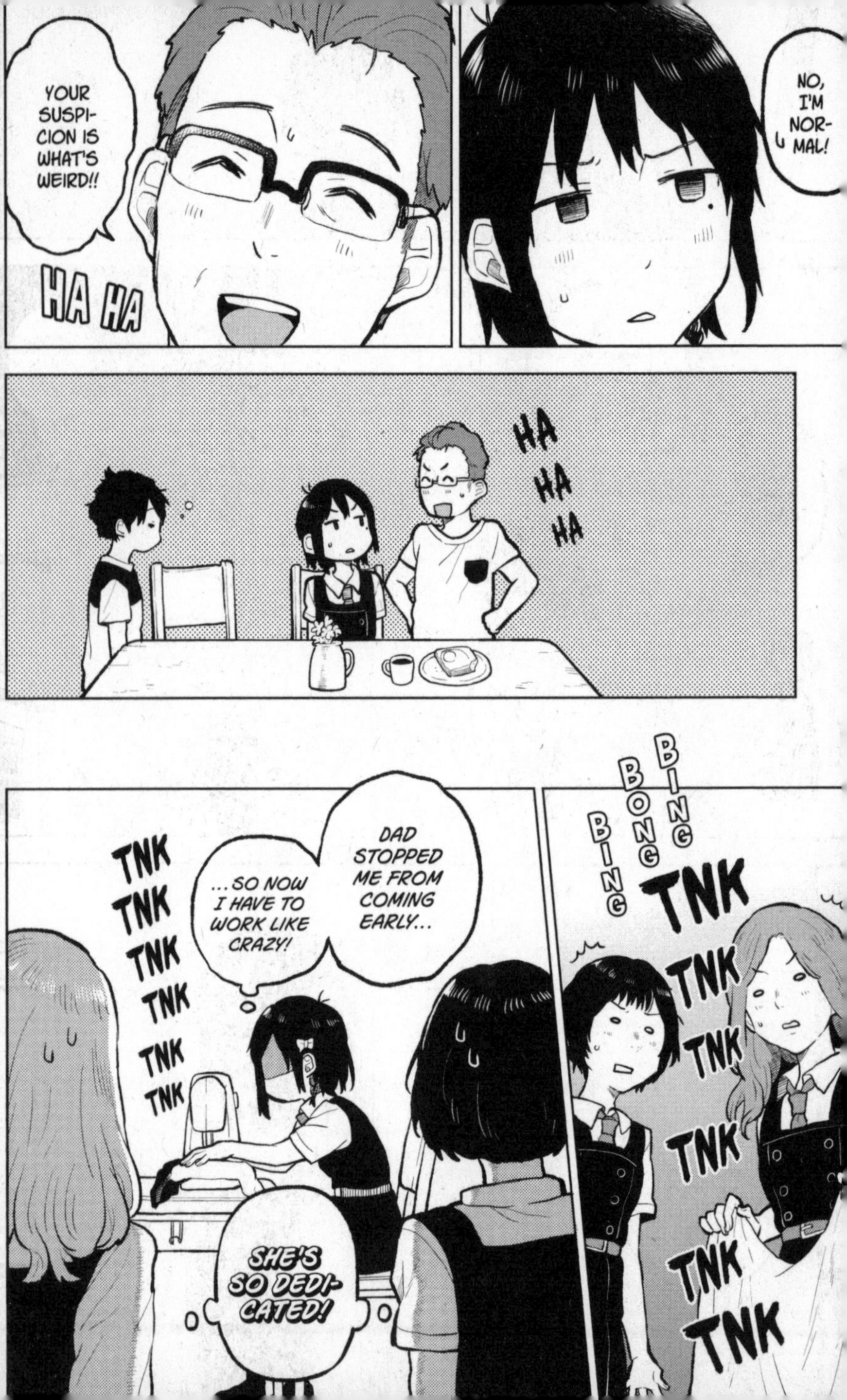
NO, I'M NOR-MAL!
YOUR SUSPI-CION IS WHAT'S WEIRD!!
HA HA
HA HA HA
BING
BONG
BING
TNK TNK TNK TNK TNK TNK
DAD STOPPED ME FROM COMING EARLY...
...SO NOW I HAVE TO WORK LIKE CRAZY!
TNK TNK TNK TNK TNK TNK
SHE'S SO DEDI-CATED!

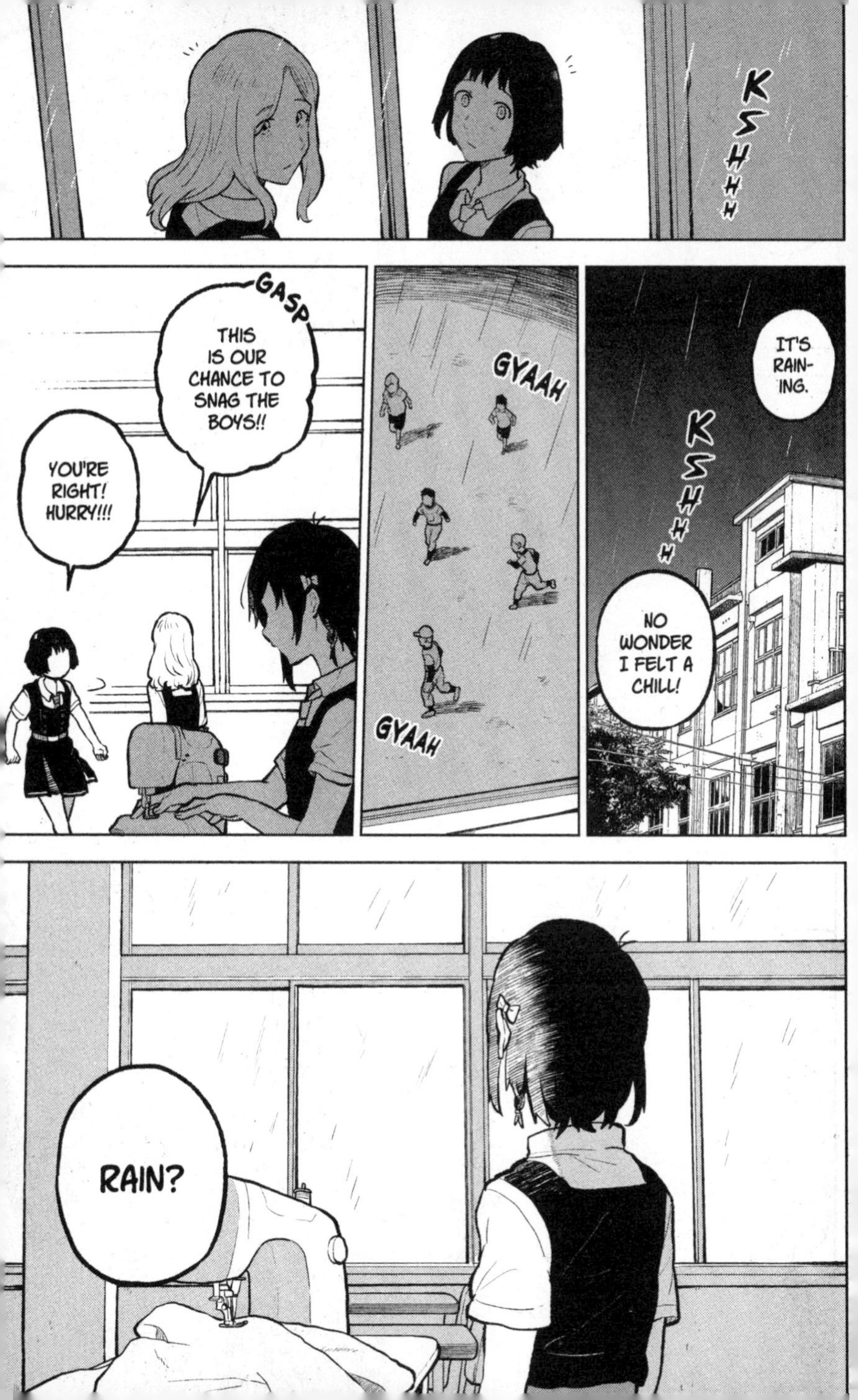
KSHHHH
IT'S RAIN-ING.
KSHHHH
NO WONDER I FELT A CHILL!
GYAAH
GYAAH
GASP
THIS IS OUR CHANCE TO SNAG THE BOYS!!
YOU'RE RIGHT! HURRY!!!
RAIN?

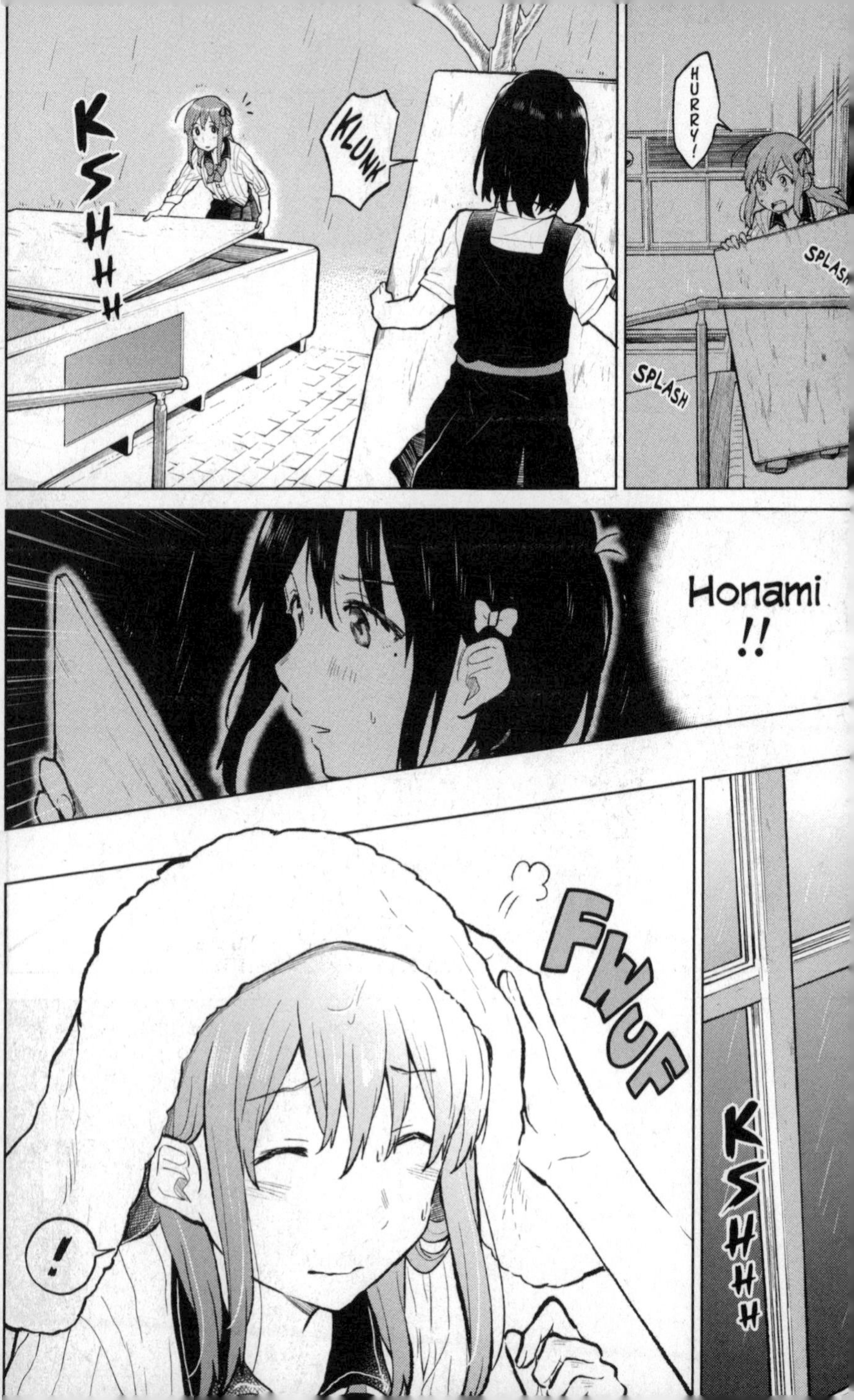
HURRY!
SPLASH
SPLASH
KLUNK
KSHHHH
Honami !!
KSHHHH
FWUF
!

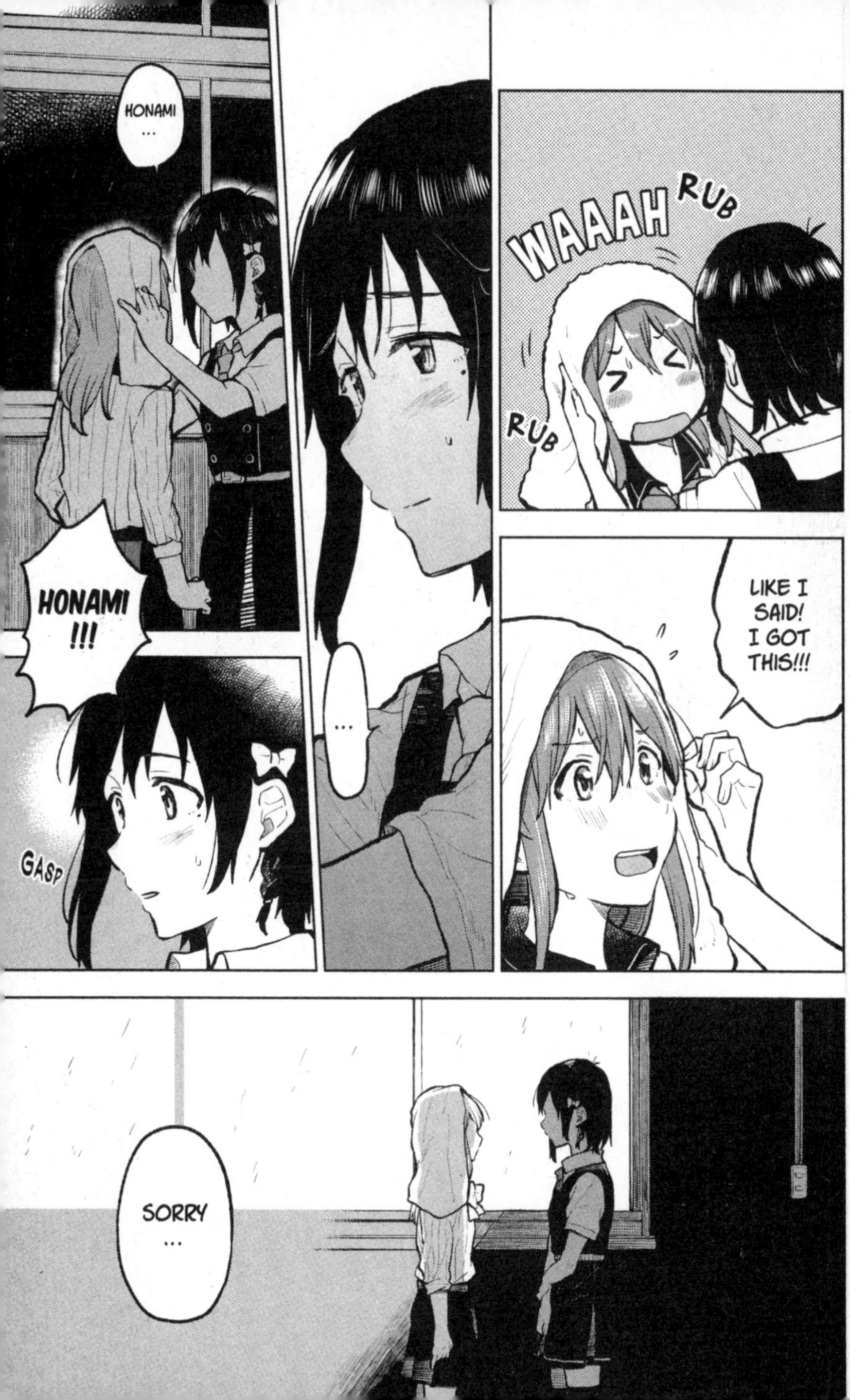
WAAAH
RUB
RUB
LIKE I SAID! I GOT THIS!!!
...
HONAMI ...
HONAMI !!!
GASP
SORRY ...

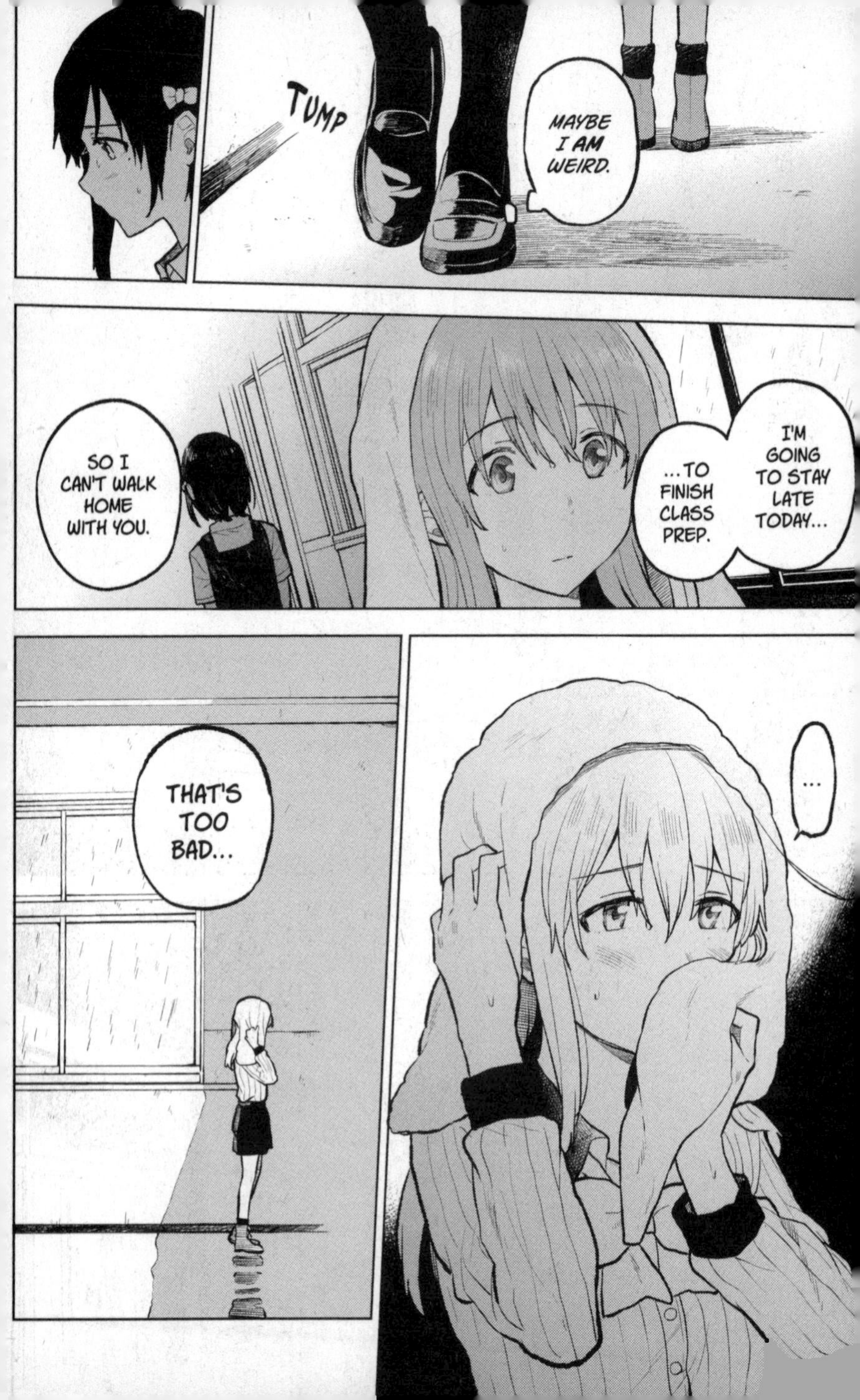
MAYBE I AM WEIRD.
TUMP
I'M GOING TO STAY LATE TODAY...
...TO FINISH CLASS PREP.
SO I CAN'T WALK HOME WITH YOU.
...
THAT'S TOO BAD...

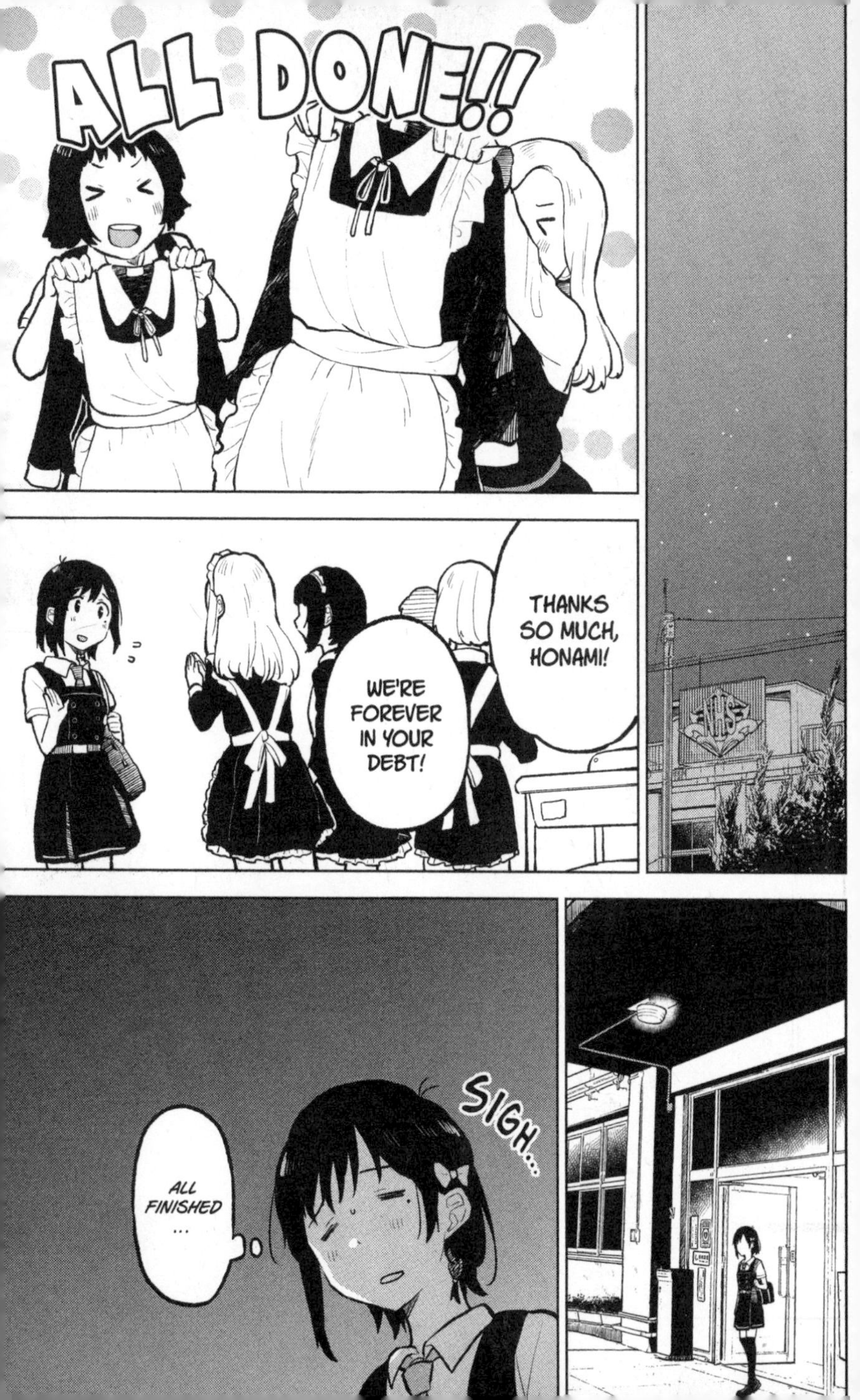
ALL DONE!!
THANKS SO MUCH, HONAMI!
WE'RE FOREVER IN YOUR DEBT!
SIGH...
ALL FINISHED ...

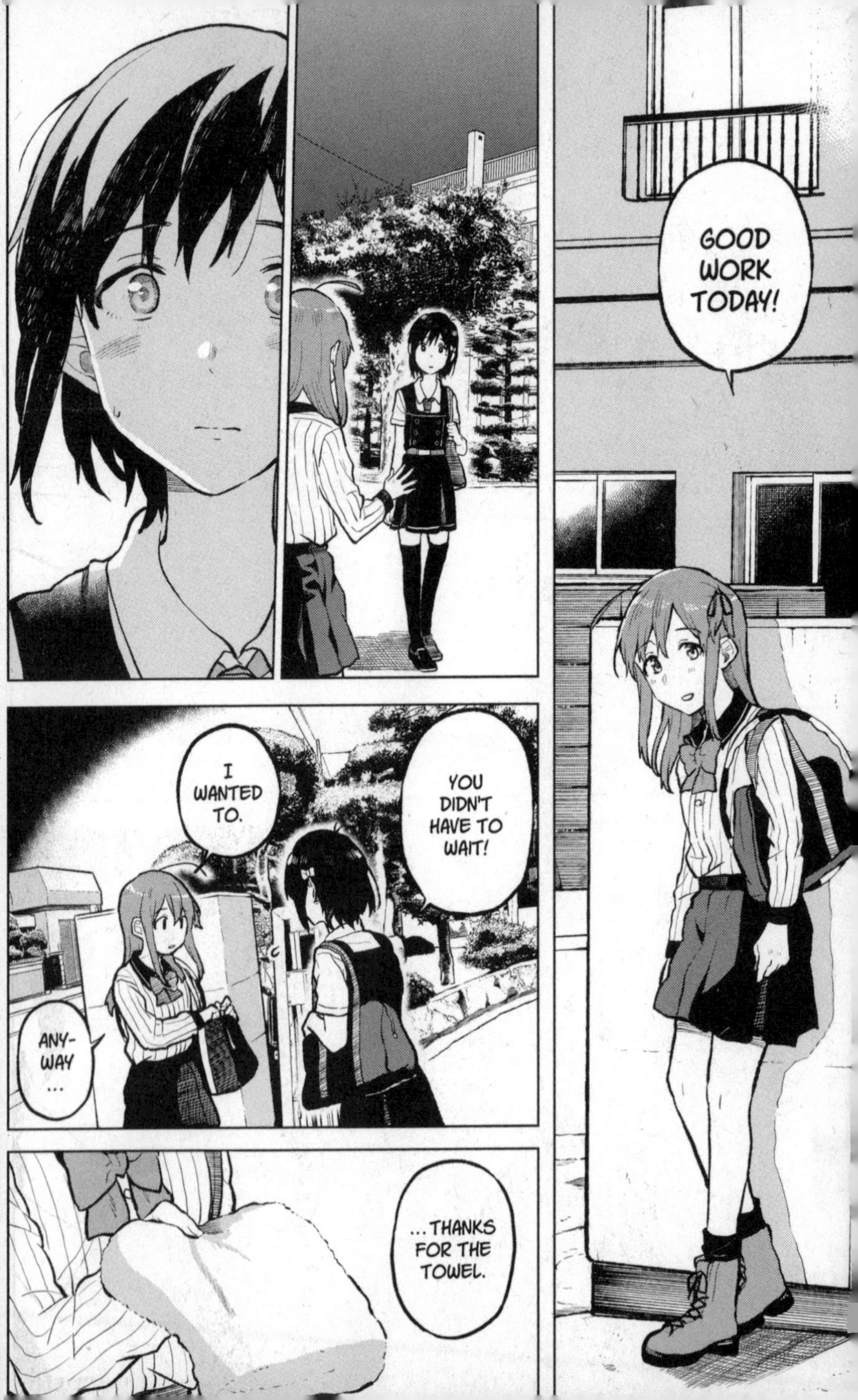
GOOD WORK TODAY!
YOU DIDN'T HAVE TO WAIT!
I WANTED TO.
ANY-WAY ...
...THANKS FOR THE TOWEL.

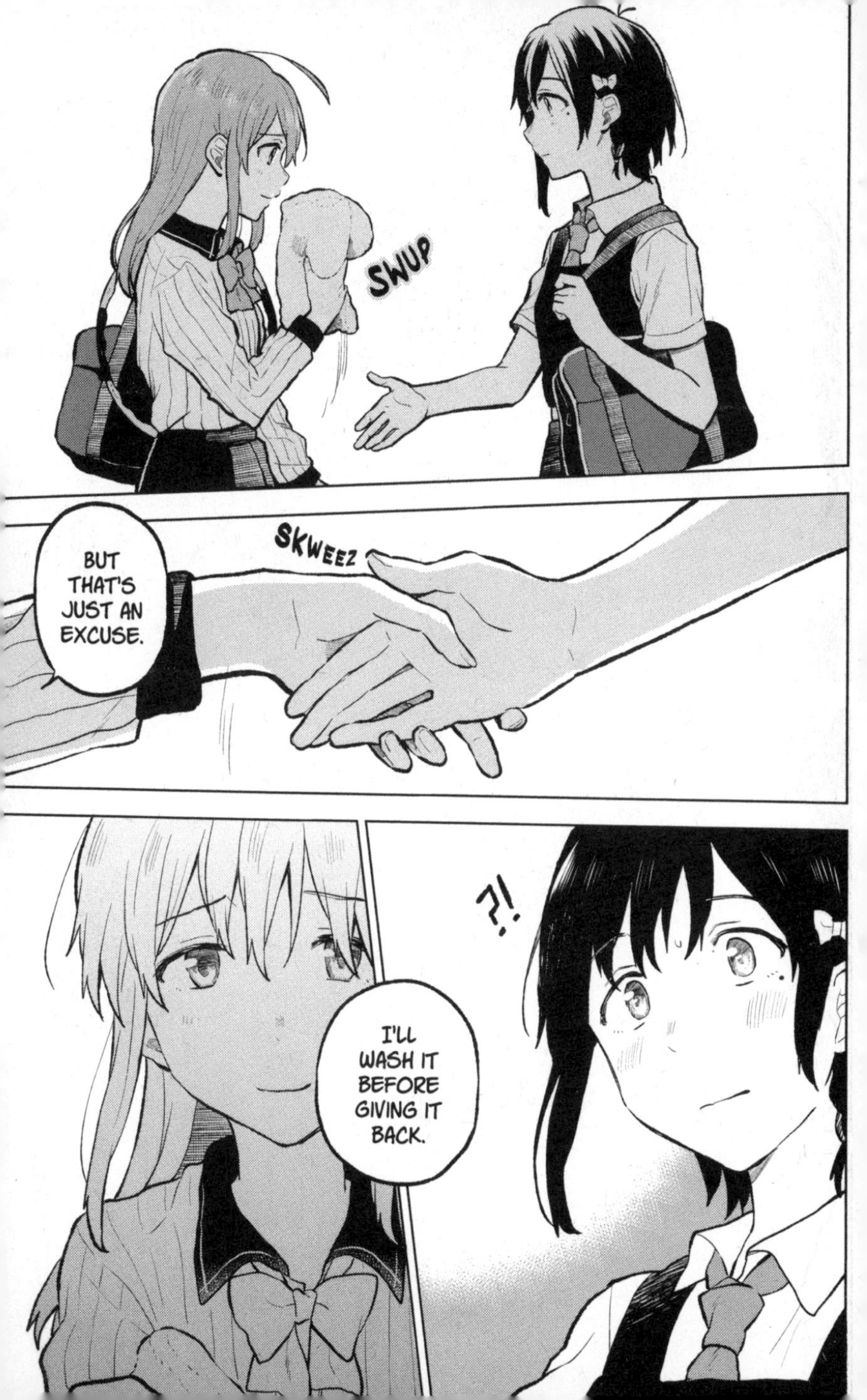
SWUP
SKWEEZ
BUT THAT'S JUST AN EXCUSE.
?!
I'LL WASH IT BEFORE GIVING IT BACK.

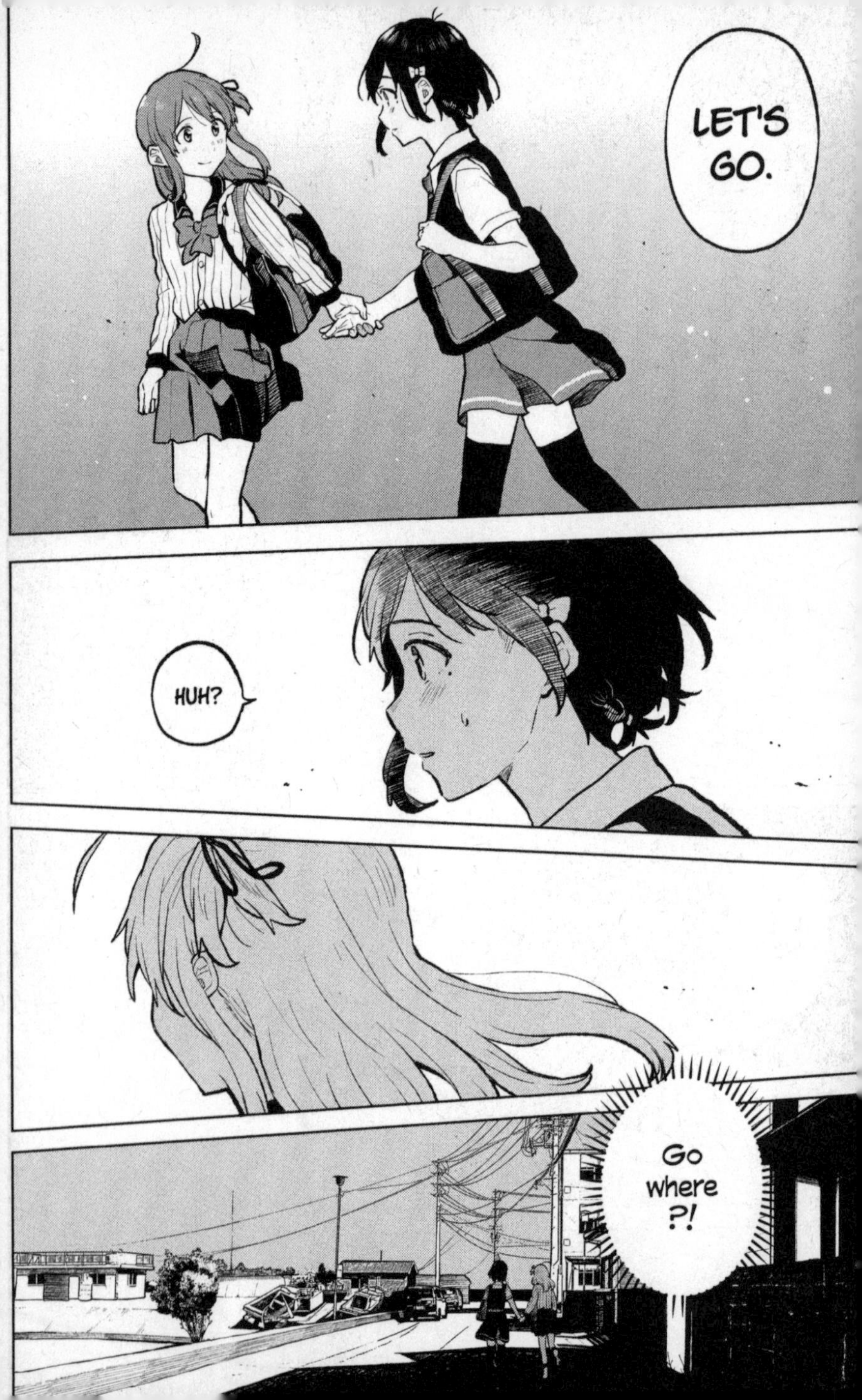
LET'S GO.
HUH?
Go where ?!

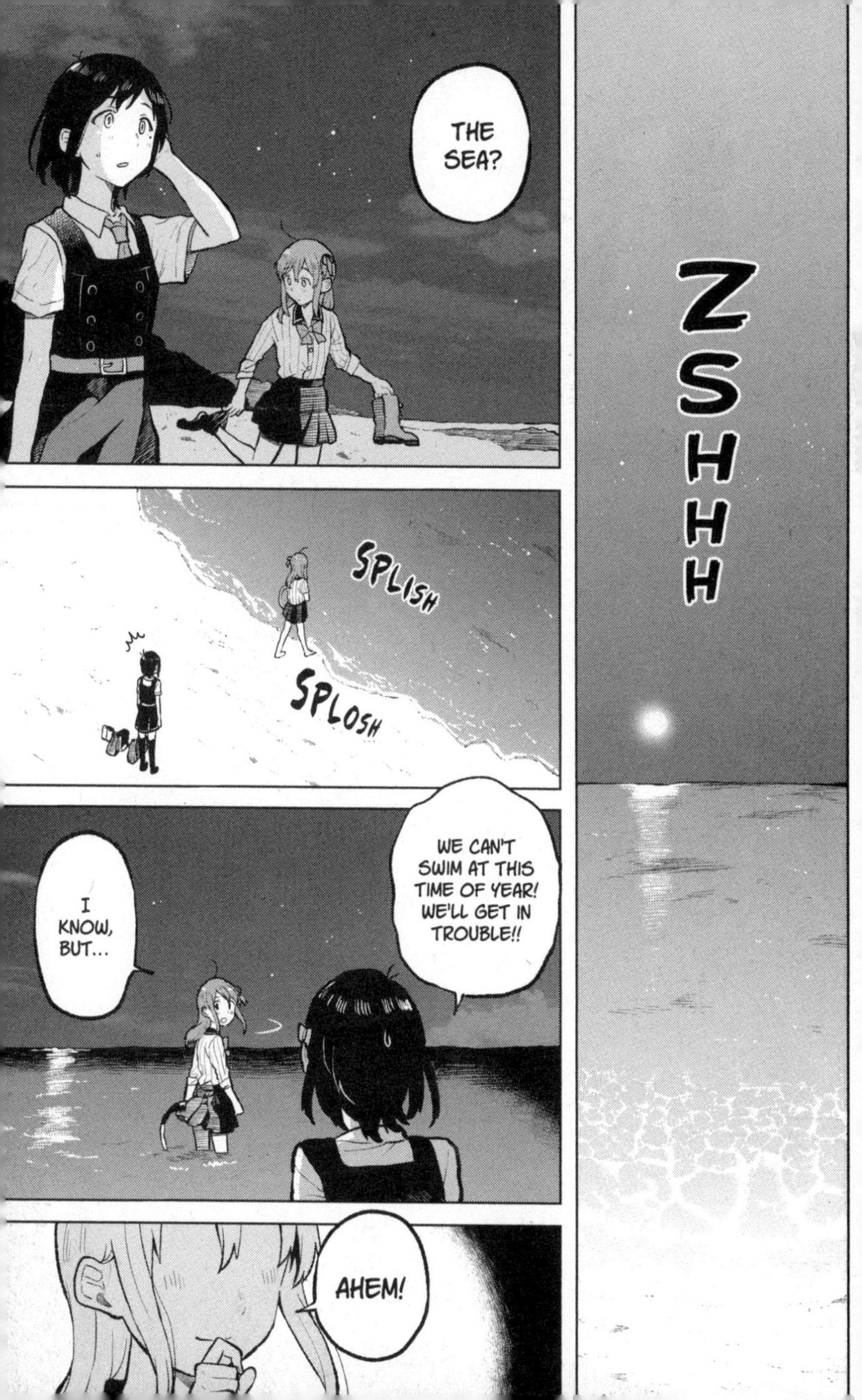
ZSHHH
THE SEA?
SPLISH
SPLOSH
WE CAN'T SWIM AT THIS TIME OF YEAR! WE'LL GET IN TROUBLE!!
I KNOW, BUT...
AHEM!

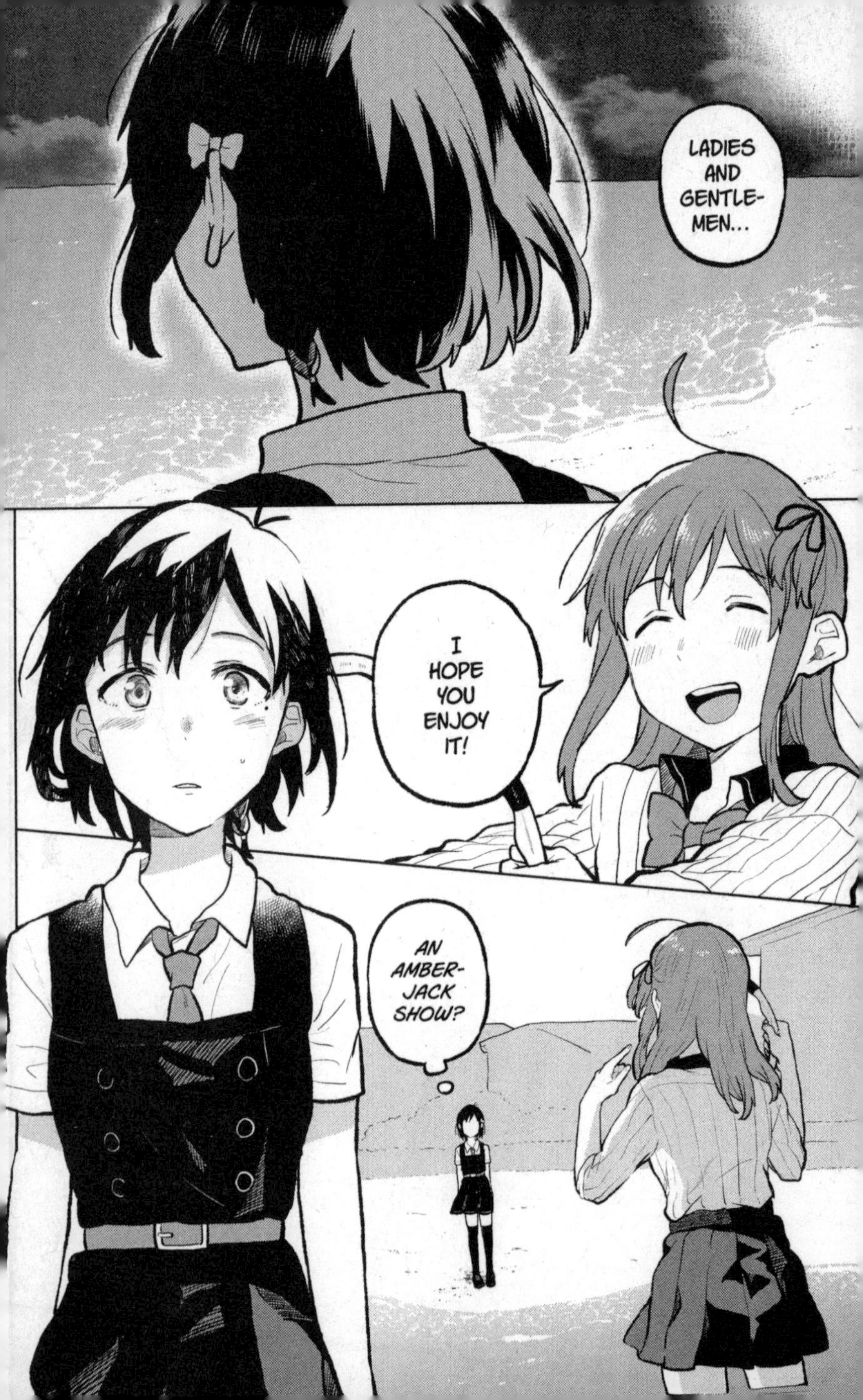
LADIES AND GENTLE-MEN...
I HOPE YOU ENJOY IT!
AN AMBER-JACK SHOW?

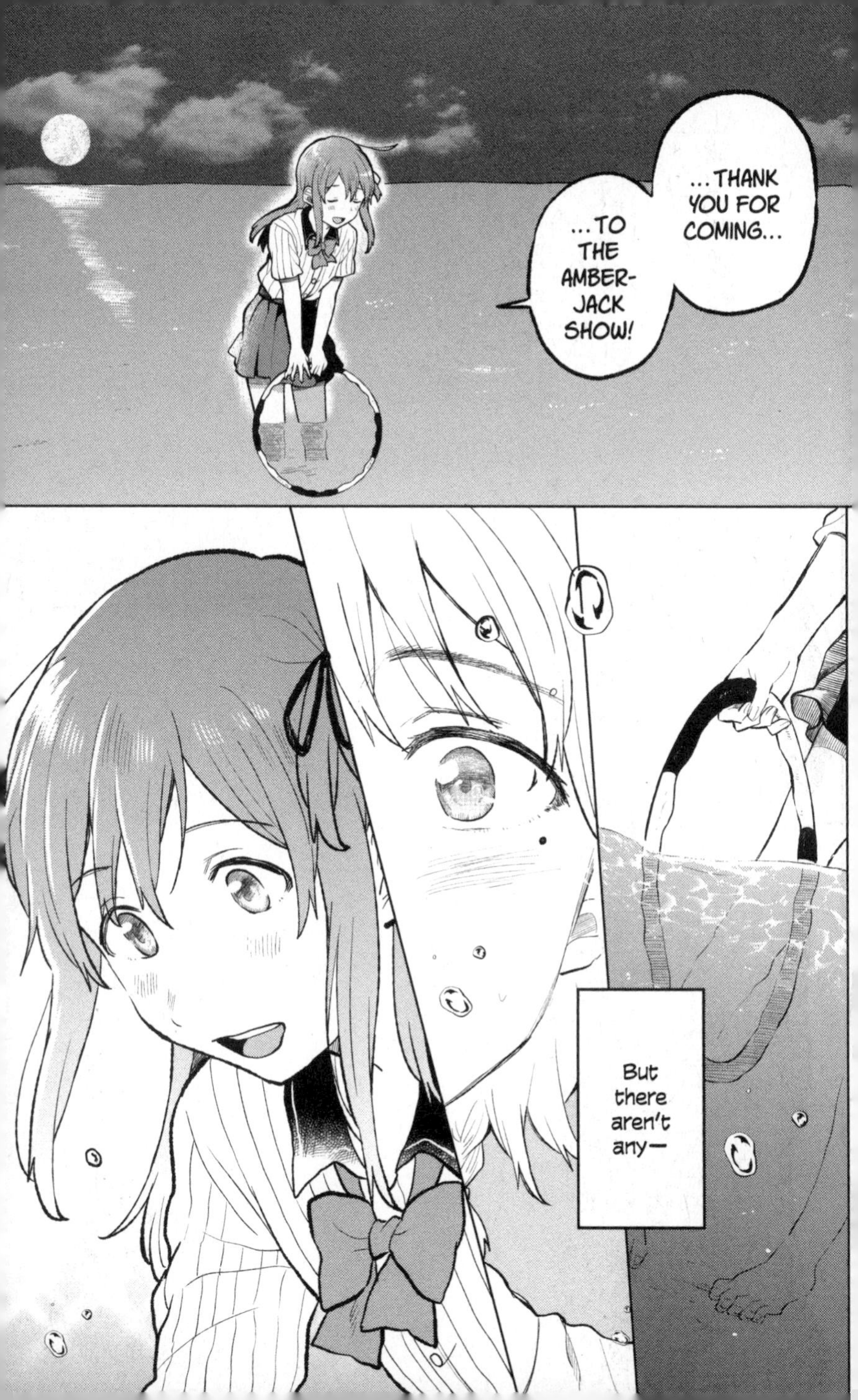
...THANK YOU FOR COMING...
...TO THE AMBER-JACK SHOW!
But there aren't any—

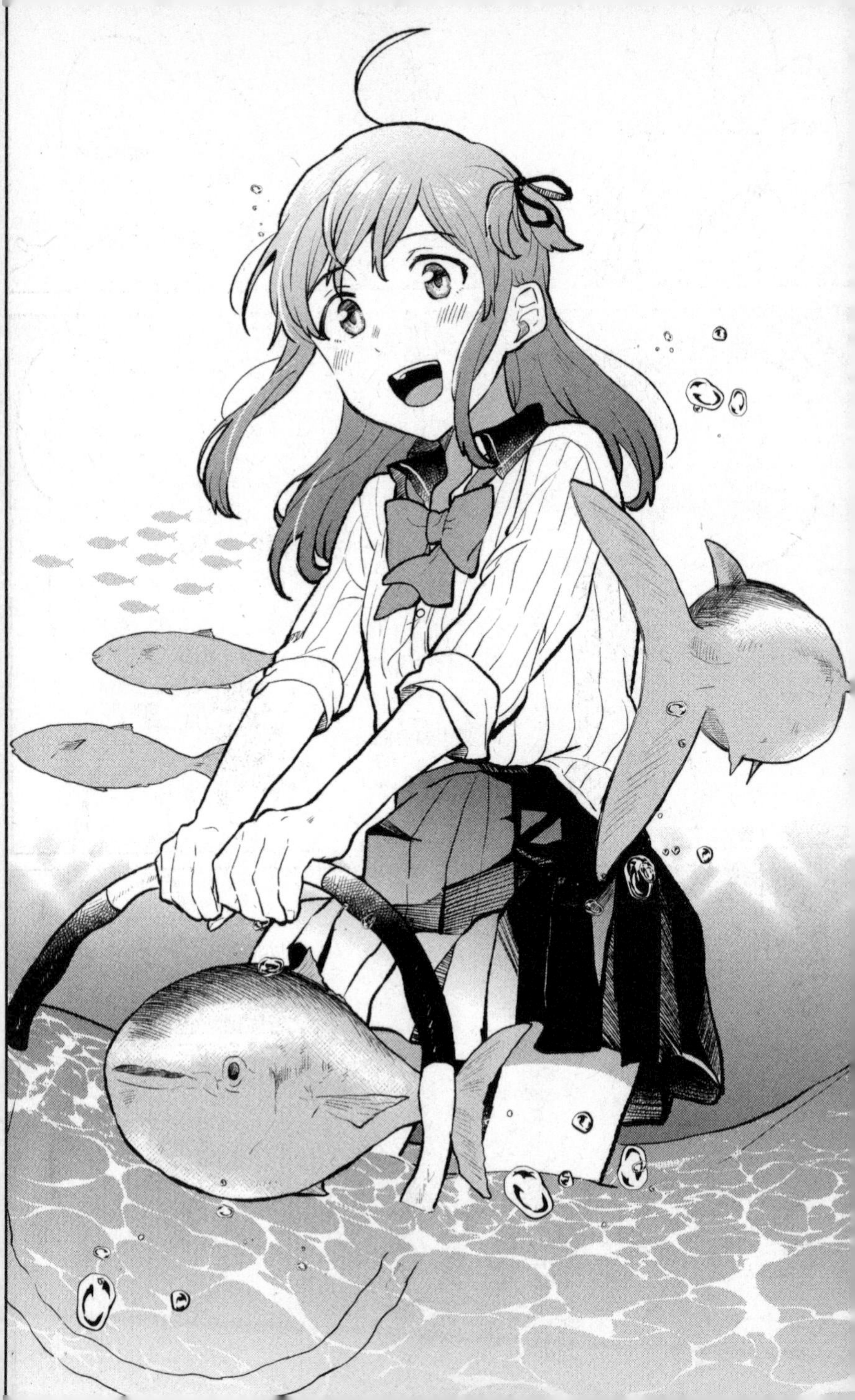

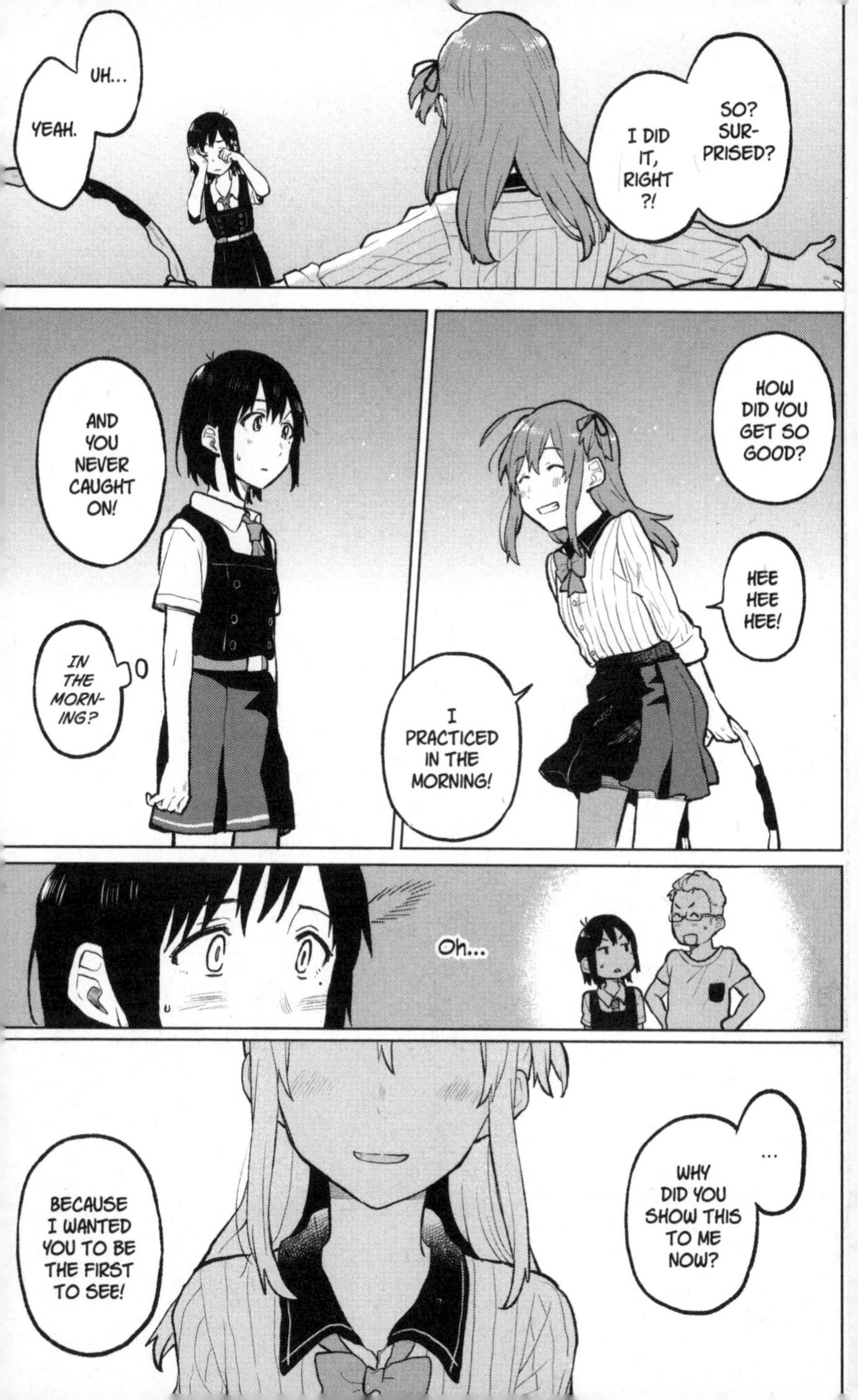
SO? SURPRISED?
I DID IT, RIGHT?!
UH... YEAH.
HOW DID YOU GET SO GOOD?
HEE HEE HEE!
I PRACTICED IN THE MORNING!
AND YOU NEVER CAUGHT ON!
IN THE MORNING?
Oh...
... WHY DID YOU SHOW THIS TO ME NOW?
BECAUSE I WANTED YOU TO BE THE FIRST TO SEE!

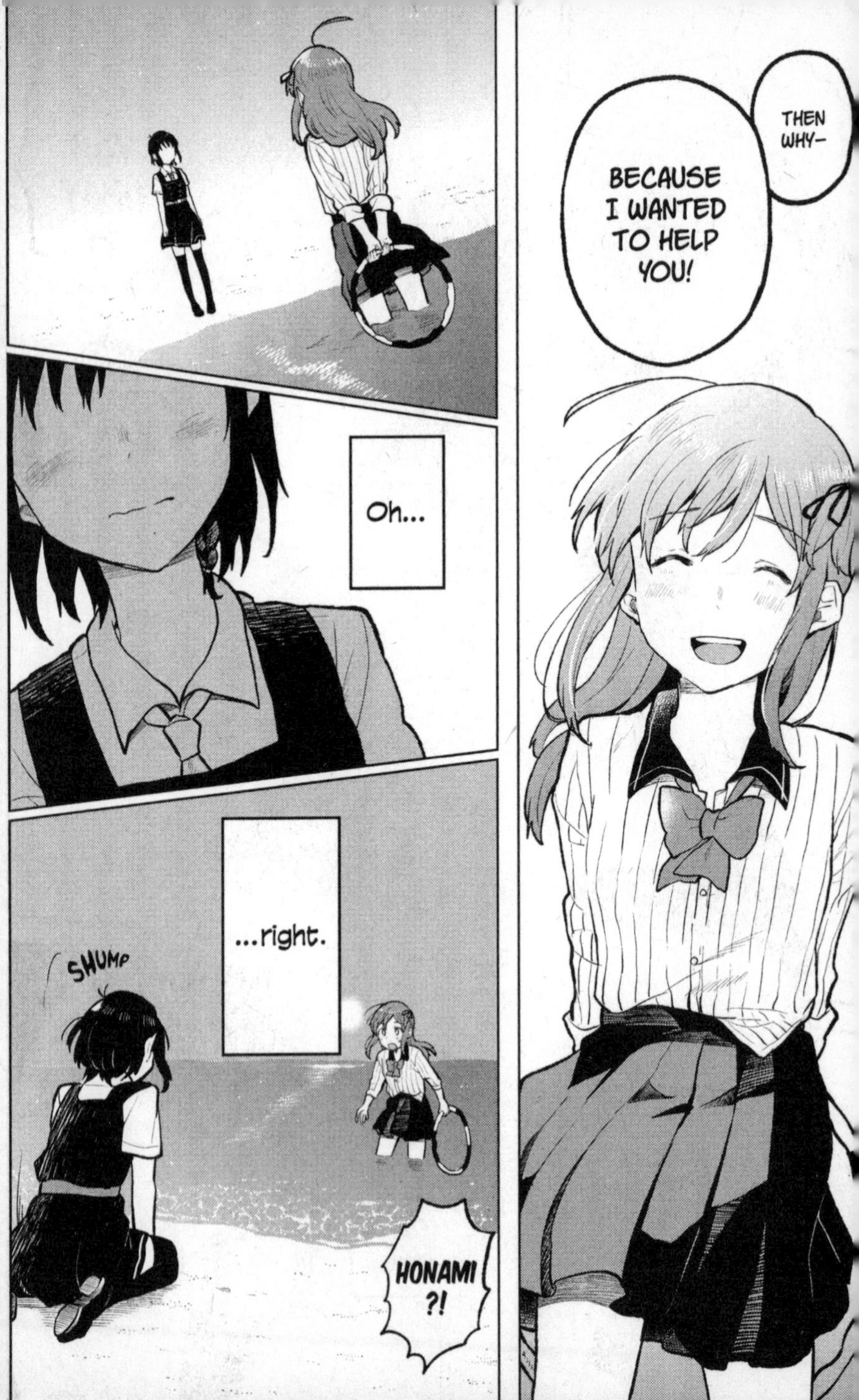
THEN WHY—
BECAUSE I WANTED TO HELP YOU!
Oh...
...right.
SHUMP
HONAMI ?!

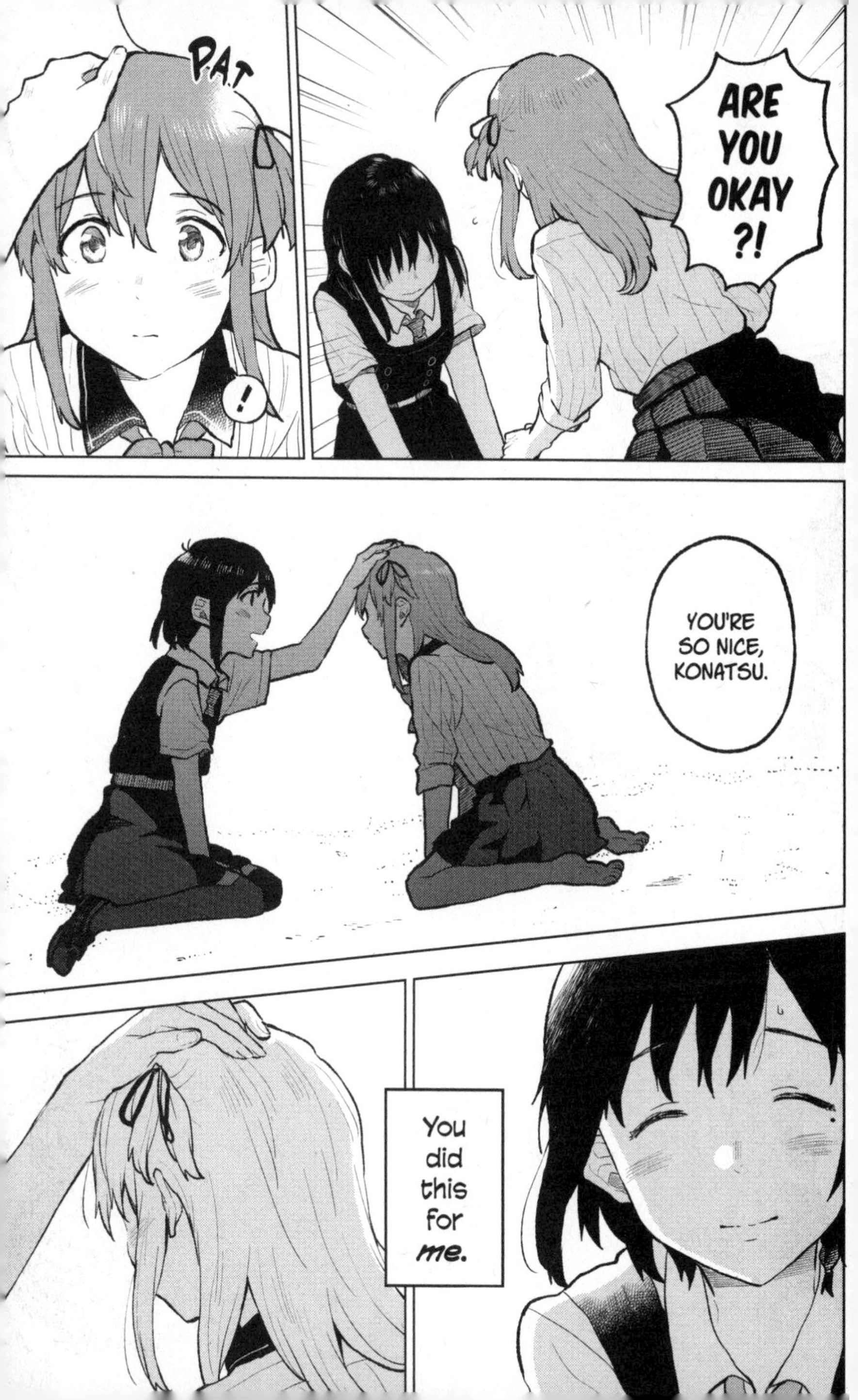
ARE YOU OKAY ?!
PAT
!
YOU'RE SO NICE, KONATSU.
You did this for *me.*

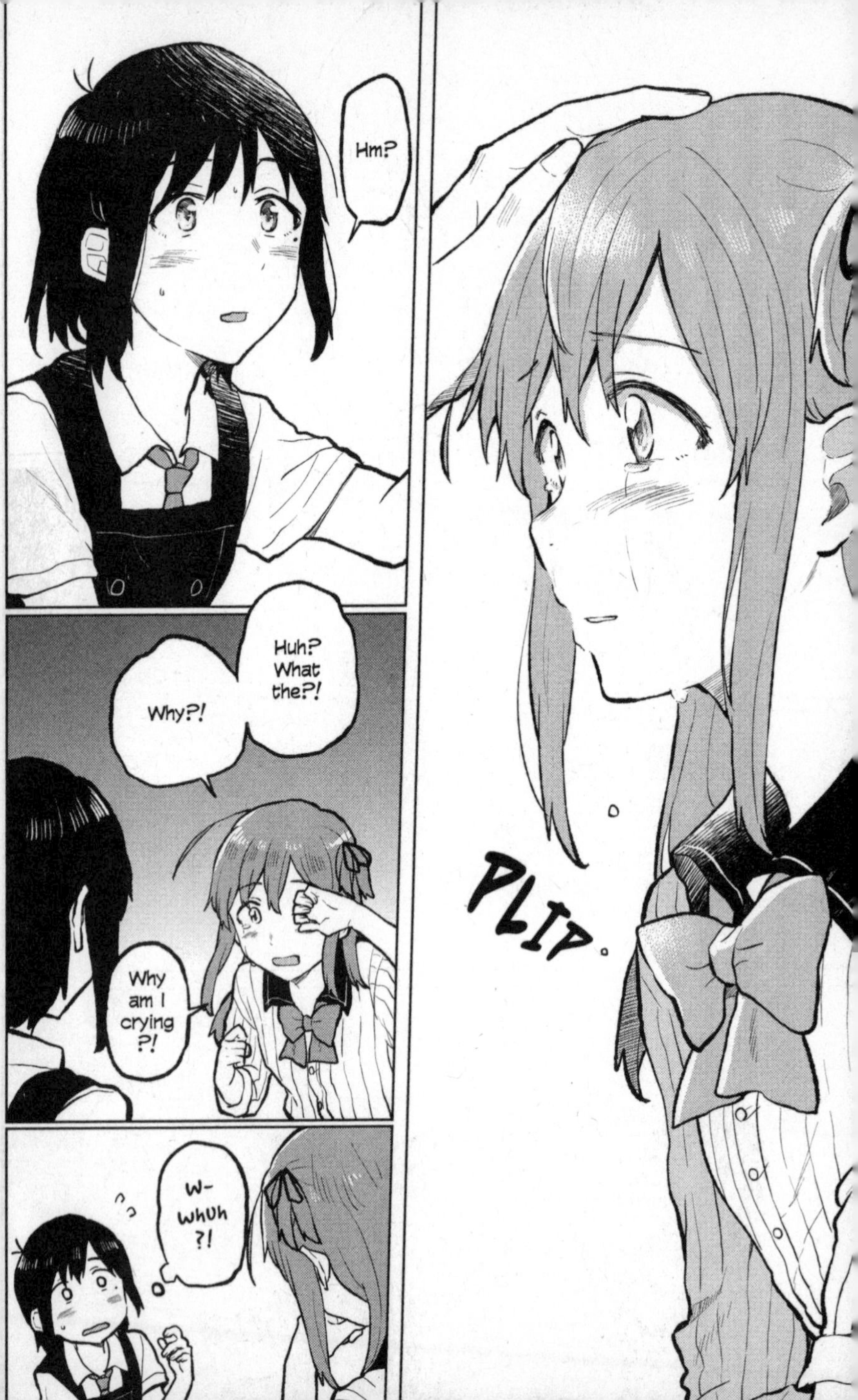
PLIP
Hm?
Huh? What the?!
Why?!
Why am I crying ?!
W-Whuh ?!

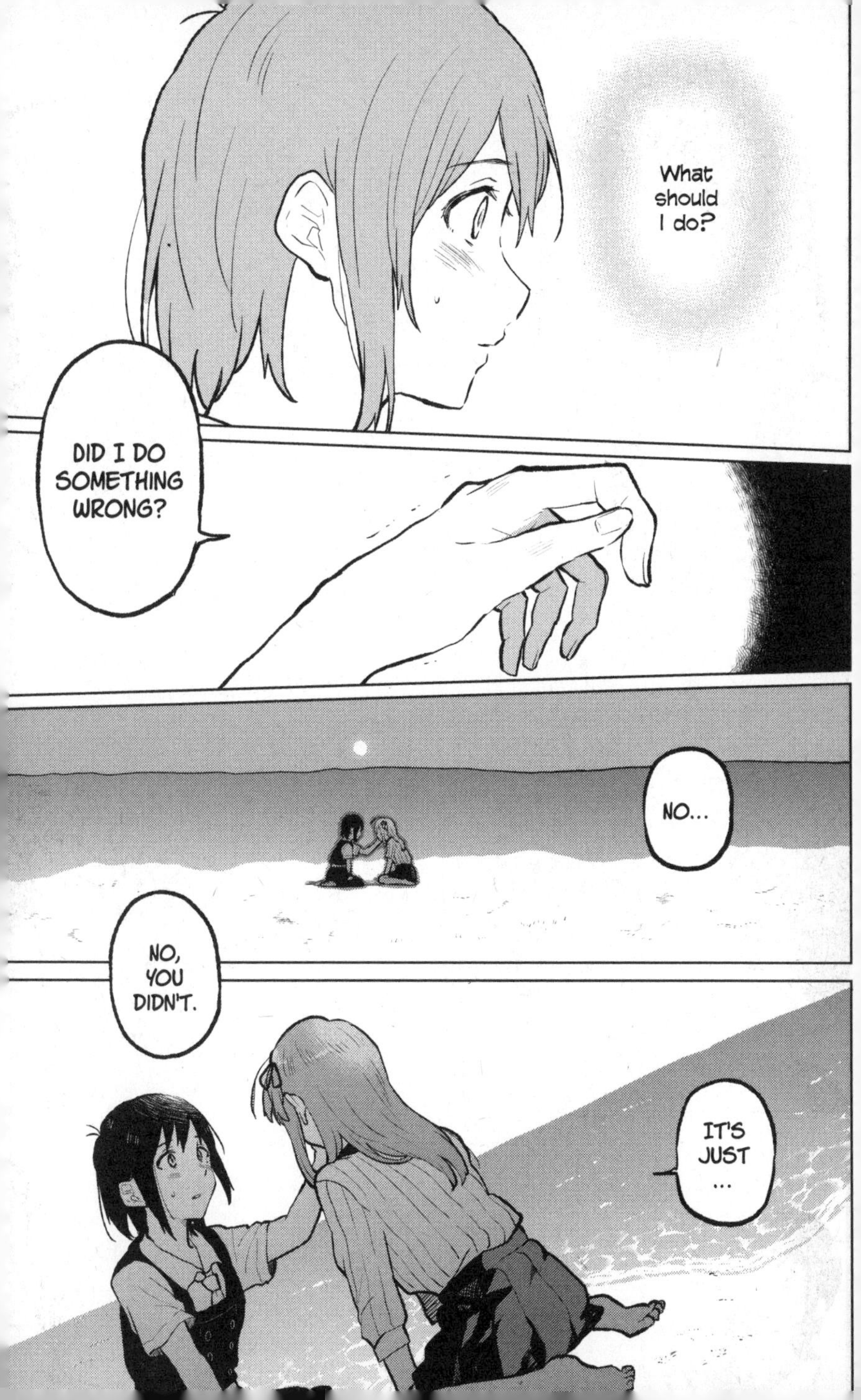
What should I do?
DID I DO SOMETHING WRONG?
NO...
NO, YOU DIDN'T.
IT'S JUST ...

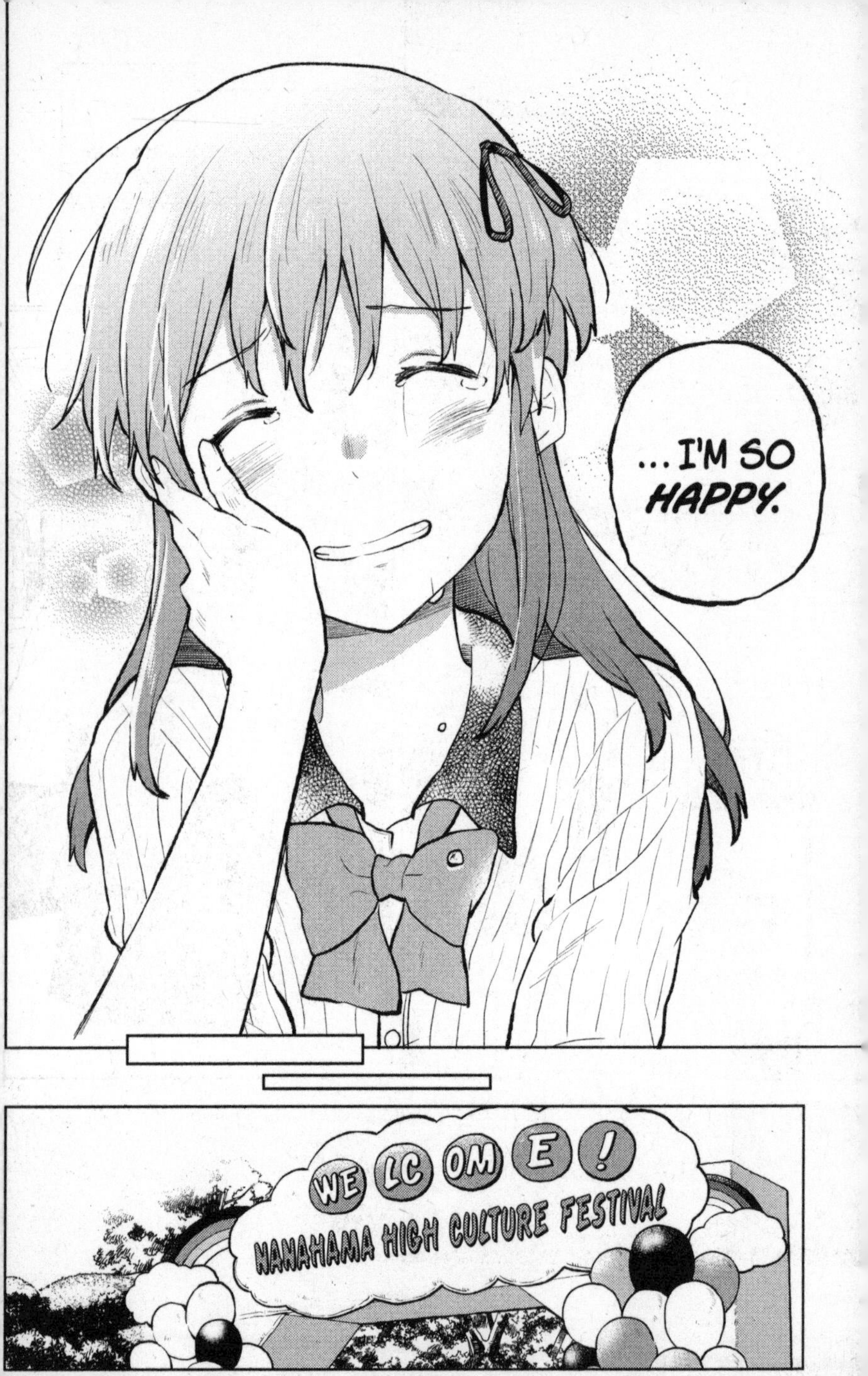
... I'M SO HAPPY.
WELCOME!
NANAHAMA HIGH CULTURE FESTIVAL

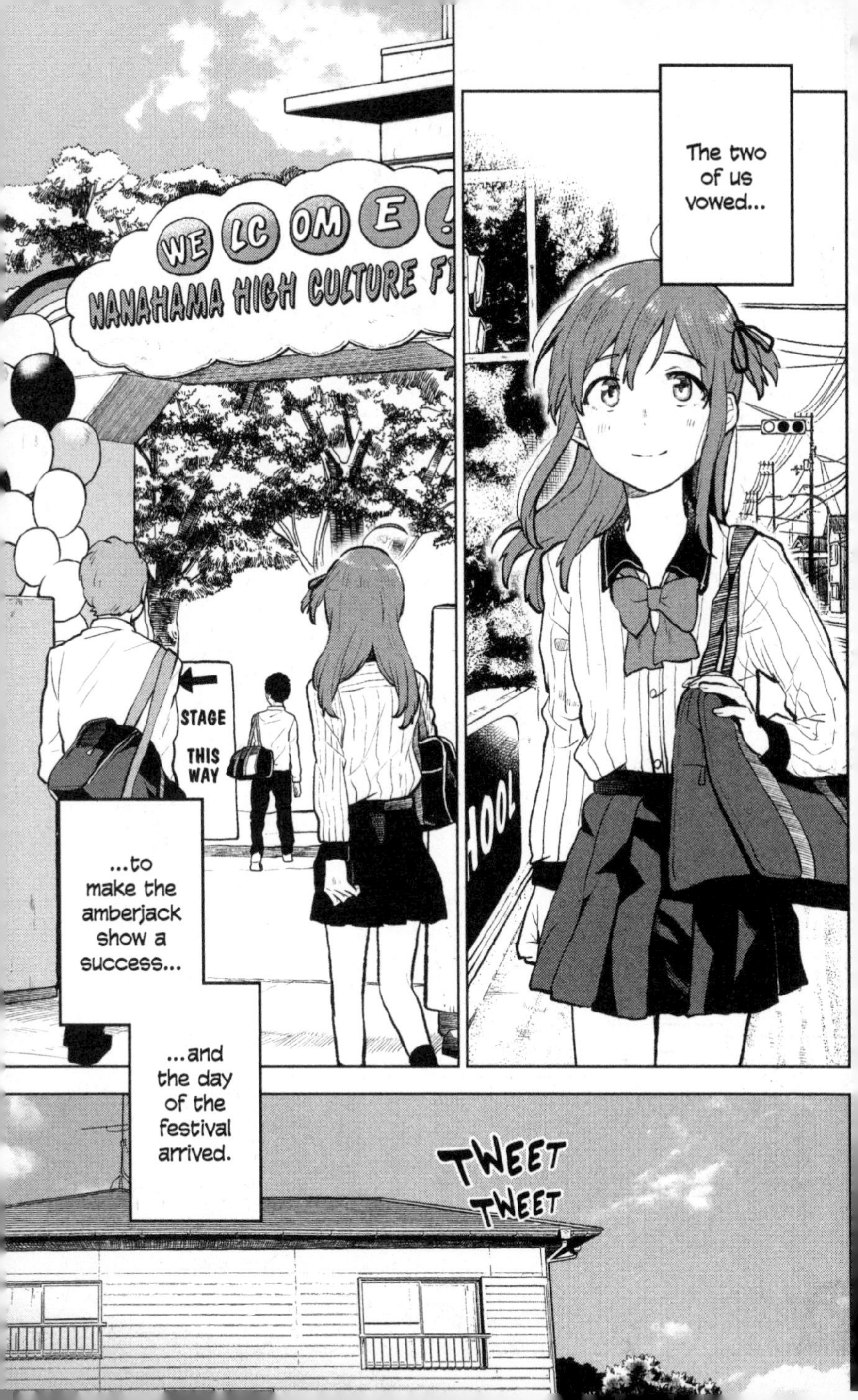

The two of us vowed...
WELCOME!
NANAHAMA HIGH CULTURE F
STAGE THIS WAY
...to make the amberjack show a success...
...and the day of the festival arrived.
TWEET TWEET

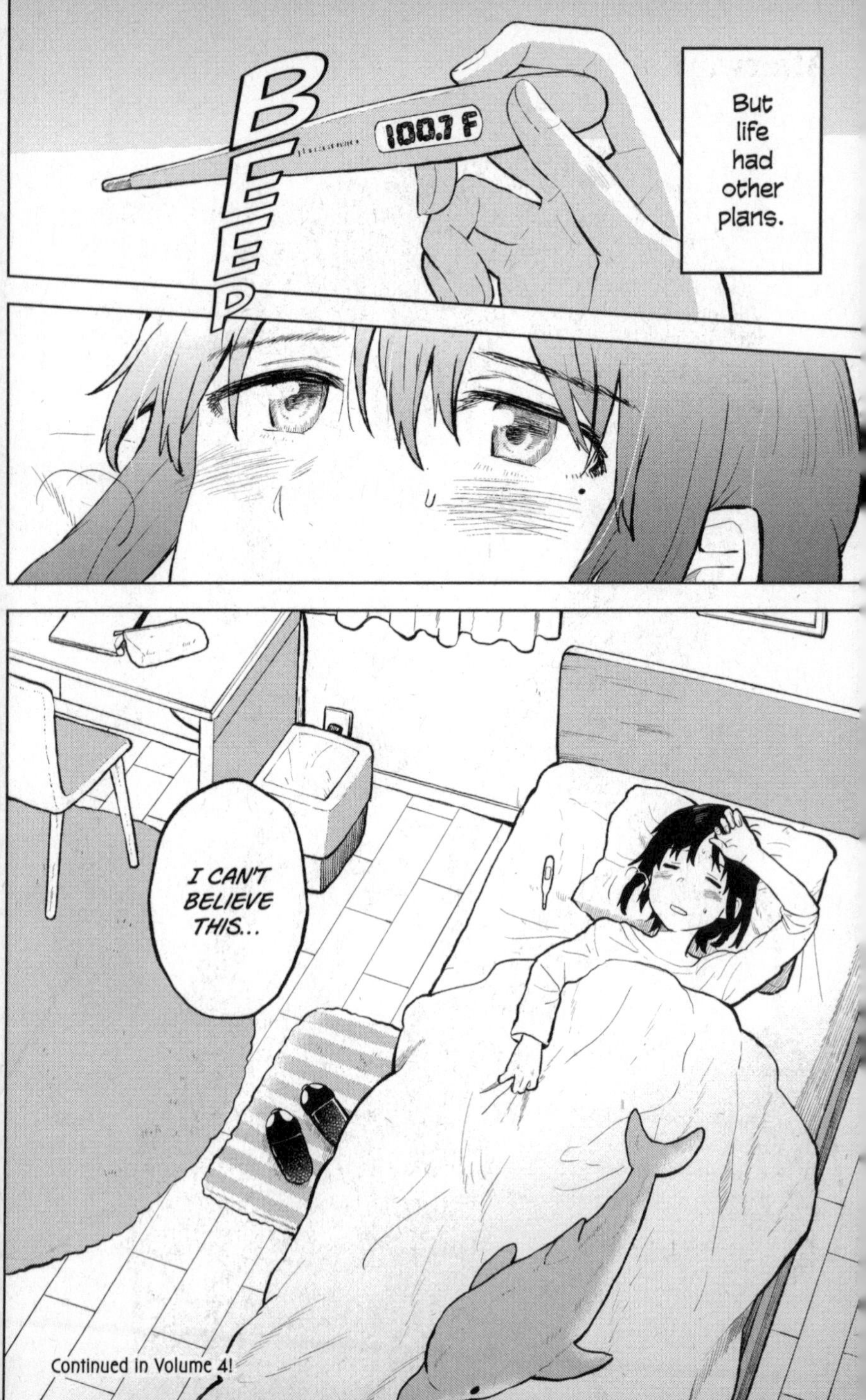
But life had other plans.
BEEP
100.7 F
I CAN'T BELIEVE THIS...

Continued in Volume 4!

Afterword

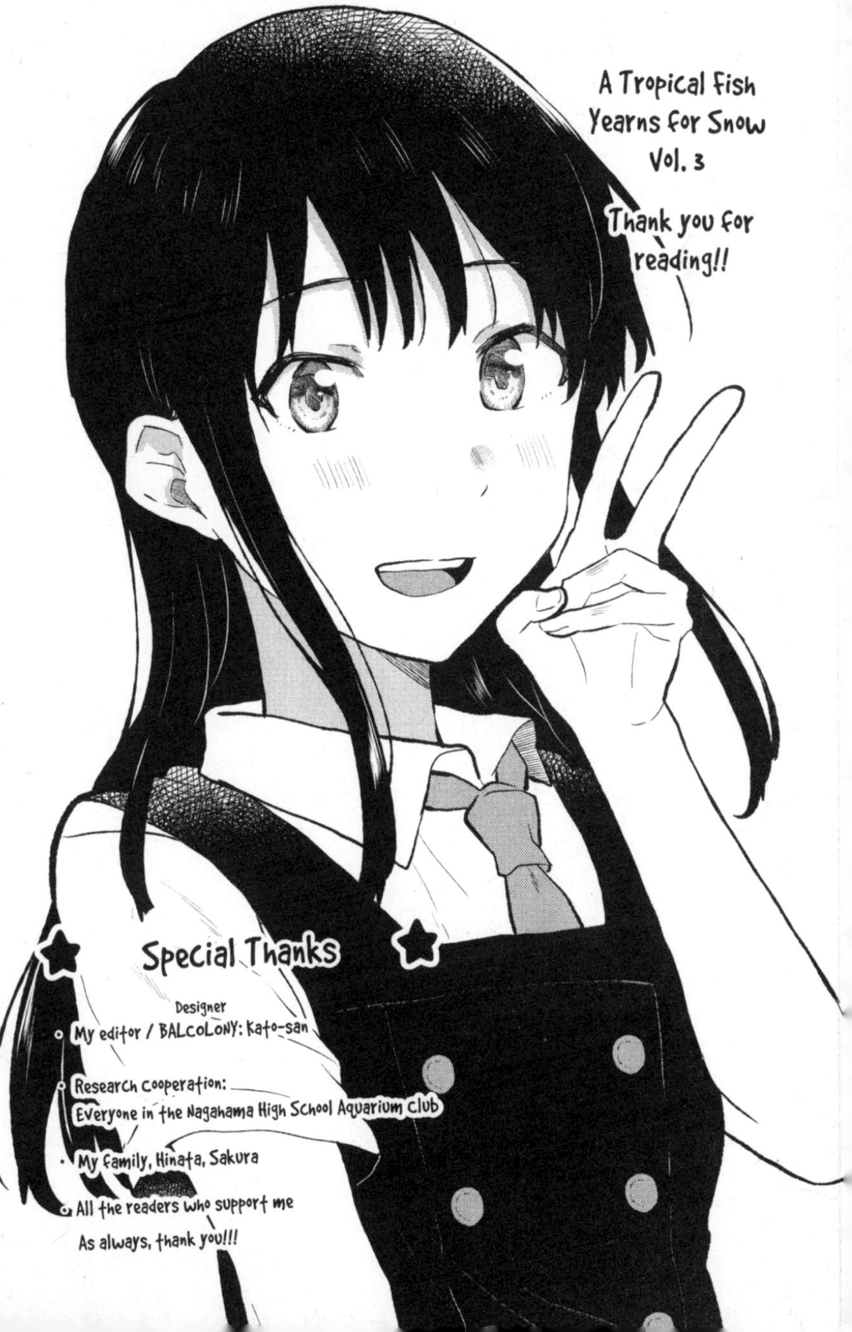
A Tropical Fish Yearns for Snow Vol. 3
Thank you for reading!!
Special Thanks
Designer
My editor / BALCOLONY: Kato-san
Research cooperation: Everyone in the Nagahama High School Aquarium Club
My family, Hinata, Sakura
All the readers who support me
As always, thank you!!!

A Tropical Fish Yearns for Snow vol. 3 Bonus Manga — Writer: Makoto Hagino

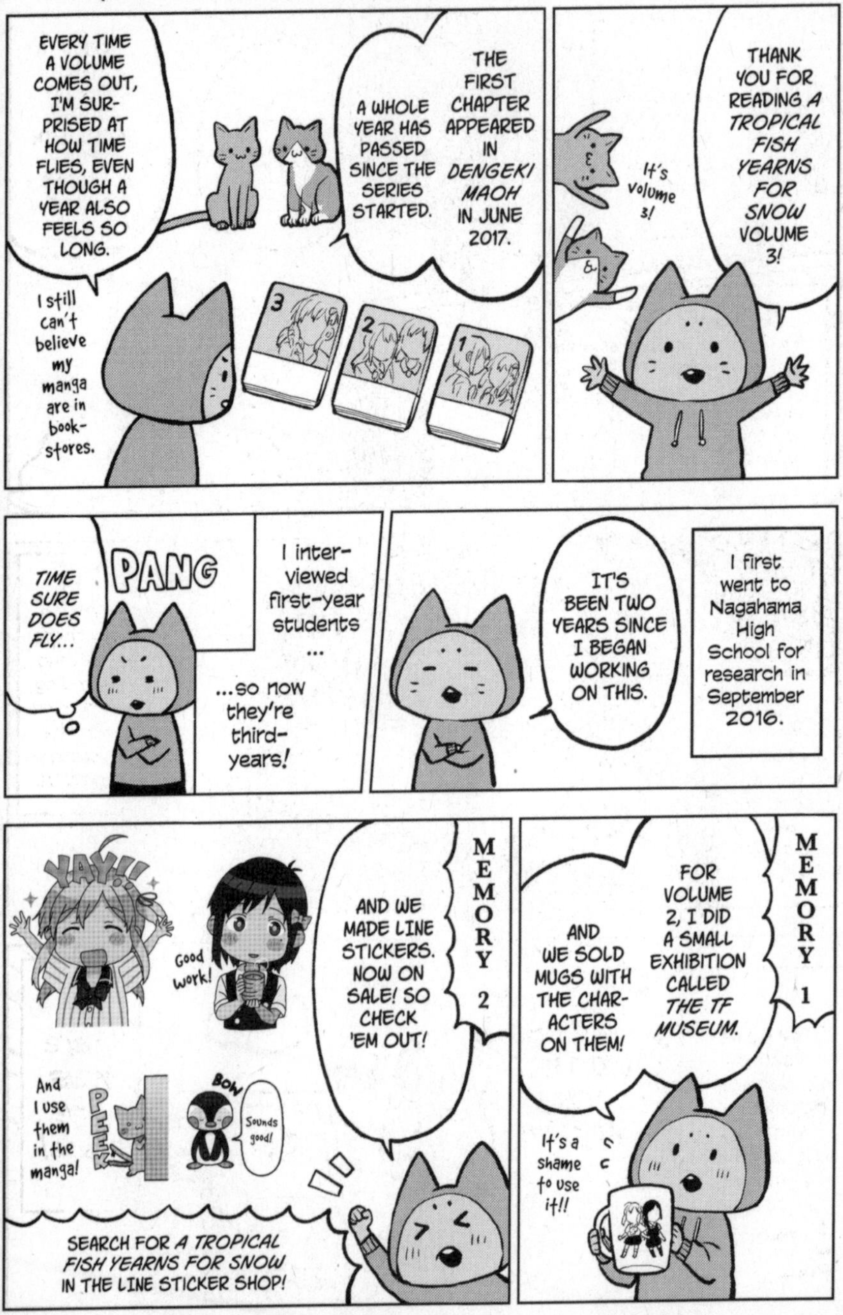
THANK YOU FOR READING *A TROPICAL FISH YEARNS FOR SNOW* VOLUME 3!
It's volume 3!
THE FIRST CHAPTER APPEARED IN *DENGEKI MAOH* IN JUNE 2017.
A WHOLE YEAR HAS PASSED SINCE THE SERIES STARTED.
EVERY TIME A VOLUME COMES OUT, I'M SURPRISED AT HOW TIME FLIES, EVEN THOUGH A YEAR ALSO FEELS SO LONG.
I still can't believe my manga are in bookstores.
3
2
1
I first went to Nagahama High School for research in September 2016.
IT'S BEEN TWO YEARS SINCE I BEGAN WORKING ON THIS.
I interviewed first-year students...
...so now they're third-years!
PANG
TIME SURE DOES FLY...
MEMORY 1
FOR VOLUME 2, I DID A SMALL EXHIBITION CALLED *THE TF MUSEUM.*
AND WE SOLD MUGS WITH THE CHARACTERS ON THEM!
It's a shame to use it!!
MEMORY 2
AND WE MADE LINE STICKERS. NOW ON SALE! SO CHECK 'EM OUT!
YAY!!
Good work!
BOW
Sounds good!
PEEK
And I use them in the manga!
SEARCH FOR *A TROPICAL FISH YEARNS FOR SNOW* IN THE LINE STICKER SHOP!

A Surprise Revelation, Part 2

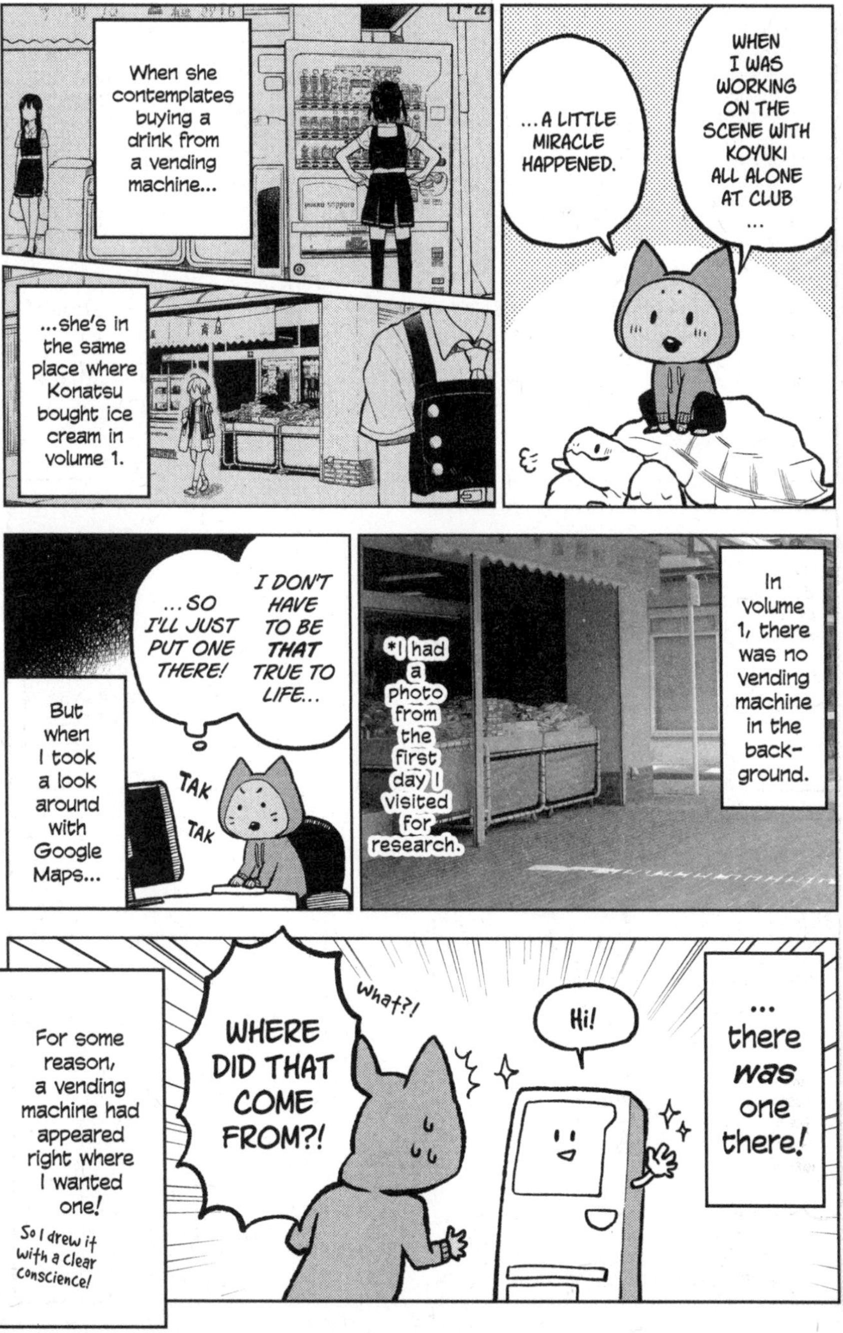
WHEN I WAS WORKING ON THE SCENE WITH KOYUKI ALL ALONE AT CLUB...
...A LITTLE MIRACLE HAPPENED.
When she contemplates buying a drink from a vending machine...
...she's in the same place where Konatsu bought ice cream in volume 1.
In volume 1, there was no vending machine in the back-ground.
*I had a photo from the first day I visited for research.
I DON'T HAVE TO BE *THAT* TRUE TO LIFE...
...SO I'LL JUST PUT ONE THERE!
TAK
TAK
But when I took a look around with Google Maps...
...there *was* one there!
Hi!
What?!
WHERE DID THAT COME FROM?!
For some reason, a vending machine had appeared right where I wanted one!
So I drew it with a clear conscience!

A TROPICAL FISH YEARNS FOR SNOW
Vol. 3
VIZ Media Edition

STORY AND ART BY
MAKOTO HAGINO

English Translation & Adaptation/John Werry
Touch-Up Art & Lettering/Eve Grandt
Design/Yukiko Whitley
Editor/Pancha Diaz

NETTAIGYO WA YUKI NI KOGARERU Vol. 3
©MAKOTO HAGINO 2018
First published in Japan in 2018 by KADOKAWA CORPORATION, Tokyo.
English translation rights arranged with KADOKAWA CORPORATION, Tokyo.

Printed in Canada

Published by VIZ Media, LLC
P.O. Box 77010
San Francisco, CA 94107

10 9 8 7 6 5 4 3 2 1
First printing, May 2020

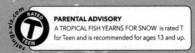

PARENTAL ADVISORY
A TROPICAL FISH YEARNS FOR SNOW is rated T
for Teen and is recommended for ages 13 and up.

viz.com

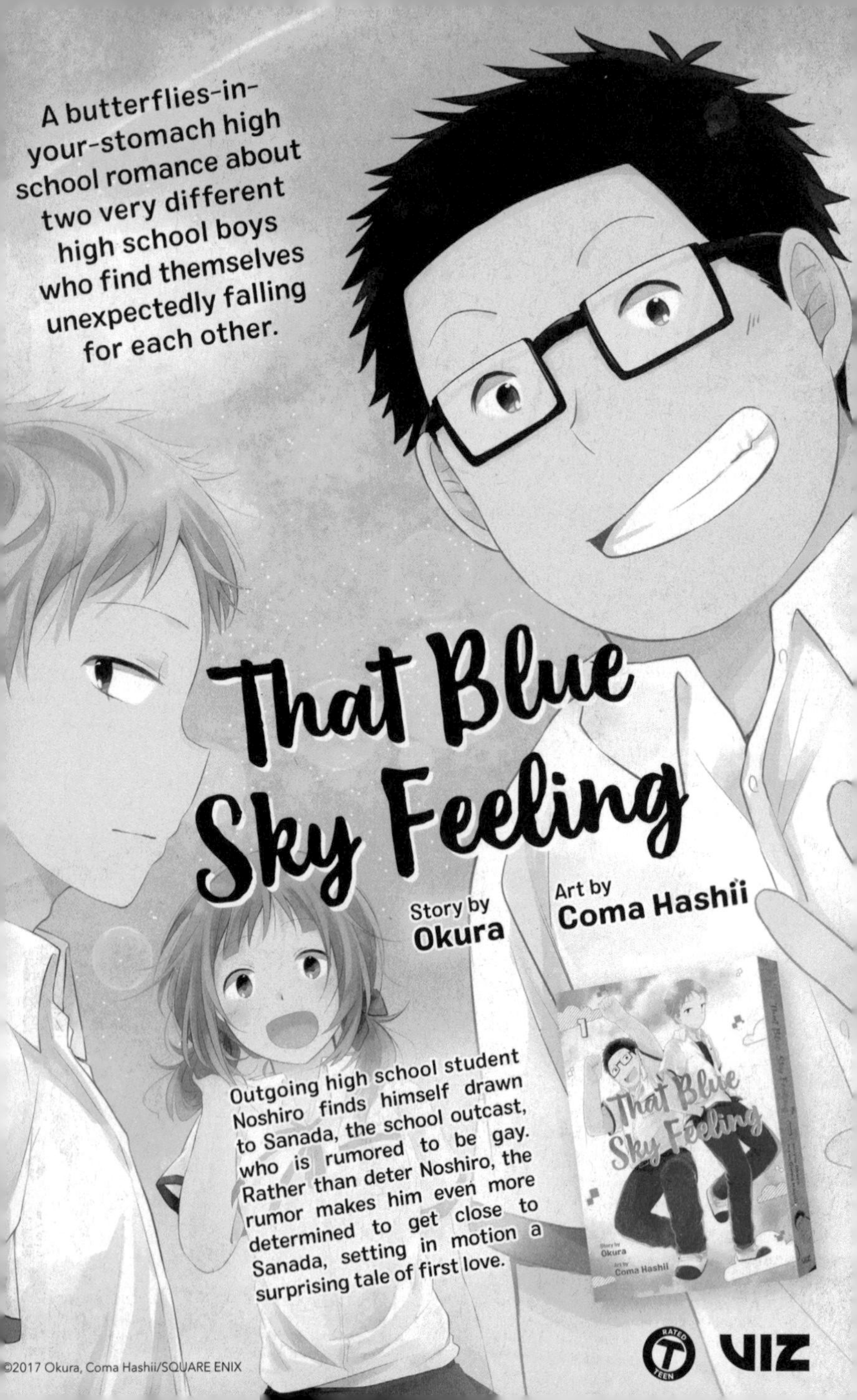
A butterflies-in-your-stomach high school romance about two very different high school boys who find themselves unexpectedly falling for each other.
That Blue Sky Feeling
Story by Okura
Art by Coma Hashii
Outgoing high school student Noshiro finds himself drawn to Sanada, the school outcast, who is rumored to be gay. Rather than deter Noshiro, the rumor makes him even more determined to get close to Sanada, setting in motion a surprising tale of first love.
RATED T TEEN
VIZ
©2017 Okura, Coma Hashii/SQUARE ENIX

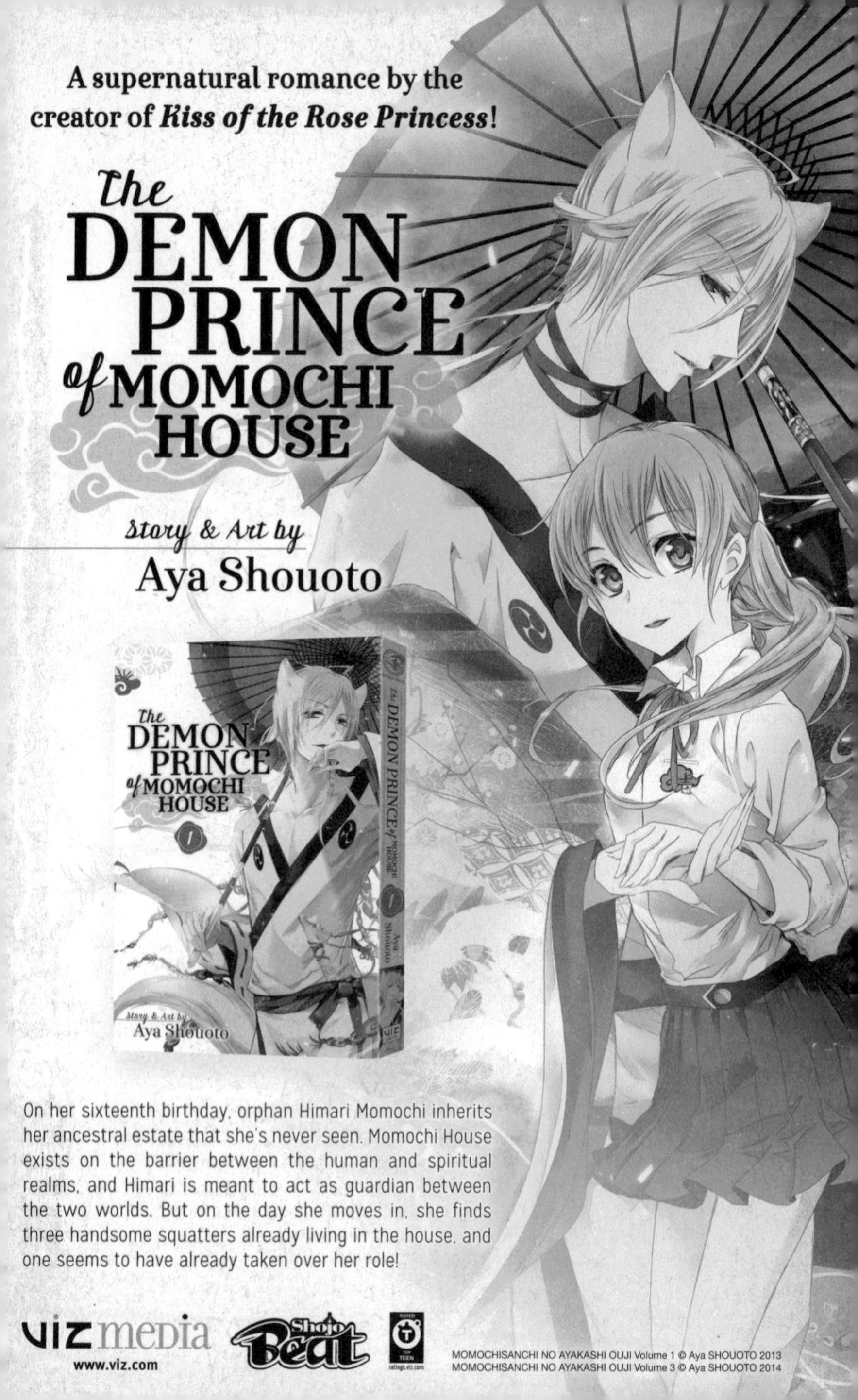
A supernatural romance by the creator of Kiss of the Rose Princess!
The DEMON PRINCE of MOMOCHI HOUSE
Story & Art by
Aya Shouoto
The DEMON PRINCE of MOMOCHI HOUSE
1
Story & Art by
Aya Shouoto
On her sixteenth birthday, orphan Himari Momochi inherits her ancestral estate that she's never seen. Momochi House exists on the barrier between the human and spiritual realms, and Himari is meant to act as guardian between the two worlds. But on the day she moves in, she finds three handsome squatters already living in the house, and one seems to have already taken over her role!
viz media
www.viz.com
Shojo Beat
RATED T FOR TEEN
ratings.viz.com
MOMOCHISANCHI NO AYAKASHI OUJI Volume 1 © Aya SHOUOTO 2013
MOMOCHISANCHI NO AYAKASHI OUJI Volume 3 © Aya SHOUOTO 2014

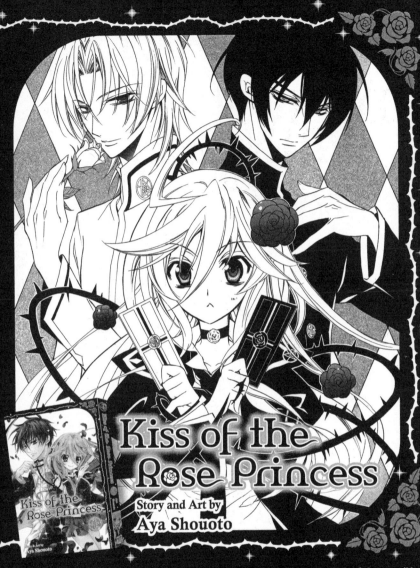

Kiss of the Rose Princess

Story and Art by
Aya Shouoto

Anise Yamamoto has been told that if she ever removes the rose choker given to her by her father, a terrible punishment will befall her. Unfortunately she loses that choker when a bat-like being named Ninufa falls from the sky and hits her. Ninufa gives Anise four cards representing four knights whom she can summon with a kiss. But now that she has these gorgeous men at her beck and call, what exactly is her quest?!

This is the last page.

A Tropical Fish Yearns for Snow **has been printed in the original Japanese format to preserve the orientation of the artwork.**

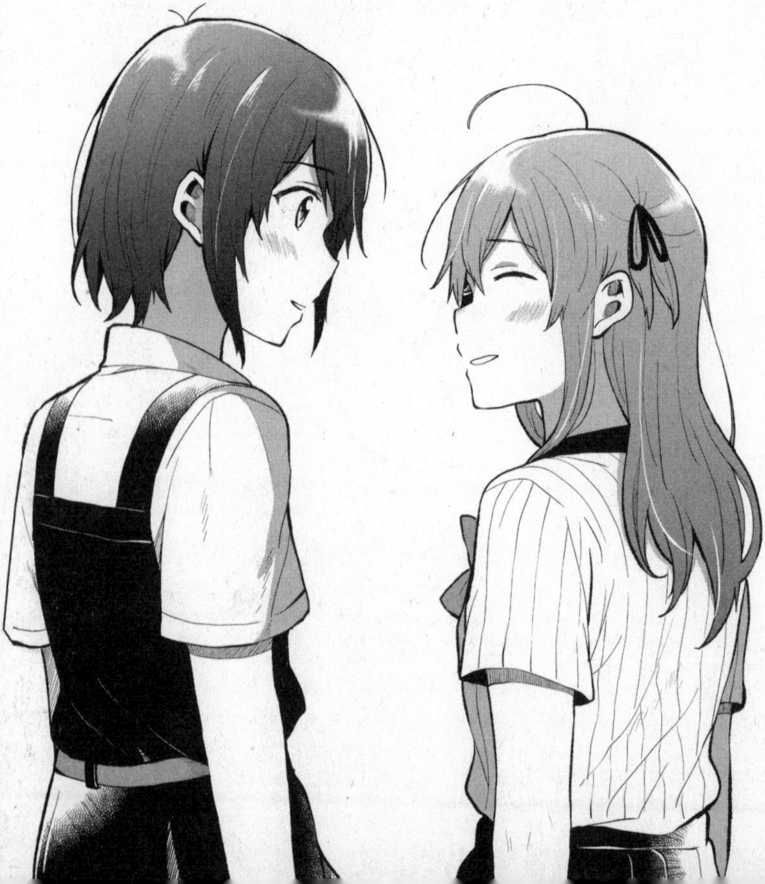